GIORDANO BRUNO
AND THE
EMBASSY AFFAIR

John Bossy was born in London in 1933 and educated
mainly by the Second World War, the Society of Jesus
and the University of Cambridge. Since then he has lived
and lectured in London and Belfast, has been a member
of the Institute for Advanced Study at Princeton, and
since 1979 has been professor of history at the
University of York. His main contributions to
knowledge have been an edition of H.O. Evennett's *The
Spirit of the Counter-Reformation* (1968), *The English
Catholic Community, 1570–1850* (1975) and *Christianity in the West, 1400–1700* (1985), which has been
translated into various European languages.

John Bossy

GIORDANO BRUNO AND THE EMBASSY AFFAIR

V

VINTAGE

VINTAGE

20 Vauxhall Bridge Road, London SW1V 2SA

London Melbourne Sydney Auckland Johannesburg
and agencies throughout the world

First published by Yale University Press, 1991
Vintage edition 1992

3 5 7 9 10 8 6 4 2

Printed and bound in Great Britain by
Cox & Wyman Ltd, Reading

ISBN 0 09 914381 X

FOR PETE AND BELINDA,
WITH LOVE AND GRATITUDE

Illustrations

Contents

Melior est canis vivens leone mortuo.

A live dog is better than a dead lion.

Ecclesiastes 9: 4

Pazzo sarrebe l'istorico, che, trattando la sua materia, volesse ordinar vocaboli stimati novi e riformar i vecchi, e far di modo che il lettore sii piú trattenuto a osservarlo e interpretarlo come gramatico, che intenderlo come istorico.

A historian would be an imbecile if, in expounding his subject, he should decide to invent a brand new set of terms and to abolish the old ones; whence his reader would have more ado to keep track of him as a grammarian, than to understand him as a historian.

Giordano Bruno, *La cena de le Ceneri*
(*DI*, p. 121)

Preface

AT THE BEGINNING of my career as a historian, which is now some time ago, I wrote a Ph.D. thesis on the relations, political and other, between France and the Elizabethan Catholics. This not being the kind of subject workers at the cutting edge of history were writing about in the 1960s, I turned, on finishing it, to other things. In the spring of 1983 I used a sabbatical term in London to see whether or not I would like to return to the subject, and decided that I would: it had the advantage that, potentially at least, I seemed to know as much about it as there was to be known, which could not be said of the topics I had been writing about in the meantime. One of the persons about whom I did not seem to know as much as might be known has become the principal subject of this book. I had made his acquaintance during the 1950s, then forgotten about him for twenty years or so. As I retraced the steps I had taken while writing my thesis, he presented himself to me again, in the guise of a problem to which I could not think of an answer.

It was not for some four years, while I was investigating the doings of Michel de Castelnau in the London of the 1580s, that a possible answer began to dawn; I was challenged, or challenged myself, to begin writing a book on the subject without knowing what the answer would be. This seemed a fair test of the idea, which I had become interested in exploring, that the superiority of narrative to other sorts of historical writing was that you, meaning the author as well as the reader, did not necessarily know, and perhaps ought in principle not to know, the end before you started. In that condition I began to write the book in November 1987: it was some six months, after I had written the first part, before I concluded, not only that I knew what the answer was, but that I could prove it before a bench of sceptical judges. What would have happened to the book if I had found a different answer, or none at all, is an intriguing but now needless speculation.

I have to say that I have cheated by making some alterations to the text of part one after the discovery recorded at the beginning of part two; but I have kept them as few as possible in the hope, perhaps vain, of saving the principle about narration mentioned above. The rest of the book, though it has been subject to more afterthoughts and rearrangements and has required me to make myself familiar with subjects I had not anticipated, has run fairly easily. With the help of two sabbatical terms, for which I am grateful to my colleagues in the history department of the University of York, the book was substantially finished in March 1990.

I should like to thank Ingrid Heseltine for bouncing me into starting it; Silvano Cavazza, Simon Ditchfield, John Fisher, Mary Flannery, Thomas Kselman, Donald Logan, Graham Parry, Jonathan Powis, Bill Sheils and Rita Sturlese for various kinds of help in getting on with it; Nick Furbank and the anonymous reader of Yale University Press especially, Clare Cully, Simon Ditchfield, Mary Heimann and Helen Weinstein for reading and criticising the manuscript; Angela Bailey for typing it; David Whiteley of the J.B. Morrell Library of the University of York for some fine photographs; and Amanda Lillie for introducing me to the wonderful library of the Warburg Institute.

I also wish to thank the British Library Board for permission to publish the Texts nos. 2, 5, 6–8, 11, 11a, 13, 14 and 17, Figures 2, 5 and 8, Plates IV–VI, and the emblem on the title page of part two; the Controller of H.M. Stationery Office for Texts nos. 3, 4, 9, 10, 15, 16 and 18 and Plates I–III, which are Crown copyright material in the Public Record Office; the Bibliothèque Nationale, Paris, for the correspondence of Castelnau and others; the Biblioteca Ambrosiana, Milan, for the correspondence of Jacopo Corbinelli, and the Institute of Mediaeval Studies of Notre Dame University for very kindly providing me with a microfilm of it; the Guildhall Library, London, and John Fisher for the engraving by Wenceslaus Hollar on which the back jacket illustration is based and Figures 1, 9–10; the Worshipful Company of Mercers, London, for Figure 7; the Bibliothèque Publique et Universitaire de la Ville de Genève for Plate VIIa; University College London Library and Susan Stead for Plate VIIb; the Württembergische Landesbibliothek, Stuttgart, for Plate VIIc; the Herzog-August-Bibliothek, Wolfenbüttel, for Plate VIII; and very particularly the V.I. Lenin State Library of the USSR, Moscow, and Professor V.Y. Deryagin for Plates IX and X, and for their most generous provision of a set of photographs of the Ms. from which these are taken.

Lastly I thank Clare Cully for drawing the elegant maps in Figures 3 and 4 and the plan in Figure 11; for doing the index; and for all sorts of other tokens of companionship.

John Bossy
York, February 1991

A Note on Dates

In 1582, POPE Gregory XIII introduced a new calendar, the Gregorian calendar or New Style, in place of the existing one, the Julian calendar or Old Style. From 15 October 1582 the Gregorian calendar was ten days in advance of the Julian; besides this, moveable feasts like Easter occurred at different times in the two calendars. The new calendar came into force immediately in Italy, in France at Christmas 1582, and in the Catholic states of the Empire in October 1583. It did not come into force in England until 1752. There was, therefore, during the years covered by this book, a difference of ten days between the date in England and the date in most parts of the continent where the events narrated occurred – the date in England being the earlier – and an additional difference in the dates of moveable feasts. Representatives of Catholic powers in England dated letters in the new style, and English representatives abroad in the old. Catholics in England, whether native or foreign, were likely in many circumstances to use the Gregorian calendar. All this causes difficulties both for historians and for readers.

In the *text* of the book, I have used the old-style date alone for events occurring in England after 5/15 October 1582, including those, such as letters written by Catholic diplomats in England, where the author or participant himself used new style. For dates where the style being used is a problem or may be in doubt I use both styles (as 1/11 April 1584); this is in particular the case on pp. 42–5.

Except where I explicitly state otherwise, I use the new-style date alone for all events occurring across the Channel after the Gregorian calendar was adopted in the country in question. For events in the Holy Roman Empire after October 1583, and for the letters home of Sir Edward Stafford, English ambassador in Paris from that date, I use both styles.

In the *footnotes*, and in the separate *Notes* and the section *Texts*, I have dated *all* letters written after 5/15 October 1582 according to both styles (as, 1/11–iv–1584).

I treat all years as beginning on 1 January.

The account of the adoption of the Gregorian calendar in A. Cappelli, *Cronologia, cronografia e calendario perpetuo* (Milan, 1929; 5th edn, 1983), pp. 28–31, needs some modification in the light of *CSP Foreign 1582*, p. xlviii.

Abbreviations used in the Footnotes

Bibliographical details are given in *Sources and Literature*, pp. 282–9.

BA	Biblioteca Ambrosiana, Milan
BL	British Library, Department of Manuscripts, followed by title of collection
BN	Bibliothèque Nationale, Paris, Département des Manuscrits: ff – fonds français; V^{c}C – Cinq Cents de Colbert
Blet, *Ragazzoni*	*Girolamo Ragazzoni, évêque de Bergame, nonce en France . . . 1583–1586*, ed. Pierre Blet
Cabala	Giordano Bruno, *Cabala del cavallo pegaseo*: *DI*, pp. 833–923
Candelaio	Giordano Bruno, *Il candelaio*, ed. I. Guerrini Angrisani, 1976
Causa	Giordano Bruno, *De la causa, principio e uno*: the first reference given is to *DI*, pp. 172–342; the second is to the edition of Giovanni Aquilecchia, 1973
Cena	Giordano Bruno, *La cena de le Ceneri*: the first reference is to *DI*, pp. 1–171; the second is to the edition of Giovanni Aquilecchia, 1955
Chéruel	A. Chéruel, *Marie Stuart et Catherine de Médicis*
CSP	*Calendars of State Papers of the Reign of Queen Elizabeth*, followed by title of series and dates covered by volume
DBI	*Dizionario biografico degli Italiani*

DI	Giordano Bruno, *Dialoghi italiani*, ed. Giovanni Gentile: third edition by Giovanni Aquilecchia, 1958
Documenti	*Documenti della vita di Giordano Bruno*
DNB	*Dictionary of National Biography*
Eroici furori	Giordano Bruno, *De gli eroici furori*: *DI*, pp. 925–1178
Firpo, 'Processo'	Luigi Firpo, 'Il processo di Giordano Bruno', parts i and ii
Florio	John Florio, *Queen Anna's New World of Words*
HMC	Historical Manuscripts Commission, followed by title of collection
Infinito	Giordano Bruno, *De l'infinito universo e mondi*: *DI*, pp. 343–537
Leicester's Commonwealth	*Leicester's Commonwealth: the Copy of a Letter written by a Master of Art of Cambridge*, ed. D.C. Peck, 1985
Murdin	*A Collection of State Papers . . . left by William Cecill Lord Burghley*, ed. William Murdin
NS	new style
ODCC	F.L. Cross, *Oxford Dictionary of the Christian Church*
OL	*Jordani Bruni Nolani opera latine conscripta*, volume and part
OS	old style
Pastor, *History*	Ludwig von Pastor, *History of the Popes*
Philip Howard	*The Ven. Philip Howard Earl of Arundel, 1557–1595*, ed. J.H. Pollen and W. MacMahon
PRO	Public Record Office, London: SP – State Papers, followed by call number of series and volume number
Sigillus	Giordano Bruno, *Ars reminiscendi: Triginta sigilla et . . . Sigillus sigillorum*: OL ii^2, 67–217
Sommario	*Il sommario del processo di Giordano Bruno*, ed. Angelo Mercati: the items are numbered and are cited by number
Spaccio	Giordano Bruno, *Spaccio della bestia trionfante*: *DI*, pp. 547–831

Texts	Refers to the *Texts* at pp. 187–247, which are cited by number
Yates, *Bruno*	Frances Yates, *Giordano Bruno and the Hermetic Tradition*
Yates, *Florio*	Frances Yates, *John Florio: the Life of an Italian in Shakespeare's England*
Yates, 'New Documents'	Frances Yates, 'Giordano Bruno: some New Documents'
Yates, 'Religious Policy'	Frances Yates, 'The Religious Policy of Giordano Bruno'

To the Reader

THIS BOOK TELLS A STORY, and because it tells a story I cannot, dear reader, reveal to you here and now what happens in it. If you wish to find out what the story is you will have to read the book from beginning to end; which you may easily do, for it is not very long. I can, however, tell you one or two things about it. Its time is a few years in the middle of the reign of Queen Elizabeth I; to be exact, between the spring of 1583 and the autumn of 1586. Its place is mostly London, with a few excursions up and down the Thames; sometimes it is Paris, and it ends there. Its principal characters are, in order of dignity, an English secretary of state, a French ambassador, a celebrated Italian philosopher later burned for heresy, and a spy. There are smaller parts for two crowned heads, Queen Elizabeth and King Henri III of France; for other councillors, ambassadors and servants; for a couple of poets, various Italians, some conspirators and a number of domestic servants. It deals with high matters of state, of public and private salvation. I should be inclined to classify it as a tragi-comedy, and it could be said to have a moral.

Although many of these features would have qualified it, a few years later, to be put on the stage at Blackfriars or Bankside, the story differs from that of *Hamlet* or *Measure for Measure* in being, or aspiring to be, true. It was imprudent of me to claim, in the original edition of the book, that it was true without qualification: it is easy to see how it could be shown to be false. But I have proceeded on the assumption that it is true, which time may confirm or contradict. I am a historian, not a writer of fiction, and have written the book in the conviction that the duty of a historian is to tell true stories about the past. It is often said that historians cannot do this, or have something better to do. One of my motives in writing the book has been to intimate that both these opinions are false. They are taught by two sorts of people, who come to the same position from opposite points of the compass. There are those, few of them Leninists, who have gone along with the Leninist notion, promoted thirty years ago by E.H.Carr, that facts are one thing and historical facts another. A historian's facts are those which he has invited to perform on the scene as actors in his expository drama, and which he has made up, in the cosmetic if not quite in the colloquial sense, to do his job for him. They are, at best, like research workers in some collective project: necessary, respected but earthbound collaborators in the historian's creative operations; deserving of an honourable mention in his acknowledgments, but not of a place on his title-page or a share in his royalties. Now that the Soviet empire it was designed to sustain has fallen down, this construction too might have rusted away in peace had it not been taken over and polished up by a corps of conservationists waving the banner of discourse. Discourse is a capacious box in which the outsider may find, among a variety of harmless or useful objects, inflammable substances like universal rules of rhetoric and subliminal messages confirming the arrangements of power. It gives off, when these are ignited, a sort of phlogiston of occult meanings which animates all communicative matter. If you are a historian it decides what is to count as a fact, and constitutes the object you think you are recording. When you put down your pen it will tell you what you have said, which will generally turn out to be much what Carr would have predicted.[1]

Patrick Collinson, from Cambridge, says he finds Carr's distinction between facts and historical facts 'mercifully meaningless'; from Aix-en-Provence Paul Veyne, who is not an enemy of discourse, says none the less that history is the narration of true events.[2] I might leave well alone and get on with my story. But I should like, before I do, to say something myself about facts. There does seem room for a distinction between real facts – all those states of affairs which are or have been so – and true facts – facts about which, one way or another, the question has arisen whether they are real or not. Since truth is a matter of propositions, somebody must make a proposition before a real fact becomes a true fact. But the proposer does not make, or help to make, the fact a true fact; he acknowledges, willy-nilly, that it is so. If it was not real, then it will not be true.

Readers of detective stories, who knew this already, may like to know that my story is a detective story too. It is like all such stories

1 E.H. Carr, *What is History?* (1961; 2 edn by R.W. Davies, London, 1987), ch. i; Hayden White, *Tropics of Discourse* (Baltimore, 1978), chs. ii & iii; J.-M. Adam, *Le Texte narratif: traité d'analyse textuelle des récits* (?Paris, 1985), especially pp. 186–203.

2 Patrick Collinson, *De Republica Anglorum: or, History with the Politics Put Back* (Cambridge, 1990), p. 10; Paul Veyne, *Comment on écrit l'histoire* (1971; abridged edn, Paris, 1979), pp. 10, 18 f, 35.

in being about a single fact. You may appreciate detective stories, and nevertheless think that one fact is not much to write a history book about. You may agree with Sartre, in *La Nausée*, that one existent can never justify the existence of another existent, or words to that effect: he meant people, not facts, but the point is the same. The main thing to be said about this is that my fact, if it is true, partakes of the absolute, even of the sacred. It is not up to me to decide whether it counts as a fact, or to toss a coin about how it may properly be described. It was there before I found it, just as it is. It was there during the 380 or so years from when the last person who knew it died until a couple of years ago. It will still be there when you and I, dear reader, are dead and gone. If it is not true, it will never have been there in the first place. What we think about it, what the most ingenious among us have thought or may think in the future, will not have made any difference at all.

That being so, it is possibly not up to me, either, to claim that my fact is quite important. That may indeed be entirely a matter of opinion. I cannot imagine any large historical hypothesis it would tend to support or falsify. All the same, some naive calculations may not be out of place. Off the top of our heads, we can think of some criteria for deciding whether a fact, if true, is important. I can think of three: 1. whether it has to do with an important person; 2. how difficult it is to find out; and 3. how many other 'facts', believed to be true by how many people for how long, etc., it is incompatible with the truth of. The first test, by itself, sounds dubious, since a lot of facts about Shakespeare are probably unimportant; and if we do not want to give too much aid and comfort to investigative journalists we had better hope that the third is more reliable that the second. But there is something to be said for all of them, and personally I think you will find that my fact will pass them all. Important or not, I present it to you as a true fact in a true story.

Perhaps it is more likely than it used to be that you will need to know something about the state of the world in which my story occurred. Europe in the mid-1580s may, with due precaution, be thought of as something like Europe in the late 1930s. The hostility of believers in incompatible doctrines of salvation, set on foot by the Protestant Reformation, had induced a state of warfare, actual or potential, throughout most of the West. This was now building up to a grand military confrontation, the most memorable incident of which occurred in 1588 when King Philip of Spain sent his Armada against Queen Elizabeth of England. In the spring of 1583, the state of formal warfare did not extend much beyond the Netherlands, where the Spaniards were having considerable success in rolling back a Protestant rebellion; as it turned out, the rebellion was to be saved by, among other things, the failure of the Armada, and before long to establish its legitimacy in the form of the Dutch Republic. There was a good deal of scattered fighting on and around the seas of the world: from the Pacific coast of Spanish America, whence Sir Francis Drake had returned with his plunder; to the Azores in the Atlantic, where the Spaniards had just smashed up an expedition sent from France to recapture the islands from King Philip, who had acquired them in 1580; to the narrow seas between England and the continent, where more or less confessional piracy prevailed.

More to the point of my story was the state of undeclared civil war between Protestants and Catholics which existed throughout north-western Europe except in the Netherlands, where it had been declared. In France it had gone on openly for much of the previous twenty years, though it was for the moment officially in suspense; there existed in the south a Protestant state within the state, in which the young Henri of Navarre reigned. It was only kept underground in England by extreme vigilance and careful statesmanship on the part of Queen Elizabeth and her government. The queen's problems were in some respects more dangerous than those of King Henri III of France. In the first place, just when the Huguenot movement in France appeared to have shot its bolt, England had suddenly, and most unexpectedly, become the scene of a full-scale Catholic revival. In the second, Elizabeth had in the person of Mary, Queen of Scots, the head of a Catholic opposition present in the country. She was the presumed heir to Elizabeth's throne, as Henri of Navarre was to become to Henri III's in 1584; the fact that she was in custody, and her opposition clandestine, made her a good deal more dangerous to Elizabeth than Henri of Navarre was to Henri III at a time when political assassination was becoming something of a commonplace. There was also the difference that Mary was queen, or ex-queen, of Scotland and that, though she had been expelled by a Protestant rebellion fifteen years before (whence her presence in England), the state of Scotland was so subject to sudden and incomprehensible changes that no one could be sure that she would not somehow be triumphantly reinstated. At the moment her seventeen-year-old son James was presiding inscrutably over a snake-pit of baronial feuds on the accidents of which it still appeared to depend whether the country's future would lie with Protestant England or with Catholic France: if indeed England was to have a Protestant future, which, if Mary or Catholicism or historic francophilia returned to power in Scotland, seemed a question.

It was true that the present condition of French affairs made a successful intervention against English or Protestant influence in Scotland unlikely; but that condition could not last for ever, and one could not tell when, and in what direction, it might be resolved. In 1583 Henri III was getting on relatively well with his Protestants, and correspondingly ill with a massive body of intransigent Catholics, under the leadership of the Duke of Guise and his fellow-members of the House of Lorraine, who regarded the king, with some reason, as a problematic defender of the Catholic faith. This body was to acquire a formal political organisation, as the Catholic League or Holy Union, in the spring of 1585; during the next three years it moved steadily towards an outright civil war against the crown, which may be said to have broken out in Paris in the early summer of 1588. This led very shortly to the assassination of both the Duke of Guise and the king, and precipitated the country into at least five years of absolute chaos.

In the spring of 1583 the air of north-west Europe was, if not thick with the cries of the massacred and martyred, thick with the expectation of massacre and martyrdom. Catholics in France pointed at pictures of priests dismembered in England to show what would happen if they allowed a Protestant to inherit the crown of France. Protestants in England, with equal or greater justice, looked for Mary Tudor's fires of Smithfield to be relit if the Catholic Mary Stuart succeeded to the Protestant Elizabeth. Close parallels in the abstract, the two situations were locked together in the concrete by the circumstances that Mary was a first cousin of the Duke of Guise and an ornament of the House of Lorraine; and that a sizeable body of her English followers was accumulating in those parts of France where the House of Lorraine was most powerful, which also happened to be the parts of France most convenient for an invasion of England. There they waited impatiently for the duke, the pope and King Philip to get their powers together for a decisive intervention across the Channel, which would recover England for Mary, for Catholicism and for themselves. In the Netherlands, in France, in the islands of the Atlantic, events were running in their favour; it could not be long before the tide began to wash away the dykes of Protestant England.

As there were English and Scottish Catholics in France, so there were Dutch and French Protestants in England, and French and Italian Protestants in Geneva. Although Italian Protestantism was a weak plant which the pope's inquisition had not had much trouble in eradicating, Italians had had several centuries' experience in the practice of political exile, and Protestants, dissident intellectuals, and members of political factions defeated by the Habsburg and Spanish power now controlling the peninsula proliferated north of the Alps. Alongside traditional migrants like artists and businessmen, they could be found anywhere from Oxford to Moscow; but since

Italian dissidents had traditionally found shelter in France, those among them who were not strictly refugees for religion were more likely to be found there than elsewhere. One of them, Piero Strozzi, had led the catastrophic invasion of the Azores.

Memories of the 1930s, which may be evoked by such refugees, will perhaps stir more acutely in England at the climate of espionage and treason in which these often moved. In the heavy atmosphere of undeclared doctrinal warfare which prevailed before lightning finally struck, the traitor, the conspirator, the spy, the counter-spy, and the *agent-provocateur* were a normal recourse of governments. As usual, there was room in the profession for idealists and ideologues, for confidence men and talented technicians; as usual, the relation between their doings and conventional diplomatic activity was sometimes intimate and sometimes adversarial. I do not think they were redundant, or that they cancelled each other out; and I have the impression that Queen Elizabeth's government managed them more capably than others, thanks mainly to the flair and dedication brought to the business by Sir Francis Walsingham, her secretary of state. This was just as well, for of the two main conventional powers in the field, on whose strength the resolution of this crisis would ultimately depend, England seemed to be the one whose domestic foundations were insecure.

With that I have brought you to the argument of my story, which begins as an Italian exile knocks at the gate of a French ambassador in London.

——PART I——

A Dog in the Night-time

'Is there any point to which you would
wish to draw my attention?'
'To the curious incident of the dog in the
night-time.'
'The dog did nothing in the night-time.'
'That was the curious incident', remarked
Sherlock Holmes.

Arthur Conan Doyle, 'Silver Blaze', in
The Memoirs of Sherlock Holmes

Figure 1. Salisbury Court and vicinity, c. 1560. From the map attributed (wrongly) to Ralph Agas. Salisbury Court appears towards the top right-hand corner. I assume that the building drawn at the bottom of it, abutting on to the taller square building which must be Salisbury/Buckhurst House, is meant to be Castelnau's house. Paget Place became Leicester House. 'Arundel Place' should refer to the very large building at the far left.

I

SALISBURY COURT

London, April–May 1583

IN THE SPRING of 1583 Michel de Castelnau, seigneur de Mauvissière in Touraine, had been living in London for nearly eight years as ambassador to Queen Elizabeth from King Henri III of France. He was a genial and civilised man in his sixties, who had grown up in the reign of Francis I and was possibly more interested in letters than in diplomacy. He was a friend of Ronsard and of most of the other ornaments of the French Renaissance, and had done some translating, and even some acting, himself. He had come to politics and warfare in the early years of the Wars of Religion, in which he had had an excellent record as an adviser to Catherine de Médicis and an effective frustrator of Huguenot enterprises against the crown. He had been on several missions abroad before being sent as ambassador to England in 1575. He was a rarity among his kind in being genuinely interested in England and the English, though he could not speak the language; in spite of disasters both political and personal, he visibly enjoyed his long stay in London a great deal.

He had been sent to England as one who got on with Elizabeth and her councillors, and this he, generally speaking, continued to do, though he was often on fairly difficult terms with the more Protestant among them. This was not because he was in any obvious way a Catholic zealot: he was too attracted to normal pleasures, too intellectually curious, probably too interested in astrology, and in general far too old a hand for the strenuous faith of the Counter-Reformation. He sometimes gave the impression of being a very imperfect Catholic. The impression was misleading. Although in his personal relations he was more or less colour-blind to religious difference, he had nevertheless acquired a severe distaste for the more aggressive forms of political Protestantism, and his experience of it had uncovered in him a bedrock of Catholic allegiance which might otherwise have remained submerged. The discovery had been assisted by

his marriage, which had occurred at the same time as his appointment
to London and in evident connection with it: his wife Marie Bochetel,
who was at least thirty years younger than he was, was the heiress of
a distinguished, wealthy and extremely Catholic family of royal
servants.

She had, unusually I think for a sixteenth-century diplomatic
household, spent most of the first six years of his embassy with him
in London, and had borne four children there, two boys and two
girls; she had been in France for the past two years, and when she
returned in the summer of 1583 the boys remained there. The
younger girl, Elisabeth, had been boarded out with Catholic friends
near Richmond, and stayed there; the elder, Katherine-Marie, now
about five, came back with her mother and enlivened the household
for the next two years. Sadly, Madame de Mauvissière did not, for
she now went through a series of miscarriages and unhappy preg-
nancies, and for most of the time was ill and in bed; she died in
childbirth shortly after their return to France, in December 1586. Her
fate seems more than usually depressing, for she was a young
woman of spirit, had her own friends and made her own financial
and sometimes political arrangements. She was Catholic by family
tradition and in England, I think, by romantic inclination; her
differences with her husband on this score, which never impaired
their mutual affection and diminished with time, no doubt help to
account for the extraordinary variety of opinions which prevailed
among the members of their numerous household.[1]

They lived at the western end of the City, in a house called
Salisbury Court. The court itself was a sort of rough square in the
jumble of buildings between Fleet Street and the Thames. A short
lane joined it to Fleet Street, which it entered opposite Shoe Lane,
and through another exit in the south-west corner you could pass
through to Water Lane, and thence down the hill to the river another
fifty yards away. It had got its name from a large keep-like building
at the south-east corner, which had belonged to the bishop of
Salisbury before Sir Richard Sackville acquired it in 1564; this was
now called Buckhurst House from the family title, and in 1583 it was
at some stage of transformation into the elegant mansion which it
became in the seventeenth century. Then, it had a fine garden

---

1   J. le Laboureur (ed.), *Mémoires de Michel de Castelnau*, 3rd edn by J. Godefroy (3 vols;
    Brussels, 1731), iii, 67–171; G. Hubault, *Michel de Castelnau, ambassadeur en Angleterre*
    (Paris, 1859; repr. Geneva, 1970), pp. 1–26. There is a lot of value on Castelnau's politics
    in A. Chéruel, *Marie Stuart et Catherine de Médicis* (Paris, 1858). I have drawn here and
    there on my unpublished study of Castelnau's embassy, which is intended to form the
    first part of a book on relations between France and English Catholics during the wars of
    religion; I refer to it, where necessary, as 'Castelnau in London'.

Figure 2. Portrait of Michel de Castelnau, from *Les Mémoires de Messire Michel de Castelnau, seigneur de Mauvissière* (Paris, 1621). Since the manuscript of Castelnau's memoirs was given to the publisher by his son Jacques, the portrait ought to be a reasonable likeness.

running down to the river; in the 1580s the river end of the property was more of a mess, but where the lane came to the waterside there was a set of river-stairs, which took their name from the house. The stairs have a part in our story; the house does not. To the east of Salisbury Court stood St Bride's church and churchyard and the ex-palace of Bridewell, now a house of correction; to the west, the large riverside complex of the Temple, and then a string of aristocratic houses running with their gardens, between the Strand and the river, as far as the palace of Whitehall.

The ambassador's house must have been the largest property actually facing on to the court, and I think it should probably be identified with a long and rambling-looking building which occupies most of the north side of the court in Richard Newcourt's map of the 1640s (Figure 9). The drawing is crude, but if it is of the right house it is the only evidence we have of what it looked like. It shows, at best, two and a half storeys, which must be too few since the embassy had a gallery; it also shows an archway running through the building which would have covered the main entrance. Newcourt's map is not topographically precise, and it becomes obvious from the accurate survey of the area done immediately after the Great Fire of 1666 (in which the house was burned down) that if it was what he had meant to represent he had put it on the wrong side of the court. There it appears in its correct place along the south side, filling the space between the passage towards Water Lane and Buckhurst House, which it adjoined. From Castelnau's description of his land-lady as 'la marquise' it also emerges that the house had been part of the Salisbury House property, and when Sir Richard Sackville died in 1566 had passed as a dower house to his widow; she had promptly remarried that ninety-year-old pillar of early Tudor government, William Paulet, Marquis of Winchester, and therefore did not need it for long. It had been used as the French embassy since 1568, and either the marchioness or Castelnau's predecessor may have ex-tended it westwards. By 1580 it seems to have acquired some kind of a cloister or arcade on the side facing the court, since on one occasion Castelnau was met 'walking under his lodging' in the court. The garden, which it certainly had, appears on the 1666 plan and covered about half the distance between the house and the river: it had the larger garden of Buckhurst House on one side and the lane going down to the river on the other. It was possible to get into the house from the lane, presumably through a door in the garden wall; which was convenient, as not everyone wanted to be seen going in at the front gate. It sounds and looks spacious and comfortable, though not particularly grand: Castelnau said it was an old building, which is what it looks like on the maps.[2] It was known simply as Salisbury Court, and is one of the principal personages in our story.

By 1583 Castelnau was a well-established figure on the English scene, and had a large number of friends, and acquaintances both political and literary, whom he entertained to excellent dinners. As a political influence, he was a good deal less intimate with the queen and her councillors than he had been a couple of years before, when a marriage between Elizabeth and his king's younger brother, François, Duke of Alençon and Anjou, had been on the table. Since the failure of that enterprise, in which he had invested a great deal of various kinds, he had been doing his best to cultivate the goodwill of Elizabeth's prisoner and putative successor Mary, Queen of Scots. Recently, a lot of his energy had gone into creating a means of communication with Mary's establishment at Sheffield, and this was

2   See 'A Note on Castelnau's House', below, pp. 248–9; Figures 1 and 9–11.

now running fairly smoothly. Officially he was trying to negotiate an agreement between Mary and Elizabeth which would lead to Mary's release on agreed conditions; actually, he was prepared to facilitate almost any scheme Mary had in mind for securing her liberation, including any enterprise for her forcible rescue which might be mounted by her relations of the House of Lorraine. He wanted Mary out of English hands, not so much for any consequences her liberation might have in England, as for the prospect which would then arise of restoring French influence or control over Scotland. Castelnau believed that a restoration of this kind, and the effort which would be required to achieve it, was the right way to solve the external and internal problems which beset his country in his time, and had deprived it of its rightful grandeur among the nations of Christendom. What he was up to with Mary was a matter of extreme concern to the ministers of Queen Elizabeth, and especially to Sir Francis Walsingham, who was paying a number of informants to find out.[3]

On 28 March or, according to the pope's new calendar which had been in operation in France since the beginning of the year, on 7 April 1583 the English ambassador in Paris reported a visit from one Dr Jordano Bruno Nolano, 'a professor in philosophy . . . whose religion I cannot commend'. Giordano Bruno, who has a reputation in England as a founder of modern culture and another in Italy as a morning star of the *Risorgimento*, was one of the brighter lights in the intellectual firmament of Europe in the age of Montaigne and Shakespeare. He was a refugee Dominican friar from the kingdom of Naples who had spent the last few years teaching and philosophising in France and was now leaving for England. He was not much of a doctor, since he had never taught in any university faculty higher than that of arts; but he was genuinely learned in a slightly old-fashioned way, which is explained by his background in the tradition of Thomas Aquinas, though inclined to cut corners on less familiar paths. Professionally he taught astronomy and Aristotle's physics. He had also written poetry, and recently published a comedy; in conversation he was voluble, witty, iconoclastic and opinionated. At present he was known to the public as an expert in the art of memory, which he taught more as an occult science than as a technical skill; but his life's work was still mostly in front of him. He was thirty-five, a small, dark man with a bit of a beard and,

3   I refer to 'Castelnau in London'; Conyers Read, *Mr Secretary Walsingham* (3 vols; Oxford, 1925–7), ii, 366–99.

according to the least implausible of his portraits (Figure 5), a thin moustache.[4]

Why he was going to England is not very clear. He was on personal terms with Henri III, and had a stipend from him as a 'reader', whatever exactly that meant. He was not popular in the university of Paris, and may very well have been in difficulty as a runaway friar, but there is no sign that anyone was persecuting him on either score. He said that he had asked the king for leave of absence 'per i tumulti', but there were no serious civil or religious disturbances in Paris in 1583. Whether he had made any proposal about where he might spend his sabbatical we do not know, but the king gave him a letter to Castelnau apparently recommending him to lodge Bruno in Salisbury Court. This was ideal for Bruno, and possibly a convenience for the king. We shall find no reason for thinking that Henri III sent Bruno to London on any kind of political or religious mission. It would be much more likely that he had found Bruno's presence in Paris embarrassing and invited him to go to England until the embarrassment had blown over: he had done this to other Italian exiles. But until we find some reason why he should have done this to Bruno we ought to accept what Bruno said, that the idea came from him.[5] He was certainly glad to see England, and the prospect of getting time to write without having to give lectures was as welcome to him as to any other academic. He was still the king's servant, and we may observe from the English ambassador's parting shot that he was going over to England as a Catholic.

Whatever exactly was in Henri III's letter, when Bruno presented it at Salisbury Court Castelnau was happy to take him in: Bruno looked his kind of person, could make him laugh, instruct him on poetry and the stars, and add a powerful attraction to his dinner table. As one of Bruno's friends later remarked, he was an agreeable companion and an enjoyer of life. He must have settled into the house some time in April, and begun to write.

*   *   *

4   The principal studies of Bruno in English are Yates, *Bruno*, and *The Art of Memory* (London, 1966); and Dorothea Waley Singer, *Giordano Bruno, his Life and Work* (New York, 1950). The article on Bruno in *DBI*, xiv, (by G. Aquilecchia, 1972) gives the state of factual knowledge; M. Ciliberto, *Giordano Bruno* (Rome-Bari, 1990) is a philosophical account with some valuable biographical matter and a good bibliography. For Bruno's move to England, *Texts*, no. 1, and Yates, *Bruno*, pp. 203–4; for his appearance, *Documenti*, pp. 69, 76 and possibly Figure 5.

5   *Texts*, no. 1; against Yates, 'Religious Policy' pp. 192–7, and in agreement with Ciliberto, *Giordano Bruno*, p. 28. I shall be discussing the relation between Bruno and Henri III in due course. If the king had wanted to get Bruno out of the way, there would have been a precedent in the case of Piero Capponi, a Florentine enemy of Grand Duke Cosimo of Tuscany, encouraged to go to England in 1576: Castelnau to Henri III, 14-iv-1576 (BN V^cC 337, p. 629).

Bruno was not the only unconventional resident of Salisbury Court at this time. On about 20 April, the first of a number of interesting messages from the house arrived on Sir Francis Walsingham's desk. It came from one Henry Fagot, and consisted of six separate items, each dated and signed, written on 18 and 19 April, reporting things that were happening in the house. On the 14th the post had arrived from France with a letter to Castelnau from the Duke of Guise encouraging him to pursue vigorously his secret operations in favour of the Queen of Scots, and granting him in return the revenues of a substantial French benefice. On 19 April an old man called Pierre had brought Castelnau a separate letter from somebody asking him to pass on to King James of Scotland a message that he should be patient a little longer since Catholic help was on the way and, apparently, asking for a pair of pistols. I should think the writer was the Duke of Lennox, who had recently been the head of a brief anti-English régime in Scotland, but had been obliged to withdraw to France. On 18 April a Scot called William Fowler had turned up, as he regularly did, with news about the doings of the chief ministers of the Scottish Church: he was pretending to be a Protestant, and actually in the pay of the French. On the 19th Monsieur Throckmorton had come to dinner, having recently conveyed a sizeable sum of money from Castelnau to Mary; at midnight Lord Henry Howard had turned up, no doubt via the garden, and told Castelnau that a Scot who was living in the embassy was about to be put in prison as a Catholic.[6]

A week later Fagot sent another communication of the same kind. On 22 April one William Herle had paid a visit, and had talked with apparent frankness to Castelnau about the dishonesty of English policy towards France and the likelihood that Henri III and Philip II would join together against Elizabeth. Herle did jobs for Castelnau but, said Fagot, did not trust him; a conscientious reader may have noticed him already, meeting Castelnau in the court outside as he came by from the river one summer's day four years before. A Fleming had come from Mendoza, the Spanish ambassador, to confirm the rumour about an impending agreement between the Duke of Anjou and King Philip. (The duke had been running an unsuccessful intervention in the Netherlands, and the implication was that he would be abandoning the cause of the Dutch rebels.) On 24 April Fowler had arrived again, bringing Castelnau two spectacular rings from the Duke of Lennox, which he was to send to Mary. Castelnau had also had a letter from his wife in Paris: she would shortly be coming over; she had had a conversation with the Duke of Guise, who had said that he expected to be in Scotland very soon; meanwhile Castelnau was to keep his relations with Mary extremely secret, and to cheer her up as much as possible. Talking to an English lord whom Fagot could not identify, Castelnau had predicted a Catholic coup in Scotland very shortly, to be run by Guise and Lennox. On the 25th Monsieur du Bex, the Duke of Anjou's envoy, had left for Flanders; he had told Castelnau that the duke had given up hope of getting anything out of Elizabeth, and proposed to marry a daughter of the King of Spain.[7]

Since Fagot did not write again for a while, we can pause to think about the significance of his messages. It is not often that we can observe so closely the comings and goings in the house of a sixteenth-century ambassador, and since that was apparently what Fagot had been asked to do he was doing an excellent job. The substance of what he had to say was extremely worthwhile, though not all of it was new. About Scotland, in which his employers had originally been interested, Fagot gave chapter and verse for what Walsingham was already hearing from Fowler, who was in his pay. His other news was hotter: the reports about contact between the Spaniards and the Duke of Anjou, who was widely expected to do something of the kind after the failure of an attempted coup in Antwerp in January, were mistaken about the duke but interesting about communications between Mendoza and Castelnau, a matter of nervous speculation to Elizabeth and her Council; the information that Castelnau was meeting English Catholics like Howard and Throckmorton, and communicating with Mary through the latter, was I think absolute news to Walsingham, and extremely valuable, though for the time being he was too preoccupied with Scotland to do anything much about it. The main source of Fagot's knowledge sounds like dinner-table or after-dinner conversation, but he had been present at some fairly confidential interviews, and had been able to find out what was in some of Castelnau's most private letters. The general drift of his reports, that Castelnau was actively collaborating in schemes for the restoration of Catholicism, in Scotland certainly and in England possibly, was alarmingly convincing. From an English point of view, Fagot was the right man in the right place at the right time.

Who exactly was he? We must be content for the time being with the evidence of the letters themselves, since there is no reference to such a person in Castelnau's correspondence of the period, nor in the voluminous reports of his doings which were daily arriving in Walsingham's office from Fowler and others. From his letters we can

---

7 *Texts*, no. 3; Herle appears in 'A Note on Castelnau's House', below, pp. 248–9.

deduce four things about Fagot.[8] The first is that, although he wrote in French, French was not his native language. He was not, as one might think from a first reading of his letters, semi-literate; he was simply not French. His French is not at all bad, but has been mainly picked up by conversation, and he writes the language incorrectly in a way that even a sixteenth-century Frenchman could not have done. This can be shown by his difficulties with verbs. Fagot gets the number and person of a verb wrong when the sound is not distinctive: 'ceulx qui *pense* ce faire'; 'deulx bagues . . . dont je ne *connoist* les pierres'. He often gets the agreement of his tenses wrong: 'il connoissoit fort bien que son Altesse ne *requert* aultre chosse'; 'pour avoir esté en une maison . . . apres que ledit Irlandois *estoit* mis en prison'. He gets a conjugation wrong: 'le ve Monsieur du Boys *parta* de Londres'. He uses an active instead of a reflexive verb: 'et [se] contoit cela entre luy et ung lord'. Few of these phrases could have been written by an educated Frenchman, and some of them not by an uneducated one.

I think it is fairly easy to demonstrate that Fagot was an Italian. He certainly knew Italian, because he reports a conversation taking place in it; he practically always spells *italien* with an *a*; later, in France, he described an acquaintance as being 'de mon pays'. He addresses Walsingham as *Monseigneur*, which I do not think a Frenchman would have done except to a person of much higher formal rank than Sir Francis; and as *vostre exelence*, which is surely a pure Italianism. One would expect an Italian to have difficulties with the mute final *e* in French. Fagot is actually quite good at this, but he goes wrong when a final vowel which sounds to him like *e* is actually something else. This does not matter when the vowel is *é* because his omission of the accent in all except Text no. 16 is not at all unusual. It does matter when the vowel is *ai*, and he falls down on this fairly regularly: he writes *je* for *j'ai* five times, *ne* for *n'ai* once, and *e* or *es* for *ai* or *ais* in verb endings eight times (all except one in Text no. 15). He cannot always remember whether to spell *livre* with a *v* or a *b*; and he regularly uses Italianisms which were rare, though possible, in sixteenth-century French: *patrie* (for *pays*), *trionfe, monopole* (meaning conspiratorial activity). The only other language of which he reveals any influence is Spanish: at least I assume that explains his fairly frequent use of *en* instead of *à*. His French seems to get a little better as he goes along; we shall see that from the autumn of 1583 the household contained a first-class language-teacher.[9]

Three further things about Fagot can be easily demonstrated, not

8 All references to the letters will be to the versions printed in the *Texts*, below, as there numbered.
9 John Florio: below, p. 24.

all of them from these early letters; I put them down baldly as they
come to mind. Firstly, it follows from the previous point that his
name was not Fagot. It sounds, in any case, like a pseudonym,
probably emblematic or anagrammatic; if it was an anagram I have
failed to solve it. Full Christian names were rarely used in signing
sixteenth-century letters; a constant repetition of the signature in
Fagot's first two letters suggests that the writer was trying it out.
Secondly, he was a priest. In later letters we find him hearing a
confession, discussing with the succeeding ambassador his experiences as a priest in London, and acting as almoner to a French
nobleman. Thirdly, he was extremely hostile to the pope, and to
Catholics whom he regarded as papists, which was a strong term in
his vocabulary. Text no. 2 begins with what sounds like a complaint
about using the Gregorian calendar ('les jours qui se content par le
commandement du pape') and ends with a description of Lord Henry
Howard as a 'Catholique Romain et papiste'. No. 4 contains an
attack on 'livres papistes', which are elaborated in No. 13 as 'livres
papalz diffamatoires'. Here he also speaks disparagingly of 'l'eglise
papalle'. One might have supposed that Fagot was pandering to
Walsingham in taking this line, but he used the same tone when he
wrote to Elizabeth's less godly ministers. Whoever he was, Fagot
was a spontaneous anti-papalist of a very intense kind.

One final deduction can be made. It seems pretty obvious that,
when he began writing his letters, Fagot had not been at Salisbury
Court for very long. He describes two regular visitors, William
Fowler and William Herle, as if he had just met them for the first
time: he would soon get to know Herle rather well. He does not
know people's names. It is also fairly clear from the diary-like form
of his first two communications, a form he later abandoned, and
from the pedantic dating of the first item in No. 2, that these were
Fagot's first efforts as an informer. I infer that he was a newcomer
both to the house and to the profession of spying, and had either
entered the household as a spy or become one shortly after he
arrived. One consequence of this is that we can hardly take as
applying to Fagot the occasional mention of a priest in the house
dating from a good deal earlier: there is an otherwise tempting
reference by the Duke of Anjou to 'le petit prêtre de Mauvissière' in a
letter probably written to Elizabeth in 1581.[10] I conclude that Fagot

10 HMC *Hatfield*, ii, 476: Anjou to Elizabeth, undated, sending her a portrait of himself in
    the hope 'que. . . vostre majesté eut envoyé le petit pretre de Mauvissière pour vous
    espouzer par parolle de prezant'. This cannot have been written after 1582. Throughout
    Castelnau's embassy, references to chaplains in the house are few and far between,
    though references to mass being said there are quite frequent.

was an Italian priest of anti-papal convictions, writing under an alias, who had come to live in Salisbury Court shortly before the middle of April 1583.

Fagot wrote nothing for a while after 25 April, and when he did he wrote more coherently and more knowledgeably. The letter is not dated. He says that it is 'longtemps' since he wrote, but since he had hitherto written twice in less than a week there seems no need to date No. 4 later than middle or late May.[11] After saying that he had not written because he had had nothing worth writing, he gave a detailed account of an operation being run by Castelnau's butler and cook, whose names, we learn later, were Girault de la Chassaigne and René Leduc: this involved the clandestine import of Catholic books into England from France, and the export of surplus items of Catholic church furniture picked up for a song in London. He described those who were engaged in the traffic: Pierre Pithou the carrier; 'ung . . . nomme Mestre Herson', evidently English, who sold the books in England; and the porter, 'Jehan Folk dit Renard en francoys' (Foxe? Fuchs?), who had an English wife and dug out the church stuff in London. It was, he claimed, a large and valuable business, and at the moment those engaged in it were extremely worried that government searchers were going to investigate an inn called the Half Moon, across the river in Southwark, where they had arranged to land a large consignment of books shortly to arrive. They had spent a lot of money paying the landlord of the Half Moon and the searchers at Rye and elsewhere, and were looking for salesmen for the books in England. The traffic in books passing through the embassy was to become a regular feature of Fagot's communications: he evidently disliked it very much, partly for political reasons and partly because it seemed such a money-spinner, and the butler Girault became an especial bugbear of his.

This was worthwhile information but, for Walsingham, not half so worthwhile as Fagot's next contribution. He had made friends with Castelnau's secretary, and the secretary had let it be understood that if it was made worth his while he would be willing to pass on anything Walsingham wanted to know about his master's affairs, in particular Castelnau's secret correspondence with Mary and the cipher in which it was written. In a passage where Fagot's French is particularly obscure, he seems to say that the secretary had also said that he could arrange for Walsingham to see the contents of packets going to Mary, to put in or take out whatever he thought fit, and to see that they were resealed so that Mary would not know that they

11 *Texts*, no. 4, with note on the date; ibid. n. 2 for the Half Moon.

had been seen.[12] Ideally we should pause a moment here, to register a whistle of appreciation at the receiving end, for this was an amazing coup: it raised Fagot's status at a stroke from that of an apprentice spy to that of an agent of the highest importance. But let us finish the letter. Fagot concluded by repeating that Lord Henry Howard and Francis Throckmorton were Castelnau's go-betweens with Mary, and that they visited him and he them at night; confirmed the news about Anjou's Spanish marriage from Mendoza himself, who had reported it on a visit to the house; and passed on a message from the secretary to Walsingham that Fowler was double-crossing him.

In the matter of the secretary there can be no doubt that Fagot was telling the truth. Castelnau's secretary did become a mole in Walsingham's service at this time, and Fagot may claim the credit for recruiting him. From the earlier letters it looks as if he had been telling Fagot sensitive information almost as soon as he entered the house, and that the conversation to which he refers here was only the most explicit of several. The secretary's career as a mole, and its consequences, are not particularly our business here, but a couple of things need to be said about him. The first is that he was not the person he has been supposed to be since, one hundred and fifty years ago, Prince Alexander Labanoff in his edition of Queen Mary's correspondence revealed that one of Castelnau's secretaries had been a spy. He was not, that is, Jean Arnault, seigneur de Chérelles, who had done the job for the first six years of Castelnau's embassy and was to do it for Castelnau's successor.[13] Arnault has often been vilified for his dishonourable conduct, but he was entirely innocent: he was not in London between 1581 and 1585. The culprit was Nicolas Leclerc, seigneur de Courcelles, who was secretary for most of the intervening period. The second thing is that Courcelles was not just a scribe: he had almost complete charge of Castelnau's operations concerning Mary and English Catholics, in which Castelnau wanted to be personally involved as little as possible, and he had the reputation of a Catholic zealot. Turning Courcelles was a priceless tactical achievement of Elizabethan policy: it led to the

---

12 The obscure sentence runs: 'et fault que vous sachiez qu'apres que votre exelence a visité auchun pacquet pour adresser vers Icelle [Mary] qui ne laisse [*sic*, presumably meaning *qu'il ne laissera* or *faillira*] a y remectre d'autre dans ledit pacquet et que cela n'est congneu nullement'. I have taken the liberty of assuming that Walsingham would have wanted to take letters out of any packet he inspected, as well as to put them in; but this is not what Fagot says, and something more sophisticated may have been intended. It could be that what the secretary had been suggesting to Fagot was the sort of inspired alteration of Mary's in-letters which Walsingham has often been alleged to have resorted to during the Babington Plot of 1586.

13 A. Labanoff (ed.), *Lettres, instructions et mémoires de Marie Stuart* (7 vols; London, 1844), v, 429; vi, 26, 150 n. 1.

arrest of Francis Throckmorton, and to the collapse of a promising scheme for a Catholic enterprise in support of Mary, which caused Elizabeth more alarm than anything else in her reign except the actual Armada of 1588. I apologise for these dogmatic statements, which I shall try to defend at another time; they are relevant to our story because they show that Fagot's career as a spy was an extremely serious matter.[14]

Having pulled off this coup, he wrote no more for about six months, between May and November 1583. He had done his bit for the time being, and was free to turn to other things.

14   For the story of Courcelles I refer to 'Castelnau in London'.

2

ON THE RIVER

London and Oxford, Spring and Summer 1583

AT THE END of April there had arrived in England a Polish magnate known as the Palatine Albert Laski. Castelnau reported him as trying to persuade the English to stop selling arms to the Russians, but he seems to have come mainly to see the world, as part of a tour of the west which was intended to include France: he had been in France ten years earlier in a delegation from the Poles to Henri III, then Duke of Anjou, whom they had elected King of Poland. Elizabeth, though puzzled to know what he was up to, entertained Laski at court; Henri III, who had had trouble with him during his brief reign in Poland and also thought him a fool, absolutely refused to let him land in France. Castelnau was at this time extremely preoccupied with what was going on in Scotland, and needed to fend him off. Laski was a Catholic, and lived as such at Winchester House in Southwark, which Elizabeth lent him, with a household full of Italians: Castelnau says that he used Laski's Italians to intimate to the prince that he would not be welcome in France. The two finally met at a tournament which took place at Greenwich about the beginning of June, and had a stiff conversation about Polish matters.[15]

For Giordano Bruno, of whose presence in the house the reader may need reminding, Laski's visit was an important event, since it brought him out of his retirement at Salisbury Court and introduced him to the English. I think that Castelnau probably told him to cope with Laski, and since, except for Fagot, he was the only Italian in the

---

15   The brief accounts of the visit by Camden and Anthony Wood, used by Singer, *Giordano Bruno*, p. 32, and by Yates, *Bruno*, p. 206 can be elaborated from five letters of Castelnau to Henri III and Catherine de Médicis between 5/15-v-1583 and 3/13-vi-1583 (Chéruel, pp. 239, 244, 248, 255, 262−3), and three from Henri III to Castelnau between 7/17-v-1583 and 15/25-vii-1583 (BN V^{c}C 473, pp. 409, 415, 433). There is a splendid engraving of Winchester House in Wenceslaus Hollar's 'Long View of London' of 1647: it certainly was, as Castelnau said (below, n. 24), 'ung fort honneste logis'.

house, used him to pass his messages to Laski's Italians. We can be pretty certain that Bruno was present at the interview at Greenwich, since he later said that Castelnau often took him to court as his 'gentilhuomo', and this would be a very appropriate occasion. If so it was his first sight of Elizabeth, and his introduction to the world of Elizabethan knightly romance on which he became both an expert and an influence.[16] Shortly after that Elizabeth sent Laski off for further entertainment to Oxford with her most polished courtier, Sir Philip Sidney; Bruno was invited as well, and was surely delighted to go along. Castelnau made no difficulty. The trip was evidently one of those Arcadian happenings that agreeably punctuated the drama of Elizabethan politics. The party went up and down the river in the queen's barge, with music. Sidney was in charge of it, and Bruno now began a rather intense relationship with him, and in the end dedicated to him those of his works written in England which were not dedicated to Castelnau. I should think Bruno was responsible for a report about Sidney's sympathetic attitude to Queen Mary and to Catholicism which Castelnau passed on to Mary in August.[17] It sounds implausible, but perhaps Sidney was in a mellow mood.

When the party got to Oxford Bruno succeeded in stealing most of the limelight, disputing with the dons and no doubt enlivening dinner at high table. He had a public disputation with the Rector of Lincoln, and got a great deal of free publicity. He also met clever undergraduates like the poet Samuel Daniel, and two other distinguished Italians, the professor of civil law Alberico Gentili and the language teacher John Florio; he and Florio became great friends, and when Madame de Mauvissière returned to Salisbury Court in August or so, Florio settled there too as tutor to the five-year-old Katherine-Marie.[18] Presumably Bruno was still in the party during its return to London when they stopped at Mortlake on 15 June to see the very learned philosopher and seance-organiser John Dee. Dee was, superficially at least, a man after Bruno's own heart; he had been Sidney's tutor, and was reputed to have the best library in the country. Bruno may or may not have been disappointed when Laski took Dee back to Poland, by sea as Castelnau had predicted, in September. He had had a very nice time in Oxford, and on the way there and back; he had also got an invitation to come back and give some lectures. He did go back, it is not clear exactly when, and started two sets of lectures, one on astronomy, and one on the

---

16 *Texts*, no. 1; Yates, *Bruno*, pp. 204, 288–92.

17 Yates, *Bruno*, pp. 206–11; Castelnau to Mary, *c.* 6/16-viii-1583 (Hatfield House, Cecil Papers, 162, ff. 21–2; HMC *Hatfield*, iii, 9, dated from Chéruel, p. 282); J.O. Halliwell (ed), *The Private Diary of John Dee* (Camden Society, xix, 1842), p. 20.

18 Yates, *Florio*, pp. 87 ff; Joan Rees, *Samuel Daniel* (Liverpool, 1964), pp. 2–5.

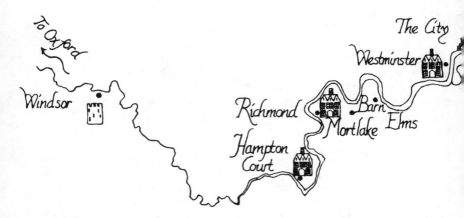

Figure 3.   Map of the Thames from Windsor to Gravesend.

immortality of the soul. The lectures caused a sensation because of his Neapolitan pronunciation of Latin (*chentrum* and *chirculus* and *circumferenchia*, reported one attender, the future archbishop George Abbot), because of his exposition of the Copernican system, and also because of his extensive plagiarism from the renaissance guru Marsilio Ficino. When this was found out he was invited to stop, and returned to London in a state of high indignation about Oxford pedantry.[19]

Bruno was to dine out on his feud with Oxford for some time to come. He claimed himself that it was mainly about his championship of Copernicus against bibliolaters and Aristotelians, and I expect this was true; but I think he had also fallen foul of ill-feeling in the university against its invasion by the nobility and gentry, which accounted for the presence of most of the Italians there. Hence he could be sure of a welcome in the different intellectual climate of London, where his expulsion from Oxford seems to have made him something of a hero. Launched by Sidney and his friends, he began to socialise widely: Castelnau was no longer his only source of dinner. He must also have begun to think of writing for a new audience. So far the only thing he had written in England, if he had

---

19 Yates, *Bruno*, pp. 207–9; P.J. French, *John Dee: the World of an Elizabethan Magus* (London, 1972), pp. 27, 97 f, 127 ff, 151 n. 4; Dee's *Diary*, p. 20.

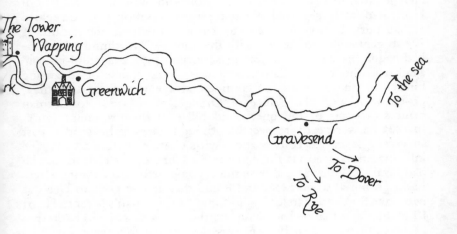

not brought it with him from France, was a knotty work called the *Sigillus sigillorum* or *Seal of Seals*, which combined the art of memorisation, a sort of contemplative magic and some rude though inscrutable remarks about contemporary Christian thought into the 'more obscure theology' of which he rightly claimed to be a master. He must have published it on his return on London. Written in Latin and dedicated to Castelnau, it was designed to appeal to an academic audience, if any, and he published it with a self-advertising letter to the vice-chancellor of Oxford.[20] That done, he was free to launch himself upon his true vocation, the social-philosophical, semi-dramatic dialogue, written in Italian for the poetry-reading public, with lots of jokes at the expense of pedants and the uncivilised. It took him a while to get going, perhaps because he did not immediately tumble to the idea, perhaps because he was too busy socialising around Christmas and New Year. Once started, he did not stop until he had left England for good.

We can record another consequence, or probable consequence, of the Palatine's visit. Elizabeth had taken steps to make sure she knew

20   Yates, *Art of Memory*, pp. 239–59. The *Sigillus* is in *OL* ii², pp. 67–217.

what he was doing, and when settling him in Southwark had attached to him a competent servant, the same William Herle whom Fagot had lately reported as having a conversation with Castelnau at Salisbury Court. We need to know something about him. A Welsh gentleman connected with the house of Northumberland, he had begun his career in the public service in 1571 as a 'stool-pigeon' against Catholic conspirators, and was in the course of advancing himself to the positions of confidential agent of Lord Burghley, go-between with the Prince of Orange, ambassador to German princes, servant of the queen and pillar of the Protestant cause. In 1583 he was nearly respectable, though traces of his shadier past survived, as in the conversation with Castelnau. On 20 May he informed the queen via the courtier Sir Christopher Hatton that he had been to Winchester House the evening before to enquire where Laski proposed to go next, and found that he had gone to Dee's at Mortlake for the day to look at his library. Castelnau's letter to Henri III, telling him that he had passed on the king's message to Laski that he was not wanted in France, was written the following day, so I imagine some collusion betweeen Castelnau and Herle in the affairs of the Palatine.[21] Laski had brought together Bruno and Sidney; it seems that he may have done the same for Herle and Fagot. We may suppose that since April Fagot had been observing Herle's relations with Castelnau, without quite knowing which side Herle was on. He must have found it out at just about this time: somewhere around the end of May or a little later. He had a serious talk with Herle, and from this point their relations became very close. By the middle of November, as we shall see in a moment, Herle had become the channel through which Fagot's information passed to Burghley and Walsingham, and from Herle's account it seems evident that this relationship had begun during the previous summer.[22] Since Fagot had met Herle for the first time on 22 April, the serious talk must have occurred some time between May and say August. I think it had probably not happened when Fagot had written his third letter, containing the news about Courcelles, which I have dated to late May; otherwise Fagot, as he did later, could have passed his news to Herle by word of mouth. I suspect the arrangement was Walsingham's reaction to the importance of the news in that letter,

---

21 Above, p. 15. Read, *Lord Burghley and Queen Elizabeth*, index, Herle, William; *CSP Foreign 1583–1584* to *1586–1587 (Holland and Flanders)*, indexes; Charles Wilson, *Queen Elizabeth and the Netherlands* (London, 1970), p. 84 and *passim*. Description from Read, p. 45; in the index he describes Herle as 'agent-provocateur', which may be harsh. Wilson calls him an 'ingenious intriguer', and he seems to have been trying to blackmail Burghley in 1585. Sir Harris Nicolas, *Memoirs of the Life of Times of Sir Christopher Hatton* (London, 1847), pp. 324 ff, 331; Castelnau to Henri III, 21/31-v-1583 (Chéruel, p. 255). Dee's *Diary*, p. 20, says that Laski visited him on 18/28 May.

22 *Texts*, no. 5.

which called for a more careful cover than Fagot had so far had; hence one might date the serious talk to some time in June. It so happens that Herle, in his letter to Hatton of 20 May, when he had finished with the doings of the Palatine said that he had 'somewhat to impart with you herein by mouth at my next attendance on you'.[23] I find it hard to resist the notion that what Herle had to impart was the contents of a conversation with Fagot: not the serious talk itself, since Herle would have known better than to breathe a word of that to Hatton, even if his letter was finally destined for the queen; but a stimulating conversation about confidential matters which would suggest to Walsingham that Herle, though a servant of Burghley, not of himself, was the right man to serve as a go-between with Fagot. He had a lot of relevant experience to pass on to an apprentice in the trade. If this was so we might conclude that the conversation had taken place at Winchester House on the day when Laski had gone to see Dee at Mortlake; as an Italian, Fagot was as likely a carrier as Bruno for Castelnau's message from Henri III to Laski, which must have been delivered to Laski's Italian secretary at almost exactly this time.[24]

23 Nicolas, *Hatton*, p. 331.
24 Castelnau to Henri III, 5/15-v-1583 (Chéruel, p. 240), suggests that somebody from the house had been to Winchester House and talked to Herle about Laski: 'L'on a fait bailler ung fort honneste logis audit Lasqui, et a esté jusques à présent bien receu et caressé de ceux qui ont eu la charge de le recepvoir.' Fagot's first chat with Herle had been fairly confidential, see *Texts*, no. 3: 'Nottez quil est facteur de monseigneur lambassadeur et ne ce fie gueres en luy.'

3

CONFESSIONS

London, November 1583–Easter 1584

FOR THE HOUSEHOLD at Salisbury Court, the winter of 1583–4, which had begun so auspiciously with the return of Castelnau's wife and daughter from France, turned out to be a time of dramatic and distressing events. These began with the arrest of Francis Throckmorton about 20 November, and proceeded through his interrogation and confession under torture in the Tower to the expulsion of Mendoza from the country in January and the barely avoided expulsion of Castelnau after that. Throckmorton was eventually tried in May and executed in July on a well-substantiated charge of treasonable conspiracy to procure a Catholic invasion of the country. This was, directly and indirectly, the result of Fagot's revelations, and he and Walsingham must have been delighted. Elizabeth, who saw herself faced with the nightmare of an agreement between Spain and France to overthrow her, was a good deal less delighted; for a month or so, the atmosphere at court was not far from panic. Having been a sleeper since May or June, Fagot was brought into service again, partly to help with Throckmorton's arrest, but mostly to find out on which side Castelnau would jump in the confrontation that seemed to be impending.

As I have explained, he was now to communicate, not in writing, but verbally through Herle, and we are fortunate to have three or four reports from Herle of what Fagot had to say. The first of these was written on Friday 15 November, from 'my lodging at the Bull's Head without Temple Bar', where we can imagine Herle and Fagot having just had a good dinner.[25] It contained five items of information. The first was about Archibald Douglas, a frequenter of both Walsingham and Castelnau in whom Herle had been interested for some time. Douglas was a Scotsman of inscrutable perfidy who had

---

25 *Texts*, no. 5, which I take with no. 6, written the following day.

helped to blow up Queen Mary's husband, Lord Darnley, in 1565. Castelnau, who found him an excellent source of knowledge about Scotland, claimed that he was on Mary's side, though Mary thought he was being deceived. Herle thought he was right, and that Douglas was working as a 'counter-miner' against the English interest in Scotland; he reported in his letter that Douglas had tried to bribe him to work for the other side. This was probably rather ancient news, and must have come from Herle himself, since so far Fagot had not mentioned Douglas at all; when he did, a while later, his judgment was the same as Herle's.[26] It was mistaken.

The second thing in the letter was a reasonably accurate sketch of what has become known as the Throckmorton plot: an invasion by the Duke of Guise, with the assistance of Spain and of a simultaneous rising by the English Catholic nobility and gentry, intended to put Mary on the throne and get rid of Elizabeth by assassination. It seems likely that this was the first hard information the English Council had had about what Throckmorton was up to, although Herle did not mention Throckmorton in connection with the enterprise, and seems to have thought it was being organised by Douglas. In substance I am sure the news came from Fagot; he had also said to Herle that, if the English scheme was successful, he thought the Duke of Guise was likely to succeed as King of France when the House of Valois died out as it promised shortly to do.

The third item, undoubtedly from Fagot, was a well-nourished polemic against Lord Henry Howard. Howard had actually been less involved than Throckmorton either with Mary or with Castelnau, but both Fagot and Herle had reason to be nervous of him. He was in some respects the senior representative of the most powerful tradi-tionalist family in sixteenth-century England, a position which had fallen upon him because of the execution of his brother the fourth Duke of Norfolk in 1572, for treasonably conspiring with Mary, whom he proposed to marry, to launch a *coup d'état* in the Catholic interest. (Herle had played a prominent and not very honourable part in the undercover operations which had led to his downfall.) Since then Lord Henry, though a poor relation and single, had been a substitute father to the duke's children. He was generally, and legitimately, held to be the most learned of Elizabethan noblemen, and wrote a great deal on matters of politics and religion; he was a courtier intermittently much in favour with Elizabeth; and he was a convinced Catholic, though sceptical both in theory and in practice of the political claims of the papacy. He was detested by all suppor-ters of the Protestant cause, and Fagot's report reflects their opinions as well as gossip at Salisbury Court. He said that Howard was thought to be a priest, and a cardinal *in petto*, no less; more plausibly, he claimed to recount what Howard had been saying and doing at the time of the marriage negotiations between Elizabeth and Anjou, in which he had indeed been deeply involved. Howard, Fagot said, had advised Anjou's agent Jean Simier that the strategy for pulling off the marriage was to organise the papists in its favour and to demand freedom of religion in England as one of the terms, on the grounds that Elizabeth 'was not resolved of what religion yet to be of'; when it was achieved they would secure the triumph of Catholicism by a massacre of the Protestant nobility. Fagot, or Herle, had been particularly incensed by Howard's comment about Elizabeth, which he thought evidence of his 'blasphemy and vile nature'. A second letter, sent the following day, mentioned a book about prophecy which Howard had published in the summer, and suggested that it should be submitted to an official censor on the grounds that it contained matter of heresy and treason.[27] Fagot concluded his diatribe against Howard with the news that a relation of his, obviously meaning his eldest nephew Philip, Earl of Arundel, had been in touch with the Catholics overseas, and was now harbouring the head of the Jesuit mission in his house. He promised full details as soon as possible, and had required Herle not to reveal the information to anybody except one of Elizabeth's most intimate councillors, and then '*sub sigillo confessionis*'.[28]

About Francis Throckmorton, who had not been recently seen around the embassy, Herle could only repeat what he had passed on from Fagot during the summer about his sinister intimacy with Castelnau, and insist that he was 'a party very busy and an enemy to the present state'. Between Herle's obsession with Archibald Douglas and Fagot's with Howard, Throckmorton might well have escaped

---

27 Linda Levy Peck, *Northampton: Patronage and Politics at the Court of James I* (London, 1982) is a fine political biography of Howard, which concentrates on his later period of power and explains how he achieved it. She has (pp. 6–13) a good brief account of Howard's doings in our period; Howard and the papacy, pp. 111–13. Also *DNB*; Neville Williams, *Thomas Howard Fourth Duke of Norfolk* (London, 1964); and my own 'English Catholics and the French Marriage', *Recusant History*, v (1959), 2–16. The book was *A defensative against the Poyson of supposed Prophecies* (London: John Charlewood, 1583); Peck, *Northampton*, p. 12.

28 J.H. Pollen and W. MacMahon (ed.), *The Ven. Philip Howard, Earl of Arundel, 1557–1595*, (Catholic Record Society, xxi, 1919) is a compendium of knowledge which fails to leave any very clear impression. The earl was not converted to Catholicism until September 1584. He was now living at Arundel House in the Strand, close to Salisbury Court; but this cannot have been what Fagot meant, since Herle said that he had sent somebody down 'into the country' to inquire; it was probably Arundel Castle. Arundel House acquired a priest about a year later (*Philip Howard*, p. 67), and two years after that became the residence of the Jesuit Robert Southwell: C. Devlin, *Robert Southwell* (London, 1956), pp. 132 ff.

notice entirely had not Fagot volunteered two rather insignificant-sounding pieces of information. The first was that Castelnau had wined and dined Throckmorton's Protestant cousin Arthur the previous Sunday; Arthur was an honest soul of no great pretensions who had a position at court as Esquire of the Body to Elizabeth and was lodging nearby in the Strand. There were various reasons why Castelnau might have invited him at this time, some of them political, some of them not: Arthur was friendly with his cousin in spite of their differences in religion, and he had also been on the Laski expedition to Oxford. The other piece of news about the family turned out to be important: it was that Francis's Catholic brother Thomas, who was supposed to be in France but had actually been in England since about August, was planning to leave the country secretly with 'one Digby of Lincoln's Inn' in the next day or two.[29]

The last thing Herle reported was the arrival in England of a Sicilian nobleman, Don Gaston de Spinola, sent from the Netherlands by the Prince of Parma to explore the chances of a settlement with Elizabeth. This was not tremendously confidential news, and we do not need to discuss it; one might have supposed that Herle had found it out from some other source than Fagot, had not his letter of the following day described Don Gaston as the product of a Genoese father, a Spanish mother, and a Sicilian upbringing, 'which is the worst commixture that ever was'. This was surely the voice of an Italian informant who was neither Genoese nor Sicilian.

This fairly substantial budget of news from Salisbury Court indicates that Fagot had by now got a firmer grasp of the political scene than he had had at the time of his first letters; it also indicates that he had acquired a fixation on Henry Howard which was not doing much good for the objectivity of his information. How far it was responsible for the arrests of Throckmorton and Howard, which occurred either on 16, or between 18 and 20 November (I doubt if they would have been made on the 17th, which was the queen's Accession Day and a national holiday), is a point which I shall leave to be investigated in due course. For the moment it seems enough to say that the achievement was partly Fagot's and partly Courcelles's; that Fagot, having recruited Courcelles in the first place, could claim the credit for both contributions; and that but for him it seems unlikely that Howard would have been arrested at all.

When they were both in custody the government's interest shifted

29   On Francis Throckmorton, of whom we know rather little, there is something in A.L. Rowse, *Ralegh and the Throckmortons* (London, 1962), a lively history of the family in the 16th century, mainly on the Protestant side. For the conspiracy, Read, *Walsingham*, ii, 380–90. Arthur and Francis, Rowse, pp. 71, 73; Arthur and the trip to Oxford, pp. 79 f; Arthur at court, pp. 77, 79.

to finding out how Castelnau was taking the matter, and on this subject Herle sent a further communication on Saturday 23. Along with a fair amount of matter from other sources, it contained an account, evidently from Fagot, of the state of affairs in Salisbury Court after Throckmorton's arrest. On the morning of Thursday 21, Castelnau had sent Courcelles to fetch Douglas, and they had had a long and private discussion in Castelnau's chamber. According to Fagot, they were talking about the last letter Castelnau had received from Mary, which he and Courcelles were convinced Walsingham had opened on the way. It sounds as if Castelnau thought that the purloining of this letter had precipitated Throckmorton's arrest, though it must have been part of Mary's official correspondence and hence unlikely to contain anything confidential. If this was what he did think, as far as we can see he was mistaken; perhaps Fagot had got the wrong end of the stick, or perhaps Courcelles was muddying the waters. Unlike Courcelles, Castelnau can have had no idea why exactly Throckmorton had been arrested at this time, and may have suspected that Douglas had had something to do with it. Anyway, after Douglas had been sent away Castelnau and Courcelles were left wondering what to do: whatever was in the letter they were worried about, it seems to have been an obstacle to what Castelnau had in mind, which was, according to Fagot, to demand audience of the queen, and 'by some course of terrification to withdraw Her Majesty from proceeding too far in examining those Actions that are broken forth, and the deciphering of their greater friends not yet discovered'. Herle must have meant that, if the English had no good evidence against Throckmorton and Howard, Castelnau proposed to make a strong complaint to Elizabeth that the arrests had been an act of enmity against himself and Henri III, inspired no doubt by Leicester and Walsingham, and that if she proceeded to torture she would force his king into a Catholic alliance with King Philip against her. The 'greater friends' whom Castelnau would be anxious to protect would be the Earl of Arundel and the Earl of Northumberland, both of whom would shortly be interrogated about their connections with Throckmorton. In actual fact Castelnau kept his head down, which may mean either that Fagot's information was wrong (which I doubt) or that Castelnau decided, correctly, that Elizabeth had too much evidence against himself. Herle also said, on his own behalf or on Fagot's, that he was glad the queen had now got something to hang Lord Henry Howard for, since he was an unquiet and dangerous spirit; and, I think from Fagot, that there had been rejoicing in Spain on the premature news that an assassination plot against Elizabeth had been successful. Urged on by the pope, the Catholic powers were now committed to murder and treachery as instruments of their cause: seeing 'of late' a well-known court Catholic, Charles Arundell, at a perfumier's in Abchurch Lane in the City (at the news of the arrests Arundell had fled to France), Herle had immediately thought of a plot to poison the queen through the nose, 'she having her senses of smelling so perfect'.[30]

Like his previous communication of a week before, so much of this as came from Fagot revealed (I think) both precise and valuable information about Castelnau, and a tendency to let his feelings over-stimulate his imagination: he had surely invented the story about the 'triumphs' in Spain, which must have made a strong impression on Elizabeth since she quoted it back to Castelnau when they met.[31] He did not manage to produce anything against Arundel or Northumberland, about whom Herle was looking for evidence in December: the Jesuit story proved a *canard*. Nor, so far as I know, did he get a copy of the 'scandalous verses', no doubt against the Earl of Leicester and his friends, which Herle thought he ought to be able to come by.[32] After the immediate stir over the arrests had died down, what the English needed to know – which was where Henri III stood in the matter – would have to come from a more professional source than Fagot.

He did, however, continue to broadcast intermittently during the next few months: three communications of his exist from between Christmas 1583 and Easter 1584, two of them sent directly and one via Herle. The first must have been written immediately after New Year, since it asked for his New Year's gift; this was presumably why on this occasion he wrote rather than sending a message. It is in the snippety style of his first letters, though it only has one signature. He said that Sir James Croft, Controller of the Queen's Household and a barely concealed Catholic, had a Catholic servant called Edward Morris who was in Castelnau's pay and passing him information from court; reported an Irish gentleman in the Fleet Prison, whom it sounds as if he had been visiting in his priestly capacity, as thanking God that Throckmorton had not confessed all he knew, since if he had done all the Catholics would be in the soup; and announced that Girault had arrived with another consignment of books which Anthony Babington was going to sell. He warned Walsingham against Douglas, Pithou and Laurent Feron, the embassy clerk; and said he had something up his sleeve which he would

---

30 *Texts*, no. 7. On Arundell, 'English Catholics and the French Marriage' (above, n. 27); he had been very close to Henry Howard, though they seem to have drifted apart. Not to be confused with Philip Howard, Earl of Arundel.

31 Castelnau to Henri III, 9/19-xii-1583; to Mary, *c.* 10/20-xii-1583 (BL Harleian 1582, ff. 329–31, 377 f).

32 *Texts*, no. 8.

communicate later.[33] In February or early March he sent via Herle a list of people haunting the embassy: a former servant of Mendoza, who had left the country in January; 'one Victor a French monk serving one Noel'; and Sylvanus Scory, whom we know to have been frequenting Salisbury Court since before Christmas. Scory was the son of the least respected bishop of the Elizabethan Church, John Scory of Hereford, and in the service of the Earl of Leicester; he had been converted to Catholicism on the continent. Fagot said Scory had had 'secret and long conference' with Castelnau, and had heard him say that as soon as his father died and he had his inheritance he would go abroad again. Fagot also said, or Herle reported on his own account, that Courcelles had been making a lot of unofficial trips to the court at Greenwich by night.[34]

All this was fairly minor intelligence, though some of it, like the news about Anthony Babington, would come in handy later. Fagot had nothing to say about the most interesting of the clandestine goings-on at the embassy during this period, the visit or visits of the supposed assassin William Parry; we shall come to Parry in a moment. After these *faits-divers* Fagot's next effort, and the last thing we have from him for about a year, seems to show him trying to recapture the headlines. In one respect at least it was sensational; as a piece of intelligence I would not vouch for it.[35]

It was probably written on 16 March, and unlike all his other communications was addressed to the queen herself, whom Fagot described as Queen of England, France and Ireland. It concerned a Spanish merchant called Pedro de Zubiaur, who had worked for Mendoza and seems to have been left in charge of his affairs after his expulsion in January. Zubiaur, Fagot said, had come to him several times, presumably since the beginning of Lent early in February, asking him to hear his confession. He had put him off until the previous day, I think Palm Sunday new style, then had heard him. So shocked had he been by what he had heard that he felt obliged, in

33 *Texts*, no. 9. 'Monsieur Morice' is identified as Edward Morris by *CSP Foreign 1585–1586*, p. 543; Feron as the embassy clerk by Castelnau to Queen Mary, [iv]–1585 (BL Harleian 1582, f. 371 v: 'Leurant [sic: *possibly* Laurant] qui escript tout devant moy et en ma presence'. Fagot presumably also had something to do with the interception of a letter from Girault to his wife in Paris, 24-i/3-ii-1584 (PRO SP 12/168, no. 5), which was mainly about trafficking in hose and shirts; this may possibly have been a code, and if so the letter was probably to Thomas Morgan.

34 *Texts*, no. 10: for Henry Noel, ibid. n. 3. Scory's relations with Castelnau can be pursued in his examination of 14/24-ii-1585 (PRO SP 12/176, no. 53); Castelnau to Walsingham, 21-vi/1-vii-1585, 5/15-vii-1585 and 8/18-vii-1585 (*CSP Foreign 1584–85*, pp. 547, 584, 589); and Scory to Castelnau, 5/15-i-1587 (BN V^{c}C 472, p. 249). John Aubrey has a brief life of him: *Brief Lives*, ed. R. Barber (Woodbridge, Suffolk, 1982), pp. 280 f; he was treated rather sharply in *Leicester's Commonwealth*, pp. 234 f and n, p. 245.

35 *Texts*, nos. 11 and 11a, and note to no. 11 on the date.

return for the favours the queen had shown him 'non seullement de bouche mais aussy de coeur et de vos bons moyens', to pass it on immediately to her. What Zubiaur had said was that he had been charged by Mendoza, along with four others of whom the only one whose name Fagot knew was called Philip Courtois,[36] with the job of assassinating the queen by whatever means they could contrive: Fagot added an imaginative list, perhaps derived from Herle, which included poisoning her underwear and smelling-bottle. Fearing that she might not believe him, he invited her to consult the Council, who would vouch for his record as a source of reliable information: he would sooner die than tell her anything but the pure and simple truth. He then described his confessional interrogation of Zubiaur, of which he subjoined a circumstantial account which would be extremely interesting for no other reason than that such accounts are rare. He had gone through the Ten Commandments with him, and Zubiaur had performed excellently on all of them except 'Thou Shalt Not Kill'. Despite all Fagot's eloquence he had refused to budge from his purpose, had said that it was in the cause of the true Catholic religion and the salvation of an infinite number of souls, and that he was sure his own soul would go straight to heaven 'quant il n'auroit faict aultre chosse que cela'. As he was talking about it Zubiaur had worked himself up into a rage about the queen until he was grinding his teeth and giving Fagot quite a fright. He had promised to bring the others along, only Fagot would have to wait until two of them arrived from Spain, which he expected them to do shortly (in the account of the confession they were described as being three, and with Parma in the Netherlands). He and Courtois would be coming next Wednesday to make their Easter communion 'et leur reconsillier'. This could mean that Fagot had postponed absolving Zubiaur until then, but I think it means that they proposed to receive communion together, and forgive each others' trespasses as a token of commitment to their holy enterprise.

To Elizabeth Fagot signed himself: 'Votre humble affexioné, Celuy que connoissez'. As he signed the account of the confession with his usual signature written in a particularly bold style, we are surely to deduce not only, as the text of the letter claims, that he had met and talked to Elizabeth, but also that Elizabeth knew who he was, though she might not hitherto have known him as Fagot. After the signature he added a blessing; an appeal to keep his secret ('gardez mon secret car je vous suys fidelle et découvriray aultres chosses'); and an elegant request for some more of her 'bons moyens'

36 Courtois was, Herle had thought, the name of the Spaniard described as haunting the embassy in Fagot's previous information: *Texts*, no. 10.

('Vide humilitatem meam et laborem meam; et cognoce me, quia ego sum pauper sed fidelis'). This last was a skilful selection from Psalm 24: 16–18: originally Fagot's pen had run on with the second half of verse 18 ('et dimitte omnia delicta mea'), but he had hastily crossed it out. Even Fagot had to draw the line at asking Elizabeth to forgive his sins.

What are we to make of the substance of this communication? I think we can take it that Zubiaur had made his Easter confession to Fagot: after Mendoza's departure, he was no doubt the most accessible priest. There are details in Fagot's account which do not sound invented, like Zubiaur's saying that it was something over five months since his last confession, and when questioned on the eighth commandment answering 'that he had borne false witness (in a suit) against one of his brothers-in-law but with the intention of securing a better settlement'. The story of the plot is another matter. There is one immediate difficulty in it: Zubiaur could not have been proposing to make his Easter communion on the Wednesday if Fagot had not given him absolution, and Fagot ought not to have absolved him if his sentiments were as described. Fagot drew a veil over this part of the confession, but implied that he had not absolved him, which casts doubt on the story about the communion. I do not think this is a pedantic point; still, the principal objection to the story is that it was, as Fagot admitted, quite extraordinarily unlikely. It is extremely hard to swallow the idea that a group of Spanish conspirators would have discussed their intentions with a priest of uncertain reliability in, of all places, the French embassy, and even under the seal of confession. Walsingham presumably did not swallow it, for it does not seem that he passed the message on to the queen or, at a time when she and the Council were still in a state of intense nervousness about plots, that any investigation was made of Zubiaur.

I can think of two reasons why Fagot might have thought that the tale, if it was a tale, would go down better than it apparently did. The first is that he must have heard from Castelnau what an impression he had made upon Elizabeth with his story (if it was a story, and his) about the glee in Spain over her supposed assassination; the vein would have seemed worth exploiting.[37] The second is that he was working from a model which was fresh in everybody's mind, the case of the (presumably) spurious conspirator William Parry. Some time in January Parry had arrived in London with a story of how he had taken a religious vow to assassinate the queen, and had solemnised it in the Jesuit Collège de Clermont in Paris by going to confession and receiving communion with two cardinals as his sponsors. He had reported all this to Elizabeth on his return to England and was, at the time Fagot wrote, awaiting a letter of encouragement and indulgence from the pope, which duly reached him at Greenwich at the end of March. Parry and his doings were well known at Salisbury Court, through which he had been communicating with a fellow-conspirator in Paris called Thomas Morgan, whom we shall meet again; they would have been particularly well known to Fagot if, as I am inclined to think, he was the priest in London to whom Parry said he had put the matter as a case of conscience. The priest had turned him down, as Fagot turned down Zubiaur. We can build nothing on the speculation that this was the secret matter which Fagot had promised to communicate in his New Year letter. But we can reasonably guess that he thought the topic was a hot one, and that it would strike an original note to reveal such a scheme in the guise of the priest in the case.[38]

Zubiaur was indeed arrested and put in the Tower, but a year later and on different charges.[39] I am fairly confident that Fagot's story about him was an invention. This is worth knowing, not for the sake of Zubiaur's or Mendoza's reputation, but because it suggests that Fagot was a man with a powerful imagination. I wonder whether he got a rebuke from Walsingham, who did not really need him for the time being. In any case, he now ceased transmitting for a year.

---

38 See the account of Parry's trial in W. Cobbett (ed.), *State Trials* (2 vols; London, 1809), i, 1095 ff; L. Hicks, 'The Strange Case of Dr William Parry', *Studies* (Dublin), xxxvii (1948), 343–62. The speculation about Parry and Fagot arises from Parry to Thomas Morgan, 12/22-ii-1584 (*CSP Domestic Addenda 1580–1625*, p. 113): 'I laboured, by conference with a singular man on this side, to be fully informed what might be done in conscience in that case, for the common good. I was learnedly overruled, and assured that it ought not to fall into the thought of a good Christian.' Hicks (p. 356) has a slightly fuller version of this passage. I show in 'Castelnau in London' that Parry visited Salisbury Court at this time.

39 *CSP Domestic 1581–1590*, pp. 240, 284, 305; *Philip Howard*, pp. 130, 131, 137. Pollen here (p. 130 n) says that he was arrested about June 1584, but I cannot find evidence for this; in his later confessions he showed himself aggressively anti-English, but he was not accused of conspiring to assassinate the queen.

4

DIALOGUES, AND
A SMALL RIOT

London, Early 1584 to Early 1585

DURING THIS TIME Bruno was in full spate. He wrote and published his two most famous dialogues, *La cena de le Ceneri* and the *Spaccio della bestia trionfante;* two further cosmological dialogues elaborating what he had said in the first (*De la causa, principio e uno* and *De l'infinito universo e mondi*); and possibly another as an appendix to the second (*Cabala del cavallo pegaseo*). All five were written in Italian and published in London by John Charlewood, who the year before had published Bruno's *Sigillus* and also Henry Howard's book against prophecies. The three cosmological dialogues were published as from Venice, the other two as from Paris: which was not mainly to escape censorship or to avoid making difficulties for Castelnau but, as Bruno said later, because the publisher advised him that they would sell better with a foreign imprint.[40] They were designed to put himself and his radical views on the physical and moral universe before an English lay public quaintly embodied in the *Cena de le Ceneri* in the character 'Smitho', and to help down the theoretical pill with a good deal of comic or quasi-dramatic business.

I shall admit that, in this sizeable body of writing, what I am interested in at the moment is not the abstract or symbolic exposition of Bruno's ideas of which it mainly consists, but whatever in the dialogues may evoke the circumstances in which they were written. This choice also has the advantage of allowing us to concentrate on the dialogue most generous in such evocations, the first to be written and by common consent one of the masterpieces of European literature, the *Cena de le Ceneri* or *Ash Wednesday Supper*.[41] In

40 *Documenti*, p. 91.
41 *DI*, pp. 1–171; I also refer to the Aquilecchia edition (Turin, 1955), which has the advantages of using the original spelling and of printing the texts of the two versions in parallel. The second reference is to this edition; on its own I refer to it as '*Cena* (Aquilecchia)'. I realise that the term 'tetralogue' is a joke (*Cena*, p. 24/87), but it seems convenient to use it.

structure the *Cena* is a Chinese box in three layers. It begins with a *Proemio* dedicated to Castelnau. Here there is a rhetorical exposition of the sort of work it is and is not, and an explanation of the title; an argument for each of the five dialogues of which the work consists; and a description for Castelnau's benefit of some of its characteristics (lightness, variety), intentions (to teach the stupid and malicious a lesson) and defects (standing too close to the subject to paint it properly). It ends with an expression of gratitude to Castelnau for being Bruno's only support in this otherwise barbarous country, a discreet request for cash and an encomium upon Henri III.

Dialogue i is a kind of preface. It sets the scene for the second layer of the work, the 'tetralogue' or four-sided dialogue between Smitho, a serious and enquiring English gentleman, Prudenzio, a classicist pedant, Frulla, a rude servant, and Teofilo, the narrator. Teofilo is an *alter ego* of Bruno, who does not here appear in his own person. After he has (rather lubriciously) invoked the English muses, Teofilo narrates the origins of the third layer of the work, the Supper of the title, which is supposed to have happened already; he has been a silent presence at these events. He begins with the arrival at Salisbury Court of Bruno's friend and fellow-inmate, John Florio, and a friend of his, the medic and musician Matthew Gwynne; they bring a message from the poet and courtier Fulke Greville inviting Bruno to a meal in his lodgings at Whitehall during which the Copernican theory will be discussed. In the tetralogue Teofilo puts the dispute of new truth and old error into the context of a world which needs to be rescued from the vice, conflict, blind controversy and slaughter which are caused by everybody's persistence in traditional wisdom. He presents Bruno as its saviour, if it will listen to him.

Dialogue ii, which takes us fully into the third layer of the work, is a sort of dramatic or perhaps epic prologue to the Supper. After recording the arrangements made between Greville and Bruno, it launches into a marvellous account of the journey of Bruno and Florio, along with Teofilo as shadow-narrator, from Salisbury Court to Whitehall; they go in the dark, via Buckhurst Stairs and the river, on a ramshackle boat whose boatmen shortly dump them on the shore; its being low tide, they splodge around in deep mud, eventually get by back alleys up to the Strand, and proceed on foot through a crowd of Londoners taking the evening air, who knock them about severely on the way. This passage leads into a paean of praise for Elizabeth, her Council, Leicester, Walsingham and Philip Sidney, and a torrent of abuse for the London *plebs*. They finally arrive at Greville's apartment in the palace and, after an odd and rather disgusting passage about passing around the drinking-cup, sit down at table.

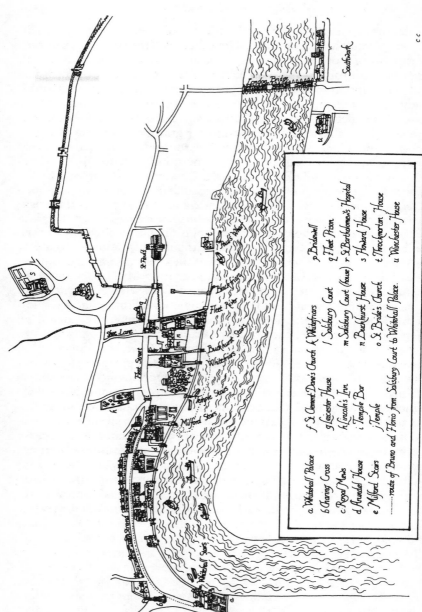

Figure 4. Map of the Thames from Westminster to London Bridge (with Bruno's and Florio's route from Salisbury Court to Whitehall).

a. Whitehall Palace
b. Charing Cross
c. Royal News
d. Arundel House
e. Milford Stairs

f. St Clement Dane's Church
g. Leicester House
h. Lincoln's Inn
i. Temple Bar
j. Temple

k. Whitefriars
l. Salisbury Court
m. Salisbury Court (House)
n. Buckhurst House
o. St Bride's Church

p. Bridewell
q. Fleet Prison
r. St Bartholomew's Hospital
s. Howard House
t. Throckmorton House
u. Winchester House

------ route of Bruno and Florio from Salisbury Court to Whitehall Palace.

In Dialogue iii we are at the Supper. The philosophical or Aristotelian objections to Copernicus are stated by the first of Bruno's two English academic opponents, Nundinio; they are discussed and rejected. The only distraction from this is a page or two of tetralogue at the beginning about the utility or otherwise of the English language, and whether Bruno understands it; this issue arises because Nundinio's propositions are apparently stated in English and not recorded by Teofilo, who seems to give the gist of them in Latin.

In Dialogue iv the narration of the Supper continues, with large interpolations from the tetralogue. The subject is theological objections to Copernicus, which are not, however, raised by the other English academic, Torquato, or discussed at the Supper. They are raised by Smitho in the tetralogue, and answered by Teofilo along the lines that the Bible is not a philosophical work, and that an infinite universe, which Bruno maintains though Copernicus had not done so, is more appropriate in Christian theology than a finite or Aristotelian one. When he gets back to his narration of the Supper, Teofilo has no more to record than a number of offensive personal remarks from Torquato, which give Bruno the opportunity of presenting himself as a persecuted follower of truth. Since he is being especially persecuted by Oxford, the history of his second visit there is now recounted. On this note the Supper breaks up, and the party goes home, without incident, to Salisbury Court.

In Dialogue v the tetralogue concludes with a fairly continuous account from Teofilo of Bruno's philosophy of universal motion in the universe and universal mutability on earth, all matter being conserved; this comes in the form of explanations to Smitho, intended to enable him to answer objections. It ends on the topic of the different motions of the earth, which Bruno leaves in rather a tangle.

At this point Prudenzio the humanist is invited to conclude the work with an epilogue which balances the *Proemio*. This consists of a series of adjurations: to Bruno to follow his genius, avoid degrading himself by ignoble frequentations, and stick to Castelnau who, one may hope, will keep supplying him with funds to finish his work; to the English nobility to give him hospitality and send him home with torchbearers, or at least a lamp to guide him in the dark; to the pedants, to get their money back from their incompetent teachers; to the Thames watermen to do their job properly; to the London *plebs* to leave off beating up foreigners; and to everybody to contribute to a better dialogue next time, or hold their peace. The passage has a mock-liturgical character vaguely reminiscent of the exorcisms in the Catholic baptismal rite, and along with a mention of Catholic burial concludes a series of sacramental or liturgical references which crop up from time to time throughout the work.

*   *   *

The first requirement in the telling of a true story is to establish a true chronology, and I now intend to spend a little time establishing a true chronology for the *Cena*. That means various things: the chronology of the fictional events narrated in the dialogue; the chronology of whatever events in real life these fictional events may imitate or evoke; and the chronology of the actual composition of the dialogue, an event in real life which may imitate a fictional event implied in it. Sorting these things out may be, even in this fairly simple case, a finicky and possibly a boring business. Why do I need to do it? The general answer is because, in keeping with the principle just stated, it is what I have been doing all along, and shall need to go on doing systematically. You never know when you may need it, but you can be sure you will need it sometime. The particular answer is that Bruno's *Cena de le Ceneri* is not, say, Sidney's *Arcadia*: Bruno is not only imitating the real world, but the real world in the place where he is writing, and at a time immediately preceding the time he is writing about it. We should be amazingly complacent if we did not follow his cues. I have to admit that the reasons why the operation may always be finicky are multiplied by two by a complication peculiar to the time; but, as Bruno said himself at one of the more life-imitating moments in the *Cena*, everything worthwhile is difficult.

We observe for a start that Bruno was extremely careful about the sequence of his fictional events. Florio and Gwynne arrive at Salisbury Court with Greville's request to Bruno to explain his Copernican views; Bruno sees Greville, and they arrange a learned meal, which will take place 'mercoldí ad otto giorni', which seems to mean on Wednesday week; this will be Ash Wednesday, the first day of Lent. The journey to Whitehall, and the Supper, take place on the evening of Ash Wednesday, starting rather late; presumably the guests return to Salisbury Court in the small hours. Not long after this the parties to the tetralogue, who do not include Bruno, meet at the house of Smitho, and Teofilo begins his narration, which is what the work purports to record. This takes up five meetings, which occur on successive days. On the first day, according to the first published version, Teofilo dates the bringing of Greville's original invitation by Florio and Gwynne 'circa quindeci giorni passati', about a fortnight ago; in the second version this is changed to 'a i dí passati', some days ago,[42] but I shall proceed on the original statement.

---

42 *Cena*, pp. 26, 544/90, 279, 281. The second version not only fudges the dating; it omits the location of Bruno in Castelnau's house, and a commendation from Prudenzio of the historicity of Teofilo's narration: 'Ab origine, ab ovo: a tempore, loco et personis optime exorditum.'

This gives a clear narrative time-scale, as follows: the invitation arrives some ten days before Ash Wednesday, say Sexagesima Sunday; Bruno sees Greville a day or two after that, which is either the Wednesday before Ash Wednesday or a few days earlier (the editor of the *Cena*, Giovanni Aquilecchia, thinks the first, but the second is surely the natural reading); supper, Ash Wednesday evening probably into Thursday morning; tetralogue *chez* Smithó, beginning say the next Sunday or Monday and finishing towards the end of the week. The whole sequence of events takes roughly three weeks, from about Sexagesima Sunday to about the second Sunday in Lent. All these events, including the last, are fictional, but they will nevertheless help us to find out exactly when the dialogue was written. We certainly cannot say that Giordano Bruno actually began writing the work *La cena de le Ceneri* on the second Sunday in Lent, or on whichever day we choose as appropriate for the morrow or so of the end of the tetralogue. I should have thought we could say that he did not begin to write it earlier, and it would seem to me implausible to argue that he began to write a considerable time afterwards: the *Cena* must have been published reasonably early in 1584, otherwise we cannot find space for the rest of his publications during the year. Since the text is not enormously long, and Bruno was not a slow writer, it seems to me virtually certain that he had finished it by Easter.[43]

The reader may think that this gives a perfectly clear absolute chronology for the narrated time of the dialogue and the actual time when the text was composed. Alas, it does not. Everything turns on Ash Wednesday 1584, and no one, so far as I know, has observed that in England Ash Wednesday 1584 occurred twice, and its date depended upon which calendar one was using. According to the Julian calendar, or old style, which despite the best efforts of John Dee was still the official calendar in England, Ash Wednesday occurred on 4 March and Easter on 19 April. According to the Gregorian calendar, or new style, used by this time over most of the continent, and by Catholics, they occurred on 15 February and 1 April. Since 15 February, new style, was the same day as 5 February, old style, the two sets of dates were actually a whole month apart. If

43 Aquilecchia, in his *Cena*, p. 115 n, has a tighter dating: invitation a week before Ash Wednesday, writing begun a week after. This identifies the day of the invitation with the day of Nolanus's meeting with Greville, and that with the Wednesday before Ash Wednesday; both assumptions seem to me unlikely. It also assumes that Bruno mixed up the date of the beginning of his own narration with that of the beginning of Teofilo's ('circa quindeci giorni': on Aquilecchia's chronology Teofilo would have begun his narrative about ten days after the invitation). This also seems to me improbable, considering the claim made in the original version for circumstantial accuracy (previous note). I expect this is a trivial point, but we may as well try to get it as right as we can.

we suppose that Bruno's Ash Wednesday was old style, we get a time for the narrated events of the dialogue and the actual period of writing it which runs from about 23 February/4 March to about 19/29 April; if we suppose that it was new style, the terminal dates are about 26 January/5 February and 22 March/1 April.[44]

Everybody seems to have supposed that Bruno was thinking in new style, and this was certainly followed in the embassy, as Fagot makes clear in his first letter. But it was not Bruno but Greville who fixed the date of the supper ('mercoldí ad otto giorni, che sarà de le Ceneri'), and even a fictional Greville must have been using old style, both in his conversation and in his household. Hence I think the pair of dates we need is the first one. Bruno was writing for an English audience; both the supper and the tetralogue are set in English houses; and this is how he must have expected to be understood. It would make no sense for him to represent himself as beginning around 15/25 February the narrative of a sequence of events which could not have started until a week later. It is true that during his interrogation in Venice he said that, while he was living in Protestant countries, he had not been able to remember which were fasting days; but this cannot have been true of his stay in England, because he was living in a Catholic house and because abstinence, at least, had not been abolished in England. There was no ecclesiastical obligation to celebrate Lent, but there was a statutory obligation to abstain enacted by parliament in 1563, which could in theory only be evaded by a royal licence: the French embassy had actually applied for one in 1581. Ash Wednesday had not disappeared from the English calendar.[45]

I therefore assume that the date Bruno wished to be ascribed to his *cena* was 4/14 March 1584; which is of course not to say that such an event, or anything resembling it, actually happened on that day. Indeed we have Bruno's own statement to support us in assuming that it did not, and if we attend carefully to what he said I think we shall find that it solves our problem. In Venice the inquisitors asked him what he meant by the title of the book, which they thought provocatively un-Catholic; he said that he had called it the *Cena de le Ceneri* because he had had a discussion of the kind with some medics at dinner in the ambassador's house on Ash Wednesday.[46] This event

---

44 The dates are in fact exactly four weeks apart, though they do not look as if they are; this is because 1584 was a Leap Year, but in the old style 29 February did not fall in Lent, whereas in the new style it did.

45 Aquilecchia's dating of the supper to 4/14 February, which is actually a day out because he has forgotten the Leap Year, seems to be followed by everybody. *Documenti*, pp. 115 f (Bruno and fasting); *Acts of the Privy Council*, new series, ed. J.R. Dasent (London, 1890–), xii (1896), 329.

46 *Documenti*, p. 121.

is much more likely to have happened than anything like the *cena* of the dialogue; if it did, it would have happened on 5/15 February, since Ash Wednesday would have been celebrated in Salisbury Court on that date. I shall cite in favour of this date what Bruno said about his title in dedicating the book to Castelnau. He was not, he said, alluding to Psalm 101: 10 – 'Cinerem tanquam panem manducabam (I ate ashes instead of bread)' – and so making reflections on the cuisine. He meant the day on which the *cena* had occurred – 'nel primo giorno de la quarantana, detto da nostri preti DIES CINERUM, et talvolta giorno del MEMENTO' (on the first day of Lent, called by our priests Ash Wednesday, or sometimes Memento Day).[47] 'Memento' is the first word of the injunction spoken by the priest to the participant in the ceremony of that day as he rubs ashes on his forehead. One might think from this placing of the *cena* in its liturgical context that Bruno was associating it with a performance of the Ash Wednesday rite which can only have taken place at Salisbury Court, and on 5/15 February. The deduction is certainly not compulsory, but I think it is more likely than not that the idea of the dialogue was set going by something that happened at Salisbury Court on 5/15 February; this does not affect my assumption that while he was writing it the date he had in mind was 4/14 March. We have in short a real-life dialogue which has occurred at Salisbury Court on Ash Wednesday 1584, new style, and a fictional dialogue which occurs at Whitehall on Ash Wednesday 1584, old style, or four weeks later. The conclusion that Bruno wrote the *Cena de le Ceneri* between say 15/25 March and 19/29 April seems to me moderately well established, and I shall assume it hereafter.[48]

Bruno had not finished with the text of the *Cena* when it was published, I assume in May, for there were two successive printed versions.[49] Between the two he rewrote the beginning of dialogue i and a great deal of dialogue ii. The changes made the work more 'poetical' and less 'historical' (by leaving out some of the narrative detail, and putting in the invocation to the English muses), more decorous and less racy (by reducing the part given to Frulla), and possibly more Protestant and less Catholic (by leaving out a drinking-

---

47 *Cena*, pp. 9/69–7-. The text is: 'Memento homo quia pulvis es, et ad pulverem reverteris'; it comes from Genesis 3: 19, cf. Ecclesiastes 3: 20, a chapter to which Bruno was extremely partial.

48 This is against Aquilecchia's conclusion that the dialogue was 'composto o iniziato' on 11/21 or 12/22 February.

49 Appendices I and II to *Cena* (Aquilecchia), pp. 275–305; based on Aquilecchia's 'La lezione definitiva della "Cena de le Ceneri" di Giordano Bruno', *Atti della Accademia nazionale dei Lincei: Memorie, Classe di scienze morali, etc.*[8], iii (1950), 207–43. There has been some feeling that Aquilecchia's reconstruction is over-critical: cf. R. Tissoni, in *Giornale storico della letteratura italiana*, cxxxvi (1959), 558–63.

scene which may have been a satire on communion in both kinds, and putting in what may be some jokes about the Catholic penitential system). A political explanation of this has been suggested, but I do not find it very convincing.[50] The problems with the original version look more literary than political, in that it was in various ways rather strong meat for the audience of intelligent laymen for which it was written, and I should guess that the main influence on the revision was Philip Sidney, who receives a eulogy in both versions. We do not know how much of Sidney Bruno was seeing at this time, and the only time we know that he came to Salisbury Court was in July, when the rewriting had presumably already been done.[51] But they had other ways of keeping in touch, and from the general character of the revisions, and also from the next dialogue, I think a contribution from Sidney can be assumed. If the revision had political implications, Castelnau seems as likely an influence as Sidney. I have no idea when the second version was published: a case could be made out that it was published after *De la causa*, perhaps in July.

Bruno's second and third dialogues, *De la causa, principio e uno* (Of the Cause, the Beginning and the One) and *De l'infinito universo e mondi* (Of the infinite universe and the plurality of worlds), will not detain us so long, for in them he was mostly concerned with high theory. Here he was for the first time positively expounding his own conception of the universe. This has been described as 'ultra-Copernican', meaning that Bruno took the heliocentric doctrine defended in the *Cena* as a point of departure for a number of exciting speculative assertions which were neither Aristotelian nor Copernican: notably that the universe was infinite and homogeneous, and that all spatial position in it was relative. In *De la causa*, as Aquilecchia has explained in his edition, Bruno was conducting a relatively formal and well-mannered argument with Aristotle, whose principle of the duality of form and matter he was seeking to subvert.[52]

Since he was thinking so hard about fundamentals, he did not have much time for the sociable comedy of the *Cena*. He did, however, come back to it in the first dialogue of the *Causa*, which was written after the four theoretical ones.[53] Since most of this deals with the

50 *Cena* (Aquilecchia), p. 49, from 'La lezione definitiva, pp. 224 f; cf. Michele Ciliberto's introduction to his edition of the *Spaccio* (Milan, 1985), p. 17. The question is discussed below, pp. 169 f.

51 Castelnau to Henri III, 18/28-vii-1584 (Chéruel, p. 317).

52 For *De la causa*, I refer to *DI*, pp. 172–342, and to the Aquilecchia edition (Turin, 1973). For *De l'infinito*, *DI*, pp. 343–537; Gentile was surely mistaken in putting a comma in the title after 'infinito', so turning the word into a noun. On the substance and method of the *Causa*, see Aquilecchia's introduction, pp. xi f, xxxix f.

53 Ibid. pp. xii, 8.

hostile reception he says had been accorded to the *Cena*, I doubt if it can have been written much before late June, whereas the other four may easily have been written directly after the *Cena*, say in May and early June. *De l'infinito* would then have followed in July–August or thereabouts: I doubt if Bruno had much of a summer holiday in 1584.

Outside the first dialogue of the *Causa*, two points emerge from these texts about Bruno's exterior life during 1584. We hear something about how he is getting on at Salisbury Court from the two dedications to Castelnau, in which he expresses gratitude for hospitality and for defending him against enemies. He slips into *De la causa* a conventional eulogy of Madame de Mauvissière and of Katherine-Marie, Florio's pupil. The dedication of *De l'infinito* distinguishes Bruno from the other members of the household as the one who does not give service but receives it, and by whose fame rather than by success in his own career or by the greatness of his family Castelnau will be eternally remembered.[54] There may be nothing much to be extracted from such elegances, if elegances they are; but we have recently learned quite a lot from investigation of the name of one of the characters in the substantive dialogues of *De la causa*, who are different from those in the first. The name 'Dicsono' sticks out in this quartet like that of 'Smitho' in the *Cena*; unlike that, so far as one knows, it was the name of an actual person, called Alexander Dickson.[55]

Dickson was a young Scot who had graduated from St Andrew's seven years before and had come to London, where he had attached himself to Sidney. It seems likely that he had been on the trip to Oxford, for he became a disciple of Bruno and at the beginning of 1584 published a book called *De umbra rationis* expounding Bruno's doctrine of memory. The book was dedicated to the Earl of Leicester, and Dickson must have had a position of some kind in the earl's following. He was, however, at odds with a number of the earl's academic supporters, for in his book he had attacked the Huguenot logician Peter Ramus, and Ramus was not only the author of a rival scheme of mental discipline to which many English Protestants

---

54　*Causa*, pp. 175–7/5–8; *Infinito*, pp. 345–7, 359–63. For Castelnau's wife and daughter, *Causa*, pp. 295/122 f.

55　Dickson's history was sketched by John Durkan, in *The Bibliotheck* (Glasgow), iii (1962), 183–90; thence Yates, *Art of Memory*, pp. 260–78, and Aquilecchia, in *Causa*, pp. xliii-xlvi. The identification of Dickson's opponent with William Perkins, the most distinguished of Elizabethan Calvinist theologians, seems persuasive. Cf. Margaret Aston, *England's Iconoclasts*: i, *Laws against Images* (Oxford, 1988), pp. 34, 452–66; and now Rita Sturlese, 'Un nuovo autografo del Bruno', *Rinascimento²*, xxvii (1987), 387–91 reporting her discovery of a copy of *De umbris idearum* with a dedication from Bruno to Dickson.

subscribed; he was also a martyr for the faith, having been murdered during the massacre of St Bartholomew. Big guns were trained on Dickson from Cambridge, and public controversy ensued during the year, to which Bruno added his mite by describing Ramus as an 'archpedant'.[56] The controversy was about the moral and intellectual value of mental images; it was not at all trivial, but for Bruno it was now a side-issue, which no doubt explains why he left Dickson to get on with it.

Dickson's appearance as a disciple of the Nolan philosophy in the main dialogues of *De la causa* suggests to me two things. The first is that since the trip to Oxford the previous summer the relation between Bruno and Sidney had been maturing to the point where the dedication of Bruno's later works to Sidney would become appropriate. The second is that Bruno had formed a fairly coherent view about English public affairs. He was not, in my opinion, looking for political or religious reconciliation of any kind, and he was not an instrument of a policy of reconciliation supposedly being promoted by Henri III or Castelnau:[57] he wanted Elizabeth to pursue the Protestant policy which Leicester and Walsingham represented, while stamping on the Protestant theology in which their supporters believed. I shall put the idea less baldly in due course.

It does not seem that the fracas about Ramus contributed very greatly to the public hostility to Bruno which the first dialogue of *De la causa* claims to document.[58] Dickson does not appear in it; the three characters seem to be roughly identifiable as Bruno, Florio and Sidney, and the subject is the reception of the *Cena de le Ceneri*. The third character, called Armesso, makes much the same complaints about the *Cena* as we have attributed to Sidney: its mixture of noble and ignoble matter, its uncivilised air of taking indiscriminate vengeance, and its general malediction on the English, which has raised hackles. Bruno complains that the campaign against him, which he says has included unspecified scandal from a malicious woman, has forced him to give up his social dinners and keep his head down at the embassy, where the servants are growling at him. He offers by way of an olive-branch a back-handed compliment to the intellectual eminence of the university of Oxford in the thirteenth century, and ends with another panegyric on Elizabeth. This time she is commended for successfully defending herself against the wicked slanders and enterprises of her enemies, so that while the Seine runs with blood and the other rivers of Europe boil, the Thames continues to

56 *Causa*, p. 260/92. In his early days Castelnau had translated into French a work of Ramus, *De moribus veterum Gallorum*: Hubault, *Castelnau*, p. 2.
57 Aquilecchia, in *Causa*, pp. xli ff, from Yates, 'The Religious Policy of Giordano Bruno'.
58 *Causa*, pp. 191–224/29–59.

wind untroubled down to the sea, rising and falling peacefully with the tide.[59] The reference is clearly to Throckmorton; the passage must have been written at just about the time he was executed.[60]

How much of Bruno's account of the fall-out from the publication of the *Cena* is true, and how much of it 'tropological' or a publicity stunt, is anybody's guess. He would not have rewritten it if there had not been some unfavourable reaction, and we may assume that he had received some Protestant flak as a result of Dickson's polemic against Ramus. Otherwise I should think he made a good deal of it up; and he was certainly not going out of his way to be nice to Protestant theologians when he gave Dickson a star part in his new production, put into the first dialogue of the *Causa* a substitute for the lost drinking-scene almost equally disgusting, and dragged in to *De l'infinito* one of the attacks on the consequences of preaching predestination to the masses which became a recurrent feature of his later works.[61] His feelings about Protestant politics, as one may gather from the evocation of Throckmorton and his plot, were another matter entirely. He had no reason to argue with Sidney about that.

At this point our story is briefly interrupted by the sort of difficulty that might happen to any property-holder.[62] Castelnau had been having problems about dilapidations with his landlady, the Marchioness of Winchester, and an argument with a neighbour, Dr Bailey, about what Castelnau said was part of his stables. These disputes had made some kind of a stir around Salisbury Court, but were put into the shade when another neighbour, William Gryce, who was clerk of the Royal Mews at the other end of the Strand, began rebuilding. There is nothing like building work for souring relations between neighbours, and Gryce and his builders were not tactful men. They smashed Castelnau's drains, covered his windows with filth and took away his light. (I record his side of the story, because it is the only one we have.) When the embassy staff complained, they were abused

59   *Causa*, pp. 197, 199, 204–5, 214/35, 37, 41–3, 49 (literary objections); 176/6 (woman: Aquilecchia does not think the implication was sexual); 194/32 f (confined to embassy); 176/6 (servants); 209 f/46 (mediaeval Oxford); 222–3/58–9 (Elizabeth and the Thames). I am sure that Émile Namer, pp. 76 f, and Sidney Greenberg, p. 107, (see *Sources and Literature*, 3) are right against Yates, *Bruno*, p. 288, and Aquilecchia, *Causa*, p. 58 n, in taking the efforts of Elizabeth's enemies to 'desmetterla' as political ('atteindre', 'dethrone'), not simply moral.

60   10/20 July: *Holinshed's Chronicles* (6 vols; London, 1807–8), iv, 548.

61   *Causa*, p. 198/36 (hair in the soup, etc.); *Infinito*, pp. 385–6.

62   Described in Castelnau to Walsingham and the Council, 7/17–16/26-viii-1584 (*CSP Foreign 1584–85*, pp. 11–24; Yates, *Florio*, pp. 63–5).

as French dogs and invited to fight it out; I imagine they threw some filth too, or undermined the scaffolding. Crowds assembled in the street. On 9 August Gryce, who as a royal servant claimed to have the queen's authority to teach the French a lesson, brought along some armed toughs, who were perhaps the bricklayers grabbing whatever they could lay their hands on. Sticks, stones and (according to Castelnau) crossbow-bolts demolished the embassy windows and bombarded the valets in the kitchen. One *garçon* (according to Castelnau a foundling boy whom he was charitably bringing up) had an eye knocked out. The crowd then got into the house and rampaged up and down, chasing Courcelles and Florio out of their chambers, smashing up the parlour and terrifying Madame, who was in bed.

When they had gone Castelnau sent Florio off to Walsingham with a furious letter. The Council very promptly had a string of Gryce's builders arrested, and sent a man along to pacify the neighbourhood.[63] Probably, as Castelnau implied, some of the other neighbours were quite happy to see Gryce taken down a peg. After a day or two Walsingham sent to ask Castelnau to petition for the builders to be released, which he amiably did. Peace returned to Salisbury Court. Gryce finished his extension; the sewers were re-opened, the windows mended, the parlour put to rights. Florio and Katherine-Marie got back to their lessons; Courcelles to his correspondence, his rendezvous and his now occasional treachery; Girault, who I imagine had had something to do with causing the riot, to his cellar and his money-making schemes. Madame went stoically through the series of miscarriages which were her lot during the year, helped by the loan of a gentle ass from the Walsinghams, which enabled her to get out to the country and to visit her friend, Sir Francis's daughter Lady Sidney, at Barn Elms. Castelnau himself, whose embassy had been in low water since Throckmorton's arrest and was coming to an end, was persuaded by the Council's prompt action to drop his suspicion that the riot had been officially inspired; a number of pleasures were put in his way, including a hunting trip to Windsor, when Elizabeth, Leicester and Sidney were particularly nice to him.[64] Fagot kept his head down; Bruno, who does not seem to have been much distracted by the noise from contemplating the infinity of the universe, no doubt repeated across the dinner-table what he had said before about the barbarity of the English and the folly of converting them to

63   I had supposed from Castelnau's description (to the Council, 16/26-viii-1584) of this man as 'Mr. William Houl', that this was Herle, but Herle was on a mission to Emden at the time (*CSP Foreign 1583–84*, pp. 546, 626; *1584–85*, pp. 88, 155).

64   Castelnau to Burghley, 29-viii/8-ix-1584; to Walsingham, 30-viii/9-ix-1584 (*CSP Foreign 1584–85*, pp. 36, 38); to Henri III, 8/18-ix-1584 (Chéruel, pp. 327–31).

justification by faith. So far as I know, the incident was of no importance in our story; but you never can tell.

Some time after this, Bruno began the longest of all his dialogues, the *Spaccio della bestia trionfante*. It looks like another piece of deference to Sidney, since it was dedicated to him and, while to some extent a return to the conversational manner of the *Cena*, is a great deal more high-minded in tone. It must have been written in the autumn: in the dedication, which I suppose was written after the rest of the book, Bruno mentions that he will soon be leaving England, which indicates a date after 4 November, when Castelnau received his instructions to return to France.[65] It is again in Chinese box form, and recounts a council among the gods, reminiscent of the Council of Trent, about reforming themselves and the heavens in order to prevent a *Götterdämmerung* impending upon them for the vices of their past conduct. Most of it is an exhaustive astronomical allegory in which the traditional figures which represent the constellations are removed from their places for their evil conduct, replaced by more acceptable virtues, and sent off to redeem themselves by battling against vicious and malevolent forces on earth. The Beast of the title has been variously interpreted; something vaguely apocalyptic is implied, but it is not given any concrete reality apart from the various vices in which it is embodied. The work is famous for its evocation of the ancient and true Egyptian religion, of which Judaism and Christianity are treated as corruptions; the civic religion of Rome seems to be regarded as its nearest available representative. Its relentless abstraction makes it difficult to reduce its message to anything fairly particular. A lot of it seems to me to be about the restitution of true religion, morality and politics in Italy in face of the backruptcy of modern Rome; but it certainly gives plenty of scope to Bruno's animus against Reformation theology, and this aspect of it has been stressed by its latest commentator.[66] I have already said that I do not think that in Bruno's mind the two targets were at all incompatible. I am not entirely sure that Sidney thought they were incompatible either, for Sidney's views on Protestant theology seem something of a mystery; but in any case Bruno never supposed that

---

65 *DI*, pp. 547–831. For Bruno's impending departure, *Spaccio*, p. 549; cf. Henri III to Castelnau, 19/29-x-1584 (BN ff 3305, f. 56), Castelnau to Henri III, 4/14-xi-1584 (Chéruel, p. 347).

66 Ciliberto, introduction to the *Spaccio*, pp. 7–59. A. Ingegno's account of the book in *La sommersa nave della religione* (Naples, 1984), p. 33, as 'una sorta di anti-Evangelo' is true but unspecific.

those to whom he dedicated his books would necessarily agree with everything that was in them.

From a literary point of view the _Spaccio_ suffers from a floppy structure and insufficient effort to bring it to life. The outer dialogue is a shadowy affair, which is not very clearly distinguished from the council of the gods and seems to get in the way. Among the gods, Momus keeps things relatively lively with satirical interjections, and Jove behaves like one of the more amiable popes. If Bruno meant to accommodate one of the criticisms of the _Cena_ by imposing a unity of tone, he certainly achieved that; the cost, for most readers, will be a good deal of boredom. Perhaps it is anachronistic to feel that the _Spaccio_ only comes alive when it is reasonably clear what Bruno is talking about, as in his passages about the Egyptian religion and reformed theology, or when a precise reference seems reasonably close to the surface, as in a piece about the worthiness of dissimulation as a protector of truth.[67] The design elaborated in the argument, which involves proceeding through the entire catalogue of the constellations, is not entirely carried out; at the end a panegyric on Henri III seems to have taken the place of what was originally intended.[68] I imagine that this was partly due to exhaustion, and partly to the prospect of having to return to France in the near future.

If this is so, the two short and hasty dialogues which go under the title _Cabala del cavallo pegaseo_ (meaning something like 'An Oracle from the Winged Horse'), or one of them, will presumably have been composed during an unexpected delay in his departure.[69] They were published together fairly early in 1585, but perhaps written at different times. In his preface, Bruno said he had found a sketch for the first of them on a sheet of paper he had used as a cover for the manuscript of the _Spaccio_, and it seems to be a sort of theological appendix to the previous work.[70] It advances the claims of the ass, a figure of holy ignorance, to replace the Great Bear in the place left vacant in the reformed firmament next to the most eminent of its constellations, that of truth (which has replaced _Ursa Minor_, including Polaris). Apart from this probably ironical gesture towards a theological _via negativa_, and an embodiment of the doctrine of the

---

67 _Spaccio_, pp. 622 ff, 707 f.
68 Compare the _Argument_, p. 570, with the text, pp. 823–9; also pointed out by Ciliberto, _La ruota del tempo_ (Rome, 1986), p. 145.
69 _Cabala del cavallo pegaseo, con l'aggiunta dell' Asino cillenico: DI_, pp. 833–923.
70 _Epistola dedicatoria. . . al rev^{mo}. Don Sapatino. . ._, p. 836: 'al fine, non avendo altro da ispedire, più per caso che per consiglio, ho volti gli occhi ad un cartaccio che avevo altre volte spreggiato e messo per copertura di que' scritti (_Spaccio_): trovai che conteneva in parte quel tanto che vi vederete presentato.'

transmigration of souls, the *Cabala* is memorable as a return to the comic vein which Bruno had been neglecting. The spoof dedicatory epistle, the elegantly satirical 'Declamation to the pious reader', and the second dialogue, which portrays the holy ass trying to get into the Pythagorean Academy like Bruno trying to get into Oxford or the Sorbonne, are a lot funnier than anything he had written since the second dialogue of the *Cena*. There was probably a serious intention behind this somewhere, but it hardly had time to emerge: the first dialogue stopped in its tracks, as if Bruno had had a sudden call to do something else, and the whole thing reads as if it had been knocked up at the request of a publisher who wanted something more saleable than the *Spaccio*. Among other connotations too numerous to mention, the ass is something to do with the horse Pegasus, upon which Perseus rescued Andromeda from the sea-monster; something to do with Christ's entry into Jerusalem; and something to do with the transmigration of souls, which appealed to Bruno as a substitute for purgatory. What all this would have amounted to if expounded in a full-length dialogue is very hard to say. Bruno later said that it had not gone down well, and disowned it.[71]

---

71 *De comparatione imaginum,* OL ii³, 237–8, and *DI,* p. 835 n. 1: 'Nos particulari stylo de illo (*sc.* asino) scripsimus, quod, quia vulgo displicuit et sapientibus propter sinistrum sensum non placuit, opus est suppressum.' Which means, I think, that it could easily be taken, as it was probably intended, as a satire on Christianity. N. Ordine, *La cabala dell'Asino* (Naples, 1987) tries to distinguish positive and negative aspects to the figure of the ass; I expect the distinction ought to be made, but Bruno does not offer much help in making it.

5

LAST DAYS IN ARCADIA

Paris and London, February–September 1585

AT MUCH THE time when Bruno was putting together the *Cabala*,
probably towards the end of February, Fagot finally emerged from
his silence: he was in Paris, and writing in an elegant new hand a
letter to the English ambassador, Sir Edward Stafford.[72] Much of it
repeats what he had said two years ago about the import of seditious
Catholic literture by Girault and Leduc; the subject had just been
made newsworthy by the arrest of the agent William Parry, who had
been, among other things, a distributor of such books. Parry was
tried for treason, and executed on 2 March. Fagot was now able to
add a good deal about the Paris end of the operation: it was run, he
said, by Thomas Morgan from his lodgings 'auprès l'église St
Hilaire du Mont', where he was lodging possibly with Girault's
wife, with the help of another Englishman, probably the recent
émigré Charles Arundell. Morgan provided the funds. He also, Fagot
said, conducted his correspondence with England through Castelnau
and his packets, the link being one of the secretaries of the French
secretary of state, Villeroy: I think he meant Jean Arnault. Castelnau
was about to be replaced in London by Guillaume de l'Aubépine,
baron de Châteauneuf: Girault, who was also in Paris, had been
taken on by Châteauneuf to run his household. Girault would
shortly be leaving for England to look for a new house for him in the
same area as Salisbury Court, 'du long de la rivière'; he would fill it
with Catholic fanatics like himself. Fagot suggested that they put a
ban on any embassy in this quarter, since it was far too easy for
people and goods to come and go unobserved, and that they arrest
Girault, who was going over via Calais. They should ban anything
going in or out of the embassy without being searched. He began

---

72 *Texts*, no. 13. The signature is 'Henry', and the contents make it evident that it was by
Fagot.

and ended with an emotional appeal to Stafford and Walsingham to act on his information, and so defend the 'repos public de [leur] patrie' from the grave danger of civil war being stirred up by the enemies of the queen and the state. He sounds in excellent form.

As far as we know Fagot had not been in Paris since his introduction to espionage in April 1583: indeed we do not actually know that he had ever been there before, though he sounds rather at home in the city. So we may ask what he was doing there. The obvious answer is that, in view of Castelnau's impending return, he had come to see if there was a chance of his being re-employed by Châteauneuf, and to look for something else if there was not. This was obviously what Girault had been doing, and it looks as if they may have come over together. Courcelles had also been in Paris around the same time, and on the same errand; in fact, Arnault got the job as Châteauneuf's secretary, and Courcelles returned to London at the end of February.[73] We may wonder how Castelnau was getting on without most of his staff: actually he was waiting for the end of his wife's latest pregnancy and, having little to do, was about to start writing his memoirs.

This was surely the main reason for Fagot's trip to Paris; but it is tempting to speculate that there was something else to it. The new thing in Fagot's letter is the information about Thomas Morgan. In the world in which Fagot was now moving, Morgan was a large figure. He served Queen Mary as a sort of secretary of state in exile, and was a good deal more active in her cause than her official representative in Paris, James Beaton, Archbishop of Glasgow.[74] Although he was the principal organiser of conspiracies against Elizabeth, and had been using Salisbury Court as a post-box for a long time, Fagot had not hitherto found occasion to mention him. According to William Parry's confession, Morgan had been the author of Parry's assassination scheme, and shortly after Parry's arrest, which occurred on 8 February, Elizabeth wrote a formal letter to Henri III to demand his extradition. Fagot had done nothing to earn his money for nearly a year, and since he was probably going to Paris anyway I am inclined to think that Walsingham had asked him

---

73 I refer to 'Castelnau in London' for the story of Courcelles; but see Arnault to Walsingham, 16/26-ii-1585, 4/14-iii-1585 (PRO SP 78/13, nos. 31, 49 bis; *CSP Foreign 1584–85*, pp. 285, 323); Thomas Morgan to Mary, 5/15-i-1585 (Murdin, p. 456, misdated to 1586).

74 Leo Hicks, *An Elizabethan Problem* (London, 1964), assembles the available information about Morgan and his friend Charles Paget, but the book is marred by over-reliance on Jesuit evidence and a prior conviction that Morgan was an English agent. The argument is greatly weakened by the revision (above, p. 20) about Castelnau's secretaries; cf. Hicks, pp. 177–84 (but see below, pp. 66–8). Mark Greengrass, 'Mary, Dowager Queen of France', *The Innes Review*, xxxviii (1987), 171–88, offers a new start.

to keep an eye on Morgan until the request for his extradition had gone through. Although one would imagine that Stafford, as ambassador, knew where Morgan was to be found before Fagot told him, there does seem to be a fairly close relation between Fagot's letter to him and Morgan's arrest: he was taken into custody by royal guards on the night of 9 March and, though not sent over to England, put in the Bastille.[75] Fagot's letter is not dated, but some time about 6 March seems most likely, and that was the date on which Stafford put a watch on Morgan's house in preparation for his arrest.

The suggestion would explain, what is otherwise a problem, why the letter was sent to Stafford. I do not think it likely that Fagot did this on his own initiative. He was working for Walsingham, and both of them were extremely careful about security. Walsingham was in general adamant that his agents, when in Paris, should not reveal themselves to Stafford, whom he deeply mistrusted; he was later to regret that Fagot and Stafford had been put in touch with one another. But only Stafford could get Morgan arrested, so Walsingham, if he thought Fagot could help, would have had to make an exception in this case. The new handwriting would help to cover his tracks, and he did not use his full signature. The letter was sent on by Stafford, and apparently arrived in Walsingham's office on 8/18 March, when it was endorsed in the usual way, though without Fagot's name. One may suppose that it had been sent over with Stafford's letter to Walsingham of 1/11 March, when he reported Morgan's arrest.

If this was the underside of Fagot's trip to Paris, which I think very probable but not certain, he had done what he had been asked to do with his usual competence, and could relax in Paris for a while. He may also have sent Stafford at this time a copy of a story which he had picked up about a Catholic girl called by the French Jehanne Garlac. This girl had escaped from England disguised as a boy and taken ship as a sailor from Ireland to Bordeaux where, having been discovered by the Jesuit provincial, she had been received with great solemnity into a convent. The story had been sent from Bordeaux, perhaps to the Jesuit college in Paris or perhaps to Thomas Morgan, as a contribution to Catholic edification and propaganda. The copyist does not seem to have altered the text, though he may have left some of it out, and did not make any comment on it. I identify him with reasonable confidence as Fagot from the location of the piece in the British Library, and from the handwriting, both of

---

75 Walsingham to Stafford, 12/22-ii-1585, Stafford to Walsingham, 24-ii/6-iii-1585, 1/11-iii-1585 (*CSP Foreign 1584–85*, pp. 277, 301, 309).

which are very close to those of Fagot's previous letter to Stafford. I think he may have got the story from Girault.[76]

Bruno's last production in England, and the last of his major Italian writings, was *De gli eroici furori* (Of Heroic Passions), a defence of Platonic and intellectual love in the guise of a commentary, like Dante's *Vita nuova*, on a number of sonnets most of which he seems recently to have written. It must have been composed in the spring or early summer of 1585, and published in London by about August. It was dedicated to Sidney as a poet, though unless Bruno's English was better than we suppose he must have known more about this via Florio than at first hand.[77] The formal subject of the work is about as soporific as that of the *Spaccio*, and Bruno had not Dante's talent for the genre; but a number of brighter moments occur. He enlivens his dedication by a vicious polemic against the moronic boringness and physical disgustingness of women; and by the mildly incompatible confession that he had thought of calling the piece a *Canticle* on the model of the Song of Solomon, but had been deterred by the handle he would have given to doubters of the *bona fides* of his priesthood.[78] The book is made more palatable by a political and personal subtext, which is signalled in the dedication when Bruno excepts English ladies from his general contempt for the sex. After his invocation of the English muses in the *Cena* he could hardly have done otherwise. His own experience with the muses, he explains, has been chequered. In Italy he had been obliged to neglect them in order to defend himself against the envious, the ignorant and the malicious, and because of 'censors' who had chained his intellect 'beneath the rule of a most vile and senseless hypocrisy'. The speech is attributed to the Neapolitan poet Luigi Tansillo, but is plainly autobiographical and about Bruno's experiences as a Dominican. He narrates the migration of the muses from Italy to the north, where they are cured of the blindness inflicted by Circe/Rome through the intervention of Diana/Elizabeth, who opens the vessel of truth and beauty and sprinkles them with its water. Bruno is here as good as his word, and responds to the occasion with real poetry. Elizabeth ends as the instrument of divine government of the ocean and the heavens, and thence of earth, the vehicle of divine judgement on the ignorance,

---

76 *Texts*, no. 14.
77 *DI*, pp. 925–1178. On Bruno and Sidney, ibid. pp. 947–8; John Buxton, *Sir Philip Sidney and the English Renaissance* (London, 1954), pp. 164–5, 180–1.
78 *Eroici furori*, pp. 927–30, 932: Yates, 'Religious Policy', p. 185, thinks these clerical 'pharisees' are English Protestants; it seems to me that they are mainly in the Church of Rome.

slavery and malevolence of Rome;[79] Bruno, as a martyr to intellectual beauty playing Actaeon to her Diana. The Thames, where she rules with her chorus of nymphs, a supernatural river rising towards the godhead as well as flowing down from it, is the vale of wisdom and the river of eternal life. Bruno's obsession with the river had grown since the *Cena*: he reminds me of Spenser's *Prothalamion*.[80] He was shortly going to have to leave it. So indeed was Sidney, who had been planning to go with Francis Drake on an expedition to the West Indies, but was sent instead by Elizabeth to the Netherlands, where he died fighting the Spaniards in October 1586.

Castelnau's return to France had been decided upon in October 1584 but did not actually occur until the following September. He got a postponement of six months on the grounds of his wife's health (she had just become pregnant again), and it appears that a daughter was born live in June 1585 and died shortly after. His replacement, Châteauneuf, arrived in London on 28 July; Castelnau, held up by his wife's condition and by trouble about the very large debts he was leaving behind, finally left on or soon after 23 September. He and Châteauneuf proved an unhappy tandem, and Castelnau spent most of the summer on farewell visits and writing his memoirs.[81]

After his expedition to Paris, Fagot must have arrived back at Salisbury Court somewhere about Easter (11/21 April, same day in the two styles), and remained in residence thereafter. There was no question of his staying on permanently with Châteauneuf, but some time between Châteauneuf's arrival and the beginning of September he asked Fagot to come and see him. In view of Châteauneuf's reputation as a Catholic hardliner, Fagot must have been rather nervous, and the interview did not go at all well, though it might have gone worse. He wrote Walsingham an extremely circumstantial account of it, which I reproduce more or less *verbatim*:

> *Châteauneuf* Catholics are persecuted in England. Especially priests. Everybody knows you are a priest. Have you not been afraid to walk about the streets?

79 *Eroici furori*, pp. 955–7, 1165–78 (the beginning and end of the work); Gentile's identification of the Circe with Rome (p. 1171) is surely correct.
80 *Eroici furori*, pp. 946, 1168 ff.
81 Above n. 65; Jean de Vulcob to Castelnau, Paris, 15/25-vii-1585 (BN V^C 472, p. 141), congratulating him on the birth of a 'belle fille'. Châteauneuf's arrival: A. Teulet (ed.), *Relations politiques de la France et de l'Espagne avec l'Écosse au XVIe siècle* (5 vols; Paris, 1862), iv, 79, misdating by a year. Castelnau to Archibald Douglas, London, 22-ix/2-x-1585 (HMC *Hatfield*, iii, 110) dates the departure, and attributes the delay to the condition of Castelnau's wife.

Fagot I have not found this a problem.

Châteauneuf I see. (*Pause*) Is there anybody who frequents the embassy who you think is a traitor or a spy?

Fagot I don't know any such people. It is not part of my job.

Châteauneuf Quite. But maybe you have some idea, or have heard something?

Fagot Not a thing.

Châteauneuf On your conscience, is not M. Archibald [Douglas] a traitor?

Fagot If he is, I know nothing about it.

Châteauneuf Why is M. Douglas so thick with M. de Mauvissière?

Fagot I've no idea.

Châteauneuf Yes you have, but you won't say. (*Pause, while Châteauneuf thinks of torture*) Very well. What about Maître Geoffroy [Le Brumen] the [Huguenot] doctor? In France they say he's a double agent, works both for the Huguenots and the pope. They don't trust Laurent [Feron] or Florio much either.

(*An Italian called Brancaleone, possibly a priest, who has been standing around, comes up to Châteauneuf.*)

Brancaleone I've been told by people here that the Queen of England is extremely sorry that M. de Mauvissière is leaving, and would give a fortune not to have had you come in his place.

Châteauneuf Shut up. We are getting off the point. Monsieur, I should like the benefit of your experience on behalf of the two priests I have brought with me. One is French and one is Italian, and the Italian is a distinguished preacher in both languages. It is time there was some preaching in this house.

[Fagot does not record his reply, but tells Walsingham he has talked to the Italian, who is a trouble-maker and intends to write a best-seller about his experiences in England. Perhaps he is Brancaleone].

Châteauneuf By God, I will have no Protestants in my house, as M. de Mauvissière has done. They have been spying on him, and anyway it is a disgrace and a scandal. The king knows all about it, and M. de Mauvissière will get a rocket when he goes home. The king has absolutely forbidden me to employ Protestants, and you will know that he has just issued an edict committing himself to the restoration of unity of religion in France.

[Fagot seems to have said nothing, but must have been tempted to say that it was not his Protestant servants who had been betraying M. de Mauvissière.]

Châteauneuf I believe there is a lot of church stuff going cheap somewhere around London. I should like to buy some to donate to poor churches in France.

Fagot I will take you there on Monday.
Châteauneuf You should have gone into the book-importing business, like Girault. He has made a fortune.
Fagot Girault and I do not have much in common.

Fagot ended his letter with another blast against Girault ('a plague in the kingdom') and a farewell to Walsingham. He was and would be his faithful servant to his dying day, and hoped to be able to serve him better in France than he had done in England, since he would be hobnobbing with the king's councillors. 'Please drop me a line about this. God save the Queen of England and her Council. Do not forget me. Henry Fagot.'[82]

Despite the ironic ring of Châteauneuf's first enquiries, and his evident lack of enthusiasm for Fagot's performance as a priest, it does not sound as if he thought he was actually a spy himself, which must have taken a weight off Fagot's mind. There was no doubt more to the conversation that he recorded (Châteauneuf must surely have enquired into his mysterious background), but he seems to have managed to give the impression that he was an unworldly type and a reasonably good Catholic who was stonewalling out of loyalty to Castelnau.

Although Fagot had said goodbye to Walsingham, and through him to Elizabeth, this was not quite the last they were to hear of him before his departure. Castelnau had enormous debts in London, which his government was doggedly refusing to pay, and though he himself still had diplomatic immunity his servants were liable to arrest. Florio was given a power of attorney, and protected by an arrangement with Châteauneuf whereby he was taken on as Châteauneuf's servant but excused from living in the house: since he was a Protestant, Châteauneuf wanted him out, and had no reason to employ him himself. But Girault, who was loading Castelnau's goods on to a French boat at Gravesend, had a court order taken out against him in London to stop him leaving the country; and Fagot himself was actually arrested and put in jail.[83] Walsingham sent to have him released, but the Lord Mayor stuck to the law and said he

---

82 *Texts*, no. 15, with note on date. Henri III did not employ Protestants in his own household, which makes Fagot's account very plausible in that respect: Jacqueline Boucher, *La Cour de Henri III* (n.p., 1986), p. 180. The implication is that Feron as well as Florio was a Protestant.

83 For Girault, Castelnau to Florio, [13/23]-ix-1585, to Walsingham, 14/24-ix-1585 (Yates, *Florio*, pp. 68–70; *CSP Foreign 1585–86*, pp. 260, 24); the letter to Florio is undated, but must have been written on the Monday. For Fagot, Thomas Pullison, Lord Mayor of London, to Walsingham, 9/19-ix-1585 (PRO SP 12/182, f. 18); Fagot is described as 'Mauvissière's priest'. The records of the Lord Mayor's Court in the Corporation of London Records Office, where traces of the case should have survived, are very deficient for this year, and have nothing.

could not release him without the agreement of the plaintiff, a Frenchman whom he could not locate. There was an exciting scene at the Lord Mayor's house, which featured Fagot fetched up from the cells, and Castelnau in a rage trying without success to grab him, said the Lord Mayor, 'out of my hands'. So Fagot must have spent another night or so in jail before the Privy Council got its way, or the plaintiff was squared. Girault got away smartly from Gravesend, and the ship passed Dover on Tuesday, 14 September; it was attacked by Dutch pirates off Le Havre. Fagot spent his last week at Salisbury Court, then left with Castelnau, his wife and the remains of his household for France.[84]

---

84   The departure of Girault and the boat is dated by the examination of a number of English youths taken off it at Dover, 14/24 and 15/25-ix-1585 (PRO SP 12/182, nos. 15–19). Castelnau's journey: Yates, *Florio*, p. 71; Castelnau to Douglas, 22-ix/2-x-1585, to Burghley, St Leu-la-Forêt, 20/30-x-1585 (HMC *Hatfield*, iii, 110; *CSP Foreign 1585–86*, p. 97). It sounds from Castelnau's route to Paris as if they had crossed from Rye to Dieppe.

6

UNDER THE VOLCANO

Paris, November 1585 to November 1586

AFTER THE HIGH LIFE in London, the eight months or so that Bruno spent back in Paris must have seemed rather a come-down.[85] The city and the court were in an extremely nervous state, awaiting a further eruption of Catholic fundamentalism, and neither was especially pleased to see him; as a Neapolitan, he would have recognised a smell of the last days of Pompeii. Castelnau's career went into a decline, as Châteauneuf had predicted, and Bruno must have parted from him almost as soon as they got back to Paris. In his Venetian examination, Bruno was discreet about what happened next, saying that he passed the time 'with those *signori* whom I knew', and lived mostly at his own expense. We know he took lodgings near the Collège de Cambrai, on the left bank, and that during the winter he did a lot of reading in the library of the Abbey of St Victor, made famous by Rabelais; or at least that he did a lot of talking to the librarian, who recorded his conversation.[86] In the spring he became involved in a ludicrous dispute with a fellow-countryman, the Salernitan Fabrizio Mordente, a mathematician who was interested in squaring the circle and had invented a compass to draw it. In May Bruno was allowed by the university to set up a disputation in the Collège de Cambrai, in which his anti-Aristotelian view of the universe was defended by a pupil; he seems to have run away from it when the distinguished audience turned against him. At some point he approached the papal nuncio and the Spanish ambassador with a view to regularising his status in Rome by getting retrospective

---

85 *Texts*, no. 1; Yates, *Bruno*, pp. 291–305, and 'New Documents', which elaborates on Rita Calderini De-Marchi, *Jacopo Corbinelli et les érudits français* (Milan, 1914). Both of them are based on the volume of Corbinelli's letters to Gianvincenzo Pinelli, BA T 167 sup, which I use later.

86 The librarian Cotin's diary, extracts from which are printed in *Documenti*, pp. 39–46; I have not seen the original, which is in BN ff 20309.

permission to abandon his Dominican habit and live as a secular priest.[87] In the meantime he was having an agreeably social time with a set of Italian friends, whose connections in high places kept him in touch with public affairs. The ones we know about were the wealthy *abbé commendataire* and politico Piero Delbene, who was now acting as go-between for the king and Henri of Navarre and was Navarre's unofficial agent in Paris; and a learned Florentine *émigré*, Jacopo Corbinelli. Corbinelli had been tutor both to Henri III and to his now deceased brother the Duke of Anjou, was in the king's employment as *lecteur* or literary adviser, and had his finger on the pulse of the court and of the intellectual scene.[88] He had recently published the first edition of Dante's *De vulgari eloquentia*.

Disheartened, so it seems, by the failure of his disputation and of his approach to the nuncio, and alarmed by the rumblings of the volcano, Bruno left France in June 1586. He went to Germany, I suspect to Frankfurt and to the house of Horatio Pallavicino, a Genoese exile now resident in England and there as Elizabeth's agent negotiating the recruitment of a German Protestant army to invade France in support of Navarre and the Huguenots. He says that he tried to get a job in the Catholic cities of Mainz and Wiesbaden; he then tried the arts faculty of the Lutheran university of Marburg, where he matriculated on 25 July but was turned down by the rector on theological grounds; a month later he had been accepted by, of all places, Luther's university of Wittenberg, on the strength of a reference from his Oxford acquaintance Alberico Gentili, who was teaching law there. Since Gentili acted as secretary to Pallavicino around this time, and had possibly come to Germany with him, I presume that Bruno's applications to German Protestant universities had support from Pallavicino; Pallavicino had recently visited both the Elector of Saxony and the Landgrave of Hesse, the sovereigns of the two universities in question, and was on excellent terms with both of them.[89] We leave Bruno lecturing on Aristotle and Raymond

---

87 *Documenti*, pp. 104, 133.
88 For this side of Bruno's life during the year, see Yates, 'New Documents'; Corbinelli remarked, in a letter of 27-v/6-vi-1586, that Bruno was a 'piacevol compagnietto, epicuro per la vita' (translated above, p. 14).
89 *Documenti*, p. 85. Bruno does not mention the attempt at Marburg, for which see Singer, *Giordano Bruno*, pp. 139–41; Gentili and Pallavicino, *CSP Foreign 1585–86*, p. 652. Pallavicino stayed at Frankfurt from 31-iii/10-iv-1586 to 7/17-iv-1587, except for a trip to see the Elector in June 1586; he saw the Landgrave on his way to Frankfurt, and again on the the way home (Ibid. pp. 515, 652; *1586–88*, pp. 14, 41, 274, 281 etc). Bruno did not admit to having been in Frankfurt at this time, but his trips to Mainz, Wiesbaden and Marburg suggest it; he spent a lot of time in the city a couple of years later. It would have been dangerous for him to confess a connection with Pallavicino, because Pallavicino had been formally excommunicated as a heretic, and all contact with him was prohibited early in 1587: Lawrence Stone, *An Elizabethan: Sir Horatio Palavicino* (Oxford, 1956), pp. 8–10; *CSP Foreign 1585–86*, pp. 222, 224.

Lull in Wittenberg and preparing to put his philosophy into Latin hexameters; five years later he left Germany for Venice on the trip which led to his trial and his death.

Fagot had also arrived in Paris with Castelnau at the beginning of November, and had also, to Castelnau's 'great regret', to leave his service. He did not take long to find another billet: in a letter written probably in January he said that he had had an interview with the grand almoner of the Duke of Guise, who was a fellow-Italian and perhaps a member of the influential Gondi family; he had recommended him to the duke's nephew, the Duke of Montpensier, one of whose almoners he now was. If Fagot intended to pursue his career in intelligence, this was a fairly strategic situation: the duke was a Catholic Bourbon, Henri of Navarre's cousin and a middle-of-the-road man who was friendly with Sir Edward Stafford; the duke's mother was the most energetic organiser of the Catholic League in Paris, and the Hôtel de Montpensier one of its recognised centres, though the duke does not seem to have lived there. The letter was written to Walsingham to remind him of Fagot's existence and the opportunities offered by his new situation. It must have been sent by Stafford, and except for the implication that Walsingham was still paying him a salary did not contain much in the way of useful intelligence. Fagot reported on an Antwerper called Alexander who was living in his house and acting as a courier between Mendoza, now Spanish ambassador in Paris, and the Prince of Parma in the Netherlands; and he added something to his account of the doings of Girault as a financial operator on behalf of English Catholics in France. The most entertaining thing in the letter was a farcical report on the unnamed Italian preacher whose arrival in London with Châteauneuf Fagot had reported in his last: he had, Fagot said, invented a feeble cipher in which to send intelligence to the pope, and Fagot must have raised a laugh in Walsingham's office by explaining it (for each vowel, you put the next letter of the alphabet) and addressing the letter to Walsingham in it ('Mpnsfkgnfxr lf Sfgrbttbkrf Pxxbl Skngbng'). He included his usual protestation of loyalty to Elizabeth, and a request for a sub.[90]

We do not know that the letter to Walsingham led to anything, and no later one has survived if Fagot wrote any. But if he was still receiving English money, which is what the letter says, he must have been doing something for it while he was in Paris, and the presumption must be that he was doing it for the English ambassador, Sir

Edward Stafford. He must have sent Walsingham's letter via Stafford, and his new employment, if that is quite the word, put him in the way of serving him. Stafford had close relations with the Bourbon clan, in one of whose households he had been a page, and he must have known Montpensier quite well. In the early months of 1586 he was putting a great deal of effort into a scheme to bribe the duke and one of his Catholic cousins to desert the court of Henri III and join their relative the King of Navarre in an interdenominational family front against the League. His intrigue, which was of a type fairly common during the Wars of Religion, did not come off: loyalty to Henri III, or simply cold feet, caused Montpensier to slip out of it at the last minute.[91] Unless Fagot's position was an absolute sinecure, which is not what he said to Walsingham, he can hardly fail to have had some small part in it somewhere; if he had, he would have come across Bruno's friend the *abbé* Delbene, who along with Stafford was the principal mover in the scheme.

Nevertheless, the only reasonably hard fact here is that Fagot sent his letter to Walsingham by Stafford, and it may be that there is no absolutely irrecusable evidence that Fagot worked for Stafford during 1586. What there is, is a communication received by Stafford, of which we shall have to try to determine whether it came from Fagot or not.[92] It must have been written between the middle of September and the middle of November, new style, and is virtually certain to have arrived early in November. It is now to be found in the same volume of the Cottonian Mss. in the British Library as Fagot's previous communication, or two previous communications, to Stafford, though not very close to them. This means that it found its way to Walsingham's office, where it was endorsed: 'Secrete French advertisments'. It is an extremely peculiar piece: I cannot think of anything quite like it in the confetti of similar papers which was clogging up the political machinery of Europe during these years. If we judge it by Fagot's standards it was rather long; it incorporated as *pièces justificatives* three disparate pieces of advice or intelligence. One of these, originally in French, had for no obvious reason been rendered into a laborious and incorrect Italian translation. Most of it consisted of stale news and needless advice; but at the end it conveyed one piece of extremely hot intelligence. Since it is hard to think of a brief descriptive title for it I shall refer to it, where necessary, as Text no. 17.

It began, without a preamble, with a copy of the advice in French

91 *CSP Foreign 1585–86*, pp. 554, 575, 587 (April 1586) and *passim* thereafter; Stafford's upbringing with Henri, Prince of Condé, ibid. *1586–88*, p. 129.
92 *Texts*, no. 17.

and Italian, a fairly crackpot scheme to win the war in the Netherlands by sending troops to burn the harvest simultaneously in the
two loyalist, or 'malcontent', provinces of Flanders and Brabant.
The writer suggested two other schemes for bringing confusion to
the enemy: setting fire to the arsenal at Antwerp, which he knew
a Huguenot gentleman willing to do; and mounting an invasion
of Italy. This, he said, was easier than you might think, since the
Spaniards, who controlled the country from Milan to Sicily, had
denuded it of troops in order to pursue the war in the Netherlands
and to defend the West Indies against Drake; he claimed to have
some hot news about Spanish troop movements. All one would need
to do would be to raise an extra force in Germany under cover of
Pallavicino's mission recruiting soldiers for France, and send them
down over the Alps instead. This would not, he claimed implausibly,
cost much or take much time; the pro-papal Italians would be taken
completely by surprise, and the others, living under a regime of
tyranny and torture, would revolt. There was a French magnate
available who had just been all round Italy and would be the man to
lead the enterprise: he may have meant the Duke of Nevers, a
member of the Gonzaga family, Dukes of Mantua, who had recently
been on a short trip to Rome.[93] What the writer seems to have had in
mind was something like Charles V's sack of Rome in 1527.

Two more documents followed: the first an extract from a letter
by an Italian merchant in Lyon about the effect on Spanish policy of
Drake's ravages in the West Indies; the second a whole letter in Latin,
probably written to the reporter himself and retailing the contents of
a letter from Rome about aggressive designs of the pope. According
to this, Sixtus V was weighing up the advantages of supporting the
Duke of Savoy in a strike against Geneva or launching an enterprise
of invasion and assassination against Elizabeth, and had just despatched an aggressively political nuncio to the Emperor Rudolf II.
The first document must have been meant to support what the writer
had said about the overstretching of Spanish forces; the second,
together with a piece of stop-press that the Duke of Savoy had now
come to terms with Geneva, gave weight to his last passage, which
contained the only really hard intelligence in the piece. À propos of
enterprises against Elizabeth, the writer said that he had been talking
to an 'honest man' who had been visiting Queen Mary's servant
Thomas Morgan, still in the Bastille after a year and a half. He had
been visiting him 'comme malade', so he was presumably a doctor or
a priest. Morgan had told his visitor of a great conspiracy against

93   June, 1585: A. Lynn Martin, *Henri III and the Jesuit Politicians* (Geneva, 1973), pp. 135,
140 f.

Elizabeth being financed by Spanish money and run by the Duke of Guise and Mary's ambassador in Paris, the Archbishop of Glasgow. This, he conceded, was no news in itself since the conspiracy had been blown by other means, but it showed that Morgan, the key man in anti-Elizabethan conspiracies, could be tempted to change sides. He was extremely fed up with being in prison, and if Elizabeth could get him out he would tell her all he knew. He was angry with Guise and Glasgow for leaving him to stew in jail, and his long imprisonment had 'dompté ce [sic: son] zèle papistic'. Morgan had also been talking to a Huguenot gentleman called the Comte de la Magnane, likewise in the Bastille, who had been soothing his enmity against the queen.

Ignoring for the moment the rest of the communication, we have two reasons for taking the information about Thomas Morgan seriously. It was probably true, or sufficiently close to the truth to give the notion of springing him a reasonable chance of coming off. Although Morgan was something of a martyr to the Catholic population of Paris, no authority on that side had been anxious to press Henri III for his release. Guise and Glasgow suspected him of double-crossing them, and the papacy was prevented from intervening by a fear of exposing Gregory XIII's involvement with him in the operations of William Parry.[94] There was a feud among English Catholic exiles in Paris between supporters and enemies of Morgan which both Walsingham and Stafford had been working to embitter. During 1586 Morgan and Walsingham had been playing hide-and-seek with one another through a third party, to whom Morgan had expressed an interest in contacting Burghley.[95] It is extremely likely that he had been fishing for an offer of the kind proposed; which is not to say that, then or at any other time, he was betraying, or prepared to betray, the Queen of Scots.

It was also taken seriously by Stafford. It opened up a matter which, from the middle of September 1586, had driven off the front pages in Paris even the galloping progress of the disintegration of the country. At this point the news had arrived of the exposure in England of Anthony Babington's conspiracy to liberate Mary and, probably, to assassinate Elizabeth, which was expected to precipitate, according to one's point of view, the righteous execution or cruel

94 Charles Paget to Mary, Paris, 5/15-ii, 31-iii/10-iv-1586 (Murdin, pp. 463–7, 506–10; also pp. 479, 503); for the Roman side, Blet, *Ragazzoni*, pp. 379 ff; Hicks, *An Elizabethan Problem*, pp. 151–6.

95 Confession of Gilbert Gifford, the party in question, Paris, 4/14-viii-1588 (HMC *Hatfield*, iii, 347, 349; cf. *CSP Domestic Addenda 1580–1625*, pp. 221 ff). The best introduction to all this is Cuthbert Butler and J.H. Pollen, 'Dr Gifford in 1586', *The Month*, ciii (1904), 243–258, 348–366.

martyrdom of the Queen of Scots.[96] Morgan, Bastille-bound as he was, had once again been active in mounting the conspiracy, and was assumed to have other such schemes up his sleeve; Elizabeth sent over another man to Paris to demand his extradition. Stafford's intelligence about him was therefore timely, and on 16 November he sent it on to Burghley and told him he was doing something about it. 'I . . . have a means in hand to see if, by one that is great with Morgan, and doth sometimes haunt him in the Bastille, there is, under fair promises and hope of liberty (for he is very weary to be where he is), anything to be drawn.'[97] It is obvious that the author of Text no. 17 was the means in question, and unlikely that Stafford had lost much time after receiving it. In London it was taken seriously too: Burghley took the news to the queen, and a few weeks later she was quoting it at Henri III's minister Bellièvre, who had come over to London with the mission of saving Mary while declining to surrender Morgan as she had asked. She sounds as if she had been rather tempted to act upon Stafford's suggestion.[98]

If there were not grounds for thinking that Fagot might have put together this odd communication, I should not have described it at such length. But since the pursuit of its author will take us rather far afield, I shall ask the reader to satisfy his curiosity for the time being with what we can find out about him without more ado. After reporting to Burghley his response to the scheme about Morgan, Stafford went on to say that he expected opposition from Walsingham:

> But Master Secretary, that will let nothing that good is to be done by my means, I am afraid will both cross me in the matter, and alienate the person's mind, whom he is acquainted withal, that dealeth in it. I fear it because such things have been done to me twice or thrice already both with that person that dealeth in this and others that have dealt with me in other things.

When some of Walsingham's correspondents in Paris had told him they were in touch with Stafford, 'he would never deal with them after'.[99] For the moment we can ignore the reasons for the feud between Stafford and Walsingham, and stick to the facts recorded.

---

96   J.H. Pollen (ed.), *Mary, Queen of Scots, and the Babington Plot* (Scottish History Society[3], iii; Edinburgh, 1922).

97   *Texts*, no. 18.

98   '. . . et quant a Morgand que depuis troys moys il luy [Elizabeth] à mandé que si il luy plairoit accorder sa grace, qu'il luy descouvriroit toute la conspiration de la Royne d'Escosse': Bellièvre and Châteauneuf to Henri III, London, 8/18-xii-1586 (BN ff 15892, ff. 44–6). This passage was originally printed by Agnes Strickland in 1843; thence to Hicks, *An Elizabethan Problem*, p. 151. I was quite excited by finding it in Paris in May 1989.

99   *Texts*, no. 18.

Stafford tells us that the author of No. 17 was 'acquainted' with Walsingham, and had been a correspondent of Walsingham's before he began to work for Stafford; which narrows the field rather a lot, since such transitions were not common. He was also, obviously, *au fait* about Morgan, and sounds as if he had known him at first-hand before his entry into the Bastille. Both facts are very compatible with Fagot's career as a spy.

Other facts about the author, which may be discovered from the piece itself, are less compatible: he showed proficiency in Latin, fair proficiency in French, but not much proficiency in Italian; and he wrote in a different hand from either of those we know Fagot to have used. We also have no reason for supposing that Fagot had access to confidential information, even rather ancient confidential information, from Rome, and from his general posture towards popes and papists it may seem unlikely. I have therefore to leave the story of Fagot in the air, for we do not hear from him again. Either about January 1586, with the joke about Châteauneuf's priest and his cipher, or in the November following, with the scheme of springing Morgan from the Bastille, he disappeared into the universe, like Melchisedech, as mysteriously as he had arrived in April 1583.

We know what had happened to Bruno in the meantime: he had gone to Germany, in June. And that, so far as we are concerned, was the end of *his* story: the history of his doings in Germany is in better hands than mine.[100] However, we may return to his final period in Paris to observe one thing about it, which will remind us that his and Fagot's histories, separate as they were, were nevertheless being performed upon the same stage and at the same time. In London the stage was Salisbury Court, and the two actions were connected by the person of Castelnau; in Paris we have no scene smaller than the city itself, but we do have a character who may seem to perform something of the double-headed role of Castelnau. This character is Piero Delbene. We know from Frances Yates how intimate were Bruno and Delbene at this time. They were both members of a close and learned circle which revolved around the Florentine literary scholar and servant of Henri III Jacopo Corbinelli, in which Bruno said at his trial that he 'spent most of his time' during these months; two of his works written and published at this time, one of them rather substantial, were dedicated to Delbene. Bruno did not

---

100 I refer to Dr Rita Sturlese, author of 'Su Bruno e Tycho Brahe', and of the *Bibliografia e censimento* of existing copies of early editions of Bruno, for which see *Sources and Literature*, 4.

dedicate at random: Delbene was rich, at least his family was, and Bruno must have gravitated into his orbit soon after he left Castelnau.[101]

As well as being a man of literary interests, Delbene was a man with a political position: he was Henri of Navarre's quasi-official agent in Paris and at the court of Henri III. Since the two kings were theoretically at war, this was a delicate situation, but it seems to have suited Delbene's talents. It put him in close relations with Stafford, which went through their ups and downs, and in more remote relations with Walsingham, with whom he corresponded through Navarre's agent in London. This being so, it is not surprising that we have some indication that he dealt with Fagot as well, in the scheme to get the Duke of Montpensier to change sides, which he concocted with Stafford at just about the time Fagot entered the duke's service.[102] It was the kind of scheme Fagot would have relished helping along.

We have likewise reason, perhaps rather better reason, for supposing that Delbene had something to do with the author of Text no. 17 and his message. For one thing, Protestant gentlemen in the Bastille for political reasons were rather Delbene's department. For another, we find Stafford's single reference to the scheme for springing Morgan from the prison, and to its author, sandwiched in his letter to Burghley of 6/16 November 1586 immediately between two items about Delbene. In one of them Stafford complained, with a good deal of heat, that since the failure of the Montpensier scheme Delbene had been feeding Walsingham, behind his back, with information intended to discredit him as not sufficiently enthusiastic for the Protestant cause in France. The other, more amicable, item was a report on progress made with a commission Delbene had undertaken for him, and for his correspondent Lord Burghley, during the autumn.[103]

Burghley had a grandson called William Cecil, a difficult youth who had started a continental tour the year before. In the course of it he had gone off on an unauthorised trip to Rome; in Rome, he had been looked after by one of the cardinals of the Holy Office, a member of a historic Roman family and politically connected with France, Cardinal Savelli. Savelli had managed things so that young Cecil was able to return home in the summer of 1586 unscathed

---

101   Yates, 'New Documents', and above, p. 63. Lauro A. Colliard, *Un dottore dell'Ateneo patavino alla Corte di Francia: Pierre d'Elbène (1550–1590)* (Verona, 1972) is a strange compilation useful for establishing Delbene as a literary man-about-town, but hardly otherwise.

102   Above, pp. 64–5.

103   Stafford to Burghley, 6/16-xi-1586 (CSP Foreign 1586–88, p. 125); *Texts*, no. 18.

and, despite a lot of speculation, still a Protestant. Burghley was extremely relieved and grateful that nothing worse had happened, and asked Stafford to use his Catholic contacts in Paris to convey to the cardinal his thanks. Delbene turned out to be the right man, for in spite of his Protestant connections and (I imagine) his own neutrality his background was Florentine Catholic, and his mother's family had a branch in Rome; he passed the message, no doubt with due circumlocution, to a Roman cousin, and the cousin passed it to Savelli. Savelli sent back an extremely civil reply, which he evidently felt no need to disguise, even to the principal counsellor of an excommunicate princess. He said that he had been glad to do what he could for young William, and would do any further service for Burghley that he might; he hoped that things might so turn out that he would have opportunity to show more generally his admiration for the English, and in particular for Burghley, 'whom he esteemeth above all the rest'. He meant, I am sure, not only Elizabeth's more rebarbative counsellors like Walsingham, but also those of the English Catholic colony in Rome, like William Allen, who had been publicly denouncing Burghley to the Catholic world.[104]

The letter arrived in Paris two days after Stafford had written his previous letter to Burghley; somebody brought it to Stafford, and he and the messenger seem to have had a convivial evening together. They concluded that Savelli was cultivating the English with a view to acquiring Queen Elizabeth's support at the next conclave and, when he had become pope, launching a radically fresh departure in papal policy. Since the party who brought the letter does not seem to have been Delbene himself, one might wonder whether he was not the author of Text no. 17, who had just been reporting to Stafford confidential matters from Rome.[105] It is hard to know whether he would have thought the prospect of a liberal pope a help or a hindrance to his projected invasion of Italy; but in the meantime the notion was a tolerable joke.

104   Conyers Read, *Lord Burghley and Queen Elizabeth* (London, 1960), pp. 350–1 and nn. 43 and 46; Burghley to Stafford, 2/12-x-1586 (Murdin, p. 56); Stafford to Burghley, 29-vii/8-viii-1586, 9/19-xi-1586 (*CSP Domestic Addenda 1580–1625*, p. 183; *CSP Foreign 1586–88*, pp. 136f.).

105   Stafford's description of the event in the last letter cited indicates that Delbene did not bring the letter himself: 'Yesterday the Abbot of Albene had news . . . I saw the letter . . . We that read this last point . . .' Cardinal (Jacopo) Savelli had been *papabile* at the death of Gregory XIII in 1585, and did indeed take an independent line over England; but he died about three weeks after this: Pastor, *History*, xix, 13; xx, 515; xxi, 235; Hicks, 'An Elizabethan Propagandist', p. 186.

—PART II—

Veritas Filia Temporis

Preceding page: emblem of *Veritas temporis filia*, from Geffrey Whitney, *A Choice of Emblems and Other Devises* (Leyden: Plantin, 1586) p. 4.

I

A COINCIDENCE OF OPPOSITES

i   *A Priest in the House*

WE HAVE NOW FOLLOWED the careers of two men, in London and Paris, during three years or so in the 1580s. They had quite a lot in common. Both of them were Italians, and both of them were Catholic priests. Both of them came to stay in Castelnau's house in London in or about April 1583, and served in his household thereafter. Both of them were extremely hostile to the papacy, to Spain, and to Catholic conspiracies in England. Both of them met Queen Elizabeth in person and wrote of her with extravagant loyalty. Both of them left England for Paris with Castelnau in September 1585, and both of them left his service shortly after getting there. In the course of 1586, one of them left Paris for the last time, and the other disappeared.

Two accounts of this twinship seem possible. Either there were two men very close to each other in background, feelings, experience and movements, who lived in the same household for two and a half years; in which case they must have either become extremely friendly or got on each other's nerves. Or the two men were the same man.

The documentary evidence must, in principle, be in favour of the first hypothesis, since separate bodies of documents relate to the two individuals, and nowhere visibly intersect. Some kind of principle of economy must be in favour of the second. In choosing between them I think there are four considerations, partly documentary and partly rational, to be borne in mind.

1. We do not have a name for one of the individuals. 'Henry Fagot' was a pseudonym, and we have no real name to attach to the person who wrote under it. After he left England, when he seems to have stopped using it, we have no name for him at all. If there was such a person, we really have three careers to trace, not two, and no evidence whatever has appeared for one of them. As well as having no real name, Fagot has no real biography: he appears from no-

where, disappears into space, says (at least directly) nothing about himself, and exists only in the role of a man passing intelligence and asking for his reward. It is certainly possible that evidence may turn up which would give him a real existence; but on what we have at the moment he looks a spurious person.

2.   On the eve of Castelnau's departure from London, there was only one priest in his house. This emerges from Fagot's account of his interview with the incoming ambassador Châteauneuf.[1] Châteauneuf asked him whether he was not afraid to go about the streets of London, 'pour autant que j'estois cestuillà qui debvoit estre congnu entre tous les autres' (since I was the one [inhabitant of the embassy] who ought to be known among all the others). From Fagot's reply, where he said that nobody had done him any harm 'pour mon office', it is obvious that what he was concealing inside the circumlocution was 'priest'. We do not actually need to infer this, because Fagot had started to write 'le pr [*estre*]' before realising that this was a careless admission, and crossing it out. 'Priest' was what Châteauneuf had said; he went on to say that he had brought with him two priests, one Italian and one apparently French. He asked Fagot to tell him how he had dealt with the situation in England, and to advise the new priests how they should deal with it themselves ('. . . me demanda comment je me gouvernois, et que je donnasses instruction a ses prestres comment il falloit qu'il [*sic*] se gouvernassent . . .'). It seems quite evident from this that there was only one priest in the house, and that he was Fagot. It would be very natural to conclude that Fagot had been the only priest in the house for some time, but that does not necessarily follow. What does follow, surely, is that when Castelnau went home he only had one priest to take with him. Since both Bruno and Fagot went home with him, they must have been the same person.

It might be held that there was another priest in the house in the summer of 1585 (that is, Bruno), but that Châteauneuf did not know about him, or did not know he was a priest. Consider the probabilities. Châteauneuf had arrived in London in a state of deep suspicion about his predecessor's conduct of his household: he was convinced that it was full of Protestants, spies and traitors. He needed to make a thorough investigation of it in order to find out what members of it, if any, he would want to keep on; he also, on his own account or possibly under instructions from Villeroy or somebody else at home, wanted to find out because he wanted to find out. After Castelnau's return he wrote home, via his wife, damning descriptions of Castelnau's conduct from a Catholic point of view, which unfor-

1   *Texts*, no. 15; above, pp. 58–60.

tunately have not survived. Castelnau must have provided him with a list of the establishment when he arrived; it is conceivable that he had left Bruno off it, or that he was disguised as the gentleman-servant he later claimed to have been. But it is not conceivable that, in a household which was radically split on religious and political lines, one of the Leaguers would not have told Châteauneuf the truth. Girault had been hobnobbing with him since the spring, and had obviously briefed him on the household; he would certainly have told him about Bruno. I should think he had told Châteauneuf as much about Bruno as Fagot had told Walsingham about Girault. In any case, supposing he had wanted to, Castelnau could not possibly have concealed Bruno's existence from Châteauneuf: for two whole years Bruno had been trumpeting from the rooftops where he lived and on what familiar terms he stood with Castelnau. Châteauneuf would have been deaf and blind if he had not noticed; and Henri III, Catherine de Médicis, Villeroy, Bellièvre and the rest of the French councillors would have been deaf and blind if they had not told him. If Fagot was not Bruno, then Châteauneuf would have asked him to say what he knew about him, as he did about Douglas, Le Brumen, Feron and Florio. He did not ask him because he had Bruno in front of him. In fact, Fagot's account of the interview, though discreet, suggests to me that Châteauneuf knew perfectly well who he was talking to, and that he was talking to Bruno. The first thing he asked Fagot was whether he was not afraid, as a known priest, to go about the streets of London: the framing of the question might suggest that Châteauneuf, or Brancaleone, or somebody, had been reading the second dialogue of the *Cena de le Ceneri*, with its dramatic account of Bruno and Florio being beaten up by the London *plebe* on their way down the Strand, or some other of Bruno's evocations of the thuggishness of the English masses. Later, when he asked Fagot to give the new priests instruction on how to get by in London, Châteauneuf added that Fagot would do himself a bit of good by co-operating in this way ('. . . et qu'il me seroit chosse salutaire . . .'). The implication was that Fagot was in some kind of a jam which Châteauneuf could help with, or exploit: the threat would apply very pertinently to a refugee Dominican who had been in trouble with the Inquisition and could expect to be in more trouble if Henri III, whose councillor Châteauneuf was, did not continue to protect him when he got back to France.

Nobody is compelled to agree with my reading of these overtones of Fagot's account of the interview, still less with my opinion that the actual interrogation contained a great deal more about Bruno's doings, which Fagot left out because he was much too fly to put anything in writing which would identify him as Bruno. But the

identification of Fagot as Bruno does not depend on my interpretation of these passages in the letter, though the interpretation seems to
me to become persuasive once the identification is established. It
depends on those passages which make it apparent that Fagot was the
only priest in the house; or, if one wants to take the evidence at its
least possible valuation, that Châteauneuf believed that there was
only one priest in the house, and that he cannot plausibly be
supposed to have been mistaken.

3. If Fagot and Bruno, being the people we know them to have
been, living in the same house over a period of two and a half years,
had been two separate individuals, it is inconceivable that neither of
them should ever, during this time, have mentioned the other's
existence. Or rather: it is not inconceivable that Bruno, in his
published writings which are all we have, found no occasion to
mention another Italian priest in the embassy whose views were
similar to his own. One might think that he would have been just the
fellow to find a spot in one of Bruno's dialogues, perhaps a seat in the
boat as it set off in the dark from Buckhurst Stairs; still, Bruno could
certainly have had reasons for not mentioning him. It is, on the other
hand, quite inconceivable that Fagot, who was employed to report
what was going on in Salisbury Court and probably among mutual
acquaintances in Paris as well, should never at any point have
mentioned Bruno: never have passed any information from him,
never have tried to recruit him as a spy, never have suggested that he
was a dangerous fellow, never have recorded a word of the table-talk
of the most memorable conversationalist of his time. On the grounds
of pure rational probability, this is probably the strongest argument
that Fagot and Bruno were the same person; but since of its nature it
can have no documentary basis I think that, from a historian's point
of view, it is an inferior argument to the previous one.

4. If we prove that Fagot and Bruno were the same person, we
prove that Bruno wrote all Fagot's pieces. We do not prove that he
wrote Text no. 17, because we have not proved that this was written
by Fagot. If we do not prove this our knowledge of their joint career,
if that was what it was, does not extend much beyond their return to
Paris.

This is a refinement which we do not need to attend to just now. I
consider that point 2 – the argument from the interview with
Châteauneuf – establishes sufficiently that Bruno and Fagot were the
same person. Point 3 – Fagot's silence about Bruno – removes one
potentially lethal counter-argument, and positively confirms point 2.
Together I think they are conclusive. Point 1 – about the alias – does
not add anything positive to the proof itself: it establishes that there
was no real person called Fagot, but not that the name of the person

whose name was not Fagot was Bruno. But it does remove the obstacle to identifying them presented by the separate bodies of documentary evidence, since in the circumstances separate bodies of evidence are what one might expect. It also gives us a story of how and why Bruno, being one person, passed and has passed himself off as two. How – by using an alias, and systematically avoiding writing anything under that alias which would identify him as Bruno; why – because he had adopted the profession of an English spy, and wished to pursue it successfully, and not to be found out. Since we are dealing in historical proof, a story is something we need.

The fact that Bruno and Fagot were the same person is the fact mentioned in my preface to the reader, and I shall now proceed on the assumption that its truth has been established. It will soon become necessary, and I hope a pleasure, for myself and the patient reader to reconsider the two stories we have been following as two stories about the same person. Before we start doing that I hope to clear away objections to my conclusion. There are actually very few difficulties in the evidence which stand in its way; for the most part, the two separate sources fit together very comfortably. But I can think of one factual problem and one documentary problem.

One of the bigger bombshells in Bruno's biography which follows from identifying him with Fagot is that, while he was in Salisbury Court, he functioned as a priest and was, indeed, the embassy chaplain. He said mass, heard confessions and presumably administered other sacraments, visited prisoners and I should think distributed alms, performed such other rites (as those of Ash Wednesday) as were called for. He did this certainly between the spring of 1584 and his departure from London fifteen months later, and probably all the time he was there; the only thing he does not seem to have done is preach. This is a fact whose implications we shall need to consider later. The issue which arises at the moment is that, during the investigation made about him in Venice, he explicitly denied doing this. He said that he had had no job in Castelnau's house, except that he served as his gentleman ('in casa del qual [Castelnau] non faceva altro, se non che stava per suo gentilhuomo').[2] After he left Italy, or thereabouts, he had not gone to mass because he knew that as a wilful refugee from the Order of Preachers he was excommunicate; he had sometimes gone to vespers and sermons. During his time in England he had not gone to mass for that reason, 'although mass was said in the house'; nor had he gone to hear mass or sermons outside Salisbury Court ('ne in questo tempo, ancora che si dicesse messa in

2 *Texts*, no. 1; Yates, *Bruno*, p. 204.

casa, non andavo, ne fuori a messa ne a prediche per la causa sudetta').[3]

Bruno's canon law on this point was correct, as one would expect: an apostate Dominican was subject, *latae sententiae* or without the need for a particular process, to the lesser excommunication, and on that ground prohibited both from administering the sacraments and from receiving them; he was also forbidden to attend any public worship except sermons. Bruno had therefore, on his own account, been sticking very closely to what a priest ought to have done who could not bear the disciplines of the religious life but was otherwise a faithful, law-abiding and conscientious Catholic, who might with a bit of luck get away with exclaustration and permission to live as a secular priest. We really do not need to be at all surprised that this ingratiating story was quite untrue: a great deal of what Bruno said to his inquisitors has turned out to be untrue, and who shall blame him? He was talking for his life. The historian of his *processo*, Luigi Firpo, has said of his dogmatic statements that his method was to 'deny the deniable, to justify by appropriate modifications whatever with a bit of stretching could be reconciled with Catholic dogma, and to repudiate whatever irreducible errors could be proved against him'.[4] He had even less difficulty in talking about his life outside Italy: except possibly at the very end, there were no witnesses to his conduct in England, and he could say whatever he liked. Sometimes he simply lied (as he had done to Châteauneuf in London), sometimes he equivocated. When talking about Salisbury Court, he did not say that he had not said mass, but that he had not gone to mass although mass was said in the house: both of these statements could be held to be strictly true. He said nothing at all about hearing confessions, while saying quite a lot about going to confession. Admittedly the reason he gave for not having gone to mass was spurious, but it may be that the clerk wrote down something less

---

3   *Texts*, no. 1; also *Documenti*, pp. 102, 104. For the legal situation, see *ODCC*, Excommunication; and especially P. Hofmeister, 'Die Strafen für den Apostata a Religione', *Studia Gratiana*, viii (1962), 436, 443–4. Pope Paul IV (1558) had added to the penalties, among other things, *ipso facto* deprivation of all academic degrees and excommunication of helpers and patrons, but these aggravations seem to have been withdrawn shortly afterwards. Hence it does not seem to have been an offence in itself for Bruno to teach in universities, or for Castelnau to employ him; but he was still permanently suspended from his priestly functions. Bruno's story to the Inquisition was therefore very carefully constructed in relation to the canon law. According to the Council of Trent (1563), no dealings for a settlement were possible until he had returned to his order: cf. below, pp. 131, 133–4, above, p. 77. I am most grateful to Donald Logan for help with this matter.

4   Firpo, 'Processo', (i), 557; cf. his introduction to *Scritti scelti di Giordano Bruno e di Tommaso Campanella* (2nd edn, Turin, 1968), p. 29, from V. Spampanato, *Vita di Giordano Bruno* (Messina, 1921), pp. 290–8, on the disingenuousness of Bruno's account of his stay in Geneva; *Documenti*, pp. 33–6, 44.

careful than Bruno had actually said. In short, the difficulty about Bruno's own evidence is no difficulty at all: Bruno was not telling the truth.

The documentary problem is that Fagot and Bruno wrote totally different hands. We know Fagot's handwriting rather better than we know Bruno's because, except for his first letter which only exists in an office copy, all the pieces we have from him are in his own hand, and most of them are signed. With Bruno in person we are less fortunate. He wrote an enormous amount, but precious little evidence of his compulsive 'paper-scratching' survives. The only relatively substantial piece of writing which exists in his own hand covers about a dozen leaves of a notebook written between 1589 and 1591 in Germany and Padua; half of this is a scribbled draft of a text called *De vinculo spiritus*, half is some of a work on Lullian medicine (Plates IX–X). Apart from this all we have is bits and pieces, most of them dating from his time in Germany: indeed we have only five lines of his written before 1587, four of them discovered three years ago. The bits and pieces are: 1) a signature in the Rector's Book of the Academy of Geneva, dated 20 May 1579; 2) four dedications in books, written between 1583 and 1588; 3) a couple of verses of Ecclesiastes (improved) written in the album of a friend, and another version written on a print of his home-town, Nola (Wittenberg, 1587–8); and 4) a formal letter to the pro-rector of the University of Helmstedt, dated 6/16 October 1589 (Plates VII–VIII). I have seen copies of all these except one of the dedications.[5]

As one might have expected from his origins, Bruno's taste in handwriting ran to the Roman or italic. The pages of the notebook are fairly recognisably by, though not I think in, the same hand as the Geneva signature, the dedications and the second set of verses. On these public occasions he adopted something more lapidary and print-like than his ordinary cursive scribble, but clearly the same as the numerous titles in the manuscript of *Medicina lulliana*. With exceptions like *a* for *a* in the public hand, the letter-forms are italic even when he is scribbling; the cursive *ꞃ* and the uncursive *ꞇ*, for *r*, are fairly constant in both. Almost everything that survives in

5 Bruno's handwriting is discussed and illustrated in Tocco and Vitelli's introduction to *OL* iii, pp. xvii–xxix; in Singer, *Giordano Bruno* pp. 219–22; in V. Salvestrini, *Bibliografia di Giordano Bruno*, 2nd edn by L. Firpo (Florence, 1958), nos. 224–8; and by G. Aquilecchia, in *Giornale storico della letteratura italiana*, cxxxiv (1957), 333–8; cxl (1963), 148–51. The latest addition to the corpus is Rita Sturlese, 'Un nuovo autografo del Bruno', *Rinascimento²*, xxvii (1987), 387–91, which reports and illustrates the dedication to Alexander Dickson of a copy of *De umbris idearum* (1582). This probably dates from late 1583, and is the only piece of Bruno's legitimate handwriting which we have from his years in England. 'Vergar di carte': *Eroici furori*, p. 951. I have gone into handwriting questions more fully in 'A Note on Fagot's Handwriting, and Bruno's', below, pp. 256–68; source references for Bruno's originals, pp. 269–70; Plates I–X.

Bruno's hand is in Latin; but since some passages in *De vinculo spiritus* are in Italian, we must assume that he wrote the private hand in both languages, and that the lost manuscripts of his dialogues were written in some version of it. All this is quite straightforward. But not everything we have of his was written in either of these hands. The writing of the letter to the pro-rector of Helmstedt, also in Latin, might be classified (mainly by the *r*'s) either as an elegant version of the private hand or as a cursive version of the public one; but I should hardly believe anyone who claimed to recognise it on handwriting grounds alone. There has been some doubt whether he actually wrote the text of the letter, though it is now agreed, I am sure rightly, that he did. The signature is a large, loopy and obviously Italian version of the text.[6] Formal in style, the text and especially the signature of the letter are miles away from the upright or backsloping print of his usual formal hand, of which we have examples dating from before and after it. The first version of the verses is something else again: here the signature is in the usual public hand, but the verses themselves are spiky, forward-sloping and laboriously cursive – quite unlike anything else of his that survives.

So, even from this limited corpus, we know that Bruno wrote at least three different hands, and we need not be too amazed that his hand when writing as Fagot was different from any of these. Indeed as Fagot he had two different hands: of the Texts printed at the end of this book, Nos. 3, 4, 9, 11, 11a, 15 and 16 are in one hand (Plates I–IV), Nos. 13 and (I think) 14 in another (Plate V). I shall call these FA and FB. FA is a workmanlike, rather crude version of the more traditional alternative to italic, known as 'secretary' hand (Plate I), with a tendency to spread: there are no secretary forms anywhere in Bruno's acknowledged handwriting. FB is an elegant, clearly French hand, which I think he may have picked up from Feron, the clerk in the embassy; the letter forms are mainly Roman, but sometimes Fagot uses traditional French forms for *e* (*ʓ*) and *s* (*ẑ*). No. 14 does not look quite so French as this, and has various letter-forms different from those of No. 13, such as tails on the *p*'s and *q*'s; I think that it is the same hand with self-conscious differences of detail, but nothing much depends on my opinion being correct.

I see no large theory which would cover the use of these half a dozen hands; but if we confine ourselves to Fagot we come up with the hypothesis that Fagot wrote a different hand according to whom he was writing to. All the letters to Walsingham are in FA, and all the letters in FA are to Walsingham, if one includes the one to Queen Elizabeth, which was sent to Walsingham. The pieces in FB, or the

6   Plate VIII; below, p. 269; *OL* iii, pp. xii f.

single piece if we exclude No. 14, were sent to Stafford. This seems to make perfectly good sense. Bruno had a regular hand, which had two versions, cursive for everyday and printed for special occasions; when he felt like writing differently, he did so; we know of two styles other than his regular ones. It looks as if he enjoyed experimenting with his handwriting, as he did with his identity. When he became Fagot he adopted a handwriting for him; when he began communications with Stafford he invented a new one. As his comic letter to Walsingham shows, he could have written in cipher if he had wanted to, but he evidently thought his own system both more congenial and more secure.[7] When he decided that writing was too risky, he sent his messages verbally, through Herle. It occurs to me that he may have taken a hint from Francis Throckmorton, who caused some difficulty to his prosecutors by writing some of his compromising papers in a secretary hand, and some in a Roman; but Bruno must have worked out his own system before he discovered this.[8] Since it has taken us four centuries to find him out, one must admit that the system had a good deal of merit: he was, I conclude, an extremely competent spy.

ii Communications with the Enemy

It does not follow from identifying Bruno and Fagot that Bruno was the author of Text no. 17, the puzzling communication reported by Stafford in November 1586 (Plate VI). Indeed it appears to follow that he cannot have written it, since he had been in Germany since June. However, since there is now some evidence that he may have written it, we need to follow it up. We should be glad to know whether Bruno, in 1586, looked for a Protestant invasion to liberate his country from the pope, and whether he was party to a scheme for springing Thomas Morgan from the Bastille in the interests of

---

7 Apart from *Texts*, no. 16, there is the diagram from the Moscow manuscript, f. 161 (*OL* iii, p. xx; below p. 269 f), which I think is a scheme for a number-cipher of the box type which Bruno calls, in *Texts*, no. 4, 'lettre quartallé (cartelée)'. It is somewhat more complicated than the normal one described in De Lamar Jensen, *Diplomacy and Dogmatism: Bernardino de Mendoza and the French Catholic League* (Cambridge, Mass., 1964), Appendix, pp. 231–2, and would have been rather cumbersome to use, but it looks quite efficient to me. Such schemes conventionally begin at 11, but this one begins at 58, a variation (oddly) suggested by Jensen himself; it also has 13 co-ordinates each side, instead of 9 or 10. 'The cat sat on the mat' needs about 46 single numbers instead of 34.

8 Anon., *A Discoverie of the Treasons practised and attempted . . . by Francis Throckmorton* (London, 1584; repr. in *Harleian Miscellany* (10 vols, London, 1808–13), iii, 190–200), pp. 190, 195, 199 f.

Queen Elizabeth.[9] So it will be our business to investigate the matter, even if the investigation takes some time.

Hitherto we have been trying to discover whether the author of No. 17 was Fagot, and found indications pro and con. Now that we are trying to discover whether the author was Giordano Bruno, the case is altered and we must reconsider it from the beginning. The beginning is Stafford's letter of 6/16 November 1586. If we look at it again we find that the indications that he was talking about Fagot (the 'acquaintance' with Walsingham, the passage from Walsingham to Stafford, the access to Morgan) will now serve equally well as indications that he was talking about Bruno; and one other aspect of his comment will serve a good deal better. I said that the item came, in Stafford's letter, between two different items concerning his relations with Piero Delbene, which suggested that in Stafford's mind the writer had something to do with him; so did the news about Morgan from the Huguenot gentleman in the Bastille, since such persons were in Delbene's province as agent in Paris for Henri of Navarre.[10] The second point, which may not sound very convincing in itself, is given a good deal of force by Delbene's involvement with Stafford, a year later, in an imbroglio which likewise featured the Bastille, a Huguenot prisoner in it, and Thomas Morgan.[11] The point about the sequence of thought in the letter is made a good deal stronger if the subject of the item in the middle was Bruno, since we know that Bruno and Delbene were hand-in-glove during Bruno's final visit or visits to Paris. The suppression of Bruno's name would be natural, but no more natural than that of an ordinary spy. I add that Bruno would also make a most plausible carrier of Cardinal Savelli's message from Delbene to Stafford, and an even more plausible drinking-companion for the ensuing night; but since we do not know that this person was the author of No. 17 I shall have to dismiss the hypothesis as a red-herring.[12] Ignoring it, we find that Stafford's description, which fits Fagot pretty well, fits Bruno even better.

I proceed to the indications in the text of No. 17 itself, which were mainly against the authorship of Fagot; are they equally against the authorship of Bruno? The first is the handwriting. It is a neat, almost printed, uncursive Roman hand; its French has accents, which Fagot never used before No. 16 and rarely there, and it has virtually no abbreviations. It has some minor lapses into secretary forms, one of which is corrected. I can see nothing in it, except perhaps a very

9   Above, pp. 63, 65–8.
10 *Texts*, no. 18; above, p. 70.
11 Below, n. 36.
12 Above, p. 71.

remote resemblance to the two versions of FB, which would suggest either Fagot or Bruno. But since we already have five distinct hands of Bruno, including two of Fagot, and all of them quite different, it will not perhaps seem much of a problem to suppose a sixth.[13] We may leave a provisional space for it as FC.

Then there is a question about the language of the piece: or rather two questions, one about the parts of it in French, the other about the parts in Italian. In attributing the piece to Bruno, the first is not a problem; the second is a very serious one. If we take it that Fagot's French was Bruno's French, it will seem quite likely that Bruno wrote No. 17. If we ignore the parts of it where he is copying someone else, the author writes a French which is not bad, probably rather better than most of Fagot's efforts, but not the French of a Frenchman. There are too many cases where the sound has led the spelling astray: *fain* for *faim*, *ont* for *on*, *leur* for *leurs*, *chevauls* for *chevaulx*, *soldat* for *soldats*, *conte* for *comte* and – agreeably – *papistic* for *papistique*. The writer also has various mannerisms which sound distinctly fagotian: forms of *lequel* where *qui* would be the natural thing; *que* used as a neuter subject ('Qu'est la cause . . .'); *iceluy*, instead of *ledit* or *ce*, used in a demonstrative way with a person's name ('iceluy Morgan', like 'icelluy Morice' in No. 9, and 'iceluy Girault' in No. 15); and perhaps particularly the penchant for marginal interjections of *Nota* or *Notez*, a form which has occurred rather lavishly in four of Fagot's communications, and may well seem to be a trade mark of his.[14] The writer describes Queen Elizabeth, twice, as *serenissime*, as Fagot had done in the confession letter and in his last communication. It would be very foolish to suppose that all these tricks were peculiar to Fagot, but *iceluy* and *Nota* sound as if they might have been; *papistic* would seem to identify the author as Italian. If the piece was not written by Fagot, that is by Bruno, it must have been written by somebody who resembled him a good deal.

The Italian passages are quite another matter. They are execrable, and on the face of it it is inconceivable that they could have been written by an Italian. Here we may pause to think what a peculiar composition we have in front of us. The piece starts with a page of advice about how to win the war in the Netherlands this year, picked up at best from some old soldier who had fought there. The advice is copied out for Stafford in its original French. Then it is translated, on the spot and more or less *verbatim*, into Italian.[15] For whose benefit?

13 Above, pp. 81–2.
14 *Texts*, nos. 1, 2, 4 and (in the text) 11; cf. above, pp. 16–18.
15 This is evident from the alterations, deletions and errors in the Italian version, and also from the fact that it is slightly abbreviated. It is however expanded at one point (l. 8 of

Certainly not Stafford's, whose French was as good as his English. Nor Burghley's, nor Walsingham's, nor the queen's. What did the author think he was doing? It is not as if his own Italian is any good: it is very much worse than his French. He falls down over simple verbs, simple numbers, plurals and prepositions; he invents words. He does not know the Italian for Antwerp, which is like not knowing the English for Singapore. It is a barbaric effort. But after a while you begin to feel that it is barbaric in a particular direction. *Le* comes out as *el*; *que* as *que* instead of *che*; *déjà* as *ia*; *ceux-ci* and *ceux-là* as *aquesti* and *aquelli*. His feminine for *inglese* is *inglesa*. All these are Spanish forms, and the second and fourth are impossible in Italian. The author is therefore a Spaniard; or else he is somebody seeking to give the impression that he is a Spaniard trying to write Italian. As we look further, it is the second of these alternatives that comes to mind. Quite often he gets exactly the right effect. For *attaquer* (assault), which is *assalire* or *assaltare* in Italian and *asaltar* in Spanish, he writes *assaltar*; for *amuser* (occupy), *intrattenere* or *intertenere* in Italian and *entretener* in Spanish, he writes *intretenir*; for *toute* (all, feminine), *tutta/toda*, he writes *tota*. This seems rather knowing of him. He is beginning to sound too learned for the degree of ignorance shown. Would somebody who did not know that *qu* cannot be pronounced *k* in Italian also know that *tritico*, an archaic and latinate form reminiscent of the Spanish *trigo*, was just about possible (though extremely literary) Italian for *corn*? Then there is *ove*, meaning 'where'. He gives this, five times, as his translation for *ou*, meaning 'or'; the Italian is *o*. Two things are being suggested here: the respectable Italian *over*, a form of *o* which cannot however be reduced to *ove*; and the French *où*, meaning 'where', which is the actual equivalent of *ove*. The implication is that the author has got the wrong word, and translated it to produce something that sounds quite like Italian, but which any reasonably informed reader will know is wrong. *Ove* is a quite complicated, and distinctly learned, joke. At other times our translator throws caution to the winds: in rendering *gast* and *embarquement* (*guasto* or *guastamento/imbarco* or *imbarcamento*; *gasto/embarcacion*) as *guastamente* and *imbarquamente*, he seems to be working on a mistaken principle and inventing Esperanto rather than evoking Spanish; but I can testify that these forms will sound convincingly Hispanic to a rapid reader not very competent in the language. The writer, I conclude, is pulling legs, on a basis of rather less Spanish than he would have needed to achieve a master-piece; but in any case I do not get the impression that he would have

Italian version), and an expansion corrected at l. 22. Both expansions mention that the army in question is English, which the French version does not.

been too put out by someone who doubted that his native tongue was Spanish, so long as he got the message that it could not possibly have been Italian.[16]

Since the piece was written for Stafford, and likely to circulate among Elizabeth's councillors (as it did), I think the author was trying to suggest that it had come from some servant of Don Bernardino de Mendoza, in whose household Stafford was known to have connections. It was an effective, though rather laborious, method of disguise; my impression is that the labour was rewarded by the pleasures of invention. I conclude that this entertaining effort is no obstacle to supposing that the author of Text no. 17 was Italian, and therefore no obstacle to supposing that he was Bruno. Rather, if I may say so, the contrary. Bruno's Spanish was just about up to it; and it was he, after all, who taught that translation was the source of all knowledge.[17]

When we were trying to find out whether Fagot had written this piece, the last motive for doubt was that there was no reason for supposing that Fagot had any access to confidential information from Rome, and that it seemed unlikely. Now that we are enquiring whether the author was Bruno, the case is greatly altered, for it is extremely likely that Bruno had access to such information in 1586. What makes it extremely likely is what we have discovered about Piero Delbene. We know that Delbene had means of confidential communication with Rome, since he used them to put Lord Burghley in touch with Cardinal Savelli.[18] Since we also know that Delbene and Bruno were extremely close about this time, we can readily suppose that, as long as Bruno was in Paris, what Delbene knew about Rome, Bruno knew as well. Which removes this difficulty. What we may now need to know is: how Delbene managed his confidential communication with Rome; and what he did with it besides passing messages about William Cecil. Here I can offer something new, which will repay the time we shall have to spend on it. We must remember that Delbene, like Stafford, was the representative of a Protestant power, and that the knowledge that he was in communication with Rome would have put him and his Roman

16 The reader may now turn to *Texts*, no. 17, where he will find more oddities than I have mentioned. My authorities have been S. Battaglia, G. Barberi Squarotti, *Grande dizionario della lingua italiana* (14 vols to date; Turin, 1961–88) and (from 'R' onwards, where this is at present lacking) C. Battista and G. Alessio, *Dizionario etimologico italiano* (5 vols; Florence, 1950–7); G. Devoto and G. C. Oli, *Dizionario della lingua italiana* (Florence, 1971); and Florio, *Queen Anna's New World of Words* (1611).

17 Gentile picks up some Hispanisms in Bruno, the most important being forms of 'lo che' for '(that or the) which' (*DI*, p. 302 n. 2, etc.); I presume he heard Zubiaur's confession in Spanish. *The Essays of Michel de Montaigne*, translated by Florio (1603: London, 1965 edn), p. 7.

18 Above, pp. 69, 70 f.

source in considerable difficulty and perhaps danger from the more zealous followers of either side. We shall therefore expect the lines of communication to have been kept as private as possible.

On Stafford's authority we have recorded that Delbene's correspondent in Rome was a relation of his ('his kinsman that he writ unto at Rome');[19] he did not say who the relative was, but we can find this out, and in finding it out we find out a good deal more. As it happens, he is identified from a source which was used by Frances Yates forty years ago to shed new light on what Bruno was doing in Paris at this time. The source is the Italian correspondence of his and Delbene's friend the royal *lecteur* Jacopo Corbinelli, who had a good deal to say about both of them. Corbinelli gave news of their doings in regular letters to another scholar, Gianvincenzo Pinelli, living in Padua, with whom he corresponded on literary and other matters via the Venetian ambassador in Paris.[20] This is the only series of his letters which seems to survive, but from them it emerges that he had another correspondent in Rome. This man's name was Giovanni Cavalcanti. We do not know too much about Cavalcanti, but one thing we can assume about him is that he was a reasonably close relation of Piero Delbene. The name of Delbene's mother, a capable and wealthy businesswoman who had come to France fifty years before as a maid of honour to Catherine de Médicis, was Lucrezia Cavalcanti. It was her brother Giovanni who had left Florence to make his career in Rome and founded the Roman branch of the family. This Giovanni sounds rather old to have been Corbinelli's correspondent, who was possibly his son. If they were different people, it is most unlikely that they were not closely related, the family being a new arrival in Rome. Giovanni and Corbinelli had been corresponding since at least 1572, and it is clear that they were extremely good friends. Corbinelli was indeed practically a member of the family, since he had been frequenting Madame Delbene for a very long time, and lived next door to her house in the Rue de Tournon in the suburb of St Germain-des-Prés. He had been Piero's tutor, as well as Henri III's; Madame Delbene was godmother to his children.[21] Nothing more natural than that he should keep up a correspondence with Giovanni in Rome; nor that Piero, who was a less diligent correspondent, should make use of the connection from time to time.

19   Stafford to Burghley, 9/19-xi-1586 (*CSP Foreign 1586–88*), p. 136.
20   Yates, 'New Documents', and above, p. 63.
21   For Giovanni Cavalcanti, Calderini De-Marchi, *Corbinelli*, pp. 237 f; further reference to the originals, BA T 167 sup, is given in 'A Note on Cavalcanti', below, pp. 253–5. For Madame Delbene, *DBI*, xxii (Cavalcanti, Lucrezia), xxvii (Corbinelli, Jacopo); Calderini De-Marchi, *Corbinelli*, p. 80; BA T 167 sup, ff. 77 f, 82 and *passim*.

We can get some idea of what Corbinelli and Cavalcanti were corresponding about from his letters to Pinelli in Padua, where he mentioned occasionally that he had sent Cavalcanti some newsletter or publication. All of them contained news from the Protestant side in France, the Netherlands or England. We gather that the correspondence, unlike that with Pinelli, was political.[22] We cannot find out any more through Corbinelli; but we can find out something from another source, since Corbinelli was not corresponding simply on his own account, and items from the letters were passing into other hands. Since we have discovered that the connection, or at least the Roman end of it, was used by Piero Delbene to pass Lord Burghley's message to Cardinal Savelli, we need not be too surprised to discover that two of the hands into which the letters passed were Sir Edward Stafford's. Five items from a regular political correspondence, written from Rome between February and May 1586, were sent over by Stafford to England in the form of Italian copies or Latin abstracts.[23] They reported closely the progress of political activities in Rome: the doings of envoys sent by the French Catholic League to Sixtus V, the prospects of a Catholic enterprise against Geneva or England, and the chances that the Spaniards would collaborate in either of them. The correspondence will have been destined for advisers of Henri III or Henri of Navarre, and intended to forewarn them in case the pope, now that he had excommunicated Navarre, should decide to bring the whole weight of papal power into action against one or both of them; this was what the ambassadors of the League were asking him to do. It was also of considerable interest in England, and it was a feather in Stafford's cap to have got access to it.

No great detective skill is required to show that the correspondence was Cavalcanti's with Corbinelli. One of the pieces we have, written early in May 1586, was described by the person who sent it to Stafford as being 'from Cavalcanti in Rome'; the same communication contained a copy of part of another letter written from Rome on 5 May to somebody in France by a diplomat in the papal service called Fabio Mirto Frangipani.[24] At this point Frangipani's career was a hot issue in both Rome and Paris. He had been appointed papal nuncio to France by Sixtus V in June 1585, and refused admission by Henri III on the grounds that he was a supporter of the League; the pope had retaliated by expelling the French ambassador from Rome, and a year of deadlock in papal-French relations followed. By the spring of 1586 the difficulty was being smoothed out, and Frangipani

22 BA T 167 sup, ff. 106, 170, 189 (April 1583, August 1585, November 1586); the second is printed in Calderini De-Marchi, *Corbinelli*, p. 237.
23 I have assembled these fragments in 'A Note on Cavalcanti', below, pp. 253–5.
24 See the list in 'A Note on Cavalcanti', no. 4.

arrived as nuncio in August.[25] The principal agent in accommodating the parties had been Corbinelli, who despite political differences had been friendly with Frangipani for a long time; he mentioned his efforts in two of his letters to Pinelli. It is quite obvious that the letter of which an extract was passed to Stafford was part of Frangipani's soothing correspondence with Corbinelli.[26] Cavalcanti must have sent it under cover of his own letter, which must therefore have been written to Corbinelli.

Everything is now, I hope, perfectly clear. Corbinelli's Roman correspondence was a hot political correspondence of considerable value. But Corbinelli's correspondence was also Delbene's correspondence. We might assume this on first principles: that what it conveyed was of vital interest to Henri of Navarre; that Delbene was Navarre's agent in Paris, and also something like a son to Corbinelli. But I think we can go beyond this. Delbene's handwriting often had a characteristic final *e*, and this was uniformly used in the nicely written piece which contained the Cavalcanti and Frangipani copies just mentioned, and described the first as being from Cavalcanti in Rome; so I am fairly confident that he made the copy for Stafford himself.[27] There is nothing at all surprising in this: Delbene and Stafford were working closely together at the time on the scheme for hijacking the Duke of Montpensier into Navarre's camp. One may ask why Delbene did not bring the information in person; but, as in the case of Cardinal Savelli's message, it seems that he did not think it wise to be seen frequenting Stafford's house on the Quai de la Tournelle.[28] Hence his need for a messenger; which brings us back, at last, to the author of No. 17. This is not because we know that he did the job regularly for Delbene: we know nothing of the kind. I have no idea who brought Stafford the piece discussed above, presumably around the end of May; and the reader may properly be sceptical of my hypothesis that the author of No. 17 was the man who brought the message from Cardinal Savelli on 8/18 November. But

25 The state of papal-French relations in this period, and Frangipani's part in them, are described in Pastor, *History*, xxi, 273–93; xxii, 150, n. 1; and in Blet, *Ragazzoni*, pp. 65–90.

26 Calderini De-Marchi, *Corbinelli*, pp. 69, 234, 245, 253. Since writing this I have found a letter from Frangipani to Bellièvre, Rome, 23-i/2-ii-1586 (BN ff 15908, f. 93), where he says that they have been in touch via 'Signor Jacomino', evidently Corbinelli; Bellièvre was Corbinelli's contact on Henri III's Council, and was probably the chief intended recipient of Cavalcanti's newsletters.

27 'A Note on Cavalcanti', no. 4.

28 Stafford's house, which I do not think is identified anywhere in his correspondence, is described in a case brought in the Parlement of Paris against one of his servants (Archives Nationales, Paris, X²ᴮ 1098: Parlement civil, feuilles d'audience, 8/18-viii-1584) as being 'sur le Quay de la Tournelle au logis de Madame ?Desclue', i.e., on the left bank of the Seine roughly opposite the apse of Notre-Dame.

there can be practically no doubt that our man, in composing his own complicated missive not many days before this, had been acting as some kind of a go-between for Delbene and Stafford.

So far, I have stated this supposition on the grounds that the news about Thomas Morgan's conversations with the Huguenot gentleman in the Bastille was likely to have come from Delbene, and asked the reader to be patient about the evidence for this; which I still do. I have at present something better to offer. We have not heard much yet about an item which comes towards the end of Text no. 17 and is one of the three *pièces justificatives* incorporated in it. As I described it originally, it was 'a letter in Latin, probably written to the reporter himself (that is, to the author of No. 17), and retailing the contents of a letter from Rome about aggressive designs of the pope'.[29] As the rest of my description will now make clear, the letter being abstracted was one of Cavalcanti's political letters to Corbinelli: it was in fact by date of origin No. 2 of the series sent to England by Stafford, of which the copy just mentioned was No. 4; Cavalcanti must have sent it some time in March. The letter containing the abstract of it, which is given in No. 17 without the names of either writer or addressee, cannot have been written by Corbinelli himself, for the writer said he had only been able to get a look at Cavalcanti's letter, and was quoting it from memory. We have probably seen Delbene doing this job already, and I think there can really be no doubt that he was the writer; he often wrote in such crisp humanistic Latin.[30] I have said that I think the letter was written to whoever copied it into No. 17. It cannot have been written to Stafford directly, because it refers to Elizabeth as *reginam Angliae* and was hence not written to an Englishman, though I assume that Stafford was intended to get the message in the end. Delbene described the recipient as *tu*. He was therefore an intimate of Delbene appropriate for passing on confidential information to Stafford. At this point we may remember that, seen from Stafford's end, he was an intimate of Delbene who was doing confidential work for himself, and had previously done the same for Walsingham. We may also remember that he wrote French like Fagot, went to comic lengths to disguise the fact that his native language was Italian, and had a taste and talent for linguistic adventures. I am inclined to think that this is enough to demonstrate that the author of Text no. 17 was Bruno. If so, it was one of his livelier compositions in the tragi-comic vein he commended in the preface to the *Cena de le Ceneri*.[31]

29 Above, p. 66.
30 'Heri vidi literas Romae . . . Horum verborum memini . . .'; there is a sample of Delbene's Latin, in translation, in *CSP Foreign 1586–88*, pp. 374–83.
31 *Cena*, p. 8/68.

But it will always be difficult to know exactly what one has demonstrated in such a case, and it would be rash to claim the piece definitively as Bruno's without having made a search for alternative candidates in the milieu in question. We need to adopt something like the method followed in some early propositions of Euclid where, in order to prove that a figure has a certain characteristic, he attempts to construct the same figure with a characteristic different in this respect, and shows that no such figure can be constructed.[32] Thanks to the richness of Stafford's correspondence, we know rather a lot about the milieux in which he found his agents and informants. On the Roman side there were several discontented English Catholics with whom he was in touch at this time; some of them had to do with both Walsingham and himself, and one of them, a tailor called Solomon Aldred, had useful connections in Rome, including connections with Cardinal Savelli. Some or all of the other 'persons' mentioned by Stafford in his letter of 6/16 November as having been dropped by Walsingham when they were found to be dealing with himself were among them, and Aldred seems to be mentioned as a correspondent of Walsingham's in another part of the same letter.[33] But there is no reason whatever for supposing that No. 17 was written by an Englishman, and none of these people had anything to do with Delbene, which is our principal requirement.

They can be excluded. But we can find another credible candidate who was an Italian correspondent of Walsingham's, who saw Stafford from time to time, and had an interest in papal policy and the doings of Thomas Morgan; he scores higher than Bruno in respect of the first item of No. 17, the scheme for winning the war in the Netherlands, since he was a military man. This man was another cousin of Delbene's, an old soldier called Masino Delbene (Masino being a familiar form of Tommaso), usually described as 'Captain'. Masino had been around in Paris for a long time, I think since the end of the Italian wars in 1559. He was in the service of Catherine de Médicis, and as long as Catherine had influence on French policy he was a figure to be reckoned with. He was the anti-Spanish type of Italian *émigré*, like Piero Strozzi with whom he may have fought, and correspondingly pro-English; at one time he had had an English pension, which he earned by useful service to a string of English

32 *Elements*, book i, propositions 6–8.
33 Above, p. 68; cf. Edward Grately to Walsingham, Paris, 18/28-v-1586 (*CSP Domestic Addenda 1580–1625*, p. 177). Grately, a collaborator of Gilbert Gifford, had been to see Stafford; Gifford had told him not to; he would not do so again. On Aldred, L. Hicks, 'An Elizabethan Propagandist: the Career of Solomon Aldred', *The Month*, clxxxi (1945), 181–90; Stafford to Burghley 6/16-xi-1586 (*CSP Foreign 1586–88*, p. 131), where 'one Stanley, a tailor by occupation', writing to Walsingham from Paris, sounds like Aldred.

ambassadors. We find him giving advice, which sounds like good advice, on Ireland, Scotland and the Netherlands.[34] We have two reasons for thinking that he might have been the source of the news about Thomas Morgan's availability for an offer: one is good, the other is excellent. Eight years earlier, when Morgan had just escaped from England to Paris, Masino had offered the then English ambassador a scheme to have him kidnapped and interrogated in Germany.[35] Eight months later, in the summer of 1587, he was to be sent by his cousin Piero to tell Stafford that Morgan was about to be released from the Bastille, as he was in August of that year.[36] Both these points, and the military tenor of the piece, make him an extremely probable author of No. 17; if he carried a message from Piero to Stafford about Morgan and the Bastille in July or August 1587, he is likely to have done the same in November 1586. It seems to me most implausible to suppose that we shall find a better alternative candidate than Masino Delbene.

But Masino cannot have written our text. He had not fallen out with Walsingham. He wrote, in Italian or in French, a large, vigorous hand which so far as I know never changed, and he signed or initialled what he wrote: there was no reason why he should not have done. His French, as befitted a man who had been in France for twenty years or more, was excellent, and though it preserved some Italian characteristics they bore no resemblance to the results of Bruno's long struggle with the language.[37] Masino was a soldier, not a scholar, and if he had any Latin I very much doubt if it was up to the A-level standard required to construe Piero's letter; it seems to me, in any case, incredible that his cousin should have written to him in Latin. Nor can I envisage him playing games with Italian and Spanish as the writer did in translating the advice about the Netherlands. I also think that the view of military prospects in the Netherlands and Italy is far too naive and amateurish for a man of Masino's experience: he had a very proper regard for Spanish military power.

34 He can be found *passim* in CSP Foreign, from 1575–77 to 1586–88; PRO SP 12/92, f. 41 – English pension of £60 p.a., apparently dating from 1573; BN ff 15905, f. 488 is a letter to Bellièvre, 1580, about Spanish designs on Ireland. Between February and August 1586 he wrote regularly to Walsingham (CSP Foreign 1585–86 and 1586–88, indexes and BL Harleian 1582, ff. 115–27); the latter includes a 'discourse' of August 1586 on how to resist the coming Armada. He was also writing to Pallavicino in Germany (CSP Foreign 1585–86, p. 383; 1586–88, p. 423; Stone, *Palavicino*, p. 39); cf. below, n. 38.

35 Sir Amyas Paulet to Walsingham, Paris, 8-i-1578 (A. Ogle (ed.), *A Copy-Book of Sir Amyas Paulet's Letters* (?London, 1866), p. 247). The suggestion was not adopted.

36 CSP Foreign 1586–88, pp. 376, 463. This came out in the course of a second, ferocious quarrel between Stafford and Delbene over the imprisonment in the Bastille of another Huguenot gentleman, called Salettes or La Sallette, who had come to Paris in June 1587 on a mission from Navarre. This is my reason for associating Delbene with the news from the Bastille in November 1586 (above, pp. 70, 84, 91).

37 E.g., BL Harleian 1582, ff. 115–27, and BN ff 15905, f. 488.

It seems to me very possible that Masino had something to do with the piece: he may perhaps have been the immediate source of one of the fresher news items in it, about the Duke of Savoy making peace with Geneva;[38] he may very probably have been the man intended to execute the design for spiriting Morgan out of the Bastille if Elizabeth had agreed to it, though I doubt if it would have appealed to his own mistress, Catherine de Médicis. But he did not write the piece. If my Euclidian line of argument is at all sound, Bruno wrote it.

But, as we must now admit, Bruno cannot have written it, because he has an alibi: he was at Wittenberg. He had left Paris in June, after the unsuccessful disputation at the Collège de Cambrai on 28–29 May; to be exact, he had left some time after 6 June, when Corbinelli said he was about to leave. As I have said, I think he went first to Pallavicino at Frankfurt. He was at Marburg on 25 July/4 August, where they turned him down, and matriculated at Wittenberg on 20/30 August in order to take up the teaching position he had been offered through the influence of Alberico Gentili, and probably of Pallavicino as well. We do not know that he started lecturing immediately, and at the end of August it sounds rather unlikely.[39] But his first publication at Wittenberg, *De lampade combinatoria lulliana*, published early in 1587, has an early manuscript title page dating it MDXIVC, presumably meaning 1586; this seems to mean that it was based on lectures given between August and December.[40] Hence Bruno was in no position to be passing messages to Stafford in Paris in October or November 1586. But are we quite sure of this? There is no date between 20/30 August 1586 and 13/23 March 1587 when we can be absolutely sure that Bruno was in Wittenberg. He was not an *ordinarius*: he could lecture, I take it, as and when he wanted to. The lectures on Ramon Lull, who was not on anybody's syllabus, could have been given or begun in September or December. He said that he had read Aristotle's Organum in Wittenberg for two years, but we do not have to take this any more literally than the five years he said he had lectured in Paris.[41] The

---

38 'Note' in *Texts*, no. 17, and cf. Masino's 'discourse' of August 1586 (above, n. 34: the pope has given up the enterprise of Geneva in favour of that of England); Masino probably sent the news to Pallavicino, who reported it to Walsingham on 16/26-x-1586 (*CSP Foreign 1586–88*, p. 113). Pastor, *History*, xxii, 150 n. 1, indicates that the enterprise had been given up some time after June. But this information had probably come from Cavalcanti via Piero (cf. his newsletter of 30-iv/10-v-1586, 'A Note on Cavalcanti', no. 5, reporting the postponement of the enterprise); likewise the warning in Masino to Walsingham, 19/29-v-1586 (*CSP Foreign 1585–86*, p. 641).

39 Above, p. 63. Yates, 'New Documents', p. 185 and *Bruno*, p. 304 has caused some confusion by mistranslating a letter of Corbinelli, dated 25 July/4 August, as if it meant that Bruno was in Paris on that date; the passage cannot mean this.

40 Singer, *Giordano Bruno*, pp. 140 and n. 1, 208, 220.

41 *Documenti*, p. 85; *OL* ii², pp. 358 (Ms. *Animadversiones* on the *Lampas* dated 13/23-iii-

alibi is not very firm if we have positive reason to suspect it. Do we?

Well, we have some evidence suggesting that Bruno wrote Text no. 17. We also have reason to suppose that the author had not been in Paris for a while, and had recently come back. This possibility arises from the one remaining oddity of the piece: the problem, not of the date of the piece itself, which at the outside is somewhere between the middle of September and the beginning of November 1586, but of the pieces it incorporates. The letter from Lyon about Drake is dated 26 April, and the advice about burning the harvest in the Netherlands can hardly have been written after about May. The letter from Cavalcanti, which is abstracted in Delbene's Latin, mentions 1 September as being some time in the future; it can be dated fairly exactly, since it refers to the departure from Rome for Prague of a nuncio who had arrived there before 12/22 April.[42] Either the corpus of enclosures had been put together in May 1586 or thereabouts, or it had been assembled later from pieces which had been lying around for five months or more.

The antiquity of much of the intelligence contained in the piece did not matter too much, since what mattered was the news about Morgan; but if the author had had any more up-to-date *pièces justificatives* to offer he would presumably have offered them. He seems, or somebody seems, to have been worried about this, for Stafford sent to England another version of Delbene's Latin letter, which described the Cavalcanti newsletter whose substance it conveyed as having been sent from Rome 'in the month of October 1586', when it had actually been written in March or thereabouts; the letter was doctored to remove two passages which indicated its date, and perhaps to reduce it to a bland piece of propaganda for the Protestant cause.[43] I presume that the somebody in question was somebody in Stafford's office, and the likeliest thing would seem to me to be that, at the same time as Stafford sent the original to Burghley for transmission to the queen, which was probably with his letter to Burghley of 6/16 November, he sent the warmed-up snippet to Walsingham.[44] This would be extremely compatible with

1587) and 223 (Bruno teaching at Wittenberg *privatim*). Dr Rita Sturlese has kindly confirmed to me that there is no evidence absolutely requiring us to believe that Bruno was in Wittenberg in October–November 1586.

42 No. 2 of the list in 'A Note on Cavalcanti'.

43 'A Note on Cavalcanti', nos. 1 and 2a. The title in the original is: 'Ex aliis literis Roma scriptis mense Octob. 1586'.

44 The difficulty with my reconstruction is that both the original and the snippet survive in Walsingham's papers. The snippet, which was sent with another extract from Cavalcanti's newsletters dating from the previous February, is found in PRO SP 101 (Newsletters), which would indicate that it arrived in the Secretary's office in the normal

Figure 5.   Portrait of Giordano Bruno. According to Salvestrini, *Bibliografia di Giordano Bruno*, no. 5, 'the only known portrait of Bruno'; said to be a re-engraving made in Paris of a lost print hailing from Munich. Its authenticity seems doubtful.

the state of Stafford's relations with Walsingham, and with the author of No. 17's being an ex-correspondent of Walsingham's who had defected to Stafford in Paris. Stafford, while withholding from Walsingham the person's real information about Morgan, would have been sending him some rubbish to keep him happy, persuade him that the writer was still at work, and perhaps get him another instalment of his wages. This is a hypothetical construction; but it is built around what seems to me a fairly hard fact, that our author had

---

way. The original (*Texts*, no. 17) is in BL Cottonian Nero B vi, a collection of Walsingham's French papers, but the connection with Stafford to Burghley, 6/16 November (*Text* no. 18), and its rabid polemic against Walsingham surely makes it clear that Stafford sent it to Burghley. Since it is not found with Stafford's letter to Burghley (in PRO SP 78), one may presume that Burghley did not give it to Walsingham at the same time as this letter; it seems most likely that Walsingham got it after Elizabeth had seen it (above, p. 68). Stafford wrote three letters to Walsingham, which do not seem to survive, on the same day as he wrote to Burghley (*CSP Foreign 1586–88*, p. 132) and it seems the natural thing to suppose that he sent the snippet to Walsingham in one of them. There would have been no point in his sending both the original and the snippet to the same person.

been doing intelligence work in Paris between March and May 1586, but had not done any between May and about October. This is of course another reason for thinking he might be Bruno, since Bruno had left Paris in June. As in other cases, what appeared to be a reason for thinking that Bruno could not have written the piece turns out on investigation to be a reason why he could have done.

I sum up. The author of No. 17 was a close friend of Piero Delbene, but not Masino Delbene. He had worked for both Walsingham and Stafford. He had a close interest in Thomas Morgan. Not being a Frenchman or a Spaniard, he was probably an Italian, though he was anxious to conceal this. He wrote French like Fagot. He had considerable linguistic talents and a leaning towards the comic. He had very possibly been away from Paris for most of the time between May and November 1586. I really think that this is quite enough. Bruno wrote Text no. 17, which is therefore the last of his Fagot letters. Bruno therefore came back to Paris, probably for a rather short while, in October-November 1586. There is no real difficulty about this, any more than there is about the trip we now know he made from London in the spring of 1585.[45]

I think we have now cleared up all the difficulties which present themselves against identifying Fagot as Bruno; and also against including the last of our texts in the canon of Bruno's and Fagot's works. Our two stories, which are still two, are now two stories about the same person. The next question is whether, if we put them together, they form a convincing or followable narrative of three and a half years in the life of a single individual, Giordano Bruno the Nolan.

45   Above, pp. 54-7.

2

BRUNO AT LARGE

i London

BRUNO ARRIVED AT Salisbury Court on or just before 13 April 1583. He brought a letter from Henri III suggesting or requiring that Castelnau take him into his household, which he was happy to do. We do not know whether the letter mentioned that Bruno was a priest or invited Castelnau to employ him as such; or whether Castelnau was in need of a priest; or whether Bruno began to say mass in the house immediately. Perhaps we could take Bruno's statement to the inquisitors, and his trips to Oxford, as evidence against all three assumptions; in that case he would have begun his career as chaplain to the household by early 1584, at the latest.

Shortly after his arrival, and probably on 17 April, Castelnau sent him to make his presence known to Walsingham. When they met, Walsingham invited him to act as a spy on Castelnau's dealings with Mary and the Catholics. He offered him a salary, and Bruno seems to have been happy to agree. Which of the two was responsible for thinking up the name Fagot we shall never know: my guess now would be that it was Bruno, and that it was one of the jokey references to the stake which he tended to come up with on such occasions; it also has connotations of tittle-tattle which seem appropriate. Presumably Walsingham also promised to introduce him to his prospective son-in-law, Philip Sidney, and to other luminaries like his neighbour Dr Dee. Bruno went back to Salisbury Court, and settled in. During the next two months he wrote his notes to Walsingham as a change from his inscrutable book on Seals, dined, talked, walked in the gallery and the garden, listened to the conversation, read the correspondence, and recruited Castelnau's secretary, Courcelles, into English service. From the conversations he records it seems quite clear that he was representing himself as a friend of the Catholic cause. On the social front he visited the Palatine Laski across the river, passed on Castelnau's messages to him, and exchanged information on his doings with William Herle; he also came to an arrangement with Herle that Herle should pass his own messages to Walsingham, which saved him writing. I imagine he also visited Dee at Mortlake, if only to chide him for kow-towing to the papacy about the calendar. He surely accompanied Castelnau to court at the beginning of June for the tournament Elizabeth put on for Laski: Bruno must have met the queen on this occasion, if Castelnau had not introduced them already. At court he also met Philip Sidney, with whom he was to accompany the palatine to Oxford.[1]

I have nothing new to add to the story of the trips to Oxford, since there was no work for Fagot there, unless the message about Sidney's receptivity to an offer from Mary was something of the kind. But I think we can now make more of the months between his return from the first trip around the end of July and Throckmorton's arrest in the middle of November. In Oxford he had acquired a number of learned friends and admirers, and formed the beginnings of a clientele; in this he was surely encouraged by the example of Dee, who was some kind of intellectual godfather to the Oxford party, and then by his departure for Poland with the palatine, which left a vacancy in England for the position of resident guru. In London he must have started coaching Dickson on the art of memory and setting him up for the anti-Ramist polemic he launched after Christmas. He put his own claims before the public with his *Sigillus*, and especially with its prefatory manifesto to the vice-chancellor of Oxford which sounds, as George Abbot indicated, like a tube-station advertisement from an Indian quack.[2] One's impression that he was aiming at the share of the theosophical market abandoned by Dee is rather strengthened by the other piece of intellectual politicking we now know him to have been engaged in at this time: the campaign, which had to be clandestine since the victim was a friend of Salisbury Court, against Lord Henry Howard.

In the summer Howard had published a book against prophecy, called *A Defensative against the Poyson of supposed Prophecies*. The publisher was John Charlewood, who also published Bruno's *Sigillus* and all of his works written in England; Charlewood described himself on the title-page as printer to the Earl of Arundel, Howard's nephew and virtual son.[3] One might therefore think that Bruno had

---

1 Walsingham was in London on 17/27-iv-1583: C.T. Martin (ed.), *Journal of Sir Francis Walsingham* (December 1570–April 1583) (Camden Society, civ part 3, 1871; repr. 1968), p. 48. It was a Wednesday. Dee and the calendar: French, *John Dee*, p. 7.

2 Above, pp. 24–5, 47–8; Yates, *Bruno*, pp. 206–8.

3 Above, p. 30; *Short-Title Catalogue (Sources and Literature*, 4, under *Pollard*), no. 13858. I have used the two copies in BL, G 744 and 478. a. 24. There was a second edition (no.

entered the market under Howard's auspices. There is indeed a lot in
the book which could have come from Bruno himself: Howard had
the same taste for the wisdom of Solomon and especially for
Ecclesiastes, the same conviction that prophets were the enemies of
kings, something of the same penchant for mythological figures and
for Thomas Aquinas, the same identification of Christian politics
with peace and unity, that we find in Bruno's own writings. Bruno
was not at this time a defender of astrology or 'star divinity', which
Howard attacked as well.[4] In so far as Howard was conducting a
polemic against English Puritans and their institution of 'pro-
phesying', condemning political prognostication and the consultation of cunning men, or pursuing a feud with the detestable Earl of
Oxford, Bruno can have had no objection to his book. Why then did
he recommend it to the censor as containing both heresy and
treason?[5] Various things might have been the matter with it. There
was the Catholic implication, disguised but fairly plain, that visita-
tions of the Spirit should be tested by the collective authority of the
Church: not a position Bruno will have sympathised with. Then
Howard had trodden particularly hard on Bruno's corns when he
had specified, among the various forms of searching-out of secrets to
be condemned, 'rifling in the mysteries of Egypt'. This was, he said,
'utterly forbidden by the civil laws, restrayned by the rules of
pollicy, condemned by the worde of God, offensive to the common
peace of men, and no more refrainable within limits of regarde, than
the River Nilus is within a hedge of willows'.[6] Readers of Frances
Yates will know that Bruno was obsessed with the hidden messages
of ancient Egyptian worship and philosophy seemingly conveyed by
the spurious sage Hermes Trismegistus. Howard was not here, any
more than on the question of 'star divinity', wittingly attacking
Bruno: he was attacking Dee, in whose armoury of secret sciences
Hermeticism had a place. Dee was not actually mentioned in the
book, but he is fairly obviously the person suffering from 'distemper

---

13859), folio, and 'newly revised and divided into chapters', which must have come out
in the autumn, and this was probably the version that Bruno attacked. I have not seen it.
Charlewood and Bruno: G. Aquilecchia, 'Lo stampatore londinese di Giordano Bruno',
Studi di filologia italiana, xviii (1960), 102–28.

4 *Defensative*, dedicatory epistle, sig. iii-4 (prophets); A i, E 3ᵛ, F ii, F iii, M i (Solomon); A
   i (mythological figures); G iᵛ (Aquinas); Dd ii-2 (star divinity); L i, Rr i-2 (unity).

5 *Texts*, no. 6: I presume that Bruno is the 'some of good judgment' mentioned here. The
   connection with Oxford is suggested by Howard to Walsingham, 14-ix-1582 (PRO SP
   12/155, no. 44) and Raleigh to Burghley, 12/22-v-1583 (BL Lansdowne 39, no. 22).
   Oxford had possessed a 'book of babies', or (I presume) astrological nativities, which he
   sought to use for political purposes: Francis Southwell, PRO SP 12/151, no. 57.
   Oxford's relations with Howard are recounted in my 'English Catholics and the French
   Marriage'.

6 *Defensative*, A iv, Nn i-1, Rr-2ᵛ and ff. (spirits tested by the Church); F ii, G ii (rifling in
   the mysteries of Egypt).

of the brain' who communicated with angels in his dreams, cast political horoscopes, and sought to entrap Diana in the toils of his occult knowledge. Bruno, I take it, did not fancy this; nor can he have warmed to Howard's political message, which was that the Earl of Leicester and his Protestant friends had been using diabolic powers to control the queen, prevent her marrying the person she wanted to marry (Anjou), and divert her crown from its legitimate successor (Mary).[7] It may be that the notion of such political magic lodged in his mind for future use, since we shall come across it later; for the time being Bruno seems to have thought that the mantle of Dee was an intellectual inheritance which he could aspire to and therefore ought to defend. He also, I think, realised that Howard's kind of Catholicism was something that one side of Elizabeth was always attracted to, and felt himself in competition with him for her favours.

Bruno may have fed Herle with more information about Throckmorton after his return to Salisbury Court, but I am not sure that there was any, and if Bruno passed anything over at this time it has not survived. Perhaps the arrival of Madame de Mauvissière in August cramped his style, though it had the agreeable effect of bringing John Florio into the house as tutor.[8] The flow would in any case have been interrupted by his second, disastrous, trip to Oxford, whenever exactly that occurred, and by the absence of Walsingham. To his extreme irritation, Walsingham had been obliged by the queen to go to Scotland in August to try to bully King James into line, and he did not get back until the first week of October.[9] He left the various arrangements with Salisbury Court in the hands of Lord Burghley, but not very willingly, and it seems likely that Fagot was closed down for the time being. In the meantime the Catholic conspiracy had been maturing, and Herle, who had been watching the situation, must have been told to reactivate Fagot early in November. Bruno had plenty on his hands already: it is not clear that the *Sigillus* had yet been published; he had Dickson and perhaps other disciples to supervise, enemies to confute. His social diary was perhaps not as full as it became after Christmas, but it needed to be cultivated; he had his duties to Castelnau to think of, which now included or were about to include the job of chaplain in the house; no

---

7 *Defensative*, title-page, dedicatory epistle iii, sig. E-3, K i[v] and ff, L iii-4, E-4 and f. Cf. French, *John Dee*, pp. 6, 33 f, 129; Yates, *Bruno*, p. 149; Peck, *Northampton*, p. 12.

8 On the whole I think that Herle's statement (*Texts*, no. 5) that he had advertised Walsingham about Throckmorton 'this last summer' refers to the original communications in May-June rather than to anything later. For Madame de Mauvissière's return, *CSP Foreign 1583–84*, p. 23.

9 Conyers Read, *Walsingham*, ii, 205–24; dates of departure (17/27-viii) and return (between about 3/13-x and 16/26-x), pp. 207, 223–4.

doubt he wanted to think about his great revenge on the pedants, which became the *Cena de le Ceneri*. He may well have thought that he could leave the espionage to Courcelles. So I think it is more likely that the stimulus to the resumption of his career as a spy came from Herle than from his own observation of sinister dealings at Salisbury Court. But whatever the inspiration, he had now for a while to pay as much attention to what was going on in the house as he had done in April and May. He took advantage of his strategic situation to nudge the authorities in a direction he was personally keen on.

Very shortly after he resumed transmission as Fagot, Francis Throckmorton and Lord Henry Howard were arrested; we can now enquire whether Bruno was actually responsible for this. In respect of Throckmorton, there is no reasonable doubt that Bruno's early reports were the 'secret intelligence', mentioned in the government's account of his treason, on which the destruction of the conspiracy was founded. There is also no reason to disbelieve his claim that he had recruited Courcelles, who had been passing over letters between Castelnau and Mary since June. He had two things to add in November. He gave a rough outline of the invasion scheme being devised between Throckmorton and Mendoza, and a slightly garbled version of the conversations they had been having; the government later claimed that they did not know about this until very late in the day, so it may have been Bruno who had first put them up to it. He also reported that Francis's brother Thomas was about to leave the country, as he did; Francis, who was not very sanguine about the prospects for a Catholic rising, had very nearly gone with him.[10] Both these pieces of news must have encouraged Walsingham to have Throckmorton arrested, but I do not think either of them quite turned the scales. It seems clear to me that his actual decision was triggered, not by anything picked up from Mary's end as Castelnau thought, but by the news that Throckmorton was in town and had in his possession a packet of clandestine letters from Salisbury Court to Mary which he was about to send on to Sheffield. One of them, not particularly compromising in itself, had been written for Castelnau

10 *Texts*, no. 5; *A Discoverie of the Treasons*, pp. 192¹, 191² f (pp. 191 and 192 are repeated), 195, 197–9 (invasion scheme); pp. 192², 199, and Lady Margery Throckmorton to Francis, 9/19-x-1583, and her examination, 5/15-xii-1583 (PRO SP 12/163. no. 8; 164, no. 9), on Francis's brother Thomas. I presume that Thomas is the brother intended by Herle and Bruno, though another brother, George, could be meant. According to his own account Francis went off to Worcestershire after Thomas left, and if Thomas did not go until after 15/25-xi this would be impossible; but their mother in her examination made it clear that Thomas was still in London while Francis was in Worcestershire. On her evidence I feel satisfied that the brother in question was Thomas, and that Bruno's intelligence was roughly correct. Thomas was friendly with Madame de Mauvissière, as Francis was with her husband: Castelnau to Francis Throckmorton, 1-x-1581 (*CSP Foreign 1581–82*, no. 347).

by Courcelles on (?the evening of) 15 November, and that night or in the morning he must have passed Walsingham the news.[11] Bruno had nothing to do with this: Herle sent messages from him on both 15 and 16 November, but they do not contain anything of the kind. Courcelles and Bruno were separate operations at this time, and Courcelles must have passed his message another way. I conclude that, though Bruno exposed Throckmorton in the first place, and in November provided enough new evidence for the government to decide to do something, he did not actually tip Walsingham off that the 16th, or whenever it was, would be a good day to arrest him. Otherwise the downfall of Throckmorton, and the defeat of his conspiracy, was to a very considerable degree Bruno's own work. He was entitled to his New Year's wages: he must have felt extremely pleased with himself, and sucks to the pedants at Oxford.

Now that we have looked at the book about prophecy we can see why Bruno was more interested in Howard than in Throckmorton, though the evidence against him was extremely slender, and such as there was had been provided by Courcelles and not by himself. Howard was not going to be arrested for writing a book against the Earl of Oxford or John Dee; nor indeed, galling as it might be for the Earl of Leicester, for what he had done, or what the conversation at Castelnau's dinner-table said he had done, at the time of Elizabeth's marriage negotiations with Monsieur. In so far as this gossip was correct, it was extremely ancient news. Nor was it treasonable, or even 'blasphemous', though it was unfounded, to have speculated aloud that Elizabeth 'was not resolved of what religion yet to be of'. Bruno needed something better than this, and did his best to provide it. To allege that Howard was a priest, and had been created a cardinal *in petto*, was probably one of his jokes, but it had a sting in the tail; and the charge that his nephew Philip was in communication with the Catholic exiles and harbouring the head of the Jesuit mission in his house was no joke at all. His promise to provide further details and Herle's immediate response make this plain. This was the first, and so far as I know the only, occasion when Bruno acted as an informer on his fellow-priests and their harbourers in England. According to a royal proclamation of 1 April 1582, shortly to be confirmed by statute, the offence which Bruno was alleging against both the priest and his host was treasonable, and conviction upon it would have entailed the execution of both parties in a manner almost

11 The letter is Castelnau to Mary, 15/25-xi-1583 (*CSP Scotland 1581–83*, p. 654; PRO SP 53/13, no. 62): deciphered by Thomas Phellippes, and dated by him, I presume OS. I imagine the letter was taken with Throckmorton when he was arrested.

as barbarous as his own.[12] It is quite clear that this was what Bruno intended. Since nothing came of Herle's investigation, it is possible that Bruno simply made the information up, though it does not sound like it; more probably it came from talk in Salisbury Court, or via the Throckmortons (since Thomas had been got away to the continent by the Earl of Arundel's wife).[13] That Bruno meant it to be taken seriously is evident from his instruction to Herle to pass it on directly to the queen herself, and '*sub sigillo confessionis*'; that this phrase, surely Bruno's own, was as it turned out particularly ludicrous is only one of the many incidents in Bruno's history which are grave and farcical at the same time.[14]

Bruno's campaign against Howard was successful in that he was arrested, interrogated, and kept in custody for at least six months, but despite Bruno's or Herle's opinion that he was '*aut non capiendus aut non relaxandus*', he lived to fight another day. When the Jesuit story broke down Bruno had nothing to offer against him except that he had been seeing Castelnau; I doubt if Elizabeth took much notice of the rest of the tale, though some of her councillors may have done.[15] While the Earls of Arundel and Northumberland were being interrogated about their connection with Throckmorton's conspiracy, Herle gave Leicester what he had on them, but Bruno does not seem to have had much to tell him: Arundel was released, though Northumberland was not. On the other hand the story about 'triumphs' in Spain on the news of Elizabeth's assassination, which I assume he had invented, made quite an impression on the queen.[16]

Bruno had now done the job he had been hired to do, and his career as a spy had had its finest hour. There were still things that Elizabeth, Burghley and Walsingham needed to know about Castelnau, but Courcelles was the man to tell them these, as he

12 *Texts*, no. 5; above, p. 30; Philip Hughes, *The Reformation in England*, iii (London, 1954), pp. 342 ff; P.L. Hughes and J.F. Larkin (ed.), *Tudor Royal Proclamations* (3 vols; New Haven/London, 1964–69), ii, 485–91. Philip Howard had not been reconciled to Rome at this time, and other attempts to prove that he was harbouring priests failed: *Philip Howard*, pp. 44, 46–7, 50, 96.

13 Lady Margery Throckmorton to Francis Throckmorton, 9/19-x-1583 (above, n. 10).

14 *Texts*, no. 5; above, pp. 30, 34.

15 *Texts*, no. 7. Howard's interrogatories are in PRO SP 12/163, f. 93; his answers, 11/21-xii-1583 and [ ]-i-1584, in *CSP Scotland 1581–83*, pp. 675 f, and *1584–85*, pp. 21 f. The Earl of Arundel's, 24-xii-1583/3-i-1584, are in *Philip Howard*, pp. 45–8. The items in them which seem to be based on Bruno's information were questions to Howard about his meetings with Castelnau 'specially last summer', and to Arundel about contacts with the Jesuit Jasper Heywood, who fits Bruno's description. Howard was confined to the house of Sir Ralph Sadler until at least the end of May 1584; Arundel to Arundel House in the Strand until April: *Philip Howard*, pp. 48–52, 56, 103, 338; Nicolas, *Hatton*, pp. 368, 376.

16 *Texts*, nos. 7 and 8.

shortly did. Bruno passed a couple of useful messages in the New Year, but he was now free to concentrate on his writing undistracted by anything except a vigorous social round and his duties as chaplain. His social range must have been greatly widened when, over the Christmas season, Castelnau systematically wined and dined the Council, court and aristocracy with a view to smoothing over the crisis caused by Throckmorton's confessions. He must also have seen the queen again: Accession Day (17 November, probably the day after Throckmorton's arrest), and a visit by Castelnau to Hampton Court early in December, seem the likeliest occasions. We know that she knew about his services to her, and thanked him verbally for them at some point. His Elizabetholatry warmed accordingly, though it did not stop him asking for his money.[17]

Lent 1584, if we count the whole two months between Ash Wednesday new style and Easter old style, was the most important time in Bruno's life. He wrote his masterpiece, the *Cena de le Ceneri*; and he sent to Elizabeth the most amazing, if not the most truthful, of his communications – the letter about Zubiaur's confession. We may think that the success of his operation against Throckmorton had put him in a euphoric and creative mood. I hope the reader will forgive the time already spent on establishing the exact chronology of these two contributions, since fitting the two together is the most important thing we now have to do.

Below is a chronological table (Figure 6), which distinguishes between actual events and fictional events in the *Cena* which will have had more or less foundation in reality. Its purpose is to combine the sequence which led up to the confession letter and the sequence which led to the writing of the *Cena* into a single story running from Christmas 1583 to Easter 1584. I use old-style dates.

So far as I can see the first sequence began rather the earlier, and was dominated by the Spanish ambassador, Mendoza, his relations with Castelnau, with his agent Zubiaur, and with his contact Scory. In the latter months of 1583 Mendoza had frequented Salisbury Court a good deal, and so had Zubiaur, who had there become friendly with Scory. At the end of the year Scory did some valuable jobs for Mendoza: by way of his master the Earl of Leicester he got Don Gaston de Spinola his interview with the queen on behalf of the Duke of Parma; and at the end of December he organised a celebrated dinner in London at the house of Mr Customer Smith, where Mendoza met Leicester and a deal between England and Spain was

---

17 Castelnau to Henri III, 9/19-xii-1583 (Hampton Court), and 22-xii-1583/1-i-1584 (BL Harleian 1582, ff. 329 ff, 334 ff); above, p. 35; *Texts*, no. 5.

	Date OS	Date NS	
November	15–23 16–20	25–3.xii 26–30	GB's messages from SC passed via Herle to Burghley Arrest of Throckmorton and Howard
December	Late November to mid January	Early December to late January	Throckmorton and E. of Northumberland in Tower. Interrogation of Throckmorton, Howard, Es. of Northumberland and Arundel, and others
January	early 9 12 or 19 or both 20–21	middle 19 22 or 29 or both 30–31	GB's New Year letter to Walsingham Mendoza before the Council Mendoza at SC; hears mass, etc. Mendoza leaves
February (29 days)	5 between *c.* 5 and 12 *c.* 15 or later *c.* 23 24–26	15 between *c.* 15 and 22 *c.* 25 or later *c.* 4.iii 5–7.iii	*Ash Wednesday* NS. GB at dinner in SC with medics William Parry at SC GB sends information from SC via Herle **Florio and Gwynne bring invitation from Greville** **GB sees Greville**
March	4 about 8–12 15 16 18 22 *c.* 23	14 about 18–22 25 26 28 1.iv *c.* 2.iv	*Ash Wednesday* OS. **Trip to Whitehall. 'Cena' at Greville's** **'Tetralogue'** *Palm Sunday* NS. Zubiaur's confession to GB GB's confession letter to Elizabeth Zubiaur's communion *Easter Sunday* NS. ? *Cena de le Ceneri* begun
April	March to April 19	April 29	*Cena* being written *Easter Sunday* OS. *Cena* now finished
May	21	31	Trial of Throckmorton

Fictional events narrated in the Cena *are in bold.*

Figure 6. Chronological table of events.

mooted.[18] These approaches were defeated by Throckmorton's confessions, or by the use which was made of them. Bruno had helped the cause along with his tale about Spanish rejoicings on the news of Elizabeth's assassination; he now, early in January, added some information about the privy councillor most in favour of a deal with Spain, Sir James Croft. I presume that Croft's man Edward Morris had been passing messages between Croft and Mendoza as he later did between Burghley and the Duke of Parma: Bruno's report that Castelnau had been seeing a lot of him recently implied that Mendoza, Castelnau and Croft were in some kind of Catholic cahoots and that the peace-making efforts were a blind.[19] This was at roughly the time that Mendoza was summoned before the Council (9 January) and told to leave the country in fourteen days. During the interval Mendoza paid either one or two lengthy visits to Salisbury Court; on one of the Sundays he came to mass in the morning and stayed all day, trying to get Castelnau to see the sense of a tough alliance with Spain to get rid of the heretics in England, the Netherlands and France. It sounds as if he no longer had a priest in his own house.[20] I presume that Bruno said mass, and should imagine that Zubiaur and Scory came too: Scory accompanied Mendoza down to the river when he left, which was rather brave of him. If Bruno passed on any news about this meeting it has not survived. Ash Wednesday, Catholic style, was some ten days later, 5 February: Bruno signed the congregation with ashes on their foreheads, and reminded them, congenially enough, that they were dust and unto dust would return. In the evening Castelnau had some medics to dinner, certainly including the family doctor Geoffroy Le Brumen, and possibly also Florio's Oxford friend Matthew Gwynne; Bruno had an enjoyable time trouncing Aristotle and defending the Copernican system.[21] Some time after the middle of February Bruno

18 All this is from Scory's examination a year later, 14/24-ii-1585, but reported by Castelnau to Anjou, *c.* end of December 1583 (PRO SP 12/176, f. 148; BL Harleian 1582, ff. 392 f). Stafford had had an account of this letter from somebody in Anjou's service by 18/28-i-1584 (*CSP Foreign 1583–84*, p. 314).

19 Above, pp. 33–4.

20 Mendoza's visit or visits to Salisbury Court between his interview with the Council and his departure are mentioned in Castelnau to Henri III, 14/24-i-1584, to Catherine de Médicis, same date, to Henri III, 4/14-ii-1584 (BL Harleian 1582, ff. 339 f, 346, 349). The visit described in the first two letters occurred between 9/19-i and 14/24-i-1584; the visit mentioned in the third is described as 'a few days' before Mendoza's departure, and Mendoza was said to have come to mass and stayed the whole day. Castelnau's remark in a letter to Walsingham, 6/16-vii-1584 (*CSP Foreign 1583–84*, p. 592), that it was unfair to regard him as pro-Spanish 'because an ambassador once came to my lodging' should not be taken literally, since Mendoza had paid him several visits during the previous few months. Mendoza left on 20/30-i-1584 or immediately after: *Calendar of State Papers, Spanish, 1580–1586*, ed. M.A.S. Hume (London, 1896), p. 516.

21 Above, pp. 44–5.

met Herle again (?at the Bull's Head), and told him who was to be seen around the embassy these days: they included two men who had worked for Mendoza, Scory and Zubiaur's friend Philip Courtois.[22]

After this we are in the narrated time of the *Cena*, which is certainly fictional; but Bruno was so precise about it that it would be extraordinary if it had no foundation in fact at all. Ash Wednesday old style, on which the supper and conversation at Greville's rooms in Whitehall is narrated as having taken place, was 4 March; the invitation from Greville, brought to Bruno at Salisbury Court by Florio and Gwynne, is put about ten days before, say 23 or 24 February. The tetralogue *chez* Smitho, which is the least likely thing in the dialogue to have had any factual correlative, would fill something like the week after the first Sunday in Lent old style, say 9–13 March; and Bruno, I have assumed, would in real life be starting to write shortly after that. The following Sunday, 15 March, is an almost certain date for Zubiaur's confession. Though Zubiaur had been frequenting the embassy for months, Bruno had not hitherto mentioned him, which suggests that they had got on rather well. According to Bruno, he had been pestering him to hear his confession for some time, and this was almost his last chance before Easter; he and Courtois had arranged to make their Easter communion (I suppose at the embassy, though Bruno does not actually say so) on the following Wednesday, which must have been the Wednesday in Holy Week new style, 18 March old style. So we can be fairly certain that Bruno's writing of the confession letter to Elizabeth, and his beginning the writing of the *Cena*, were practically simultaneous. If anything, I should think the letter was probably written earlier: as chaplain, Bruno would have had quite a lot to do in Holy Week; after Easter he would be a relatively free man. He may also have wanted to get rid of his obligations to espionage for the time being in order to concentrate on his book. I have explained my conviction that the *Cena de le Ceneri* was written between Easter new style (22 March) and Easter old style (19 April).[23] I doubt if it would have taken him as long as that.

For the rest of 1584 Bruno was engaged in the writing and publication of his dialogues, and I have nothing more to add to the little that is known about the circumstances of this. I do have something to say about certain of their contents, but before the story modulates into a literary mode it will be as well to complete the narrative of Bruno's exterior doings from the publication of the *Spaccio* at the end of 1584 until his departure from England. There are no difficulties about the sequence of events, and we have already digested the principal consequence of combining the two stories, which was to convert Châteauneuf's interview with Fagot into an interrogation of Bruno. That occasion does indeed acquire in retrospect a position in Bruno's life-story not unlike the mark of the compass-point which he (erroneously) detected at the centre of Copernicus's diagram of the moon's orbit.[24] But apart from that there is not much to say.

After Christmas he dug out his abortive theological dialogue, the *Cabala del cavallo pegaseo* (we can see him shuffling the papers on his table and finding what he had written of it used as a cover for the *Spaccio*), but before he had got very far with it he was off to Paris on his first trip for two years. The main reason for this was certainly to sort out his future in France, and he may possibly have needed the king's permission to return. It seems to me unlikely that he was actually sent in order to get in touch with Thomas Morgan and set him up for arrest and extradition to England; but once he had told Walsingham he was going I have no doubt that Walsingham told him something of the kind would be extremely welcome. He did tell Stafford where Morgan was to be found,[25] and gave him quite a lot of other useful information; I do not think he would have revealed himself to Stafford unless Walsingham had told him to do so. How long he stayed is Paris we do not know; I imagine he was back by Easter, 11/21 April.

After this there is a gap until August; during this time I should think he added *L'asino cillenico* to the *Cabala* and published them together. He certainly now wrote his last dialogue, *De gli eroici furori*. Like Castelnau, he had time on his hands: Châteauneuf was supposed to arrive in April, but the outbreak of an insurrection by the Catholic League held him up until the end of July. Bruno had time to polish up his poems, his self-portrait as Actaeon captured by Elizabeth's Diana, and his tale of the blind muses who had left Campania to be illuminated by the queen and set free to sport among the nymphs of Thames. We have seen how he got on at his confrontation with the new ambassador. We have also seen how he spent a couple of nights in a City prison until Castelnau and Walsingham rescued him from the Lord Mayor; who, we may observe, was perfectly clear that in Bruno he had his hands on M. de Mauvissière's priest.[26] Considering

---

24 Above, pp. 58–60, 76–8; *Cena*, p. 141/201.

25 Someone has underlined the passage in *Texts*, no. 13, where Morgan's whereabouts are described, and added a triangle to mark it; this must have been done by the clerk to bring the passage to Walsingham's attention. But Morgan must already have been arrested by this time.

26 Above, p. 60, and n. 83.

the pains he had taken to conceal it, one can well understand the alarm Castelnau felt at the prospect that the fact would be ventilated in a court case in the City. Evidently in something of a state, he posted down to the Lord Mayor's house and tried to repossess Bruno by a *coup de main*. Whether Bruno found his master's discomfiture at the hands of the Lord Mayor as comic as it sounds in the telling, I cannot say. Fortunately Walsingham must have been almost as keen as Castelnau to keep Bruno's name, or whatever name he was using, out of the public eye. This little crisis over, Bruno was free to take a dignified leave of England, and of the best years of his life. It seems quite likely that he showed his appreciation for Walsingham's help by informing him that the ship on which Girault was carrying Castelnau's effects to France was also carrying half a dozen Catholic youths from Oxford to the seminary at Reims and other places.[27] They were taken off the ship at Dover and so, as it happened, escaped the beating or drowning which they would no doubt have suffered at the hands of the Dutch privateers who ransacked the ship on the other side of the Channel.

ii   *The Malcontent*

I return from these later adventures to Bruno's principal gift to posterity, the dialogues he wrote in Salisbury Court, and in particular to those of his *annus mirabilis*, 1584; I shall attempt to put some passages from them into their place in a story which is both Bruno's and Fagot's. I say, 'some passages', since I shall not be talking about the dialogues as a whole or in their main substance. In the first three, the *Cena*, *De la causa* and *De l'infinito*, the object is the exposition of Bruno's version of Copernican physics or metaphysics, which seems as perfectly independent of the doings of Fagot as the substance of the physics of an atomic spy of the 1940s was independent of his spying. This is not true of the substance of the *Spaccio*, but at the moment I shall be concerned only with whatever in that work may contribute immediately to a biographical narrative: literary texts being what they are, and Bruno being who he was, we ought not to expect too many revelations of this nature.

Since Fagot now went to sleep for a year, we have no opportunity

---

27 Their examinations, 14/24-ix-1585 to 23-ix/3-x-1585, are in PRO SP 12/182, nos. 15–19, 27, 31. The passage had been organised by Girault, but some of the students had met Castelnau at Salisbury Court, and had had a conversation with him in Latin. It is possible that Bruno was still in jail when they passed through; but if he knew about the operation I should be surprised if he did not report it. Their action was treasonable under the proclamation of 1 April 1582, above n. 12.

to relate his daily occupations to those of the author of the dialogues.
There are in any case few external events to record from the period,
except for the riot in Salisbury Court in August; Bruno's apparent
immunity to this would suggest that, unlike Courcelles and Florio
who were chased out of their rooms, he was living and writing at the
top of the house, where he would get peace and quiet and a better
view of the stars. Such incidents apart, however, I think Bruno's
texts can be induced to yield story-building material of two kinds.
From the first two dialogues, where quasi-biographical information
is fairly generously provided, I think we can extract a theme whose
frequent, not to say obsessive, recurrences are readily accounted for
by the prehistory which has been narrated. This will take our story
somewhat further. Aside from that, there are isolated passages in the
dialogues which may now be found more revealing of Bruno's
character and biography than there has been reason to think them
hitherto. These will confirm what we know already, but possibly
make it shine with a richer glow. I begin with two of the latter.

The Argument of the *Cena* contains a memorable passage describing the journey of Bruno and Florio from Salisbury Court to
Whitehall as not so much 'historical' as 'poetical' or 'tropological': by
the last term Bruno meant the method of scriptural interpretation
which takes facts of a narrative as symbolic moral statements. The
realistic details, such as their scrambling in the mud of the Thames
bank at low tide, are intended, like the actions and scenery put by a
painter in the background of his painting, to 'istoriar la figura', or
give the impression that the major dramatic event is happening in a
context of real life.[28] My interest at present is not with what may be
the relation between Bruno's and Florio's fictional journey and
anything that happened in real life; but with what it may have to say
about Fagot and his intelligence. Fagot is almost always pains-
takingly factual; but the question of whether he is doing something
to 'istoriar la figura' arises in several cases. One is the comic cipher
said to have been invented by his successor to correspond with
the pope; another is the climax of Zubiaur's confession; another
is the account (of which we do not have the original version and
which may possibly not have come from Bruno) of the Spaniards
'triumphing' on the rumour of Elizabeth's assassination. Here we
are concerned with Zubiaur's confession. I have said that I think it
practically certain that Zubiaur went to confession to Bruno, but
incredible that he confessed his assassination plot as Bruno describes
it. Here is Bruno's account of Zubiaur's answer to his confessional
interrogation:

28 *Cena*, p. 11/72.

Nottez Madame que je l'ay interrogué le plus qu'il m'a esté pocible, et premierement sur le dix commandemens de la loy, laquelle chosse c'est fort bien confessé hors mics sur *non occides* [Thou shalt not kill], car il a tousiours ceste volonté vers vostre Majesté, et luy ay fait les plus belles Remonstrances du monde sur cela. Mais il m'a respondu en somme que c'estoit pour la tranquilité de la vraye Religion catholique, apostolique et Romayne, et que resolument qu'il croyoit que son ame yroit tout droict en paradis quant il n'auroit faict aultre chosse que cela, et semble qu'il soit enragé en ce confessant comme il grichoit les dentz et me faisoit peur en le voyant . . .[29]

If we take this to be a fiction, it is rather brilliantly done until the part about Zubiaur grinding his teeth in rage, which may be thought to give the game away. The thought will be encouraged by comparison with a passage in dialogue iii of the *Cena*, where the furious pedant Torquato is reported by Frulla as likewise gnashing his teeth at the Nolan.[30] In both cases Bruno uses the wrong word for the action, and the French word invented in the letter is fairly evidently a version of the Italian word which is used in the dialogue. Torquato, among other things, 'ghigna i denti dell'ingiurie', meaning roughly 'spits out insults through his clenched or grinding teeth'. *Ghignare*, according to Florio and modern Italian, means to sneer or make a nasty face; the proper word for gnashing teeth is *digrignare*: Bruno's editors do not suggest that he was trying some poetic conceit, but that he had forgotten the right word. Zubiaur 'grichoit les dentz et me faisoit peur en le voyant': here the proper verb was *grincer*, and so far as I know there has never been a word *gricher* in French. Bruno had obviously forgotten *grincer* as well as *digrignare*, and wrote something like the Italian word that came to mind.

I imagine this repetition of a linguistic error will seem more significant to some readers than to others; but it concerns the strongest phrase in the Zubiaur passage, and to my judgment powerfully confirms the conclusion that Zubiaur's confession of an assassination plot ought to be classified among Bruno's fictions, not among Fagot's reportage. But I do not draw attention to it so much for this reason, as to show that Bruno's very careful segregation of Fagot from his real identity is not absolutely watertight, and to point out the narrative continuity between two dramatic 'figures' which cannot have been composed much more than a fortnight apart.

The second passage comes from *De la causa, principio e uno*, which must have been composed in June-July, features three characters who

29   *Texts*, no. 11.
30   *Cena*, p. 105/166.

seem to represent Bruno, Florio and Sidney, and is represented as taking place at Salisbury Court. It occurs in the first dialogue, where Bruno defends the *Cena* against a hostile English reaction to it politely expressed by Armesso/Sidney. He distinguishes himself from those 'domestic philosophers' whose only functions are to serve as light entertainment indoors, or as scarecrows out in the fields. Elitropio/Florio chips in:

> To tell you the truth, most of the world thinks that the race of philosophers is more vile than the race of domestic chaplains. Everyone knows that chaplains are hired from all sorts of riff-raff and bring the priesthood into disrepute; but they pick their philosophers out of a crowd of bestial morons who are a much worse advertisement for philosophy.[31]

This seemingly gratuitous intervention, now we know what Bruno was doing in the Castelnau household, turns out to be, not random abuse of English pedants, but a rather witty remark from the domestic tutor to one who was both domestic philosopher and domestic chaplain. Florio and Castelnau must have enjoyed the joke, so far as they could see it; Madame de Mauvissière may not have appreciated it quite so much, whence perhaps the smooth eulogies of herself and her daughter inserted into the fourth dialogue.

Fortified by these reminders of Fagot, I proceed to the larger theme. The *Cena* and *De la causa* are directed against bigoted supporters of Aristotle, like Nundinio and Torquato in the *Cena*, and humanist pedants like Prudenzio in the *Cena* and Poliinnio in *De la causa*, both of whom present a contrast to intelligent supporters like Smitho and Dicsono and sympathetic critics like Armesso. Most of the time the opposition is academic, and is feeble and stereotyped; the doctors are cartoon doctors, the humanists cartoon humanists; though they may be stupid and malevolent, the tone is usually quite amiable. It is rather as Bruno claimed in his interrogation in Venice, dinner-table joking at the expense of the medics with whom he said he had discussed Aristotle at the original Ash Wednesday supper.[32] At the same time, there is something in the air more disagreeable than this, which is in the first place detectable in two of the prefatory sonnets. The *Cena* is prefaced by a sonnet 'Al Mal Contento', 'To the Malcontent' who, says Bruno, should have taken care not to bite him if he did not want to be bitten back; people who live in glass houses, the sonnet says in various ways, should not throw stones. Even, Bruno says if I understand him correctly, if he loses the fight his

31 *Causa*, p. 202/40.
32 *Documenti*, p. 121.

vituperation will have scarred his enemy for life. The enemy should believe (selectively) in the gospel, which says, in the parable of the wheat and the cockle, that those who sow error in the world will harvest retribution from it, and their works be burned in the fire.[33] Of the five poems which precede *De la causa*, the last is a sonnet to the subject of the dialogue, the 'Cause, Beginning and One' which are Bruno's names for God. The octave evokes this deity; the sestet describes what is, or those who are, standing in the way of his own proclamation of it, or more simply of his getting on with his work. These are: 1) 'blind error, a miserly age, evil fortune'; 2) 'secret envy, vile rage (rabies)'; 3) 'zeal for iniquity, cruel hearts, impious brains and perverted enterprises (strano ardire)'.[34] Most of this suggests another sort of conflict than the hostility of academic types: more political, more perilous both to those who engage in it and to those others who may be infected, as well as more individual. It is political because the word 'malcontent' refers to political opposition, and was in 1584 principally applied by supporters of the Protestant cause to the Catholic opposition in the Netherlands for having supposedly betrayed the united front of the revolt against Spain. The 'error' which is being disseminated is not simply intellectual and private, but political and public: it leads cruel hearts and impious brains to conceive unnatural enterprises, which could not by any stretch of the imagination be said of Nundinio, or even of the rabid Torquato, though he comes fairly near. If the *Causa* sonnet was written after the text of the dialogue, Bruno would very probably have been referring, as well as to Throckmorton, to the assassination of William of Orange, which occurred on 1 July. The conflict is more perilous because it inspires the vicious retaliation which Bruno will have to defend in the text of the *Causa* from the charge of uncivilised vendetta, and because it will lead, in the natural course of justice, to the destruction of those who began it, or at least of their works. It is individual, because one person seems to be envisaged as the principal malcontent and Bruno's principal enemy. True, Bruno's problems are attributed in the first place to the general condition of the world ('blind error, a miserly age, evil fortune'). But thereafter the underground envy and canine rage seem to be the

33   *Cena*, p. 5/65:

> . . . Dal nostro campo miete penitenza
> Che vi gittò d'errori la semenza;
>
>   Matthew 13: 24–30.

34   *Causa*, p. 190/27:

> Cieco error, tempo avaro, ria fortuna,
> Sord'invidia, vil rabbia, iniquo zelo,
> Crudo cor, empio ingegno, strano ardire
> Non bastaranno a farmi l'aria bruna . . .

property of an individual enemy; the zeal for iniquity, cruelty of heart, impious brain and perverted daring, which sound more plural, sound plural as the properties of a collection of individuals, among whom the envious rager will be counted, rather than as conventional attributes of a category of person like university doctors.

From the sonnets we proceed first to the text, not of the *Cena* but of the first dialogue of *De la causa*, which was written, we remember, in June or July and after the four substantive dialogues of the work. Here Armesso disparages the venom with which Bruno has been pursuing his enemies in the *Cena*, and Bruno defends himself as one who is not conducting a vendetta unworthy of a philosopher but exercising the correction proper to a censor. In reply to an objection that the offence was private and retribution should therefore not be public Bruno, with the authority of a confessor and connoisseur of the canon law, says that a lot of sins are committed in private but punished in public. After a good deal of discussion about whom exactly, among the English, Bruno is complaining about, we come down to a particular sort of person who claims to determine all matters in heaven and on earth, though his only claim to knowledge is that of a classical humanist. The figure is embodied in the 'sacrilegious pedant', Polihimnio (or Poliinnio).[35]

Polihimnio (as I shall spell him) appears only after twenty pages of the dialogue, but it is clear that he has secretly been there all along, since Bruno had already written the four later dialogues where, in the intervals between the serious parts of the book, he is subjected to ridicule by the scoffer Gervasio. As the object of Bruno's Diogenes- or dog-like rage, he is the same character as the Malcontent of the sonnets.[36] Unlike Nundinio and Torquato, Polihimnio is not simply Bruno's standard pompous ass, though he is of course that too. He is given a history and some kind of a description. He is not a doctor but a *magister*, or rather a *dominus magister*, a *magister doctorum*; he is an *archididascalo* or archteacher in the way that Ramus had been an archpedant. He is about fifty. He has probably taught the humanities in a university. He dyes his beard.[37] He is celibate and probably homosexual. The last fact or facts emerges from a long soliloquy he

---

35 *Causa*, pp. 199–200/36–7, 204–17/41–53, especially p. 213/48. Bruno always spelt 'Polihimnio', and I retain this spelling for a reason which will emerge in a moment; Gentile's modernisation 'Poliinnio' conveys the sound, but rather diminishes the force of the name: *DI*, pp. xlvi, 254 n.

36 The identity of Polihimnio and the Malcontent depends on the repetition of the 'cinico/cane' theme in Bruno's attack on both: *Cena*, p. 5/65; *Causa*, pp. 196–7/34, 199/36, 200/37, and Gentile's notes at pp. 5 and 199. Aquilecchia (p. 37) makes a firm connection, and cites Florio ('cinico': 'dogged, currish') to the purpose.

37 *Causa*, pp. 225/61, 241/75, 254 f/87, 292/119 (*magister*); 219/55, 241/75, 260/92 (*archididascalo*); 296 f/124 (age); 213/49 (teaching); 293/121 (beard). Florio (Aquilecchia, p. 55) gives 'chiefe disciple' for 'archididascalo', which is a very rare mistake.

is given at the beginning of dialogue iv where, in a caricature of the main argument of the piece, where Bruno is expounding to Dickson his alternative to Aristotle's doctrine of matter and form, he identifies matter with women and form with men. Women are a sort of bog of desire, of unformed appetite, the source of sin and error, the downfall of great men who without them would be pure intelligence and immortal, the cause of instability and mutability.[38] Hence Polihimnio's own celibacy is a state of pure intellect.

It is also in some fairly strong sense a priestly condition, which is not the condition of the doctors of the *Cena*. The name refers to the muse of sacred music, Polyhymnia; Gervasio teases him on two occasions as *reverendissimo*, one of them after Polihimnio has demurred to the title as being 'presbyteral and clerical'.[39] The point is carefully led up to in dialogue i: the discussion of the manners of the English learned, ostensibly *à propos* of the *Cena* where there was no question of anyone but 'doctors', is nudged by Florio's remark about philosophers and chaplains and managed by Armesso so as to include among the offending classes people described as both 'priests', which might be stretched to cover most university doctors, and 'monks', which certainly cannot.[40] As a commentary on Polihimnio's celibacy, which because of the way in which the *Causa* was composed is the earlier *datum*, these descriptions make it pretty clear that the priesthood in question is of the Romish kind. So Polihimnio is some kind of a popish priest; and he is something more than a priest. He is *archididascalo*; he possesses a *pallio*; he is, on two occasions, *purpurato*, which might possibly make him a cardinal; he is, at the end of a long list of pompous epithets, a 'capro emissario del sommo pontefice Aaron'.[41] After all this preparation we should be contumacious not to accept the supreme pontiff Aaron as the supreme pontiff Gregory XIII: Polihimnio is, if I read the overtones rightly, the scapegoat upon whom the sins of the pontiff have been loaded and who should therefore be driven away, and also a Romish seminary priest in the guise of a goat. Finally, and fairly conclusively, he is the pope himself, recognisable to the meanest intelligence in a mock-humble riposte by Gervasio to one of Polihimnio's outbursts at being treated as an idiot by this whipper-snapper: 'Pax vobis, domine magister, servus servorum et scabellum pedum tuorum. (Peace be to you, lord Master, the servant of your

---

38 *Causa*, pp. 289–97/117–24; cf. pp. 215/50, 221/57, 341/162.
39 *Causa*, pp. 255/87f, 261/93.
40 *Causa*, pp. 202 f/40 f, 208 f/45 f, 213/49, 219/54.
41 *Causa*, pp. 213/49, 241/75, 255/88, 220/56: Greenberg (p. 106) has been misled by Gentile's mistaken reference (p. 220, n. 5) to Leviticus 8 (actually Leviticus 16) to translate 'emissary rams'. It seems that *porporato* in the sixteenth century was more likely to refer to civil officers than to cardinals: Aquilecchia, *Causa*, p. 80 n, citing Florio.

servants and a footstool under your feet.)' To which Polihimnio replies with a briskly pontifical malediction: 'Maledicat te Deus in saecula saeculorum. (May God curse you for all eternity.)'[42] There can be no doubt at all what this exchange is intended to indicate.

Polihimnio, it has to be said, is not totally ridiculous or unattractive: he makes a couple of good jokes, one of them about the Frenchman in a storm at sea who, when instructed by the captain to throw overboard his heaviest piece of luggage, threw his wife.[43] (But on this subject he was expressing Bruno's own sentiments, so perhaps we should not be surprised.) Pedantry apart, his papal, or archiepiscopal, or priestly, or monastic characteristics were calculated to imprint him in the minds of an audience of Protestant gentlemen, and Protestant ladies, as a figure less genially comic than Malvolio or Tartuffe. Looking around in Bruno's field of vision in the spring and summer of 1584, and giving, I hope, due weight to the consideration that fictional characters are not historical ones, I think we should be pedantic not to recognise behind the fictional portrait of Polihimnio the historical features of Lord Henry Howard.

Howard was certainly a *dominus*. He was equally certainly a *magister*, having taken his MA in Cambridge in 1564 but no higher degree; indeed he was a *magister* twice over, since he had been admitted to the same degree in Oxford. Born in 1540, he was now 43 or 44, extremely celibate, and probably homosexual. He was also extremely learned, and given to displaying his learning at length. He was, says his biographer, 'the only nobleman of the Elizabethan era to teach at a university'; for some years he had been Reader in Rhetoric (i.e., Greek and Latin) at Cambridge, and he had later lectured in civil law. He was, in short, an archetypal humanist, in Bruno's terms an archpedant. Although, as I have said, he was not very strictly, as Bruno claimed, a papist, the term would do very well, for he was a Catholic, and that by conviction rather than by inheritance, since his father and brother had been Protestants. Taking his long career as a whole, it has seemed reasonable to put this down as a natural position for a professional courtier; but he was a scholar before he was a courtier, and the source of his Catholic conviction seems to have been that sacraments were essential to Christianity and he could see no half-way state between the realism of Rome and the tokenism of 'sacramentaries'. He had an intense devotional strain; this took the form of a great deal of quasi-liturgical composition in both Latin and English, which ought to be investigated. On a rapid view, it looks as if he would have made a first-class translator into

---

42 *Causa*, p. 242/76; Michele Ciliberto, *La ruota del tempo*, pp. 123, 125 observes, truly but rather mildly, that there is nothing anti-Protestant in the attack on Polihimnio.

43 *Causa*, p. 295/122 f.

Figure 7.   Portrait of
Lord Henry Howard,
later 1st Earl of
Northampton, 1594.

English of the Catholic liturgy, if such a person had been required.[44]
It was only in Bruno's fiction that he was a priest and a cardinal, but
the scratch was not made at random: as the scholarly younger brother
of a Duke of Norfolk, he would almost certainly have become a
priest, and very possibly a cardinal, if the England of Elizabeth had
been a Catholic country. Though, or because, he was careful to
restrict his dealings with seminary priests to mass and the sacraments, had nothing directly to do with Catholic enterprises, and did
not communicate with Rome, he was the nearest thing to an official

44   Peck, *Northampton*, pp. 3, 8–9; Williams, *Thomas Howard*, p. 133; John Bossy, 'The
     Character of Elizabethan Catholicism', in T. Aston (ed.), *Crisis in Europe, 1560–1660*
     (London, 1965), p. 242; Howard to Walsingham, 12-i-1581 (PRO SP 12/147, no. 6), on
     sacraments; below, n. 49. I should say that 'domine magister' is a form of address used to
     Bruno's original pedant, Manfurio, in the *Candelaio* of 1582.

representative of English Catholicism at the court of Elizabeth: Gervasio's *reverendissimo* and *illustrissimo* were not at all beside the mark. He was a substantial figure on the Elizabethan scene, and an even more substantial figure on the Jacobean.

Bruno had numerous reasons for wanting to bite him: his Catholicism, his attack on Dee and on rifling in the mysteries of Egypt, his vendetta with the Dudleys and visceral hatred of the Protestant cause, his friendship with Castelnau and his influence upon Elizabeth. I have said that I think Bruno felt himself in competition with Howard for Elizabeth's favour.[45] He did his best to destroy him by involving him in Throckmorton's conspiracy and the harbouring of Jesuits. The attempt did not really come off, but Howard was at least temporarily in disgrace and removed from contact with Elizabeth. Bruno continued his campaign, in *De la causa*, with a mixture of triumphant ridicule and sinister insinuations. I presume that his choice of celibacy and misogyny as the point to insist on was governed by the idea that this was the most promising ground, the conspiracy story having gone off at half-cock, to put him into bad odour with Elizabeth. This would raise difficulties of a personal kind arising from Howard's supposed contempt for women in general (though Bruno ought to have considered that Elizabeth had a stake in celibacy too), and difficulties of a political kind by reminding her that he was an enemy to her government of the English church, which was probably true, and implying that he was an enemy to her government of the country, which was not true. It was not a very creditable line for Bruno to take, since he himself held most of the opinions about women which he attributed to Howard; but it seems to have struck home to the extent that Howard was constrained to write a defence of female government in the hope of restoration to favour.[46]

In case the point had not been sufficiently made, Bruno polished off the first dialogue of *De la causa* with two proofs against the views about women of the 'severe, supercilious and most savage Polihimnio': the phrase is eerily echoed in the 'proud, pedantic and cynical' of Howard's biographer. One of the proofs, *ad hominem* for a Reader in Rhetoric, was a comparison of masculine and feminine nouns which contrasted a string of masculine examples of vice and disorder with their feminine opposites. This piece of gender analysis was also, it seems quite obvious, a covert comparison between the degenerate viciousness of the Roman system (lethargy, hatred, fear, rigour, scandal, fury and error) and the happy excellence of the

---

45 Above, p. 101.
46 Peck, *Northampton*, p. 12, referring to Howard's 'Dutiful Defence of the Lawful Regiment of Women'.

English (memory, friendship, security, gentleness, peace, quiet, truth); it seems to be a recollection of the seven deadly sins and their contrary virtues, or perhaps of the twelve fruits of the Holy Ghost. The other proof was, of course, the existence of the divine Elizabeth herself: model of the cardinal virtues prudence, justice, fortitude and temperance; more wise, brave, prudent, etc. than any man of her country, or any of the great queens of history; beloved of the heavens, who defeated all attempts to displace her from her throne; the wonder of the present age; guardian of the peaceful Thames in a Europe of turbid rivers.[47] Bruno was certainly doing his best to make sure that if, as Howard had claimed in the *Defensative*, there were prophets about seeking to monopolise the ear of Diana, it would be he and not Howard whose voice would be heard.

The motives for virtually identifying Polihimnio with Howard seem to me now so strong as almost to amount to a proof that Howard dyed his beard. One need not fear the discovery of a better candidate, for I am sure that none can be found: even his warmest admirers would not suggest that William Perkins, say, could plausibly be presented to the public in the guise of the muse of sacred music, and as a doctor and a Protestant he and anyone like him must be excluded.[48] The only serious objection would be that it is trivial and misguided to look for living exemplars of fictional characters, an objection I would certainly admit in the case of most of the characters in Bruno's dialogues. We absolutely do not need to enquire how many children had Smitho or Prudenzio, Frulla or Gervasio. Others, like Dickson or the poet Luigi Tansillo in the *Eroici furori*, appear under their own names and hence are not relevant here. Yet there are others again who do not appear under their own names but under fairly recognisable pseudonyms, like Elitropio, who since the flower heliotrope was Florio's emblem is quite evidently Florio; and this is the kind of name I take Polihimnio to be. We have seen that his age, history, status, appearance and personal characteristics are detailed, which is not true of any other character in Bruno's dialogues; and although his pseudonym is not so transparent as Florio's, it is actually a good deal more transparent than that of Armesso, if we take Armesso to represent Sidney.

Polihimnio is something to do with sacred music; so was Howard. He was a composer, not of music itself, but of services for which

---

47 *Causa*, pp. 221–3/57–9; Peck, *Northampton*, p. 7.
48 Above, p. 47. It would appear from Howard's 1594 portrait that Howard dyed his hair as well as his beard: Roy Strong, *The English Icon* (London/New York, 1969), p. 208. See Figure 7.

music might have been appropriate;[49] he was also the patron and probably the friend of those who would have supplied it. William Byrd, the most distinguished composer in a distinguished age of English music, was like Howard a Catholic courtier, Elizabethan loyalist, and at this time a conformist; he is spoken of as a 'friend' by the Earl of Northumberland, whose daughter he had been teaching, and he was examined by the Council, rather gently, in the aftermath of the arrests of Throckmorton and Howard.[50] He made music with Jesuits. I do not know any contemporary evidence that he was connected with Howard at this time, but the virtual certainty that they would have been in close touch on matters liturgical and musical is turned into an actual certainty by the celebrated preface to the first book of Byrd's *Gradualia*, published twenty years later in 1605. This, though published in England, was a systematic collection of polyphonic music for the feasts of the Catholic year. The first of its two books was dedicated to Howard, who had by then become Earl of Northampton. In the dedication Byrd said that Howard had been a patron in the affairs of his family, had known and appreciated his music for a long time, and had just used his new-found position of power as privy councillor to King James to get the choristers of the Chapel Royal the first rise they had had since the reign of Edward III. He also said that Howard had been an inspiration to him while he was working on his novel project.[51] The eminent historian of Byrd's sacred music, Joseph Kerman, allows that there was probably some flattery in this, but thinks Byrd's description substantially true. It was written in a very different climate from that of the 1580s, but we cannot doubt that, in those darker years, it was quite as appropriate for Howard to appear on the stage as the muse of sacred music as in the guise of priest or monk, cardinal or pope. That being so, I think we can stand up quite unashamedly for the simple notion that, in the text of *De la causa*, Polihimnio equals Lord Henry Howard.

Secure in that conviction, I shall risk another identification. Polihimnio, Bruno indicates, is the same personage as the 'Malcontent' in the prefatory sonnet to the *Cena*. That Malcontent,

---

49 BL Cotton Titus C vi, ff. 516–82, is a series of self-composed offices in English and Latin. They are for private devotion, but contain antiphons and other texts very like some that Byrd set to music: Kerman (see next note), pp. 36 f. According to *DNB* there is similar material in BL Arundel Mss. 300 and Lambeth Palace Mss. 660.

50 Northumberland to Burghley, 15-i-1579 (BL Lansdowne 29, no. 38); William Parry to Charles Paget, 12/22-ii-1584 (PRO SP 12/168, no. 23), for Byrd's examination; also *Philip Howard*, p. 123 n (May 1584), which suggests some intimacy between Byrd and the earl. Byrd's Catholicism is splendidly dealt with in Joseph Kerman, *The Masses and Motets of William Byrd* (London, 1981), pp. 37–54 and *passim*.

51 Kerman, *William Byrd*, p. 228; the dedication is printed in Oliver Strunk, *Readings in Music History*: ii, *The Renaissance* (London/Boston, 1981 edn), pp. 137–9. Cf. *Causa*, pp. 222/58, 293/120.

Bruno's enemy who lived in a glass house and should not throw stones, who sowed error in 'our field' and would reap the retribution due, was therefore Howard: the epithet, meaning 'a political opponent of the existing regime, of Romish inspiration', was not precisely accurate but it was perfectly recognisable, especially if one were a maintainer of the Protestant cause. I repeat that the substance of the *Cena* was, even less than that of *De la causa*, a polemic against Howard and his opinions: I have no idea whether Howard accepted the Copernican revolution or not, and my hunch would be that he probably did. Nevertheless, there is a place for Howard in the dialogue, and I think it is, without much question, in the bows of the tropological taxi which took Bruno and Florio so inexpeditiously from Buckhurst Stairs to the Temple on the night of Ash Wednesday 1584.[52]

Frances Yates has observed that, if one is looking at the boat as an allegorical figure, as Bruno has invited us to do, the *signifié* which comes naturally to mind is the Roman Church. The ancient bark, relic of the Flood, riddled with woodworm, letting water at every seam, does indeed sound like the bark of St Peter: when Bruno likens it to Charon's boat ferrying the dead over the waters of Styx to the eternal rest of *lux perpetua*, I do not think there can be any reasonable doubt what he meant. There is also Florio's serenade, 'Dove senza me?' which on this reading is comic in the mouth of a Protestant refugee: it is as if he had sung to the pope 'What is life to me without thee?' from Gluck's *Orpheus and Eurydice*.[53] That does not make the two decrepit boatmen Howard and the Earl of Arundel: the latter is indeed described as being about sixty-five years old, an oddly precise age I make nothing of. They do however live beside the Temple, which suggests Arundel House; they have the manners of peasants, which equates them with Polihimnio and the error-sowing Malcontent; and they are an appropriate audience for Bruno's own serenade. The text of this, which features the rejected Saracen lover Rodomonte bewailing the inconstancy of the 'femenil ingegno', speaks to Howard's conviction that Elizabeth 'was not resolved of what religion yet to be of', and to a putative alteration in her feelings

52 *Texts*, no. 12i; above, pp. 39, 113 f.

53 Yates, *Art of Memory*, p. 302; cf. Gentile's note in *Cena*, p. 54 n. 3. But I think Yates goes astray in supposing that the passengers are 'landed. . .between the walls of an unsatisfactory convent' (like Bruno). I presume she means Blackfriars; but they do not land at Blackfriars (Dominicans), or even at Whitefriars (Carmelites), but somewhere upstream from the Temple, perhaps at Milford Stairs, next to Arundel House (and, to be fair, to Leicester House as well). Ariosto, *Orlando furioso*, viii, 76. Bruno was here recycling an image which he had coined in the *Antiprologo* to the *Candelaio* two years before: the play was described as a clapped-out boat fished up after a shipwreck and sent out unrepaired for a voyage in the open sea (*Candelaio*, p. 136); it seems an open question whether Bruno's previous usage sheds any light on his present one.

towards him which had already landed him in custody and might shortly send him to the block.[54] If Howard knew his Ariosto, as I am sure he did, he would have known that the lines in Bruno's song led directly, in *Orlando furioso*, to the polemic against women which was a source of Polihimnio's diatribe and is quoted in it. The shade of Rodomonte is in the boat already: he is a classic malcontent, and so are the boatmen.[55] Malcontent in a general sort of way; malcontent in the particular sense already mentioned; and malcontent constitutionally, as it were, in their profession as boatmen. How so? Because Howard said it in his book against prophecy. He had been venting his spleen against the Dudleys as usurpers of the English crown, actually in the case of the father (John Dudley, Duke of Northumberland), potentially in the case of the son (Robert Dudley, Earl of Leicester): 'Such Catch-poles [petty officers] as we find in Dion [Chrysostom] have ever been the brave and lustie *Malcontents*, looking one waye, like the bardgemen upon the Thames, when they bend their force, and stretch their armes another . . .'[56] I am not sure what passage from the Greek political orator Howard had in mind, but his reference to the Thames watermen was plain enough, and he was using a fashionable saying, also picked up by Francis Bacon. Generally, it applies to those who advance themselves by systematic deceit. Here it means, obviously, that a malcontent is someone who professes loyalty to his lawful master (or mistress) while secretly conspiring to overthrow him. It was a witty transposition of Bruno's to have put Howard and his quasi-son the Earl of Arundel into the same boat as Howard had put John and Robert Dudley: public

---

54 That the boatmen are 'rustici' is made much of in the *Cena* (*Texts*, no. 12i); *Causa*, p. 213/48. I confess that I cannot understand Bruno's description of the sort of *rustici* the boatmen are: 'questa e una specie di rustici, nel petto de' quali spunta tutti i sui strali il dio d'amor del popolo villano'. The god in question must be Eros/Cupid, considered as son of Aphrodite Pandemos (i.e., sensuality). If 'spunta' means that Eros's arrows have entered the breasts of the boatmen, the text presumably means that they are greedy and lazy, which seems superfluous. If, as seems more natural, it means that their breasts have proved impervious to these arrows, it presumably refers to the boatmen's refusal to go on; but why Bruno and Florio should be represented as anything to do with Aphrodite Pandemos I cannot imagine. Above, p. 30; *Orlando furioso*, xxvii, 117.

55 *Texts*, no. 12i; *Causa*, p. 292/120; *Orlando furioso*, xxvii, 117–20; xxviii, 86–7.

56 *Defensative*, sig. E-4. Howard used the same saying again in a letter to Sir Christopher Hatton written about the end of May: Nicolas, *Hatton*, p. 376. Cf. M.P. Tilley, *A Dictionary of the Proverbs in England in the Sixteenth and Seventeenth Centuries* (Ann Arbor, Mich., 1950), p. 710, no. W 143; F.P. Wilson (ed.), *Oxford Dictionary of English Proverbs* (3rd edn, Oxford, 1970), p. 484. The likeliest passages in Dio Chrysostom seem to be: *Orations* 34. 29–33, where the magistrates of the city of Tarsus are criticised for trying to get crowns and other honours with the help of the people; and *Orations* 34. 16, where the different parts of the city's constitution are described as a boat's crew pulling different ways (*Dio Chrysostom*, ed. and trans. J.W. Cohoon (5 vols; London, 1932–51 repr. 1961–4); cf. C.P. Jones, *The Roman World of Dio Chrysostom* (Cambridge, Mass./ London, 1978), pp. 80 f). Neither passage seems quite to fit.

professors of loyalty to Elizabeth and secret encompassers of her overthrow. Since their attempts had been foiled, in the Anjou marriage and Throckmorton's plot, Bruno could afford to cover them with ridicule: far from 'brave and lusty', they were aged and impotent, their arms without strength for all the obscene agitation of their torsos, their oars carrying them and their rotten boat nowhere, certainly not to Whitehall.

The seemingly tasteless joke conceals a satirical comment on their political achievements by way of the motto *Festina lente*, which both Teofilo and Prudenzio apply to them. Teofilo does so with a caricature of the emblem of Good Counsel which the motto expounded, a picture of an old and a young man representing Age and Youth, Prudence and Fortune: the sixty-five-year-old 'son' recalls the *puer senex* or bearded child, a version of the emblem in which the two were collapsed into one. There may be a particular reference here to the Anjou marriage scheme, all *lente* and no *festina* or, in Shakespeare's phrase, 'as swift as lead'. Prudenzio's sexual version is a comment on the motto itself, evoking the slow deliberation and rapid action which are required in political enterprises: 'a wisdom which', like the cannon-ball and the mulberry-tree, 'economizes all its forces for an opportunity of sudden and sure effect'. Howard and Arundel, in their efforts to overthrow Elizabeth, have shown themselves impotent and incompetent at the game, screwing themselves up to frantic activity from the word go, and achieving no consummation at all: in this respect all *festina* and no *lente*, a cannon-ball that has failed to connect.[57] I should also think that part of the moral topography of the scene is that Castelnau and his household, having been seduced from the 'right way' by Howard and Throckmorton, and covered themselves with mud in consequence, will now have to get back to Leicester and the Protestant cause, unattractive as Castelnau may find them; but that is an additional speculation which we do not need. I think we have got far enough in the understanding of Bruno's first two dialogues to realise that, besides their principal

---

57   Edgar Wind, ' "Ripeness is all" ', in *Pagan Mysteries in the Renaissance* (London, 1958), pp. 89–99, and especially 90 ff; the last quotation, from Walter Pater, is borrowed from Wind, p. 99. Probably the sources nearest at hand which may have reminded Bruno of this Renaissance commonplace were Paolo Giovio's *Imprese* (cf. below, n. 84, where the reference is to Samuel Daniel's English version; *DI*, p. 56, n. 2) and Plutarch's *De Iside et Osiride* (cited by Bruno in *Cabala*, p. 867), for the *puer senex*. He cannot have read *Love's Labour's Lost*, iii, 1, but as Wind points out it is extremely germane; so is Francis Bacon, *Essays*, xxi, 'Of Delay'. The original text of the *Cena* is: '[La barca] parea col suo *festina lente* tutta di piombo, e le braccia di que' dua vecchi rotte; i quali, benche col rimenar de la persona mostrassero la misura lunga, nulla di meno coi remi faceano i passi corti.
   Prudenzio Optime descriptum illud 'festina' con il dorso frettoloso di marinai; *'lente'* col profitto de' remi, qual mali operarii del dio de gli orti (Priapus).' *DI*, p. 56; translated in *Texts*, no. 12i. I presume a colon after *'illud'* was intended.

matter of expounding Bruno's version of Copernican truths to the English. they are also, secondarily but not marginally, instruments of the vendetta against English Catholicism which, in the guise of Fagot, he had been pursuing for the past year.

Howard probably acquired both the *Cena* and the *Causa*,[58] but whether he recognised himself in Bruno's malcontent, political duffer and sacrilegious pedant I cannot say. So far as I know he had no reason to expect an attack from Bruno, since so far as I know he had not knowingly done him any harm. He cannot have had Bruno in mind when excoriating those who 'rifled in the mysteries of Egypt': when he wrote the *Defensative* he can scarcely have known Bruno, and that side of Bruno's speculations was not really made public until the appearance of the *Spaccio*.[59] He had very possibly helped to get Bruno's works into print. Something we do not know about may of course have happened between them, on any of a number of issues; perhaps the most likely would be a dispute on 'sacramentary points', though Bruno would have had to be careful there. There is no reason to suppose that Howard knew that Bruno had betrayed him to the Council. But he was generally on the lookout for enemies, and would have been rather obtuse not to detect something of himself in the decrepit boatman or the misogynist connoisseur of sacred music. Perhaps his book on female government was his reply to Bruno, though it may not have been written until five years later.[60] In the meantime, locked up, a treason trial hanging over his head, he was in no position to bite back. He now disappears from our story as finally as the unfortunate Throckmorton.

It is open to anyone to retort that, for all the evidence in its favour, my seeing in Bruno's first two dialogues a continuation of Fagot's campaign against Howard is either too hypothetical, or misconceived in principle, or both. Time will tell. I shall try not to put more weight upon it than it can bear. Meanwhile I record one last trace of Fagot in Bruno's writings of 1584, which I defy the sternest critic to dispute. It comes from part iii of the second dialogue of the *Spaccio*

58 Rita Sturlese, *Bibliografia, censimento, e storia delle antiche stampe di Giordano Bruno* (*Quaderni del Rinascimento*, no. 5; Florence, 1987), nos. 7.17, 8.17. I conclude this from the fact that the Arundel House library, which was given to the Royal Society by Henry Howard, 6th Duke of Norfolk (d. 1684), contained copies of the two works.

59 I say this in spite of Frances Yates's detection of Egyptianism in *De umbris idearum* (Paris, 1582; Yates, *Bruno*, pp. 192–9), which Bruno had brought with him to England, and of which he may well have passed a copy on to Howard. Her argument depends mainly on what is surely a grave mistranslation of a passage in the book (ibid. p. 194 n. 1). It seems true that in Alexander Dickson's version, *De umbra rationis*, the Egyptian source of Bruno's art of memory is emphasised (ibid. p. 199, and n. 4); but that was not published until after the end of 1583. Above, pp. 47–8; Yates, *Art of Memory*, p. 260.

60 Above, n. 46; *DNB* dates it to 1589.

della bestia trionfante, and therefore dates from something like October or early November. Since the middle of dialogue i the repentant Gods, under Jove's presidency, have been reforming the heavens by getting rid of the dubious symbols of the constellations and replacing them by images of genuine virtues, of which the first is truth. They have got as far as Cassiopeia, a W-shaped symbol of pride, arrogance and military values which is to be sent back to Spain and replaced by simplicity. The opposites of simplicity, which are boastfulness and dissimulation, are therefore and thereby to be banned from heaven. There is no difficulty about banning boastfulness, but there is a difficulty about dissimulation, which as the argument says 'can *per accidens* be accepted as a virtue'.[61]

> Simplicity is a servant of Truth, and ought not for long to leave the side of her lady. [Cassiopeia had indeed stuck close to Polaris, which is now renamed Truth.] But sometimes the goddess Necessity obliges her to wander in the direction of Dissimulation, so that Simplicity or Truth shall not be trampled underfoot, or to avoid some other evil ['inconveniente']. If she deceives with moderation and system ['non senza modo et ordine'] she will also be able to deceive without error or wrong.

So, unlike boastfulness, dissimulation cannot be wholly excluded from among the virtues. 'The Gods themselves employ her from time to time; for sometimes, to protect her from Envy, Reproach and Outrage, Prudence [formerly the serpent Draco] conceals Truth inside the clothing ['vestimenti'] of Dissimulation.' Bruno, as he tended to do at such moments, here quotes Ariosto (*Orlando furioso*, iv, 1) on the 'evident benefits' of dissimulation, since we are not always among friends. Simplicity is like the face of God, and boastfulness is its exact opposite. 'This is not quite the case with honest Dissimulation ['la studiosa Dissimulatione'], whom Jove permits sometimes to present herself in heaven, not, it is true, as a goddess, but as a handmaiden of Prudence and a shield[-bearer] of Truth.' If studious dissimulation has a habit of looking insecure, it is not because she is worried about the wrath of the gods, but because she is afraid of being found out: 'since she may in the end be revealed as something different from what she purported to be, she may very easily end up being detested by him who first welcomed her'.

Well, now we know what Bruno was talking about. This is his own, self-justifying, confession, or perhaps a sort of apology to Castelnau. As with St Paul, boasting was not expedient, and Bruno

---

61 *Spaccio*, pp. 564, 705–8; on p. 708 Gentile gives the wrong reference to *Orlando furioso*, which should be as in the text below. Ciliberto, *Giordano Bruno*, pp. 5, 142, 253, 268–76 also draws attention to the autobiographical importance of this passage.

was not doing any, but a prudent commendation of honest deceit was in order. The line he now took about his conduct towards Castelnau, Throckmorton, Zubiaur and others was the line he was to take with Châteauneuf and the Venetian and Roman inquisitors. He was not found out, certainly not by Castelnau, who must be the figure conjured up in the awkward last sentence.

He will have stopped worrying about Castelnau soon afterwards, while they were setting up together an interesting occasion which, from a public point of view, must have been the climax of Bruno's career in England. It would be nice to know more than we do about the presentation to Elizabeth of an elegant volume, bound in black Morocco and bearing the arms of England, which contained the *Cena, De la causa, De l'infinito* and the *Spaccio*.[62] The existence of the volume in Elizabeth's possession, and the survival of the separate items in it, testify to the event, but we cannot tell exactly how or when it happened. The likeliest time would have been as soon as the *Spaccio* was ready, and that, since I think the manuscript had been finished about the middle of November or so, will have been some time during the Christmas season. It would have made a most appropriate Christmas present. Some time later would be possible: even if Bruno had already written the next dialogue, the *Cabala*, I doubt if he would have had the cheek to offer it to the queen. But he was in France for much of the time between New Year and Easter, and if he had begun the *Eroici furori*, which would have been most suitable, I think he would have waited until it was finished, and added it to the collection.[63]

The reasons why Bruno wanted to make the presentation are plain enough: gratitude and admiration; putting his remarkable body of writing into the public eye; reminding Elizabeth of his existence after his months in purdah; I would not exclude some hope of preferment in the Church of England or otherwise. I think he would have dedicated the *Spaccio* to her, not to Sidney, if he had not had obligations to Henri III or if Elizabeth had indicated that it would be acceptable. He will, I am quite sure, have wanted to draw her attention, not only to his literary and intellectual achievement and to his public commendation of herself and her government, but also, discreetly, to his clandestine operations on their behalf. It was the leaving present (premature, as it turned out) of a man who had a year and a half of distinguished services behind him, and wanted them to be remembered.

62 Sturlese, *Bibliografia*, pp. xxiv–xxv, and nos. 7.39, 8.20, 9.19 and 10.29. She describes the collection as 'leggendaria', I do not know why.
63 Above, pp. 51, 52 f, 57 f.

But we have to consider Castelnau's motives as well as Bruno's. Bruno did not go to court on his own, but as a gentleman-servant of the ambassador.[64] It would have been up to Castelnau to decide whether the presentation should take place, to choose what would be, from his point of view rather than Bruno's, the most appropriate time for it, and to bring the author forward with his present in his hand. It would also have been up to Castelnau to pay for the grand and expensive binding. It is a pity that his correspondence between November and February is missing; I doubt if he would have broken his rule of not mentioning Bruno, but we should know what occasions were most likely, and what else would have been happening at them.[65] Nevertheless, we can be sure that a presentation to Elizabeth of Bruno's dialogues at Christmas/New Year 1584–5, or possibly the following Easter, would have suited Castelnau extremely well. In the *Spaccio* Bruno had come relatively clean as a supporter of Protestant politics who was also a harsh critic of Protestant theology: in spite of the theology, which went down worse with Puritan clerics than with their aristocratic patrons, he was Castelnau's best evidence for presenting himself as a sympathiser with the Protestant cause. This, at that time, he rather needed to do.

During the autumn Castelnau had patched up his relations with the queen and the Council, and a good deal of amiable socialising had been going on, most of it under the patronage of the Earl of Leicester. In the middle of November, practically the anniversary of Throckmorton's arrest, he had a convivial dinner with Elizabeth, Leicester and other councillors (and perhaps with Bruno as well?). Castelnau was allowed to repudiate any connection with Jesuits and Catholic conspirators, and any unsupervised dealings with Queen Mary; they made noises about a common front against the Spaniards in which Henri III would bestir himself to do something about the Netherlands and England would launch a grand offensive enterprise on the high seas.[66] Neither party was being very candid, but Castelnau's position was weak. He was being restored to the queen's favour at the price of some public identification with the anti-popish, or at least the anti-Spanish, crusade. The pressure was hard to resist because of the skeletons in his cupboard, because he had fallen out with the Duke of Guise at home, and because the circulation through

---

64   *Documenti*, pp. 121 f; Yates, *Bruno*, p. 288: 'continually going to court with the ambassador'.

65   None of Castelnau's letters home survives between 15/25-xi-1584 (Chéruel, pp. 350 ff) and 15/25-iii-1585 (BN ff 4736, f. 270). There are letters to Walsingham of 24-xi/4-xii-1584 and 30-xii-1584/9-i-1585 (*CSP Foreign, 1584–85*, pp. 166, 208).

66   Above, p. 50; Castelnau to Henri III, 15/25-xi-1584; to Walsingham, 24-xi/4-xii-1584 (above, n. 65). I think the date (about 13 November) is too early for the presentation, likewise Accession Day, four days later.

the embassy of *Leicester's Commonwealth* gave Leicester a handle against him.[67] In these circumstances a public presentation to the queen of Bruno's works would have amounted, on Castelnau's part, to a denunciation of Malcontents, an expression of loyalty to Elizabeth, a friendly gesture towards Leicester, and a suitably obscure commendation of energetic action against the Beast. The dedication of the *Spaccio* to Sidney would imply all this, and would also dissociate Castelnau from a rebuff which Henri III had recently administered to Sidney as a negotiator for the Protestant cause;[68] Bruno's demolition of Protestant theology, he might hope, would sufficiently safeguard his Catholic rear. It would have helped if Bruno had had a copy of the revised version of the *Cena* to present; but, since what was presented was the original, it must either be that he had not got one or that the 'Protestant' character of the second version has been exaggerated.[69]

Bruno would have been happy with this, though happier if Castelnau had meant it. But he had his own fish to fry, and Castelnau, though no doubt *au fait* with the concealed messages of the polemic against Polihimnio in *De la causa* and possibly of the mud scene in the *Cena*, will not have been aware that he was presenting Elizabeth with a bill for services rendered against himself. It will surely have given Bruno a great deal of satisfaction to have so dexterously conveyed the truth inside the vestments of dissimulation.[70]

iii Paris

It would be enlarging my story beyond its natural compass to attempt to record Bruno's last period in Paris as closely as his years in London. Nevertheless we have two documents to do justice to; we have also to consider that it is from this time that we have the only surviving official reference, if one may call it so, to Bruno's career as

67 The trouble with Guise was about Castelnau's governorship of St Dizier, a town and fortress on the borders of Lorraine which Guise had had transferred to a more reliable supporter: Henri de Lorraine to Castelnau, 24-xi/4-xii and 13/23-xii-1584 (BN V^{c}C 470, pp. 3, 15). Leicester only began to complain about *Leicester's Commonwealth*, so far as the existing correspondence goes, in April (Castelnau to Henri III, 16/26-iv-1585: BN ff 4736, f. 293), but the problem had been in the air for some before that (cf. *Texts*, no. 13).

68 Below, pp. 151-2.

69 Above, pp. 45-6; below, pp. 168-70. There is no suggestion that Elizabeth's copy of the *Cena* (Sturlese, *Bibliografia*, no. 7.39) was not of what Aquilecchia calls the 'vulgata'. Otherwise one might well have supposed that the *Cena* had been rewritten for this occasion, and Aquilecchia's and Ciliberto's argument for the political implications of the revision would be vindicated.

70 Above, p. 126. There was another concealed message in the text of the *Spaccio*: see below, p. 152.

an English secret agent. The reader is entitled to an economical narrative of the decline of this career, which will naturally be a political narrative. Partly because the political chaos of this and the following years in France did not favour the survival of documents, and partly because of the clandestinity of Bruno's operations, this period of his life is one where mirages of idle conjecture seem more insistent than usual. I shall do my best to distinguish them from authentic knowledge.

The relevant things we know to start with are that Bruno spent much of his time in Paris among a group of Italians, more or less intellectual, which revolved around Piero Delbene; that this group had a political dimension, since Delbene was working for the King of Navarre and Corbinelli for the councillor Bellièvre, and operated in the field of political intelligence; that Bruno entered this field on behalf of the English ambassador, Sir Edward Stafford, and worked in it between at least March and May 1586, to the detriment of his previous relationship with Walsingham; that at the same time he made an effort to regularise his ecclesiastical situation in respect of Rome; and that he left Paris for Germany in June, and came back briefly in October and November, when he did, for Stafford's benefit and in conjunction with Delbene, his last piece of undercover work.[71]

The clue to a good deal of this is Bruno's former relation with Castelnau, whose service he left almost as soon as he got to Paris at the end of October 1585. It is easy to believe, as Bruno said, that Castelnau was sorry to see him go, but I doubt if he could afford him any longer, and Bruno was probably keen to look elsewhere. My guess is that he did what he could to provide for Bruno's future, as he had done for Florio's; when somebody identifies the grand almoner of the Duke of Guise, who got Bruno his place in the household of the Duke of Montpensier, we shall have a better idea. Bruno said he was an Italian, and I have wondered about the Gondis: even, though he was a layman, about Jérôme Gondi the *conducteur des ambassadeurs*, who had a reputation for being pro-Spanish and pro-Guise but was also a long-standing friend of Castelnau and a cousin, friend and business associate of Madame Delbene.[72] Since Bruno's account of his new appointment was given to Walsingham, he would have concealed any part in it which may have been played by Stafford.

71   Yates, *Bruno*, pp. 291–305; above, pp. 62–71, 83–97.
72   *Texts*, no. 16; Gondi to Castelnau, 14/24-vii-1584 (*CSP Foreign 1583–84*, p. 614); *DBI*, Cavalcanti, Lucrezia. Gondi's politics: P. Champion, *Charles IX: la France et le contrôle de l'Espagne* (2 vols; Paris, 1939), ii, 46, 58. Corbinelli mentions an 'Abate Gondi' as a neighbour and friend in 1581 (BA T 167 sup, f. 82). An idea of the position of an *aumônier* in a French noble clientele can be got from Mack P. Holt, 'The Household of François, Duke of Anjou', *French Historical Studies*, xiii (1984), 305–22.

Meanwhile Castelnau's career was sinking. From the moment he had left England a stream of hostile reports about the conduct of his embassy had been arriving from Châteauneuf in London: we do not know exactly what was in them, but their general drift is not hard to imagine, and Bruno must have figured somewhere in the catalogue of Castelnau's misdeeds.[73] In the prevailing climate of Catholic paranoia or triumphalism, which Bruno continued to provoke by feuding with the Sorbonne, this was very bad news. I have little doubt that, when he returned to Paris, he hoped and expected that his friendship with the king would earn him a secure and comfortable situation in France. This proved slow to materialise: before the end of December Henri III had declined to permit any new work of Bruno's to be printed by royal command; and it must have been in an attempt both to placate Catholic hostility and to recapture royal favour that Bruno now launched his scheme to negotiate a deal with Rome.[74] There was no chance whatever of his finding a niche in the Catholic France of 1586 until the incubus of his apostasy from his order was lifted.

Presumably his position with the Duke of Montpensier, though it would not have paid anything to speak of, gave him some kind of a breathing-space; he settled down in his lodgings on the *rive gauche* and got to work in the library of St Victor. There is no evidence of a connection with Delbene for a while yet, though I imagine that the friendship had begun earlier.[75] By February, in any case, Bruno was sufficiently in with Delbene and his friends to have something to do with the conveyance of their valuable Roman intelligence to Stafford. Bruno, as we know, had made contact with Stafford earlier in 1585, when he had passed him his news about Girault and the traffic in *Leicester's Commonwealth*, and possibly assisted him in the arrest of Thomas Morgan. I am sure he did not leave renewing the acquaintance very long after his return to Paris, and it would be a likely conjecture that he saw him on 9 November, when Castelnau called on Stafford and told him a tale about a plot brewing in France

---

73 The letters were actually written by Châteauneuf's wife, Marie de la Châtre, to her sister, who was in the service of Anne d'Este, mother of the Duke of Guise. The story can be followed from: Castelnau to Florio, London, [3/13]-ix-1585 (Yates, *Florio*, p. 69); to Douglas, Paris, 24-x/3-xi-1585 (HMC *Hatfield*, iii, 112); Châteauneuf to Castelnau, 25-x/4-xi-1585 (BN V^cC 472, p. 327); Morgan to Mary, 18/28-i-1586 (Murdin, p. 478); Stafford to Walsingham, 11/21-ix-1586 (CSP *Foreign 1586–88*, p. 86) – Stafford gets the news from the recipient's daughter, who is madly in love with his friend Simier; Jean Ribot, Castelnau's secretary, to Walsingham, Blois, 5/15-i-1589 (CSP *Foreign Jan.–July 1589*, p. 17).

74 *Texts*, no. 16: '. . . si Dieu me faict la grace de jamais [*sic*] estre en France . . .'; Cotin, in *Documenti*, p. 43.

75 The evidence begins in February, with Bruno's imbroglio over the mathematician Mordente: *Documenti*, p. 43; Yates, 'New Documents', pp. 178–81.

against Elizabeth: this was barely a week after his and Bruno's arrival in Paris, and he may still have had Bruno with him.[76] Without Castelnau as chaperon, Bruno would have had to be careful about haunting the ambassador's house, but contact was shortly made easier by the timely appearance at the Quai de la Tournelle of the young poet Samuel Daniel. Daniel, one of Bruno's Oxford admirers and now Florio's brother-in-law, arrived in Paris after Christmas and spent the next six months in Stafford's house, learning the business and finding out what was new on the literary scene.[77] There is no actual evidence that Daniel and Bruno were together at this time, but I think we can take it for granted: Daniel visited Castelnau, to whom he had come with a letter of introduction, and I imagine that Bruno introduced him to the Corbinelli circle. Bruno now had a good excuse to visit Stafford, and the signs of his intelligence work accumulate. Little as was in it, the surviving letter to Walsingham seems to date from January or February, and it will have been sent by Stafford; somewhere about the end of February Stafford got access to Corbinelli's Roman correspondence. After this there will have been whatever jobs, if any, fell to Bruno in Stafford's and Delbene's great scheme for bouncing the Duke of Montpensier into joining the Protestants.[78]

Perhaps we ought not to dwell too much on these un-Catholic connections, since for the time being Bruno's most urgent business was with the other side. The tale of his retainer by Montpensier shows that, in spite of the bad odours coming from Châteauneuf in London, he still had friends among mainstream Catholics and Leaguers: Montpensier's connection with Guise and his sister, and his own with the duke's grand almoner, whoever he was, sound very useful in this respect. The one pupil whom we know him to have acquired at this time, Jean Hennequin who defended his anti-Aristotelian theses at the Collège de Cambrai in May, came from a family rabidly dedicated to the cause of the League; and it seems as if Bruno had some communication with an intellectual eminence of an extremely Catholic kind, Giovanni Botero. Botero was given a part in one of the dialogues about the compass-inventor Mordente; when Mordente decided that Bruno was stealing his intellectual property he complained about it to Guise, which suggests to me that he thought Guise was an authority to whom Bruno would defer.[79]

76   Above, pp. 54–6; *CSP Foreign 1585–86*, p. 124.
77   Joan Rees, *Samuel Daniel* (Liverpool, 1964), pp. 5–8; Edward Dymoke (Daniel's patron) to Castelnau, London, 22-xi/2-xii-1585 (BN V^{c}C 472, p. 175).
78   *Texts*, no. 16, introduction; above, p. 65.
79   Yates, *Bruno*, pp. 298–9; É. Barnavi, *Le Parti de Dieu* (Brussels/Louvain, 1980), p. 81; Holt, 'The Household of François, Duke of Anjou', pp. 321 f (Hennequin). Bruno's *Due dialoghi sconosciuti e due dialoghi noti*, ed. G. Aquilecchia (Rome, 1957), p. xxi; *DBI*, xiii, Botero, Giovanni. Yates, 'New Documents', p. 185: the original (BA T 167 sup, f. 187)

Most of this is speculation ; but it is hard knowledge, established by his letters to Walsingham and, later, to Stafford, that Bruno was still cultivating English Catholic *émigrés*. This means, without any question, that when he needed to do so Bruno was passing himself off as a zealous Catholic: in 1586 such contacts were the badge of a passionate Leaguer.[80]

With some such reputation Bruno must have approached Mendoza, who was after all the representative of his sovereign Philip II, to help him in his difficulties with Rome. Mendoza does not appear to mention this, and we have to take Bruno's word for it, as given to the inquisitors in Venice; but I see no reason to doubt it, and Bruno's letter to Walsingham makes it more plausible, since it shows that at the time he wrote it he was in touch with a man working for Mendoza, an Antwerper called Alexander who was living in Bruno's house. If Bruno's account is to be believed, he had the cheek, when he met Mendoza, to appeal to their old acquaintanceship in London; Châteauneuf's campaign, if not his own experience or that of Zubiaur, must have inclined Mendoza to smell a rat, but either Bruno's cover was good enough, or his professions of repentance convincing enough, to persuade Mendoza not to turn him away.[81] Mendoza undoubtedly knew, as we know, that Bruno had acted as a priest in England, which would present a sizeable problem with Rome; but he does not himself seem to have thought it much of a difficulty. My hunch is that Bruno persuaded Mendoza to take him seriously by appearing to give him some substantial piece of confidential information, and I would hazard a guess at what it may have been. He may have told him that Jean Arnault, who had once been Castelnau's secretary in London and was now Châteauneuf's, had been recruited by Walsingham. We may suppose that Bruno saw Mendoza some time in March: carried by Charles Arundell, an object of Fagot's interest who now worked both for Mendoza and for Stafford, the information reached the queen mother before 21 March, and Arnault was instantly recalled from London, much to the detriment of Châteauneuf's and Queen Mary's affairs.[82] If Bruno,

says that Mordente 'andò con Guisa', not 'al Guisa', but it makes no difference.

80 Cf. Louis Dorléans's *Advertissement des catholiques anglois*, a powerful piece of Leaguer polemic which came out in July and was reported by Corbinelli in the letter cited in the previous note (25-vii/4-viii-1586).

81 *Documenti*, pp. 104, 133; *Texts*, no. 16. There is nothing about this in De Lamar Jensen's book on Mendoza's embassy, *Diplomacy and Dogmatism: Bernardino de Mendoza and the French Catholic League* (Cambridge, Mass., 1964).

82 James Beaton, Archbishop of Glasgow, to Queen Mary, Paris, 11/21-iii-1586; Mary to Beaton, 2/12 and 7/17-vii-1586 (*CSP Scotland 1585–86*, pp. 255 f, 518, 552; Labanoff, *Lettres de Marie Stuart*, vi, 367, 412); Hicks, *An Elizabethan Problem*, pp. 182–4. For Arundell, above, pp. 33, 54, and Conyers Read, 'The Fame of Sir Edward Stafford', *American Historical Review*, xx (1915), 292–313: Arundell working for both Stafford and Mendoza.

on his own behalf or on Stafford's or Walsingham's, did pull this off, it was one of his more brilliant coups, and killed any number of birds with one stone: the beauty and economy would suggest Walsingham, the undertone of black farce Bruno. But this is simply a hunch.

In any event Mendoza gave him a recommendation to the nuncio Ragazzoni, and by Bruno's account he besought the nuncio to write to Rome on his behalf, asking that his excommunication be lifted and that he be excused from returning to his order. The nuncio refused to do this unless he resumed his habit in the meantime, and passed him on to a Jesuit who said he could not hear his confession otherwise. Ragazzoni recorded none of this, but it sounds as if it happened. Bruno saw that he had now no chance of a secure position in France, and decided to seek his fortune in Germany.

One might think that he would have been better advised to make his approach to Rome not via Mendoza but via Henri III, but I have the impression that what was coming from this quarter was a meaningful silence, to be explained by whatever disagreeable news Châteauneuf had managed to find in London. It is at any rate a fact that, at just about the moment that Bruno left Paris for Germany, the king was earnestly appealing to Ragazzoni, and in person, on behalf of another renegade Dominican whose case was markedly similar to Bruno's. His name was Alfonso Palleologo; he had escaped from the Roman Inquisition some twenty-five years before, and he now wanted to do penance and be reconciled but not to return to Italy or to his order.[83] I expect this was just a coincidence; if not, one might float the speculation that the friar Palleologo was the friar Bruno in disguise. It is a seductive hypothesis: we have got used to Bruno as 'a man of infinite titles';[84] the name has quite a Brunian ring to it; and there was yet another renegade Italian Dominican called Paleologo who had had a career even closer to Bruno's: after twenty years as a preacher of unitarianism in eastern Europe he had been handed over by the Emperor Rudolf II and executed in Rome the year before.[85] On that reading the Palleologo story would be a notable piece of gallows humour cooked up between Bruno and Henri III himself. As with the Arnault story, there must be some sadness at turning this one down; but without supporting evidence that is what we must do. We are sent back to the conclusion that what Henri III did for

83   Blet, *Ragazzoni*, pp. 594 f (13/23–vi–1586); reply, p. 604.
84   Prefatory epistle of N.W. to Samuel Daniel, *The Worthy Tract of Paulus Jovius* (1585), in *The Complete Works . . . of Samuel Daniel*, ed. A.B. Grosart (5 vols; London, 1896; repr, New York, 1963), iv, 7.
85   Pastor, *History*, xvi, 319; xix, 302 f; xx, 268; Ivan Cloulas, 'Les Rapports de Jérôme Ragazzoni . . . avec les ecclésiastiques pendant sa nonciature en France', *Mélanges . . ./de l'/Ecole française de Rome*, lxxii (1960), 541 and n. 3; R.J.W. Evans, *Rudolf II and his World* (Oxford 1973), for the Habsburg side.

Palleologo, whoever he was, he did not do for Bruno; I think the conclusion must be right.

As his situation deteriorated on various fronts, I assume that Stafford became Bruno's main support. Although no correspondence between the two ambassadors survives, Stafford was certainly in regular touch with Pallavicino, who apart from Burghley was his closest friend and ally on the English political scene. Pallavicino had arrived in Frankfurt, to begin his negotiations for a Protestant army to go to the aid of Navarre, at the end of March; he was to leave for a trip to the Elector of Saxony at the beginning of June. He apparently had with him Bruno's friend Alberico Gentili.[86] I presume that, some time in April or May, he intimated to Stafford that he could probably do something for Bruno in Germany. It sounds as if Bruno had decided to go before the débâcle of the disputation at the Collège de Cambrai on 28–29 May, and that he had gone by the middle of June.[87] By the time Henri III was talking to the nuncio about Palleologo, I should think that Bruno was already safe in Frankfurt, free from any anxiety he may have felt that the king might turn him in, as the Emperor Rudolf had turned in the other Paleologo four years before.

There is no reason to doubt that Bruno enjoyed being in Wittenberg as much as he said he did: probably for the first time in his life, he could say more or less exactly what he wanted, especially about the pope.[88] He could also observe, particularly if he had spent some time with Pallavicino on the way, that Germany was full of professional soldiers available to be hired for an expedition against Rome. That his mind was turning in this direction is the most obvious conclusion from his authorship of No. 17. Apart from that, we cannot expect to learn much more about his doings and feelings in the autumn of 1586 than that document and Stafford's comments upon it have already told us: it is the only light we have on his final trip to Paris and our only reason for supposing that he made it. We can think of him as remembering with pleasure the work he had done for Stafford during that complicated springtime; and as taking up his career in dissimulation again, keenly but rather rustily, for the last time until 1591. We can be certain that he spent much of his visit with Delbene, though probably not with his other companions of the spring. One might hazard a guess that he stayed at Madame Delbene's, and

---

86 Above, p. 63 n. 89; Stone, *Palavicino*, pp. 26, 239 f.
87 *Camoeracensis acrotismus*, the published version of the disputation: *OL* i¹, p. 57.
88 Yates, *Bruno*, pp. 306–13; *Oratio valedictoria* (Wittenberg, 8/18–iii–1588): *OL* i¹, pp. 1–25.

picked up some of his papers there, from which he got such mileage as he could. Since he bothered to change his writing, and his reappearance was not mentioned by Corbinelli or observed by anyone else, it sounds as if he did not want his presence known. This is more than likely. His departure for Germany was no secret, and somebody must have known that he had gone to Wittenberg. The prospect of a hue and cry, raised by Frangipani and the Sorbonne and followed by a Paris mob whose manners were a good deal more violent than those of Londoners, must have daunted even him.

We cannot really know why he came back. My conjectures would be that he had left some manuscripts behind, had business with printers or booksellers, and was looking for a golden handshake from Stafford. In the nature of our evidence, the last suggestion is the only one we can at all sustain. To get something from Stafford, he would have had to put his head out far enough to come up with some genuine intelligence, and this he did. I doubt if he did much legwork for the news about Morgan, and we may as well accept what he said, that he had got it from an 'honest man' who had been charitably visiting Morgan in the Bastille. I do not think it all came from Delbene, but I assume that the two of them, perhaps with a little help from Masino, thought up between themselves the notion of springing Morgan from his prison which Bruno put to Stafford, concealed beneath a pile of five-month-old intelligence and Hispano-Italian garbage.[89]

As I have said, I think we ought to take the idea fairly seriously: we can envisage Bruno as hoping to repeat his amazing coup with Courcelles, and end his career as a secret agent on as high a note as he had started it. This time he did not pull it off, though I hope he got his money. Stafford, like Elizabeth, was right to think that Bruno was on to something. But he was also right to think that Walsingham would stand in the way: he had probably lost confidence in Bruno, and thanks to the renegade seminarist Gilbert Gifford he knew already almost as much about Morgan as Morgan could have told him in person.[90] Mary's execution was in the bag, and followed three months later. It was unquestionably what Bruno had wanted. He could be well satisfied to have done his bit towards it, and towards the defeat of papal aggression against the kingdom of Queen Elizabeth; he could leave the rest to the professionals. I doubt if he stayed for Walsingham's veto, or that he was terribly concerned. Though it had given him the best time in his life, and he would

89   Above, pp. 66, 85–7, 95–7.
90   As Henri III told Elizabeth when declining to extradite him: 'd'aultant que quant elle auroit ces deux hommes (Morgan and Charles Paget) elle ne scauroit plus gueres dadvantaige que ce qu'elle scait': to Bellièvre, 13/23-xi-1586 (BN ff 15908, f. 342).

sometimes dream of going back to the rising and falling Thames, England was now behind him. Florio had been born an Englishman, and Pallavicino would die one; but never Bruno. In front of him now, beyond the *Rifei*, the German mountains, was Italy. When he laid down his pen as an intelligencer, what was in his thoughts was not the humiliation and death of the Queen of Scots, Drake in the Indies, or the arsenal of Antwerp in flames. He saw a German army marching, like Charles V's, southward over the Alps to shatter the smug papists, receive the flowers of the persecuted and water its horses in the fountains of Rome: in Bruno's own French, 'd'assaillir ceux qui n'y pensent point, de gaigner ceux qui sont tyrannisez, gehennez et en leur biens et leur consciences'.[91]

91 *Texts*, no. 17; for the Rifei, *Spaccio*, p. 713.

3

BRUNO RECAPTURED

i Man

IT IS TIME to assemble what we have learnt about Bruno from unravelling some threads in three and a half years of his life. I must start by reminding myself and my reader that this is not a matter to be undertaken lightly. Giordano Bruno was one of the most creative minds of the sixteenth century, and possibly in the history of European thought and imagination. His reputation as a philosopher in the conventional sense has been variable, though high in some quarters, and he was certainly an acute and learned arguer. If by 'scientist' we mean a systematic observer or experimenter, he was not a scientist even by sixteenth-century standards, and he got very short shrift from one who was, the astronomer Tycho Brahe;[1] but he was an imaginative exponent of some fundamental ideas which we should now call scientific, like the infinitude and multitudinousness of the material world, the relativity of motion, and the movement of the earth round the sun in the solar system. He did not invent the concept of the universe, but he put it into general circulation. He was a considerable author in Italian prose, and sometimes in Italian verse, and has at least one literary masterpiece, the *Cena de le Ceneri*, to his credit. He was various other things too, some of which we have been observing; and he was burned alive as a relapsed heretic in Rome in February 1600. For Italians whose allegiance is to the *Risorgimento* he has been since 1860 a sort of national saint: something like Joan of Arc in France, or a combination of Shakespeare, Newton and Cranmer in England. Over his nearest rival, Galileo, he has the pull of martyrdom. His Latin works were collected and published at the expense of the nation at the end of the nineteenth century, and events in his posthumous history, like the unveiling of his statue in the

---

1 M.R. Pagnoni Sturlese, 'Su Bruno e Tycho Brahe', *Rinascimento*[2], xxx (1985), 310 f: 'Nolanus nullanus'.

Campo dei Fiori in 1889, or the publication of Angelo Mercati's edition of the *Sommario* of his trial in 1942, have precipitated moments of public drama and passion of an intensity which the English may find it hard to conceive.[2] We must therefore do our best to get him right.

We now know a good deal about Bruno that we did not know before. Indeed we now have a kind of knowledge of him which we did not have before at all. Up to now, what we have known of him as a person has come almost exclusively from two sources: his published writings; and the surviving record of his inquisitorial investigation in Venice and Rome, which began five and a half years after he finally left Paris for Germany. These sources are rich and revealing up to a point, but they have difficulties which students of Bruno have not always appreciated as they might have done. Everything Bruno wrote about himself, and almost everything autobiographical he is recorded as having said must, I am quite sure, be regarded as fiction: both his published writings and his appearances before the inquisitors were the public, theatrical performances of a fictional person. Bruno was a genius of imaginative *invenzione*: what he said of his narrative of the journey with Florio from Salisbury Court to Whitehall – that its truth was not historical but tropological – may be equally said of the entire autobiographical burden both of his writings and of his statements in Venice and Rome. Neither of them is an uncontaminated source of biographical information, though the latter, perforce, recorded a certain number of innocuous facts which were correct. The statements of the witnesses against him were, on the other hand, largely the unvarnished truth, as I think all historians of Bruno now agree, and they are our best source of knowledge about Bruno as a social person.[3] Much of their testimony has the perspicuity of a photograph or a tape-recorder. But they recorded only such things as might be of interest of

2   My two sources here are M.L. Barbera, 'La Brunomania', *Giornale critico della filosofia italiana*, lix (1980), 103–40; and Luigi Firpo, 'Il processo di Giordano Bruno', *Rivista storica italiana*, lx (1948), 542–97; lxi (1949), 1–59. This was reprinted as a book (Naples, 1949), but I use the original version, cited as 'Firpo, "Processo" (i)' and '(ii)'. See ibid. (ii), 50–9, for the polemics of the 1940s resulting from Mercati's edition of the *Sommario*. I am grateful for the knowledge of Barbera's essay to Simon Ditchfield, whose unpublished essay, 'Brunomania in Italy, 1886–1890' (Warburg Institute, 1986) has also been extremely helpful.

    On Bruno as a great writer, the judgment of the poet Giosuè Carducci needs to be recorded: '. . . ma che Giordano Bruno sia scrittore grande e commediografo almeno tollerabile, no, no e poi no.' I quote it from Barbera, p. 133, n. 230; it seems harsh, except for the comedy.

3   Cf. Firpo, 'Processo' (i), 552, on the principal witness, Giovanni Mocenigo.

inquisitors; and although the intention behind what they said he said or did was usually obvious, none of them really knew him well enough to be quite sure what was going on in his mind. He appears, on some kind of principle, to have written no private letters whatever, and precious few public ones. What I can offer now, in the documents printed at the end of this book, is the nearest substitute for these that we can expect. They represent, under the alias Fagot, Bruno himself: ultra-private (admittedly on public matters), usually unliterary, plain; Bruno in real life, Bruno from inside, Bruno doing a job. Except in obvious instances, questions of rhetoric or discourse simply do not arise. We have not had such a Bruno before.

The range of what we have found out about Bruno is certainly limited. We have found out what he did and said from his vantage point in Salisbury Court about the Catholic mission in Elizabethan England and connected matters. This sheds no light on what he thought about the infinite universe, the Copernican system, or the transmigration of souls. Since none of our additions to the canon of Bruno's writings was written in his native language, they will probably not do much for his reputation as a writer, though the confession letter must have some kind of a place in his *oeuvre* as a writer of fiction. They do not tell us whether he was a proto-Einstein or a Hermetic magician, an animist or an atomist, or whether he believed in a transcendental God. In so far as these things are what really matters about Bruno, this book will leave them very much as they now stand, in the care of his formal writings and the record of his *processo*. But everyone will agree that Bruno's writings cannot fruitfully be separated from Bruno as a person, and here there has hitherto been a gaping hole. We can now do something to fill it up, excluding some conjectures, verifying others, and adding some contributions of our own.

I doubt if anyone will hereafter be persuaded to think of Bruno as an unworldly or impractical soul, a congenital blunderer in social relations, or the creature of unmasterable passions.[4] If any of us have been tempted by Frances Yates, or by any aspect of Bruno's life, to think that he may have been insane, we shall have to confess our mistake.[5] I can quite confidently say that, at least between the ages of 35 and 39, he was not mad at all. To be vulgar, Bruno was a very smart operator. As a secret agent, he was extremely competent and extremely successful. He was observant, patient, and secure. He used his social talents, which were actually considerable, to excellent

---

4 Singer, *Giordano Bruno*, p. 9; Firpo, 'Processo' (i), 549; Yates, *Bruno*, pp. 317, 363.
5 Firpo, 'Processo' (ii), 53, quoting Mercati; Barbera, 'La Brunomania', p. 127 n. 186, quoting Lombroso. Yates, *Bruno*, p. 339, flirts with the idea of Bruno as a mad genius.

effect. He did not, on the whole, let his feelings interfere with the job. He has – perhaps he cultivated – a reputation as a talker and a boaster, but he never talked or boasted about this, then or later. Nobody found him out. Châteauneuf obviously suspected something, but if he had really discovered anything we should surely have known: it sounds to me as if he did not quite know what to look for, and took the wrong step of investigating Bruno's Catholicism rather than his political loyalty. After his return to Paris Bruno took some risks, perhaps under pressure from Châteauneuf, perhaps because he was missing Walsingham's guidance; but he had the sense to know where to stop, and got out and went to Germany. Because he was such an excellent spy, nobody has hitherto been in a position to comment on his performance; it is only clear in retrospect that he made his own comments on it in a couple of passages in his published works, and did so with legitimate complacency.

The first is the passage in the *Spaccio* about dissimulation: this is the key which opens our story, and I can only recommend the reader to go back to the place where I have quoted it, or preferably to look up the original for himself.[6] The second is at the beginning of the third dialogue of the *Cena*, and is therefore the earlier, written while his triumphs of clandestinity were still extremely fresh. Teofilo is explaining what happened at the Supper when the first pedant, Nundinio, expounded the physical objections to the Copernican system; there is a discussion about whether Bruno knows any English. Teofilo says he does not, since English is not worth a scholar's knowing. Hereupon Frulla, the servant whose part is to come up with untimely statements of demotic wisdom, says he is sure that Bruno actually does understand English, but pretends not to in order to hear what people are saying when they think he cannot understand them. I should not be at all surprised if this was the literal truth. I doubt if Bruno spoke much more than the three or four words of tourist's English to be found in the *Cena*,[7] but I should think his reading knowledge was rather better: we have the best authority for saying that he knew something of Sidney's poetry;[8] and he must have read some of Howard's book on prophecy. Florio would usually be on hand to expound. The remark is not prosaically relevant to his career as a spy, for which English was not a qualification: what it surely is, is an elegant *figura* for his career, and a

6 Above, pp. 125–6.

7 *Cena*, pp. 85 f, 144 f; cf. pp. 53/117, 78/140, 295; Firpo, *Scritti scelti*, notes to pp. 91, 93 and possibly 120.

8 Florio's comment on the sonnet to English ladies at the end of the dedication of the *Eroici furori* makes it plain that Bruno knew something of *Astrophel and Stella*: *Eroici furori*, p. 951; Buxton, *Sir Philip Sidney*, p. 164; above, p. 57.

coded statement that Bruno's social performances were under the control of an intelligent and long-range purpose. The knowledge of his expertise in dissimulation will serve us later.

We did not need the story of Fagot to tell us that Bruno was brave, or that he was witty. There is nothing here to compare with the courage of his final endurance of being burned alive for what he held to be true. But we ought not to forget that his performance as Fagot called for a good deal of courage too: if they had found him out Girault and his friends would have been happy to put a knife in his back, and so would quite a lot of people in London. His return to Paris in the autumn of 1586, though perhaps I have exaggerated the risk, was in its own way the same kind of act as his return to Venice five years later. As for wit, we can now give his talent for a certain variety of the comic more credit than hitherto. I think his best joke known so far is his reply to a question put to him by his inquisitors about a comment alleged against him that in persecuting heretics the present-day Church was not following the example of the apostles: the apostles, he volunteered, had not had to cope with 'the malignity of the world at the present time'.[9] This was only one highlight in his performance in front of the Venetian inquisitors, and from what we have seen of him an example of his favourite kind of joke: I am sure we must take the name 'Fagot' as a piece of black humour in the same vein. It is a pity we cannot add the Paleologo joke, for if that was what it was it was a stroke in the same genre; it would also have had the practical side which always appealed to him.[10] 'Practical jokes' is probably what Samuel Daniel's friend mainly meant by Bruno's 'phantasticall toyes', and though we may or may not consider Fagot's entire career as falling into the category there is a chance that it included one quite radiant example of it.[11] If Bruno did it, the practical joke about the secretary Arnault pulled off on Mendoza and Châteauneuf was a masterpiece, considering that Bruno had himself recruited the other secretary who ought to have been arrested, and considering that it worked; it has also, not incidentally, deluded historians for the past 150 years. But I am afraid there is really no evidence for this at all.

On the other hand we have collected quite a crop of straight-faced jokes of a less practical and more genial kind: the one about chaplains and philosophers in *De la causa*, the one about Châteauneuf's priest and his cipher, the comic Italian of Text no. 17. We shall shortly be appreciating one about Henri III and his devotions. There is probably

9 *Documenti*, pp. 109 f; *Sommario*, nos. 2, 18; Firpo, 'Processo' (i), 566.
10 Above, pp. 134–5.
11 Above, pp. 133–4.

too much malice in Bruno's satire on Henry Howard for much of it
to count as comedy, unless we take as comic in itself, which we may,
the passing off on Howard of his own problematic priesthood; still,
if I have interpreted it correctly, the boat scene is very funny in a
crude sort of way, and so is the story about Howard as a cardinal
(which Bruno may perhaps have believed).[12] Jokes about cardinals
were surely meat and drink to Bruno. I presume he was the source of
Daniel's story about the cardinal who, when he acquired a valuable
office made vacant by the execution for murder of the previous
incumbent, remarked that the victim had been 'crucified also for us';
I hope he was the visitor who giggled with Stafford about Cardinal
Savelli's scheme of becoming pope on an anglophile ticket.[13]

I am sure there are plenty of other jokes still lurking in his doings
and writings: Bruno was never in a hurry for his laughs. Perhaps he
does not quite make the most select circles of the comic pantheon: his
range of targets was limited, and his favourite technique was the
April fool. You also needed to be in the know to appreciate his best
jokes, which were not for the vulgar. On the other hand there is an
intense blackness about these, arising from his offering himself in the
flesh as security for the joke, for which I cannot quite think of a
parallel.[14] We must also grant him that he did not only laugh at his
own jokes: there was the joke about the boat passenger and his wife,
which was in general circulation; and if he had not found the story of
William Parry and the pope fairly comic, I doubt if he would have
imitated it in the letter about Zubiaur's confession. I should like to
think that he had had more to do with Parry than appears at the
moment; even he cannot have found Parry's execution as funny as all
that.[15]

Against Bruno's virtues and talents, now revealed or confirmed,
we have to set the discovery that he was not an honourable man.
Spying is a dishonourable profession: contrary to an impression
which has been put around, it always entails betraying your friends,
or people you have caused to believe are your friends. Bruno appears
to have had no qualms about entering it. I am sure he went into it
mainly for reasons of conviction, though he also went into it for the
money, and probably for the thrills as well. In the pursuit of it, he
systematically betrayed his master Castelnau, who did nothing but

---

12 Above, pp. 30, 39, 64, 112–25; below, pp. 151–3.
13 Samuel Daniel, prefatory epistle to *The Worthy Tract of Paulus Jovius*, p. 23: a piece full of
   Brunoism or something very like it; above, pp. 70–1.
14 There is something here not unlike Gentile's notion of the stake as the 'inveratore' or
   guarantee of Bruno's philosophy (from Barbera, 'Brunomania', p. 135); but the connection between the stake and the jokes is much more intimate than its connection with
   anything in his philosophy. Here the stake was, as it were, the stake.
15 Above, pp. 36–7 and n. 38, 117.

PROEMI-
ALE EPISTO-
la scritta all' illustrissimo et
Eccellentissimo Signor di *Mauuissi-*
ero. Caualier del' ordine del Re. et
Secretario del suo priuato conseglo, Capi-
no di cinquant'huomini d'arma. Gouernator gene
rale di S. Desiderio, et Ambasciator di
Francia in Inghilterra.

Or eccoui sig-
nor presente, non
un conuito Netta-
reo del'Altitonan-
te, per vna maestá.
Non vn Protopla-
stico, per vna huma
na desolatione. Nō
quel d'Assuero per
un misterio. Non
di Lucullo per u-
na ricchezza. Non di Licaone per un sacrilegio.
Non di Thieste per una tragedia. Non di Tantalo
per un supplicio. Non di Platone per una philo-
sophia. Non di Diogene, per una miseria. Non de
le sanguisughe, per una bagattella. Non d' un Ar-
ciprete di Poglano, per una Bernesca. Non d' vn Bo
nifacio Candelaio, per vna comedia. Ma vn conuito
si grande, si picciolo ; sí maestrale, sí disciplinale ;

A.ii.   Sí

Figure 8.   A Freudian Slip: first page of the preface to La cena de le Ceneri, original edition.

good for him, was extremely loyal to him, and regarded him as a friend. He persuaded his secretary to betray him. He procured, in so far as it was in his power to do it, the arrest, torture and execution of Francis Throckmorton, whom Castelnau said that he loved as himself, and by whose fate he was appallingly harrowed.[16] He did all this while buttering up Castelnau in three dedicatory epistles with fulsome professions of esteem, friendship and undying gratitude for looking after him and sticking up for him.[17] This was quite exceptionally disgraceful conduct, and it must gravely damage Bruno's reputation from now on. The passage about dissimulation in the *Spaccio* shows that he knew perfectly well what he was doing; the psychoanalytically inclined may think that a mistake on the first page of the preface to the *Cena de le Ceneri*, where he described Castelnau as 'Secretario' – instead of 'Conseglier' – 'del suo [Henri III's] privato conseglo', was a classic Freudian slip, since the title was much more appropriate to Walsingham, and Bruno used it of him elsewhere in the book.[18] One might well deduce that his unconscious was dedicating the book to Walsingham, not to Castelnau.

Castelnau was not the only person Bruno betrayed. He betrayed all those he informed against; he betrayed at least one person who came to him as a priest; and he betrayed, or volunteered to betray, at least one other priest and his harbourer, both of whom, if convicted, would have suffered the penalties of treason.[19] These betrayals were ramifications of his betrayal of Castelnau: one thing led to another. His betrayal of Henri III was not quite so disgraceful as his betrayal of Castelnau, as he did not share a house with him for two years and more. But unless we imagine that the king sent him to London to do what he did, which would be perfectly gratuitous, betrayal is what it was. It, too, was not simply treason in the public domain, since the king, like Castelnau, was his friend and was extremely kind to him. I shall be talking about their relations in a moment: they were creditable to Henri III, and discreditable to Bruno.

Bruno was not a congenital liar, as readers of his *processo* might suppose: he told Walsingham and Stafford the truth as he claimed to do, if sometimes more than the truth. We knew that he lied under interrogation, and we can now add one substantial lie he told in his major interrogation (the lie about his practice of the priesthood and the sacraments), and one minor interrogation (Châteauneuf's) in which he lied systematically. This is not discreditable to him, though it may make things more difficult for historians. As a free agent, I

16 Castelnau to Mary, *c.* 21-iii/1-iv-1584, *c.* 14/24-xii-1583 (BL Harleian 1582, ff. 374, 385).
17 *Cena*, pp. 17–18/79; *Causa*, pp. 175–7/5–7; *Infinito*, p. 363.
18 *Cena* (Aquilecchia), pp. 67, 248; cf. *Cena*, p. 69/131; Figure 8.
19 Above, pp. 30, 103.

think he lied fairly often and fairly naturally, as about Zubiaur; but in
the instances we have met with he was lying for a purpose, and there
can be really no doubt what the purpose was.

ii Dog

The single motive of everything we have discovered Bruno doing
was the destruction of the papacy and all its works. This is the theme
of all Fagot's letters and informations, from the grumble about the
Gregorian calendar at the beginning to the undermining of Thomas
Morgan's papistical zeal at the end. The papacy is the universal
enemy, tyrant and oppressor of bodies, consciences and property,
paymaster of assassins and traitors, would-be 'lord of the earth'.
Papists and 'Romans' are enemies, popish books enemy propaganda,
the 'église papalle' an abomination. In the light of this relentless
obsession we may suspect that those contemporaries who thought
that the pope was the 'rampant Beast' whose destruction was
prophesied in the *Spaccio della bestia trionfante* were nearer the truth
than the modern scholars who have thought that it signified
something else.[20] Bruno said in his last letter to Stafford that their
business was to 'damage and weaken the enemy by every possible
means', and he thought every sort of means justified.[21] Armed force
in the first place: the crusade against Rome fought by Drake in the
Indies and Sidney in the Netherlands, financed by Pallavicino in
Germany and France, and finally to be accomplished by the descent
of a Protestant army over the Alps. Surely we should read the
passage in the *Spaccio* about Perseus and his adventures of liberation
throughout Europe, with its invocation to labour and courage in the
fulfilment of high designs, as an exhortation to be up and doing in
the pursuit of this great enterprise, the destruction of the Beast?[22]

Where force was not available, he would use fraud.[23] This passage
in the *Spaccio* comes immediately after the hymn to dissimulation,

---

20 The contemporaries were the reader of the *Spaccio* known as the 'postillatore napoletano'
    (*DI*, pp. 570 n. 1, 739 n. 2), who was however more interested in its anti-Protestant side
    (ibid., pp. 623, 626, 654); and a belated witness at Bruno's trial (Firpo, 'Processo' (ii),
    45–6; below, p. 180). Cf. the interpretations of Yates, *Bruno*, pp. 211 ff (Hermetic
    reform) and Ciliberto, introduction to *Spaccio*, pp. 33 ff (anti-Puritan/Protestant
    polemic). The only description of the Beast in the *Spaccio* is at p. 561, where it is equated
    with the vices in general; this is surely too anodine.
21 *Texts*, no. 17: 'pource qu'on tasche de nuire et affoiblir son ennemi en toutes sortes qu'on
    peut . . .'
22 *Spaccio*, pp. 709–18, cf. p. 564; above, pp. 51, 137, below, pp. 154 f.
23 We do not have simply to deduce this from Bruno's actions, or from the dissimulation
    passage: it is stated in the *Oratio valedictoria* given, appropriately, at Wittenberg, 8/18-iii-
    1588, where he takes Minerva as his patron in the warfare against the Giants (here

and the conjunction cannot have been unintended. In the case of Fagot prudence was concealing truth inside the cloak of studious dissimulation, preventing her from being trampled underfoot, and protecting her from the envy and outrages of her enemy; and dissimulation was certainly behaving with the 'mode et ordine' required to convert her, *per accidens*, into a virtue.[24] She had worked hard in London and Paris, as she was to work hard in Venice and Rome, as handmaid of prudence, shield of truth, worthy participant in the great enterprise. There is actually a good deal more to Bruno's cult of dissimulation than may appear at first sight: it was not simply a matter of his playing Judas to Castelnau. There is also the matter of his use of his priesthood as a weapon against the enemy, which I shall come to in a moment. And it seems quite obvious that, certainly while he was in Salisbury Court and probably while he was in Paris, he was maximising his efficiency as a spy by posing, where it was useful to do so, as some kind of a Catholic zealot. If he had not done this he would not have found out half the things he did. Girault must have thought him an ally in 1583, or he would not have told him all the details of the book-import business, and it is not clear that he thought differently of him later. Bruno's reference in *De la causa* to rumblings against him among the servants might suggest that he was not getting on very well with Girault in the summer of 1584, and I have deduced from Châteauneuf's interrogation that Girault had been telling tales against him,[25] but there are several signs that throughout Bruno's career as a spy Girault continued to think that they were on the same side. In the spring of 1585 he was hobnobbing with Bruno in Paris and, presumably, introducing him to Thomas Morgan and his friends, and somebody was explaining to Bruno how Morgan ran his correspondence with England; early in 1586 somebody told Bruno about Girault's arrangements for financing English *émigrés* in France. Neither piece of information need have come from Girault himself, but both of them suggest Bruno moving in English *émigré* circles and posing as a sympathiser, which would hardly have been possible if Girault had been warning everybody

---

certainly the pope, etc.). 'Et quia maximum in bellis gerendis omnis solertiae [skill, ingenuity] mater est sapientia . . . belligerantium numen', we must be as wise as (Minerva's) serpents; 'nam nisi vigilantiae et providentiae rebus vel longe prospicientibus acumen praesidem militiae corroboravit et ornaverit', etc. (*OL* i[1], 8). I connect this with the invocation of Sagacity in the *Spaccio*, p. 716: 'Sagacità . . . (acciò ch'io (Fatica) non sia ritrovata da nemici, ed il furor di quelli non mi s'avente sopra) confondi, seguendomi, gli miei vestigi.' This whole passage smells to me almost as strongly of Fagot as the one about dissimulation; in both I am sure Bruno was thinking of Ecclesiastes 9: 16: 'Melior est sapientia quam arma bellica.'

24 Above, pp. 125–6.
25 *Causa*, p. 176/6; above, pp. 58–60, 77.

against him. His acquisition of the pious tale about Jane Garlick (if that was her name) and her escape to Bordeaux suggests the same thing, as does his capacity even at second hand to devise a scheme for springing Morgan from the Bastille. His wider contacts in Paris in 1586 – with Mendoza, with the grand almoner of the Duke of Guise, whoever he was, and with the Hennequin family – indicate that Bruno was posing in public as a favourer of the Catholic League, which he certainly in his heart abhorred.[26]

The question arises whether Bruno put anything into his published works for the purpose of substantiating the pose of a Catholic sympathiser which was necessary for his success as a spy. It arises because the tendency of recent writers has been to pick up indications of Catholic feeling in his writings and to suggest that he was some kind of Catholic at heart.[27] Given what we now know, there is a temptation to treat these as protective camouflage. As a general rule, I think the temptation should be resisted. Bruno was not a Christian. To say that he did not believe in the divinity of Christ would be putting it too feebly: he despised and detested Jesus, and had a special contempt for the Cross and for any form of the mass or the eucharist. Hence he cannot have been any sort of Catholic. Nevertheless he did say that the Catholic 'religion' pleased him more than any other version of Christianity, and we must accept that he meant this.[28] In determining exactly what he did mean, we need to distinguish. In the first place, there are, particularly in the *Cena*, a lot of spontaneous references to Catholic sacraments and practices; they are the kind of thing that naturally sprang to the pen of someone who had lived all his life among them, and was at the time earning his living as a Catholic priest.[29] They suggest, as they might well do, something of a preoccupation with the subject; but they shed no light at all on his opinions. Then there are his references to the eucharist, and one in particular. It could be, as Frances Yates maintained, that the disgusting drinking-scene in the *Cena* was intended as a polemic against communion in both kinds. I think it did express an aesthetic preference in the matter, but not that it was a considered statement in favour of Catholic practice: when he was in Germany, he went out of his way to compliment the Lutherans on their reformed eucharistic

---

26 *Texts*, nos. 13, 14, 16, 17; above, pp. 132 f.

27 Yates, 'Religious Policy'; *Bruno*, p. 304. This also seems to be the drift of Ciliberto's introduction to the *Spaccio*, of his 'Asini e pedanti', *Rinascimento*[2], xxiv (1984), 81–121, and of *La ruota del tempo* (1986).

28 *Sommario*, nos. 41–71, is a handy collection of Bruno's views on Christ and the mass; add *Sigillus*, p. 181; *Texts*, no. 12ii; *Spaccio*, p. 655, and 777 f (misinterpreted, I think, in Yates, 'Religious Policy', pp. 183–4, as simply anti-Protestant); and Ingegno, *La sommersa nave della religione*, p. 82. Preference for 'la religione catholica': *Documenti*, p. 66.

29 *Cena*, pp. 9/69, 16/77, 78 n/140 and 298, 170/230 f.

rite, which like the Anglican included communion in both kinds. He had no great interest in the subject. On the other hand it is not plausible to suppose that he put in the drinking-scene as a piece of protective camouflage: it was hardly less offensive to Catholic than to Protestant sensibilities about the eucharist, and he cannot have thought that it would do anything for his reputation as a Catholic priest.[30] Indeed I should guess that one of his reasons for suppressing it, I imagine on Castelnau's advice, was precisely that it did not. I cannot see its furthering his career in espionage.

There is more to be said about the numerous passages and statements where he expressed a fairly radical preference for a Catholic theology of salvation over a Protestant one. Although there are not so many of these as has been claimed, and I am not quite sure that any of them occur before the summer of 1584, they are thereafter so frequent and so explicit that Bruno must certainly have meant them.[31] True, he did not attack justification by faith or predestination on behalf of Catholic theologians, even on behalf of his hero Thomas Aquinas, about whom he always felt an extremely patriotic Neapolitan: he attacked them as destructive of the civic virtue he attributed to the ancient Romans, of the goods of the commonwealth, and of the human sociability which he said was the object of all law, moral as well as civil.[32] But attack them he certainly did, with a venom which has made it plausible to regard the destruction of Luther and Calvin as his main moral preoccupation at the time of his dialogues. I think this is a mistaken idea, but we need to be careful here, and a detour will be worthwhile.

Bruno's theoretical exposition of the subject comes from the first dialogue of *De l'infinito*, and so dates from the summer of 1584.[33] In discussing divine causality, Filoteo/Bruno and the eminent writer on syphilis Girolamo Fracastoro agree that God acts according to the necessity of his nature: he cannot act otherwise than he does act,

---

30 Yates, 'Religious Policy', pp. 186 f. *Texts*, no. 12ii; *Cena* (Aquilecchia), p. 303; *Oratio valedictoria*, p. 21; *Oratio consolatoria*, pp. 32–3; Cotin, in *Documenti*, p. 40. There is a prominent prose section of the poem *De immenso et innumerabilibus* (*OL* i¹, 205) which shows equal contempt for the incarnation and for the eucharist; it was pointed out by Mercati, *Sommario*, p. 76 n. 2.

31 *Infinito*, pp. 385–7; *Spaccio*, pp. 622–6, 746 f; *Cabala*, pp. 857–8; *Documenti*, pp. 40, 107–8. Ciliberto, who makes the most of these, adds to them (introduction to *Spaccio*, p. 9) an earlier passage from *Sigillus*, pp. 180–2, which I think he has misinterpreted. I agree that this is partly against Luther, but it is mainly against the religious orders, and Luther as a product of them.

32 *Spaccio*, pp. 654 ff; *Sigillus*, p. 182; cf. Jean Bodin, *Six livres de la République*, book 3, ch. vii (abridged English translation by M.J. Tooley (Oxford, n.d), pp. 96–107), though Bodin speaks of 'love', and adds love between men and God. The 'postillatore napoletano' commented adversely on this point: *Spaccio*, p. 657 nn. 2 and 3.

33 *Infinito*, pp. 383–7; Ciliberto, *Giordano Bruno*, pp. 109–15.

because he cannot will otherwise than he wills. This is a philosophical statement, not a theological one. It does not imply, philosophically, that men and women cannot do otherwise than they do, because men and women are different from God. But for Christian theologians it may or must imply this, because among the data of Christian theology are the beliefs that there is salvation, that it is the end to which moral actions refer, and that it is given by God's grace. It may seem to follow that salvation must be necessary: that is, must be caused by God's immutable will, as Calvin taught. Bruno did not believe this, because he did not believe in salvation, but he appears to think that Christian theologians ought to believe it, and to teach it among the learned (*sapienti*).[34] What they ought not to do, and what the best of them, like Thomas Aquinas, have not done, is to teach it to the *hoi polloi*, who will regard it as a licence to do what they like; so taught, it will destroy civility, law, and the goods of human society. Those who teach predestination to the masses are guilty of this grievous crime, and ought to be prevented from doing it, and persecuted if they do. Those who teach justification by faith fall under the same ban, since Bruno did not distinguish the two doctrines; in theory he probably ought to have done, since Luther did not teach that salvation was necessary in the sense that Calvin did. It is possible, though on the whole unlikely, that he did not know the difference between the doctrines; more probably, he thought that it was impossible to teach them so that the ignorant and uncouth masses would see a difference. In the circumstances of the 1580s he does seem to have made some difference between Lutherans and Calvinists, I imagine because predestination was an issue between them: when he went to Germany, he stuck to Lutherans and avoided Calvinists.[35]

In the *Spaccio*, which followed *De l'infinito*, he restated his view, but in a far more polemical way and with an immediate practical concern. In so far as this was political, we can ignore it for the moment, but it was also theological and moral: the question was about the relations between Protestant theology and the Protestant cause. Dedicated to Philip Sidney, the *Spaccio* embodied an invitation to him and his friends not to look back in their pursuit of the cause: Bruno, as I take it, was alarmed that what he assumed to be their theology would weaken their commitment to the great enterprise of destroying the papacy. So indeed was Sidney; at least, that is how I

---

34 This is not to say that we should respect them if they do: they are simply being consistent in their asininity as Christian theologians. This seems to me the doctrine of Bruno's most extended theological piece, the 'Declamazione al studioso, divoto e pio lettore' in the *Cabala*, pp. 846–58, which I take to be satirical. Cf. above, pp. 52 f.

35 *Documenti*, p. 85.

read a letter from Sidney to Walsingham, written after he had taken the plunge and gone off to fight the enemy in the Netherlands. He would never, he said, regret his resolution: even if Elizabeth's support of the cause should fail, as seemed not at all unlikely, God's would not. 'Methinks I see the great work indeed in hand, against the abusers of the world, wherein it is no greater fault to have confidence in man's power than it is too hastily to despair of God's work.'[36] I presume that Sidney was here defending the heroic virtues against potential Protestant critics, rather as he had already defended the moral vocation of the poet against them; I am not sure who, among contemporary Protestant authorities, he thought would have opposed him, though Luther would probably have done so, and Calvin might have done. Although Bruno did not bring it to a very fine point, this seems to me to have been the most immediate theological or moral issue in the *Spaccio*. In both *De l'infinito* and the *Spaccio* his defence of 'works' was a serious matter, and it cannot be the case that he took the question up in order to enhance his efficiency as a spy. I suppose I am the only person who has ever thought it might be.

By now the reader may have lost patience with me for ventilating at length a gratuitous supposition. I assure him that there is something in it; but it has been essential to give full weight to what, in his theological statements, Bruno actually did believe, if we are to put our finger fairly accurately on what he did not. There are indeed features of his anti-Protestant or anti-predestinarian passages which, in my opinion, are there as camouflage, and I intend to point them out in due course. In the meantime I offer for consideration one more passage from the *Spaccio*. It has not been cited in this context, although it is connected with those which have just been mentioned, and has been used as an index of Bruno's religious opinions. In order to understand it we need, or so I judge, to attend to Castelnau's doings, and in particular to something which happened in July 1584, some while before the *Spaccio* was written. Towards the end of that month Sidney had called at Salisbury Court to talk to Castelnau about an official visit he was due to make to France, theoretically to condole with Henri III on the death of Anjou, actually to try and stir the French up to joint intervention in the Netherlands after the blow of the assassination of William of Orange. This was not an idea which appealed either to Castelnau or to Henri III, who told Elizabeth

36 Sidney to Walsingham, March 1586, quoted by A.C. Hamilton, *Sir Philip Sidney* (Cambridge, 1977), p. 124; cf. p. 173. Sidney on the moral creativity of the poet, ibid. pp. 107–22, from the *Apology for Poetry*. The passages from the *Spaccio* are cited below, pp. 164 f.

that he was going on a pilgrimage at Lyon at the time in question and so would be unable to receive Sidney. When Castelnau took this message to Elizabeth she was ribald, and contemptuous when Castelnau explained that the king had made a vow to go to Lyon and, in fulfilling it come what might, was giving a good example of religion to his people. Such things as the king's vow, wrote Castelnau, 'do not cut much ice over here, where they have a religion which is constructed out of an assortment of heresies and self-interests, and nobody believes anything but what they please and what serves to support them in their present prosperous condition'.[37] Though this was partly flattery of the king, Castelnau did actually believe it: for the past few years his experience in England had been exposing inside his sociable exterior a rock of fairly primitive loyalty to Catholicism. Since the incident involved the two people in England to whom Bruno was closest, he must have been aware of it, and he must surely have remembered it when, towards the end of the year, he altered the planned conclusion of the *Spaccio* to include a panegyric on Henri III. Here Jove attributes to the king the place in the heavens of *Corona australis*, the third crown in heaven, after those of France and Poland, prophesied by his motto *Tertia coelo manet* (A third remains in heaven). He deserves this for being pacific, devout and pure in heart, and for not listening to people who want him to invade other countries. 'Let others therefore launch enterprises against the vacant kingdom of Portugal; let others worry about who is going to rule the Netherlands.' Not Henri III: his reward will be in heaven.[38]

This is one of Bruno's more entertaining passages. I am sure it was inspired by the incident just described, when Henri III neglected the opportunity of joining with Leicester and Sidney in the liberation of the Netherlands in order to give his people an example of true religion. If so, it was satirical: much as he liked Henri III, Bruno was the last person to take seriously the king's seasonal accesses of Catholic penitential devotion. It also contained at least two different messages, one apparent, one concealed. Castelnau had always been a vigorous opponent of the Huguenot policy of uniting France by launching a national invasion of the Netherlands, which had been stopped in 1572 by the assassination of Admiral Coligny and the

37 Castelnau to Henri III, 18/28-vii-1584, [viii]-1584 (Chéruel, p. 317; HMC *Hatfield*, iii, 43); the latter is a copy of a letter which does not survive, made officially by Jean Arnault in Paris and sent to Elizabeth by Stafford.

38 *Spaccio*, pp. 826–7. It will be seen that I disagree with the interpretations of the passage offered by Yates, 'Religious Policy', p. 194 and *Bruno*, pp. 228–9, and by Ciliberto in *Spaccio*, p. 305 n. R.B. Wernham, *Before the Armada: the Growth of English Foreign Policy, 1485–1588* (London, 1966) has a fine account of the political consequences of the assassination of Orange; I think it will be found to support the line taken here. Below, p. 164.

massacre of St Bartholomew: Bruno was adopting his master's voice in describing the Huguenots as 'rebels', 'rash, tempestuous and turbulent spirits', and their programme as 'unstable counsels'.[39] But the reason why Castelnau was against the idea, apart from the fact that it was proposed by Huguenots, was that it was in competition with his own alternative programme, which was to settle the internal conflicts of France and restore the country's position in Europe by masterminding a successful invasion of Scotland or restoring Queen Mary to her throne by other means. In pointing out that the king was too busy gaining his heavenly crown to bother about other people's kingdoms, Bruno was silently mocking Castelnau's ambitions. He was simultaneously advising the English that if the advance of papal tyranny was to be stopped they had better get their fingers out without waiting for the French. Meanwhile he had fortified his position at Salisbury Court by appearing in public as a defender of Catholic piety.

The story of Bruno and Henri III's trip to Lyon indicates the affinity between Bruno's art of dissimulation and his fertility in jokes. The object of Bruno's best jokes was to make a fool of the papacy: I think we may say that, along with military force and the art of dissimulation, ridicule was the third arm in his anti-papal crusade. The conviction that all papists were asses, which was practically the first thing brought up against him at his trial, was the principle underlying most of his jokes.[40] In a small way, the joke about the priest who had succeeded him as embassy chaplain is a very good example of it. The priest was one who 'trionfait de prêcher' (boasted of his prowess as a preacher); he was going to write a best-seller about his adventures among the English; he had invented a cipher in which to write secret intelligence to the pope, whose absurdity Bruno demonstrated by signing or addressing his letter in it: the secret name came out as 'Walsingham'. The moral of the story was that the priest was an ass, a real *idiota triumphans*, that Bruno and Walsingham were a great deal smarter, and that brains would win the day.[41] If it were possible to discover what Bruno meant by the ass

39 Castelnau had inherited Jean de Morvillier's hostility to Coligny's Netherlands scheme: G. Baguenault de Puchesse, *Jean de Morvillier* (Paris, 1870), pp. 175–6; Castelnau to Brûlart, 8-xi-1577 (BN V^cC 337, p. 701). His own views are in Castelnau to Catherine de Medici, 30-viii-1580 (BN ff 15973, f. 33), and probably in William Fowler to Walsingham, [ ]-v-1583 (*CSP Scotland 1581–83*, p. 480), reporting Castelnau's conversation; cf. Hubault, *Michel de Castelnau*, p. 111. It is true that in a late letter to Walsingham he claimed to have warned him, as ambassador in Paris, of the plot against Coligny five hours before the assassination attempt: to Walsingham, 3/13-ix-1589 (PRO SP 78/20, f. 7); but this is not easy to believe, and if true does not necessarily affect the point.

40 *Sommario*, no. 1.

41 *Texts*, nos. 15 and 16.

who was the hero of the two brief dialogues in the *Cabala del cavallo pegaseo*, and by the figures of theoretical and practical idiocy the Great Bear and Eridanus respectively, I suppose there might turn out to be some connection, but I confess I have not the least idea what Bruno meant.[42] We might, however, conclude that when he spoke of the Italian papists as being so stupid that they could be overthrown by the trick of sending into Italy a German army which they had been told was being sent to France, he was demonstrating the same faith in the practical asininity of papists as he would later show in going back to Venice: the same, justified faith he had shown throughout his career as Fagot.

There is quite good evidence that at the end of his campaign against the papacy Bruno planned to make use, as a fourth arm, of the magic arts. Antonio Corsano explained his last works, which were written between 1589 and 1591 and are indeed about magic, as showing that he intended to pull off an ultimate coup against the papacy by personally enchanting Pope Clement VIII.[43] This would explain his continuing agitation, from the moment he arrived back in Italy until the very eve of his burning, to get a private interview with the pope; and also the claim, attributed to him by his fellow-prisoners, to be more powerful than Christ and the apostles. I do not think the idea can be excluded: one might well think that having failed to shake the papacy by force, fraud or ridicule he was driven to magic as a last resort. And I doubt if we can use against it the history of the cool-headed secret agent we now know, for it seems fairly clear to me that, in exploring in *De vinculis* the ways by which affinities personal and cosmic might be manipulated for political ends, Bruno was thinking of his management of Castelnau as a model of how the thing should be done. He had in mind the sympathies created by the intelligent use of civil conversation as well as those accessible to a philosopher who understood the secrets of the universe.[44] All the same, we do not have to suppose that Bruno returned to Italy in 1591 on the presumption that the papacy could be overthrown by charm. An item from his table-talk recorded by his host Giovanni Mocenigo, in the light of an active and successful campaign against popery which had now lasted for eight years, indicates that he still hoped to achieve greatness, and the destruction of his enemy, in the baggage of some apocalyptic invasion of Italy by Henri of Navarre.

42 *Cabala*, pp. 862 f; cf. *Spaccio*, p. 809.
43 A. Corsano, *Il pensiero di Giordano Bruno nel suo svolgimento storico* (Florence, 1940), pp. 281–94. Firpo, 'Processo' (i), 549–51, seems to agree with this; Aquilecchia, *DBI*, xiv, 662 rejects it.
44 Ciliberto, *Giordano Bruno*, pp. 242–57; there are resemblances between *De vinculis* and some of Francis Bacon's *Essays*, e.g. no. xlvii.

The world, Mocenigo recorded him as saying, was in a terrible state; Catholicism, though better than any other version of Christianity, needed a complete shake-up; if it was to survive it would have to renounce force and return to preaching the gospel.

Any minute now the world would see a complete change of things, for it was impossible that such corruptions should last any longer. He hoped great things of the King of Navarre, and was in a hurry to get all his works into print and make himself famous; for when the time came he wanted to be [a] Captain, and he would not then be poor because he would be enjoying the wealth of others.[45]

If Bruno had not been such an enemy of prophets, one might think that here he had been trying on the mantle of Savonarola, that earlier Dominican dissident who had prophesied ruin for the papacy through the arrival of an avenging French monarch from over the Alps. I imagine that Bruno disliked Savonarola almost as much as Jesus, but the parallel will not have escaped him. I guess that his intention of being a *capitano* when the great day dawned was a bow in the direction of Machiavelli's remarks on Savonarola, and a statement that he meant to avoid the fate which Machiavelli had foreseen for prophets without arms.[46] Henri of Navarre was a very plausible replacement for Savonarola's Charles VIII: in 1591, he was still a Protestant, and his army would have been a Protestant army.[47] This had been Bruno's solution to the problem of the papacy in 1586, as expounded in his letter to Stafford; it had also, it seems to me, been his solution at the time of his espionage in London, his writing of the *Spaccio* and his friendship with Sidney. It was evidently still his solution in 1591. I think he remembered Castelnau, and probably also Henry Howard and John Dee, the latter having crossed his path a second time in Prague. He will have hoped for some assistance from the mysteries of Egypt, and he certainly resorted to prophecy. But neither of these was a substitute for a Protestant army.

Unlike a third Dominican dissident, Tommaso Campanella, Bruno had no great scheme for what was to happen in liberated Italy; to judge by Campanella's eugenic *City of the Sun*, this was just as well. Bruno's ambitions for himself were agreeably human. He would get his works published properly, and be known as a 'great

45 *Documenti*, p. 66; *Sommario*, no. 2. Behind Corsano, the theme goes back to the nineteenth-century interpreters who wanted to identify Bruno as a proto-Mazzini (Barbera, 'Brunomania', p. 130); this does not seem to me such a bad idea.

46 Machiavelli, *The Prince*, ch. 6. Bruno, *Documenti*, pp. 122–3, said about his claiming to be a *capitano* that he did not remember saying it, and that he had never wanted to be a soldier, since he was a philosopher. He does not sound very convincing.

47 Above, p. 66; *Texts*, no. 17; Yates, *Bruno*, pp. 340–3 – but she should not have said that Henri of Navarre had 'won his right' in 1591, which was very far from the case.

man', both guru and liberator: I imagine he envisaged the *Spaccio della bestia trionfante* as some kind of a testament for the new dispensation, though it would have needed a commentary.[48] His days of (relative) poverty would be over, 'because he would be enjoying the wealth of others'. Frances Yates has cast doubt on the evidence at this point, on the grounds that Bruno was not a mercenary man.[49] I do not think anything we have found out about him goes contrary to this claim: the requests for money in his letters to Walsingham seem perfectly reasonable, and he never possessed any property in his life. But we cannot arbitrarily repudiate one piece of Mocenigo's testimony while devoutly embracing the rest, and in the light of Bruno's conduct as Fagot I can see no problem at all. He would have had fewer scruples about living on the profits of papists than Sidney did.[50] Bruno's loathing of the pope and his minions was such that the prospect of setting himself up on some of the spoils of avarice which would be confiscated from them in the great revolution must have been very sweet: the pleasure would be in their deprivation as much as in his own possession. Since the one article of policy which emerged from his delators' reports was the confiscation of the property of the religious orders,[51] perhaps he was thinking of himself, like Luther, giving forth as a 'great man' in the refectory of an ex-convent: and why not that of San Domenico at Naples? He may not have agreed with Luther's theology, but Luther as a wrecker of the papacy was an example to us all.

The *risorgimento* image of Bruno is of a martyr for the freedom of thought, and despite the emergence in recent decades of alternative images, is probably, as represented in the work of Luigi Firpo, still the classic one. There is obviously substantial truth in it, and it is right to say that he died in defence of his claim to 'ragionare liberamente'. But if we take him to have been claiming this freedom as a right for everybody, I am sure we shall be making a mistake.[52] Some people in the sixteenth century believed this; Bruno did not. I have treated as a joke his remark to the inquisitors that he thought the Church was justified in exercising force to compel belief, owing to 'the malignity of the world at the present time';[53] but it is just conceivable that it was not a joke at all, or a different kind of joke

---

48 *Documenti*, p. 66; *Sommario*, nos. 2 and 4; Corsano, *Il pensiero di Giordano Bruno*, p. 290. Cf. *Spaccio*, p. 717: '. . . percioché per tuo (*sc.* di Ozio) mezzo accaderà, che io serva a la republica e defension de la patria piú con la mia voce ed esortazione, che con la spada, lancia e scudo il soldato . . .'

49 Yates, *Bruno*, p. 341.

50 *DNB*, Sidney, Sir Philip.

51 *Documenti*, pp. 67, 108; *Sommario*, nos. 1, 2, 6.

52 Firpo, 'Processo' (ii), 59; *Sommario*, no. 4.

53 Above, p. 142.

from the kind I imagined. In the *Spaccio* he argued that, while it was illogical for those who believed in predestination to persecute those who did not (since people were saved not by believing in predestination, but by being predestined), it was perfectly proper for those who did not believe in it to persecute those who did, since they were enemies of the human race. The gods recommended that they should be exterminated from their present life, and transmuted into pigs and asses.[54] After a good deal of hesitation I have come to the conclusion that Bruno was perfectly serious about this, though he must have wanted to postpone the persecution of predestinarians until after they had got rid of the papacy for him; but if he were not we have nevertheless now to observe that he acted very firmly on the conviction that *papists* ought to be persecuted. One may certainly claim that his actions as a secret agent in England were in the first place dedicated to the frustration of English popery in so far as it covered a political movement designed to overthrow Queen Elizabeth and her government: to that end he had successfully exposed Francis Throckmorton, recruited Courcelles into English service, denounced (if his story had been true) Pedro de Zubiaur, and planned to spring Thomas Morgan from the Bastille. This would be quite compatible with a conviction that Christianity or Catholicism ought to be spread by preaching and example, not by force. So, to a certain extent, would be his exposure of the means of introducing Catholic books into England: *Leicester's Commonwealth*, which was no doubt what Bruno had mainly in mind, was indeed a 'livre diffamatoire' and a work of political propaganda.[55] To this extent Fagot's doings were concordant with the doctrine of the *Spaccio* that in the constellation of the Pleiades unity, civility, church and other public desireables would rise, and plot (*monopolio*), mob, sect, triumvirate, faction and partiality go down: restless spirits who wandered in the nocturnal spaces of disordered affection, iniquitous enterprise, sedition and conspiracy under the dark government of perverted counsel.[56] This is the very language of the Fagot letters.

But it is not possible to defend all his doings as a secret agent on

---

54 *Spaccio*, pp. 624, 626.

55 *Texts*, no. 13; *Leicester's Commonwealth*, properly *The Copie of a letter wryten by a Master of Arte of Cambrige. . .*, most probably written by Charles Arundell, or Robert Parsons, or some combination of them and others (?Paris, 1584), has recently been edited by D.C. Peck (Athens, Ohio, 1985). It was obviously being put into circulation through Girault's import system, and Leicester was complaining bitterly to Castelnau about it at the time Bruno wrote: examination of Sylvanus Scory, 14/24-ii-1585 (PRO SP 12/176, no. 53); Castelnau to Henri III, 16/26-iv-1585, 1/11-v-1585, 6/16-v-1585 (BN ff 4736, ff. 293, 302, 307). But it should be said that Bruno's efforts to stop Catholic books getting into the country go back to the spring of 1583 (*Texts*, no. 4), when so far as I know there was nothing political coming in.

56 *Spaccio*, p. 566.

the grounds that he was simply acting to frustrate the ambitions of Catholic political activists. Among the books he was trying to stop getting into England he explicitly mentioned missals and prayer books; it is perfectly clear that he would have liked to put a stop to the import of any sort of Catholic publication, whether defamatory or political or not.[57] His spying career, so far as we know it, included betraying or attempting to betray another priest, trying to cut off the supply of funds to Catholics abroad, and possibly informing on adolescents going to join the seminary at Reims and explaining how Catholic girls might be trying to escape to convents in France. So far as it lay in his power, and at a time when he might be said to have been a member of it, he was working to demolish the Catholic mission in Elizabethan England. He was not deterred from his campaign against Lord Henry Howard by Howard's record as a Catholic loyalist, which indeed rather stimulated Bruno's bile against him. He evidently considered Howard a much more personal enemy than Throckmorton, and went to much greater lengths to procure his downfall. It is true that after Howard's arrest Bruno felt able to take the more relaxed and comic view which surfaces in the portraits of the impotent boatman and the celibate pedant Polihimnio. But the dialogues make it plainer than his delation of the book against prophecy had done that Bruno's real objection to Howard was his propagation of Romish error at the queen's elbow. Superannuated as a dangerous malcontent, he kept his place in the cast as an archteacher of monkish doctrine in *De la causa*, and in the *Spaccio* – surely – as a model of the turpitude, loquacity and imposture which ought to be supplanted in the heavens by benevolent magic, prophecy and divination.[58]

If we assume, as I do, that Bruno shared Herle's particular pleasure in Howard's arrest,[59] we approach some fairly deep water in his personality, and at the risk of wandering from the point I shall try to plumb it now. It is not simply that he was looking for matters of treason against Howard, which would entail either his execution or his disappearance into the Tower for the rest of his life. Considering the view he took of Howard's influence in England, this was perfectly normal. But the usual fate of those who were arrested in England on suspicion of treason at this time was to be interrogated under torture: judicial torture was not normal English practice, but in such cases could be authorised by royal prerogative. In these years

57 *Texts*, no. 13; cf. Castelnau to Walsingham, 20/30-vi-1584 (*CSP Foreign 1583–84*, p. 559), where he denied that he had ever imported from France 'a single book of hours'.

58 Above, pp. 30 and 100 f; *Texts*, no. 5 and 7; *Cena*, p. 5/65; *Causa*, p. 219/55; *Spaccio*, p. 818.

59 *Texts*, no. 7.

of danger to the state, and of multiplied statutory treasons, it had become relatively common. Howard was interrogated, but not under torture, I presume because Elizabeth thought the evidence against him maliciously motivated. Throckmorton was severely tortured, and under torture confessed everything. In view of what he had been up to, I can see no good reason to object to this. But Bruno, who must certainly have heard from Castelnau what Throckmorton had been through, does not seem to have been satisfied. Hence his titbit from the Irish Catholic gentleman in the Fleet, whom he had presumably been visiting as a priest, that Throckmorton had not told half of what he knew; this was a perfectly needless invitation to Walsingham to have him tortured again, and perhaps the Irish gentleman as well.[60] His delation of Zubiaur, and his fairly frequent recommendations that people should be arrested and interrogated, also suggest to me a certain gratification in this effect of his work. Like Armesso in *De la causa*, readers of Bruno will have had occasion to speculate on the same subject. In a man whose daily life must have been fairly tranquil, there was a very great deal of verbal violence: bitings, scratchings, thrashings, castrations, a pleasure in causing physical disgust.[61] In his best jokes this side of his personality created something peculiarly brilliant; elsewhere, as in his comedy the *Candelaio* or *Candlemaker*, published in Paris before he came to England, it pushed him into pornography and artistic disaster.[62] Most of the final act of the play, which is neither dramatic, nor symbolic, nor funny, consists of the public humiliation and flogging of the homosexual candlemaker Bonifacio and, especially, of the pedant Manfurio. Manfurio cannot bear the pain of his whipping, as Throckmorton could not bear the pain of his torture: in both cases, Bruno's reaction was to inflict more. So we may have our own ideas when, in *De la causa*, he presents himself to Armesso not as a vulgar avenger of personal injuries, but as a minister of public correction, in the exercise of which, he says, men become like gods.

> You know that poor Vulcan [the gods' blacksmith] has a dispensation from Jove to work on holydays; his miserable anvil has no rest from the blows of great and fierce hammers; as soon as one is lifted the other is brought down, that there may be no intermission in the lightning-flashes of justice, wherewith the unrighteous are punished.[63]

60 *Texts*, no. 9.
61 *Texts*, nos. 9, 11, 13; *Causa*, pp. 192–202/30–40; *Cena*, sonnet p. 5/65, 57/121, 78 n/298; *Sigillus*, p. 182; *Eroici furori*, pp. 927–30.
62 *Candelaio*, act v, especially pp. 323–9. Bruno must have been pleased with this because he referred to it complacently in the *Cena*, second version (p. 78 n 1/140).
63 *Causa*, pp. 200 f/37.

The image, which Bruno appears to have invented, testifies to his self-regard as a scourge of the delinquent: Romanism aside, his venomous passages on women, Jews, Protestants and Jesus demonstrate the catholicity of his victims and the pleasure he took in their discomfiture or worse. Fantasies of retribution seem to have been his daily bread.

Nobody is competent to say that Bruno was, clinically speaking, a sadist; if an argument to the contrary is needed, there is the excellent one that his penchant was very rationally discussed, in *De la causa*, by himself. However we describe his condition, I have no doubt that it was relevant to his career as Fagot: to its retributory aspect, and also to the voyeurism which it entailed. I am also inclined to think that the success of his spying had some kind of cathartic effect on his corrective passion, as I think it had a liberating effect on his creative powers. The *Spaccio* is rather chaste in this respect, probably too chaste for its own good as a work of art, and perhaps we should not put this all down to Sidney's invitation to decorum. Since the object of Fagot's retribution was the papacy and its ministers, Bruno might well have said that there was no need to interpret it by gratuitous speculations about his psyche: Rome had a long start in the business of tyranny and torture, and those like Paleologo and Pallavicino's brother Fabrizio who had suffered under it weighed down the objective scales of justice against Throckmorton and less political offenders in England.[64] With that legitimate caveat I return to my proper question, which is not whether Bruno was altogether a nice person, or whether he was entitled by his own eventual sufferings to cause such suffering to be visited upon others: it is whether Bruno believed in the use of force against English papists, in what it would be pedantic not to call their persecution. It is absolutely clear that he did. It follows that, where there had been a conflict in his mind between the defeat of the pope and the defence of freedom of thought or belief, Bruno would have chosen the defeat of the pope. But there was no such conflict: as Giovanni Gentile very properly said, Bruno was no believer in the 'autonomy of the individual conscience'.[65]

iii Politick

With one exception, I think we can say that Bruno's feelings about contemporary politics were subordinate to his feelings about the

---

64 Stone, *Palavicino*, pp. 6, 10 f, 47–63, 260 for Fabrizio Pallavicino, whose investigation, though conducted by the Holy Office, seems to have been a purely commercial and political matter, with no doctrinal aspect. This did not make it any more acceptable to the family.

65 Quoted from a review by Gentile in Barbera, 'Brunomania', p. 136 n. 251.

papacy. I do not mean that he had no political ideas as such. Fagot's letters confirm the impression he gave in his published works that he detested all kinds of subversive activity, to the extent of denouncing rebellion against the Spaniards in his own *patria* of Naples. His hatred of *novità*, *monopolio*, and of those who incited the disgusting multitude to rebel against its superiors was perfectly exemplified by the language he used about English Catholic activists and their foreign abettors. But he must have excluded rebellion against the pope from this condemnation, and though he made recommendations about the persecution of predestinarians he did not extend them, *rebus sic stantibus*, to the Huguenots in France or the participants in the Dutch Revolt. In Bruno's real life rebellions against constituted authority were legitimate and indeed laudable if the object of the rebellion was the expulsion of the pope; the passage about Naples, which comes from the *Spaccio*, may indicate that his views as an author were sterner. However, it may not. The context of the passage, if we take the preceding passages to be the context, is the need for prudent consideration of times and seasons in the undertaking of great enterprises. It may be that Bruno's message was that 1584 was not a propitious moment for attempting to restore the liberties of Naples, either because the appropriate force was not available, or because a revolt of the sort he envisaged would be a demagogic shambles. If that was what he was saying in the *Spaccio*, he had changed his mind by October 1586: there had actually been a revolt in Naples in the meantime.[66]

We have acquired a fairly extensive knowledge of Bruno's attitude to the three main powers of western Christendom in his time. He certainly appears as hostile to Spain as his published works imply: frantic about the prospect of a successful Spanish-supported coup in England, and deeply worried by the great political event of his years in England, the dramatic restoration of Spanish power in the Netherlands by his fellow-countryman Alessandro Farnese, Prince of Parma. Perhaps we can see, as time went on, the Spaniards achieving a more heroic profile in his mind: in the early part of his career as a spy, his worry seems to have been that they would achieve some kind of success in the Netherlands by doing a deal with the Duke of Anjou, with the French, or with Elizabeth; later, he seems to see them as in a position to maintain the standard of popery alone against all comers.[67] He must have been deeply gratified and relieved by the defeat of the Armada of 1588, though so far as I know he never

---

66 *Spaccio*, pp. 719–24; *Texts*, nos. 6 and 13. The revolt occurred in 1585: Ordine, *La cabala dell'Asino*, p. 120, reports a discussion about whether Bruno could have been referring to it in the *Spaccio*, which seems unlikely.

67 The division perhaps comes with the departure of Mendoza from London in January 1584, and so between *Texts*, nos. 9 and 10.

mentioned it, and at the time he was sucking up to the Habsburgs in Germany. Yet, even if we ignore his remarks about rebellion in Naples, there seems to be very little animosity in his writings towards the Spaniards as such. True, there is his description of Don Gaston de Spinola, a representative pro-Spanish Italian, as a mongrel Genoese-Spanish-Sicilian, 'which is the worst commixture that ever was', but this sounds more anti-Genoese or anti-Sicilian than anti-Spanish.[68] Spaniards as such do not qualify for the sort of detestation he felt towards papists, Jews, and women. In the *Spaccio* they are described as Atlases, examples of avarice and ambition, followers of Mars, cultivators of the martial virtues and the avenging of injuries.[69] This is really rather complimentary, and makes me wish we knew more about Bruno's relation with Bernardino de Mendoza, who was a model kind of martial person. So far as we know he cultivated Mendoza in order to spy on him and betray his servants like Zubiaur or the Netherlander Alexander; or to plant false information on him, as I have conjectured in the case of Jean Arnault. I do not think the overture for reconciliation with Rome, made to Mendoza in Paris in 1586, was genuine. But Bruno does seem to have got on with Mendoza quite well; and Mendoza was not the only Spanish ambassador he cultivated. In 1588, when he was in Prague writing a mind-bending work for the same Emperor Rudolf who had handed back Paleologo to Rome, he offered a lesser production to the Spanish ambassador there. He did not think Spanish rule was beneficial to the muses; but even this was not so much the government's fault as the priests'. Altogether I have the impression that he thought the Spaniards were serious people, and it was a pity they were on the wrong side.[70]

Despite his relatively long and on the whole satisfactory residence in France, I am not sure that he thought as well of the French. Frances Yates made Henri III the centre of Bruno's political, and to some extent intellectual, aspirations during the 1580s, and she had a good deal of evidence to substantiate her claim: two dedications, signs of royal friendship and subsidy, the letter of introduction to Castelnau and the supposed mission to England with which Bruno was entrusted, the encomium of the king as peacemaker at the end of the *Spaccio*. Bruno, we understand, was an unqualified admirer of Henri III; the king a liberal favourer of Bruno from the point at which he got to know him through their discussion of the art of

68   *Texts*, no. 6.
69   *Spaccio*, pp. 705–6, 710. The description of the Spaniards as *Atlanti* evokes: (1) holding up the world; (2) guarding the golden apples in the West; (3) the Atlantic.
70   Above, pp. 105 f, 133 f; Yates, *Bruno*, pp. 313–15; Firpo, *Scritti scelti*, introduction p. 31; *Eroici furori*, pp. 955, 1165 ff; *Oratio consolatoria*, p. 33.

memory until the spring of 1586, when he cut him off by sending a poet called Raoul Caillier to denounce his attack on Aristotle at the disputation in the Collège de Cambrai.[71] I think that Bruno's royal readership, like Corbinelli's, entailed some actual attendance on the king.[72] The evidence for this is strongest in 1582–3, and it clearly made an impression, or Henri III would not have arranged for Bruno so comfortable a situation in England. Both of them had lively minds and a demotic way of expressing themselves: I am sure they got on well. Yates's account stands up so far; and I agree with her that something went wrong between them in the spring of 1586, and roughly with her view of what that something was. I should be more specific: by my account, evil reports from Châteauneuf in London, brought to the king's attention by Villeroy, proved sufficiently accurate to bring Castelnau's establishment into disgrace, and Bruno along with it. We do not know that he had anything specially damaging to say about Bruno personally, but Bruno's obstructiveness at their interview in London cannot have disposed Châteauneuf in his favour.

In other respects we shall have to chide Dame Frances for wishful thinking. There was no mission to England. Bruno was not an agent for bringing Elizabeth and Henri III together, rather the reverse. He had absolutely no interest in the reconciliation of Catholics and Protestants, which is what she thought the mission was intended to promote. Furthermore, we must accommodate ourselves to the fact that Bruno systematically betrayed the king over a period of some three years. This may seem an excessive judgment, since one might claim that Bruno's espionage was directed, not against the king, but against the Catholic influences which were encouraging French intervention on behalf of Mary, Queen of Scots. There is something in this: I think the king, who was not informed of what Castelnau was up to in this area and disliked what he did know, would have enjoyed some of Fagot's operations. But this line of defence will not really do. As the king said to Stafford on a similar matter: 'Vous voulez faire les valets du diable, nous faire du bien devant qu'on le vous demande.' (This is the behaviour of the ministers of the devil, who do us good before we ask them to.)[73] Bruno, in his career as Fagot, had other things in mind than the glorification of Henri III,

---

71 Yates, 'Religious Policy', pp. 192–7; *The French Academies of the Sixteenth Century* (London, 1947; repr. 1988), pp. 225–34; *Bruno*, pp. 202 f, 300 f, 340 f.

72 *Texts*, no. 1; *Documenti*, p. 122; Boucher, *La Cour de Henri III*, pp. 21, 133 – she has (pp. 9–37) a persuasive personal description of the king. I take it that Bruno's 'extraordinary' lectorship is to be contrasted with Corbinelli's 'ordinary' one.

73 Chéruel, pp. 113, 120, 324; Stafford to Walsingham, 24-iii/3-iv-1587 (*CSP Foreign 1586–88*, p. 250).

and had no inhibitions about transferring his loyalty elsewhere. Hence, at the beginning of the confession letter, his description of Elizabeth as Queen of England, France and Ireland, which Henri III would not have appreciated. Hence his pressing invitation to Walsingham to employ him as a spy when he returned to France, since he would continually be hobnobbing with the king's councillors.[74] The main point can be simply stated: in April 1583 Bruno dropped Henri III for Elizabeth, while continuing to enjoy the benefits of his protection, hospitality and friendship. The king was not such a lover of 'l'Angloise' as to have forgiven him if he had found him out.

I must here say another word about the famous passage in the *Spaccio* where the king is elevated to heaven as the wearer of *Corona australis*, the southern crown. I have said that I am sure this was satirical, an exposure, in the guise of a eulogy, of the king's incapacity to do anything about resisting the growth of Spanish power in the Netherlands or elsewhere, and a covert snigger about his penchant for self-flagellation and other devotions. But there is more to it than this. Yates supposed that the 'bold, tempestuous and turbulent spirits', the rebels who disturbed the boundaries and coasts of others and wanted to give the king a third earthly crown, were the Leaguers and the House of Lorraine. But this is out of the question, since the examples given of possible crowns are those of Portugal and the Netherlands, both of which belonged to Philip II: the Duke of Guise was not planning to give either of them to Henri III. The reference is to Huguenots like Coligny, and their potential Catholic allies like the Duke of Anjou or Piero Strozzi, with whose enterprises of active intervention in the Netherlands and the Azores the king had taken extreme care to have nothing to do. On the obvious reading of the passage, Bruno was commending him for refusing to join what in England would be called the Protestant cause, at a time when, after the assassination of William of Orange, Elizabeth and Sidney were busy trying to sell it to him.[75] This was not what Bruno meant, but it was what he said.

When we have read the passage properly we can connect it, as I think it ought to be connected, with those equally famous passages in the *Spaccio* where Bruno makes vicious attacks upon predestinarians. The passages, though separate in the dialogue from the one just mentioned, are connected with it by their content, by one of Bruno's

---

74 *Texts*, nos. 11 and 15.
75 Above, pp. 151–2; *Spaccio*, pp. 826–7; Yates, 'Religious Policy', p. 194; *French Academies*, p. 228; *Bruno*, pp. 228–9. Ciliberto, in *Spaccio*, p. 34, gets the implications right, but assumes that Bruno was being serious.

Freudian slips, and in my view by the fact that they are both mainly about the Huguenots. The first awards *Corona borealis*, the northern crown, to whichever heroic prince will exterminate those who believe in justification by faith and those pedants who have taught them: those 'robbers and occupiers of the hereditary goods of others' who live in the institutions created by the works they despise, and destroy the sociability, and the certainty of rewards and punishments in this world and the next, which are necessary for the existence of commonwealths. The second elaborates the portrait of people who blow peace and concord to bits with their contradictory catechisms, destroy universities and works of public beneficence, and breed a generation of Christians with a talent for demolishing old foundations but none for raising new ones. If they are not to be exterminated, let the new pedants give up the property they have seized and abandon the desecrated sanctuaries into which they have intruded. Let them live on the cold charity of those they have taught not to believe in it, and suffer the malice and barbarism of their flocks, desperate of salvation because of the violence and murders they have committed, and disqualified from bettering their chances by acts of almsgiving, mercy or justice.[76]

These are powerful polemics against Protestantism in general and Calvinism in particular. Let us not argue whether Bruno had mainly English Puritans or French Huguenots in mind: he claimed, in talking to a French Catholic, to detest them both.[77] They are, at the least, about the Huguenots as well, and form a perfectly recognisable description of *ceux de la Religion* as seen through the eyes of a patriotic Catholic Frenchman. In the first of them Henri III was being encouraged to suppress the Protestants at home, as he was to be commended later in the book for not joining the Protestant cause abroad: he would receive the crown of the North for one and the crown of the South for the other.

Unlike the piece about *Corona australis*, the passages about *Corona borealis* were not satirical: Bruno truly believed that people who taught justification by faith and predestination to the masses ought to be shot. Nevertheless there is something wrong with them. What is wrong is that Bruno was an enemy of Protestant theology who was also an enthusiast for the Protestant cause. In a perfect world, Protestants or at least Calvinists ought to be persecuted; but not tonight. Not in England, not in France, not in the Netherlands, and not in Geneva: not until they had got rid of the pope. The dictum,

---

76 *Spaccio*, pp. 622–6, 660–5; Yates, *Bruno*, pp. 226 f. The slip, which confuses *Corona borealis* with *Corona australis*, is in *Spaccio*, p. 625.

77 Ciliberto, in *Spaccio*, pp. 29–35, argues that they are about England; remark to Cotin, *Documenti*, p. 40.

which appears in the first passage, that it was logical for anti-predestinarians to persecute predestinarians but not *vice versa*, may have been his own invention rather than, as I am inclined to think, something out of Castelnau's table talk put in to gratify his employer.[78] But for the time being, which would surely last as long as the pope did, he actively believed and collaborated in the repression, not to say persecution, of anti-predestinarian English papists by the predestinarian Walsingham. I have no doubt that he would have thought and done the same in France if the situation had arisen.

Why then did he write as he did? Well: he was the chaplain of the French embassy in London; he was about to return to France; he hoped to make a career there, presumably of a quasi-ecclesiastical kind. He had a great deal to conceal already, and planned to have more to conceal in future: he needed to cover his tracks. He disguised his belief in the Protestant cause by expounding or embroidering his genuine distaste for Protestant theology. He was not lying, but he was being dishonest; partly, I think, for Henri III's benefit, to palliate the odium of publicly supporting him, but mainly for his own. If not from the beginning, then from his arrival in London, Bruno's relation to the king had been equivocal. He liked him but did not admire him: he thought him wet in politics and absurd in his masochistic devotions and affection for Capuchins and Jesuits. He had been happy to drop him for Elizabeth. The best one could expect from him, in the church, was to maintain the excellent French tradition of converting its resources to the support of the nobility, and perhaps to abolish female religious houses, which he did not cultivate; and, in the state, to make the most of his hatred for the Duke of Guise and his boredom with the Queen of Scots. For anything better the world would have to wait for Henri of Navarre who, as Bruno judged him, was a fighter in the Protestant cause who did not believe in Protestantism either.[79]

With Bruno's attitude to Queen Elizabeth we come to something as solid and unambiguous as his detestation of the papacy. There is nothing in his life really comparable to the presentation to her of his four Italian dialogues which, as I suppose, took place over Christmas 1584, when he had just finished writing them and thought he was about to return to France. What he had heard of Elizabeth before he came to London I have no idea; but from April 1583 when he first entered her service, and certainly from the point not long after when he met her for the first time, he was her unreserved admirer and follower. Some of his dealings with Mendoza may make us a little

78 *Spaccio*, pp. 624 f.; I think Castelnau shared Ronsard's views on the subject, described in Yates, 'Religious Policy', p. 197.
79 *Documenti*, p. 122; *Sommario*, no. 212; Yates, *Bruno*, p. 341.

suspicious, but in Elizabeth's case there is really no reason to doubt the protestations of absolute fidelity of which Fagot's letters are full, or to regard the encomia in his published works as formal, or as concealing some ulterior intention. At his trial he was accused of calling her 'diva', and explained it as the kind of thing you were expected to say in England; but I am happy to agree with Frances Yates that in this case he meant what he said.[80] As long as he was in her service, that is to say during the period covered by this book, he looked up to her as the one salvation of miserable Europe, the refuge of the muses, the model of true religion, a potential slayer of the rampant Beast and a replacement for ailing Jove. Perhaps these feelings about her, and perhaps her nature, inhibited him from developing the kind of intimacy which he acquired with Henri III; perhaps he never got really close to anyone he was not betraying; or perhaps the difficulty was that unlike the King of France she knew too much about him. In the confession letter, Bruno said that the queen had shown him favour 'not only with her mouth but also with her heart', which must mean that she had thanked him for his services as warmly as she ought to have done.[81] But I doubt if she was gratified, or even amused, by the complicity he attempted to force upon her in handing her, inside the black morocco binding of the brand-new *Spaccio* and under the nose of Castelnau, a reminder of his services in the discomfiture of his master. The evidence, such as it is, suggests that she regarded employing him as a distasteful necessity, felt slightly bashful about it in relation to Castelnau, and did not approve of betraying the seal of confession even when it was done, ostensibly, on her own behalf. She was not a woman who despised the traditional sanctities of celibacy, altar and sacrament, and I suspect that, by contrast with the frustrated respect she felt for her disobedient subjects who became seminary priests and Jesuits, she viewed his manipulation of his priesthood with some disgust. According to a late source, she thought him a dreamer, a criminal and an atheist, which was how an anonymous informant described the feeling about him in England on the eve of his burning.[82] Though they had no diplomatic representation during her reign Elizabeth's relations with Venice were rather good, and by 1599–1600 her relations with Pope Clement VIII were not so bad that she could not have organised some kind of approach on his behalf if she had wanted to.

80 Above, pp. 127–9; Yates, *Bruno*, pp. 287–90; *Documenti*, p. 121.
81 *Texts*, no. 11.
82 The source (Giulio Cesare la Galla, *De phoenomenis in orbe lunae*, Venice, 1612) was found by Ludovico Limentani: Ciliberto, 'Asini e pedanti', p. 111; Salvestrini, *Bibliografia*, no. 292. Firpo, 'Processo' (ii), 46.

One-sided as it was, Bruno's relationship with Elizabeth was one of the big things in his life: besides confirming what he said about her in print we can add a good deal of reliable knowledge from his secret correspondence. On the basis of what he said in public the case has been well put by Frances Yates in a passage on Bruno as an Elizabethan: she observed that Bruno seemed to have got the climax of his most moving piece of Elizabetholatry, the passage in the *Eroici furori* where, as Diana, she brings sight to the blind muses at the end of their pilgrimage from Campania, from one of the Accession Day performances which were the high rituals of the cult of the queen.[83] I have a few things to add to the interpretation of these passages. In the light of the history of Fagot, Throckmorton and Courcelles, we can see exactly what he meant by saying in *De la causa* that heaven had so preserved and defended her that 'others' had vainly striven to dislodge her by their 'words' and 'forces'. The 'others' were the pope, the English papists and their continental allies, and Queen Mary; their 'words' were the papal bull of deposition of 1570 and the works of Catholic propaganda imported by Girault; their 'forces', those put into Catholic efforts at conspiracy and invasion which, had it been expedient for him to boast, he could have claimed off heaven a good deal of the credit for defeating.[84] He had in mind, as in his prefatory sonnet to the piece, the 'zeal for iniquity' of such as Thomas Morgan, the 'impious brain' of such as Henry Howard, and the 'perverted enterprise' of such as Francis Throckmorton.[85]

One of Bruno's Elizabethan texts occurs in the *Cena*, where the queen is portrayed as Astraea and Amphitrite, and the merits of her councillors are extolled: it was one of the passages revised in the second version, and implications about the history of Bruno's political feelings in England have been drawn from the revision. The passage comes between Bruno's and Florio's murky trip on the Thames and the walk down the Strand during which they are knocked about by the London *plebe*.[86] It is connected to the episode which follows because the warm and generous reception given to foreigners by Elizabeth, her councillors and courtiers is contrasted with the vicious xenophobia of the *plebe*; the contrast between their wisdom and security and the impotent machinations of popish watermen is also clear, and an interpolation from Frulla of the biblical story about Samuel and Saul[87] makes the connection be-

---

83 Above, n. 80; *Eroici furori*, pp. 1165–78.
84 *Causa*, p. 222/58; for the translation of this passage, above, pp. 48 f, n. 59. Yates, *Bruno*, p. 288, has been over-influenced by her discovery of a connection between it and the Accession Day performances.
85 Above, pp. 113 f.
86 *Cena*, pp. 67–70/128–131 and 286 ff.
87 Below, p. 170.

tween the two by indicating Elizabeth as the choice of heaven. The revision which has been remarked on is that, of the four servants of the queen who are mentioned individually – Burghley, Leicester, Walsingham and Sidney – Burghley is left out in the second version, while Leicester's wife is introduced. The changes give the rewritten text a fairly Protestant flavour, and Aquilecchia interprets them as an olive branch to the zealous party for offence caused by the drinking-scene and other aspects of the original version.[88] At first sight this looks a likely gambit. Bruno's politics were Protestant politics, and a cold reception of the *Cena* in Protestant quarters would be a reason for affirming them in May or June 1584. Leicester and his friends were indeed, as Protestant enthusiasts, a good deal more inter-nationalist than Burghley was. But there are arguments against a political interpretation of the revisions, and it does not seem to me the most likely. It is hard to make much of Leicester's countess in a political context, since she was not a political figure and had a low public profile; if anything, I should be inclined to connect her surprising appearance here with the seemingly most unusual fact that Leicester had invited Castelnau to meet her at dinner earlier in the year.[89] Castelnau was rather desperately making up to Leicester during the summer, and a civil reference to his wife from Bruno's pen might have done some good. It also seems most implausible to me that Bruno, at this point in his career, should have intended a public snub to Burghley: Burghley was involved as well as Walsing-ham in the *histoire de Fagot*, and Bruno's later dealings with Stafford show that he was happy to work for either of them.

There is another possibility. In the English manuscript copy of the *Cena* on which Aquilecchia mainly relied for his 'definitive' version, the catalogue of Elizabeth's servants has a cancellation of the sentence mentioning Walsingham.[90] The sentence was not omitted in the printed text of the second version as we have it; but the manuscript would appear to show that somebody had marked it for deletion on the example being copied, and I should be inclined to suppose that Bruno, having left Burghley out of his list, proposed to even things up by leaving out Walsingham as well. If I am correct, the further alteration would have been very compatible with another feature of the new version: it now attributed the welcoming attitude to foreigners, not to the Privy Council, but to Elizabeth herself. The reason for the alteration would, to my mind, be fairly plain: Fagot, as it were, had rewritten Bruno's text for professional purposes, to

88   Above, p. 46, n. 50.
89   Castelnau to Henri III, 22-xii-1583/1-i-1584; to Mary, [?i]-1584 (BL Harleian 1582, ff. 334, 387).
90   *Cena* (Aquilecchia), pp. 131, 286; 'La lezione definitiva', pp. 224 f, 232.

remove the implication that he had been in touch with the business end of the Privy Council, and to portray his reception by the queen and her entourage as a normal act of courtly hospitality to foreigners, especially Italian. Leaving Walsingham in would have been, as I rather conjecture, an oversight by the printer, or perhaps an oversight by Bruno, possibly unaware that in this courtly company Walsingham would stick out like a sore thumb. In the second case I should not be surprised if Walsingham himself had advised him to change it. This is of course a speculative proposal, but I think it is better founded than that of Aquilecchia. The reader may think it invalidated by the detail that in the first version Bruno went out of his way to insist that he did not personally know either Burghley or Leicester, and had no intention of getting to know them; the protestation disappeared in the rewrite. But perhaps Fagot thought that Bruno had been protesting too much.

What we now know about Bruno makes me want to connect this passage with one which immediately precedes it in the original version of the *Cena*, a long speech by the demotic Frulla about how writers are like princes, and prefer to start with sows' ears in order to show their majesty by turning them into silk purses; he gave the illustration of Saul, a modest youth from the tribe of Benjamin sent to look for his father's wandering she-asses, being anointed king of Israel by Samuel;[91] Saul at the time was much more interested in getting his asses back. The passage, though sparkling and funny, was left out in the second version, perhaps because Sidney, whom Elizabeth had not promoted, found it embarrassing, or perhaps because its implications about the relation between princes and holy men were tactless. Bruno found something more appropriate in the *Eroici furori*, where the model was Diana and Actaeon. But the story of Saul and Samuel meant a lot to him, for it reemerged more than once in the later dialogues in the inscrutable parables about asses and the notion of the *idiota triumphans*.[92] Bruno surely saw himself in the role of Samuel. It would be a mistake to deduce from this, and from his response to Henry Howard's attack on the profession, that Bruno thought of himself as a prophet. In Venice he took a strong line about the prophets of the Old Testament, and told his fellow-prisoners that they were phonies and trouble-makers who had, like Jesus himself, deserved the fate they often met at the hands of kings; there is no

---

91   *Cena*, pp. 64–6/283–5; 1 Samuel 9. Sidney also used the saying about princes, in respect of King Basilius and the oaf Dametas, in *The Countess of Pembroke's Arcadia*, book i, c. 3 (ed. Maurice Evans, London, 1977, pp. 78–9).

92   *Cabala*, pp. 838 ff, 846 ff, and *passim; Eroici furori*, pp. 1005 ff, 1123–6; *idiota triumphans*, above, p. 153.

reason to suppose that he had changed his views since 1584.[93]
Samuel, in the parts of the story that Bruno was interested in, was
acting not as a prophet but as a priest; and we now have very good
reason for thinking that Samuel the priest was a figure with whom,
in the spring of 1584, Bruno might be feeling he had a good deal in
common. It was as a priest that he had just sent his confession letter
to Queen Elizabeth, and not simply a priest who had heard Zubiaur's
confession, but a priest who in and by means of his letter was
blessing the queen himself, or conveying to her the blessing of God.
The letter is headed: 'En la serenissime Royne d'Angleterre, France et
Yrlande salut, bonne, longue et heureuse vie. Amen.' This is conventional, except for the 'Amen'. It ends in more solemn Latin:
'Deus adjuvat te et maneat tecum omnibus diebus vite tue. Amen.'
This is a very formal blessing, which Bruno must I think have made
up spontaneously, since I cannot find an exact source for it in the
liturgy or in comparable situations in the Old Testament. Since
Bruno wrote no other letter directly to Elizabeth, we cannot surprise
him blessing her in person again; but after he had left England he
sent, via Walsingham, a blessing to her and her Council.[94] I conclude
that, apart from the powerful personal impression she made on him,
Bruno had a rather clear view of what her position was, and of how
he related to her. He was quite justified in telling the inquisitors that
he did not think she was divine; but he did quite seriously think she
was sacred.[95] She was not sacred simply because she was a queen – I
do not think he thought Henri III was sacred in the same sense – nor
because of her virginity, which Bruno rated lower than she did. She
was sacred, partly for her queenship and for her embodiment of
virtues and characteristics he admired; but mostly for the position
she was in, where the inviolability of her person and rule symbolised
the present survival and future victory of the forces of light and truth
over those of darkness and error represented by the pope, the papacy
and the papists. Her person and rule were therefore objects of true
religion, and to speak or act against either was sacrilegious or
possibly blasphemous. The duty of a true religious was to protect
and defend her, and to frustrate her enemies; the duty of a true priest
would be to pray and sacrifice on her behalf, and to bring down upon

93 *Sommario*, nos. 41–7, 124–9; Firpo, 'Processo' (i), 585.
94 *Texts*, nos. 11, 16. There are roughly similar blessings in Judith 15: 9–12, and Psalm
     127: 5; the second would have been inappropriate because children were part of the
     blessing. I use the Vulgate numbering of the Psalms, which between Psalms 10 and 148 is
     one figure before the numbering of the Authorised Version, now generally used.
95 *Texts*, no. 11: 'vostre sacré majesté'. True, this was a cliché, but I am not sure that Bruno
     was using it as such.

her all the days of her life the help and blessing of whatever gods there were. We know that Bruno prayed for her and blessed her; we do not know whether he sacrificed for her, but I should not be surprised if he did. He certainly offered her, in the words of the canon of the mass, the sacrifice of praise.[96]

iv Priest

In trying to find out what Bruno thought about his priesthood, we now have a serious problem which we did not have before. In Venice he told his fellow-prisoners that he was an enemy of the mass, and thought transubstantiation a ridiculous idea and the Catholic ritual bestial and blasphemous. He compared the elevation of the host to hanging somebody on a gallows, or perhaps to lifting him up on a pitchfork. He told somebody who had dreamt of going to mass that that was a terrible omen; and he performed a mock mass with Ovid's *Art of Love* instead of a missal. He joked about hungry priests going off from mass to a good breakfast. He spoke particularly ill of the mass as a sacrifice, and said that Abel, the archetype of the sacrificing priest, was a criminal butcher who was rightly killed by the vegetarian Cain. A phrase he used elsewhere, apparently about Christ's passion and not directly about the mass itself, seems nevertheless to express rather exactly his attitude to it: he called it 'some kind of a cabbalistic tragedy'.[97] He also said that the breviary was full of rubbish and fables and pornographic matter, and could not be said by any decent person: whoever had put it together was an effing goat, and he certainly would not say it himself.[98] Altogether, the characteristics of the Catholic priesthood sound as beastly and perverse as one would expect of a ministry governed by the pope.

But now we know that he spent eighteen months of his mature life, at precisely the time when he was writing his most famous works, exercising this farcical and dishonest ministry professionally in London. We know that he said mass for Castelnau, his household, and such others as came, heard their confessions and gave them their Easter communions; he presumably rubbed ashes on their foreheads on Ash Wednesday and baptised Castelnau's short-lived daughter, born in July 1585.[99] He visited prisons and, I suppose, distributed

---

96 Memento of the living; *Eroici furori*, p. 1081.

97 *Sommario*, nos. 65–8, 110–16; *Spaccio*, p. 655. In the last phrase I assume that Bruno had also in mind the original meaning of the word 'tragedy': a performance by or about goats.

98 *Sommario*, nos. 158–67. The term is 'becco fottuto' (no. 158), and was also used by Bruno of Jesus: 'cane becco fottuto can' (no. 169); Firpo, 'Processo' (i), 584.

99 Above, p. 58, n. 81.

Castelnau's alms to poor Catholics. It sounds rather as if he read his breviary, if only in bed. When he said he had no job in Salisbury Court except to act as Castelnau's 'gentleman', he was not telling the truth; or rather, he was making his own the fiction about his status which Castelnau systematically maintained in public, rather as Queen Mary's travelling Jesuit Henri de Samerie was disguised as the gentleman-servant De la Rue. Bruno does not seem particularly to have wanted to preserve the secret himself, or he would not have described Castelnau, in the dedication of the *Cena*, as having welcomed him to the 'most eminent place in your house', nor, in *De la causa*, made the joke about chaplains and philosophers.[100] The confession letter seems to show him filling the role very comfortably: I presume that he had discouraged Zubiaur from making his confession to him because he was not a member of the household, rather than because he was himself an unwilling confessor.

Various suppositions about what Bruno may have felt in this situation spring to mind: that he thought it a disgusting chore, a joke, or an ideal point of vantage for pursuing his career as a spy. He might well have regarded it as a chore if Henri III had positively sent him over to do the job, but this is unlikely: the choice of chaplain, as of his other domestic officers, was surely Castelnau's own business. I assume that Bruno accepted the offer with some degree of satisfaction, as he did his post of almoner to the Duke of Montpensier. The title of the *Cena* indicates that saying mass gave him a taste of ashes, and a passage in the *Eroici furori*, that he felt like an idiot scratching the backs of other idiots; the discarded drinking-scene expresses a hyper-Erasmian disgust with the ritual and social theology of the eucharist.[101] But there were compensations. During the canon, I imagine him relieving his feelings about the words of consecration by enjoying the thought of Christ strung up on a cross or gallows as he lifted the host at the elevation; chuckling during the invocation of Abel the butcher at how justly he was slaughtered by Cain; praying for the destruction of his enemies at the commemoration of the dead and for the preservation of Elizabeth at that of the living. If he could get through this he had nothing much to worry about in the communion itself, where he would usually be alone: Castelnau was not a frequent communicant, and his wife was usually in bed. In

100 *Texts*, no. 1; *Cena*, p. 17/79; *Causa*, p. 202/40; above, pp. 79–81. For Samerie, A. Lynn Martin, *Henry III and the Jesuit Politicians* pp. 109–13; he paid a visit, perhaps investigative, to Salisbury Court in July 1584: Castelnau to Walsingham, 6/16-vii-1584 (*CSP Foreign 1583–84*, p. 592). Although J.H. Pollen described him as Mary's 'Jesuit chaplain', there is some doubt whether he was actually a priest (Martin, p. 113).

101 *Cena*, p. 9/69; *Eroici furori*, pp. 1081 f; *Texts*, no. 12ii. Cf. *Sigillus*, p. 181: 'certas. . . de Cerere et Baccho credulitates', Ceres and Bacchus being circumlocutions for bread and wine; *Candelaio*, p. 211.

view of the squeamishness about physical and social contagion expressed in the *Cena*, the absence of visible commensality or liquidity in the Roman rite must have been a blessing. When he turned to the congregation at *Dominus vobiscum* he must sometimes have noted a face to be remembered in Fagot's letters. I should think that he was worried about laughing, for one's assumption that he would have found the whole performance an enormous joke is supported by the general jocularity of his references to the sacraments.[102]

But he was not doing it for the joke but for the unbeatable cover it gave him. If we were sure that Castelnau's invitation and Bruno's interview with Walsingham had happened at roughly the same time, that is to say immediately upon his arrival in England, we could speculate that Walsingham would have set at rest any qualms he might have had about accepting the position. We cannot be sure of this; but at whatever point the invitation came to him, he had in the pursuance of his career as a spy an absolutely satisfactory justification for accepting it. He would be violating the inmost sanctities of a false religion in order to defend those of a true one. If I may quote a proverb he was keen on, he would not be one of those pusillanimous spirits who at one moment said it was a sin to spit on the floor of a church, and at another were found relieving themselves on the altar: he would be fouling the altar all the time. He said in dedicating the *Cena* to Castelnau, that the work was a conjunction of opposites, amazingly sacrilegious and amazingly religious all at once. We can see the kind of thing he meant in the confession letter, and I have no doubt that the description was meant to apply to his situation as a whole. In his life as in his work, he found the conjunction of opposites both intellectually thrilling and a very good joke: I have little doubt that his pleasure in it does a lot to account for his outburst of literary creativity in the spring of 1584.[103] Nothing, not even pulling the wool over the eyes of his inquisitors, was ever so much fun afterwards.

Perhaps Bruno did not walk up and down the gallery at Salisbury Court reciting the psalms of the breviary, or sit in his room at the top of the house, or under a tree in the garden, reading his bible: he remembered them well enough at his trial, but that may have been due to his early training as a friar. He described the Hebrews as the excrement of Egypt, and always spoke of Jews with malice and contempt. There was not much in either Testament which he

102 E.g., those in the *Cena*, above, n. 29; *Texts*, no. 5.
103 *Cena*, p. 8/68; *Causa*, dialogue v; *Spaccio*, pp. 572 f; *Eroici furori*, p. 974. The proverb was cited, from Bruno, by Florio in his *Second Fruits*: Yates, *Florio*, pp. 113 f.; in 'Religious Policy', p. 187n, she interprets it as a reference to English recusants.

thought acceptable reading. Genesis was mythological; the Law a bloody and tyrannical code cooked up in the brain of Moses, who had been a renegade from Egyptian religion; the prophets were criminal fantasists who spent their time stirring up the people to sedition against kings, and were rightly killed; Jesus was yet another prophet, who added cowardice to the other vices of the profession.[104] We have seen that he made an exception for the story of Samuel; and he made a much larger exception for the books of Wisdom which fall between the history of the kings and that of the prophets (Job to Ecclesiasticus). Although the wisdom embodied in these books was not perfect, enough that was not Jewish had got into them – as we would say, from the cultural ambience of the Middle East, as Bruno would say from the true wisdom of the Egyptians – for one to regard them, if properly handled, as some kind of repository of acceptable truth. Most of it was provided by Solomon, who under the name of Ecclesiastes had delivered Bruno's favourite dictum, that there was nothing new under the sun; most of the rest of it was embedded here and there in the Book of Psalms. The wisdom they incorporated could not be extracted by everyone: it was available to the learned and not to the vulgar; and among the supposedly learned, not to the *stulti* or asses of whom, according to Solomon, the number was infinite.[105]

The pearl inside them was what Bruno's Egyptian hero Hermes Trismegistus, in the Lament to Asclepius quoted in the *Spaccio*, had called 'the religion of the mind'.[106] The main obstacle to this religion, particularly likely to result from concentrating upon the psalms as Christians had tended to do, was to suppose that the object of worshipping the Lord in these terms was to receive from him certain kinds of immediate satisfaction. In Venice he rebuked a fellow-prisoner for blasphemy in saying Psalm 34 ('Judica, Domine, nocentes me') in order to bring down vengeance upon his enemies; the same objection would apply to a large number of other psalms, like Psalm 42, said at the beginning of mass, if they were taken in a literal or social spirit.[107] Bruno himself certainly used them in such ways, and not only when, as his fellow-prisoners reported, he cast lots by inscribing verses from the Psalms in magic circles; but we are not to expect too much consistency between his words and his actions.[108] I should think this customary use of psalms was one of the

---

104 *Spaccio*, pp. 722, 799; *Cabala*, p. 868; *Cena*, pp. 120 f/182 f; *Sommario*, nos. 41–7, 117–29, 168–77.
105 Ecclesiastes 1: 9, 15.
106 *Spaccio*, p. 785.
107 *Sommario*, no. 13.
108 *Sommario*, nos. 192–3; *Texts*, no. 11, postscript.

reasons why he claimed that the breviary was full of profane matter, though the example he quoted did not incite to malice but to concupiscence: he said the Song of Songs gave him an erection. This was a dishonest argument, since in principle he thought that a literal reading of the Song of Songs might be very good for one.[109] It ought to promote one of the two principal effects to be anticipated from a religion of the mind, which were the rational cultivation of divinity in its embodiments of nature and of justice: the nature that gave forth the glory of God and provided the pleasures of Epicurus, and the justice that rendered to every man according to his works.

Wisdom, nature and justice were united reasonably well in the person of Solomon, to whom, and not to Jesus, the kings of Tarshish and the islands had brought their gifts, albeit the Egyptians had had a larger idea of nature and the Romans a more vigorous concept of justice. And all three of them were, as a general rule, painfully dependent on the existence of true kings to maintain them. Under the shade of *Corona australis* one could dine in peace on the noonday fish, as the gods do at the end of the *Spaccio*; there one could find the terminus of stormy labours, sleep, tranquil repose, secure quiet. There, according to Fagot, resided the 'repos public de [la] patrie'. Thence you could see good things in the land of the living.[110] The psalmist had done his bit for kings, calling down blessings upon them, and praying for the triumphs over enemies which it was not proper for anyone but the Lord's anointed to ask for himself.[111] In his public writings Bruno had portrayed such true kingship in the persons of Elizabeth and, I assume satirically, of Henri III; in his private letters he drew on the language of the psalms to call down blessing and protection on the queen. There he could also have found his word for the collective forces of darkness over which true kingship would triumph: the Beast appears in Psalm 71: 9, and although St Jerome had made a mess of the verse Bruno's Hebrew may have been good enough to correct him.[112] He could of course have found it with less trouble in the Book of Revelation, but I doubt if that was a work he read very often. Who best represented the Beast for the time being, Bruno had no doubt. He was crawling about among the Malcontents: the teethgrinders like Zubiaur, Torquato and those who said 'Ha! Ha!' against the just David; the 'congrega-

---

109 *Sommario*, nos. 163, 201–5.
110 Psalm 71: 10; *Sommario*, nos. 98–9; *Spaccio*, pp. 570, 828–9; *Texts*, no. 13; Psalm 26: 13.
111 Psalms 2, 19, 71, 109 etc.
112 The *Jerusalem Bible* (London, 1966), numbering as Psalm 72, has 'the Beast' instead of the Vulgate's 'Ethiopians'; the verse immediately precedes the one about the Kings of Tarshish (above, n. 110).

tion of the malignant' whom the Lord would devour with fire; the 'pernicious angels' of the Lament to Asclepius, who mingled with mankind and tempted it to sedition and chaos on the pretext of executing justice; the 'enemies of the state, who seek its entire destruction by a civil war, and go about stirring up the people of England to revolt against their princess'.[113]

There were certainly a few teeth-grinders amongst the Elizabethan puritans, and Torquato may have been intended as one: as a class, they were more inclined to prophecy than to wisdom; they were nervous about kings and, being predestinarians, in principle a threat to civil society. But they were not what mattered to Bruno while he was in England, and not what all this was about. Bruno was not risking a knife in his back to frustrate their mild grumblings against the queen. I am not sure whether the Beast was exactly the pope, but high among the pernicious angels hovered the Howards and the Romish priests, and loud among the teeth-grinders ground those who did their work for them, Throckmortons, Morgans, Giraults and Zubiaurs. In defending Elizabeth against their machinations, Bruno had, very successfully, fought the forces of darkness with the arms of Minerva; he had not got much out of it, but he hoped that, unlike the poor sage who by his *sapientia* had saved the little city from the onslaught of a mighty king, he would not be forgotten.[114]

'All the rivers run into the sea,' said Solomon, 'and the sea is never full.' One thing that surprised Bruno when he came to England was that these words of Mediterranean wisdom were not true of the Thames. It did indeed flow into Ocean, but twice a day Ocean became full and the Thames flowed back uphill, from Greenwich to Richmond or so. Then it flowed down again, leaving at its edges the acres of mud where Florio and he floundered in the dark on the night of the *Cena*. Elizabeth was surely beloved of Ocean and the watery gods, who made this miracle happen for her. When he got used to it,

---

113 Teeth-grinders: Psalm 34: 16, the psalm Bruno complained about, above, p. 175; also 36: 12; *Texts*, nos. 11 and 13; *Cena*, p. 105/166. Otherwise, Psalms 20: 10–12, 25: 5, 34: 21, 69: 3; *Spaccio*, p. 786. Ciliberto has repeatedly claimed that by the 'angeli nocentes' of this last passage Bruno meant Luther and the Reformers: e.g., in his edn of the *Spaccio*, pp. 45–7, 270–2. I find this incompatible with the sense of the whole section pp. 776–97, and not supported by Bruno's alterations to the original of the Lament, which he was the first to point out. Bruno certainly multiplied the references to *giustizia*. But I do not think that stirring people up to warfare, fraud and unnatural evil 'come fusse giustizia' can have anything to do with the *justitia* of justification by faith; whereas the connection with the views attributed to Zubiaur in the confession letter (*Texts*, nos. 11 and 11a) seems to me fairly plain, and the connection with the legal assassination of William of Orange even plainer.

114 Ecclesiastes 9: 14–18.

the ebb and flow of the Thames came to symbolise the sacred tranquillity of England, compared with the bloody turbulence of the Seine, the Rhône and the Tiber, ferrying their loads of corpses, the anger and nervous fussing of those of the rest of the continent.[115] From the room which we have imagined at the top of Salisbury Court, he would have had a good view of the river, and we may see him during his nocturnal contemplations[116] looking down from the sky to catch the moon shining on the black water as it ran past Buckhurst Stairs. Not all the nights can have been so Stygian, nor all the watermen so prone to industrial action, as those of Ash Wednesday night, 1584: he must have enjoyed any number of trips down to the court at Greenwich with Castelnau, across to the Palatine Laski at Winchester House, up to Dee at Mortlake, and to who knows what other enjoyable rendezvous. On the way he could admire the queen's swans,[117] sing in his Neapolitan tenor, relish the thought of the papists in the Tower, smell beyond Westminster and Wapping the rutty bank where Spenser's nymphs gathered their flowers. What outrage to remember that up and down this same river, by day or after nightfall, Charon's crew was busy at the oars: barrels full of noxious books unloading at the Half Moon in Southwark; Jesuits slipping into Arundel House, students and renegades down to Gravesend; conspirators, assassins, and bearers of criminal letters moving to their destinations! And that half their comings and goings were under his nose. 'All the evil and treason which have been discovered,' to quote Fagot for the last time, 'have come from giving M. de Mauvissière a house beside the Thames.'[118] Let malcontents and teeth-grinders take their chance in the Strand with the rest of the venomous rabble, and leave Diana's river to her nymphs and her faithful lovers, her swans and her stars.

---

115 Ecclesiastes 1: 7; *Eroici furori*, pp. 946 f, 1168, 1176 f; *Texts*, no. 12i; *Causa*, p. 223, translated in Yates, *Bruno*, p. 292.

116 *Spaccio*, p. 829.

117 *Spaccio*, pp. 703 f. In prison (*Sommario*, no. 182) Bruno said that in a previous incarnation he had been a swan, which made the other prisoners laugh.

118 *Texts*, no. 13; and no. 4, n. 2, for the location of the Half Moon, which I did not know when I wrote this passage.

Epilogue

FAGOT AT THE STAKE

THIS IS THE END of my story, but it will hardly do to write a book about Bruno and say nothing about his own miserable end.[1] He returned from Germany to Venice in August 1591; was arrested on the denunciation of his host, the young patrician Giovanni Mocenigo, in May 1592; and underwent two months of inconclusive investigation by the Venetian Inquisition. In February 1593 he was transferred to Rome, where the enquiry proceeded in fits and starts for another six years. Towards the end of 1599, having all this time insisted that he was penitent and would abjure any unorthodox opinions proved against him, Bruno changed his mind and refused to abjure anything at all. Thereupon he was delivered by Pope Clement VIII to the secular authorities of the city of Rome, who had him burned alive in the Campo dei Fiori on 17 February 1600.

I have in truth very little to add to this depressing tale: it was no part of the offences charged against Bruno that he had acted as a spy on Catholics in England, since none of his judges or accusers was aware that he had done this. If they had been aware of it, it would not have been a burning matter: from the Church's point of view, the offences of officiating as a priest while under excommunication and of breaking the seal of confession would not in themselves have done much more than aggravate the offence of apostasy from his order, and earn him the rest of his life in a Roman prison. But they would have ruined his pose as a worried but well-meaning Catholic philosopher unsuited to the religious life, and if the facts had got out his *processo* would have been a good deal shorter than it was.

His conduct in England had been one of the things that had interested the Venetian inquisitors, but without any witnesses they had no means of substantiating their scepticism about his bland professions that he had always lived as a good Catholic. At one point

---

1 On which Firpo, 'Processo', is essential.

they implied that they knew something serious about it, but they did not, and Bruno came through this part of his investigation with aplomb. Perhaps he suffered a moment's flutter when, *à propos* of nothing in particular, they asked him whether during his travels he had always used his present name; but he shyly confessed that he had used his baptismal name, Filippo, when crossing the Alps to get out of Italy, and there was no more to it than that.[2] In respect of his un–Catholic life, Bruno left Venice for Rome with a good character, and the Roman inquisitors soon dropped the issue in favour of his opinions in philosophy and theology.

It did however surface once again, in a curious way and at a very late stage in the proceedings. In the summer of 1599 somebody made a deposition against Bruno to the inquisitor of the town of Vercelli in Piedmont; the gist of what he said was that while Bruno was in England he had been taken to be an atheist; and that he had written a book called *Trionfante bestia* against the pope.[3] The deposition brought new matter into the case, since the inquisitors, who had difficulty in getting hold of Bruno's books, do not seem to have known about the *Spaccio*. It was taken seriously, and found a place in his final sentence. We do not know who the informer was, or anything but the barest bones of what he had said; but he knew more about Bruno's doings in England than anybody else concerned in the investigation. He may possibly have been an English Catholic *émigré*, but it seems most likely that he was an Italian who had been in London while Bruno was there, or shortly after. I have wondered if he was not one of Châteauneuf's Italians, who would have had a motive for sticking the knife in: the priest who had been Bruno's *idiota triumphans* would be a plausible candidate.[4] Anyone of this kind would have been an extremely dangerous witness against Bruno, because he would have known that he had acted as a priest in London, and that bombshell would have blown to bits Bruno's ingratiating tale about his life abroad. The informer does not appear to have mentioned this, which may imply that he knew of Bruno's doings only at second hand; at the least, he might simply be someone who had visited Elizabeth's court some time since 1585 and picked up the gossip about him there. But he sounds to me rather nearer the bone than this; and we do not know exactly what he said, or why he

---

2 Firpo, 'Processo' (i), 557, 567, 575; (ii), 31, 42; *Documenti*, p. 126 (24-v/3-vi-1592), for the inquiry about Bruno's name, which Firpo does not mention.

3 Firpo, 'Processo' (ii), 45 f, 49. The relevant passage is from Bruno's final sentence (*Documenti*, pp. 189–95), and is therefore addressed to him: '. . . ed essendosi anco avuto notizia che nel S. Officio di Vercelli eri stato denunziato che, mentre eri in Inghilterra, eri tenuto per ateista e che avevi composto un libro di *Trionfante bestia* . . .'

4 Cf. above, pp. 59, 64, 153.

volunteered it, or most pertinently what he might have said if he had been systematically examined, as he would have been if the *processo* had gone on much longer. Bruno, one may add, did not know either.

If I were to suggest that the threatened exposure of one of his epics of dissimulation persuaded Bruno to ring down the curtain on another – that the ghost of Fagot or of Francis Throckmorton returned to point him to the stake – I should be guilty of the kind of speculation I think historians should avoid, and I have tried to avoid in this book. There is insufficient reason for any supposition of the kind. But to dismiss it is not to say that the story of Fagot has no relevance at all to Bruno's trial and death. Without the story, I wonder whether the burning would have happened.

Let me explain myself. In 1948, Bruno's history was being ventilated in Italy even more widely than usual: it was the 400th anniversary of his birth; the academic community had still to come to grips with the awkward evidence about him contained in the *Sommario* if his trial, which had been found and published by Angelo Mercati in the middle of the war; I imagine the declaration of the Italian Republic had revived the sort of *risorgimento* feelings which had turned Bruno into a national hero at the end of the nineteenth century. The observations made on all sides were surveyed in the admirably just account of Bruno's process published by Luigi Firpo at the time, and in reading it I was particularly struck by his description of one of them, which instantly rang a bell. Its author was the historian of philosophy Marino Gentile, who was mainly interested in rebutting Mercati's supposition that Bruno's professions of repentance were genuine. He took the view that Bruno's conduct of his trial was a sustained and masterly performance in the art of disinformation, its alternations of repentance and obstinacy controlled phases in a 'gioco d'astuzio' or chess-game; he also thought that Bruno, until the very end, had absolute confidence that he could persuade his inquisitors to swallow whatever garbage he cared to pass off on them. This confidence explained why he had taken the risk of coming to Venice in the first place.[5]

Gentile's account was inspired by the passages in Mocenigo's first delation, which were also among the first items to be mentioned in the *Sommario*, where Bruno was reported as saying that all friars were asses and that Catholic doctrines were 'dottrini d'asini'.[6] The

---

5 Firpo, 'Processo' (ii), 55–6, cf. 48 n. 1. I have not managed to see the original, 'Rileggendo il Bruno', *Humanitas* (Brescia), iii (1948), 1154–64 (Salvestrini, *Bibliografia*, no. 1701). I am grateful to Simon Ditchfield for the exact reference, and for the information that Marino Gentile was no relation of Giovanni Gentile, philosopher and editor of Bruno's dialogues.

6 *Documenti*, p. 60, also p. 67; *Sommario*, nos. 1, 2, 3.

friars would have included most of his inquisitors, and the implication was that people who believed in the dogmas of Catholicism could be persuaded to believe anything whatever. On this assumption, Gentile held, Bruno had conducted his defence. Firpo thought this a superficial view, I think because it did not seem quite serious; but now that we know about Bruno's almost equally sustained performance as Fagot, I think we ought to recognise it as probably correct. Not only do we know that Bruno was capable of carrying out, over a period of years and in circumstances not much less dangerous, an adventure in systematic dissimulation of this kind; we know that in 1591 he had pulled it off once already. He had perfectly good reason to think that papists were gullible boobies whom he could bamboozle as much as he wished: why should he not pull it off again? He thought he was the most intelligent man of his time, and he was in the *plus ultra* frame of mind which he had described and commended in the *Cena de le Ceneri*, when Florio and he had stood in the Strand wondering whether to go forward to Whitehall or back to Salisbury Court. 'O *passi graviora!*', 'We have got out of tighter corners than this', had been the motto then. It was not quite so appropriate now, since a chess-game with the Inquisition was riskier than anything he had yet done: it was the practical joke to end all his practical jokes. He did not exactly throw himself at it; but he put himself in the way of it, and, as on the pavement of the Strand, fate intervened to give him his chance. Even his talents might not be sufficient to win. If so,

> not only he who wins is praised, but also he who does not die as a coward and a poltroon. Not only the one who gains the prize is to be honoured, but also the other who has run so well that he is judged worthy and sufficient to have gained it, although he has lost. And they are contemptible who, in the middle of the race, give up in despair and, though last, do not go on to reach the finish with the best nerve and strength they have left. Let perseverance triumph, for, if the effort is so great, the reward will not be trivial. Everything worthwhile is difficult.[7]

He played the game with his customary skill for seven years in the prisons of Venice and Rome. Some time in or after September 1599, either his sense of invulnerability deserted him, or he concluded that the game was not worth the candle. I do not know why this happened. Probably the matters of principle between Bruno and Rome could not have been evaded for ever. It depends on what we think he was up to. We might judge that, if success in the game

7 *Cena*, pp. 60–4/124–7; passage quoted, pp. 63–4/126.

meant setting himself up in Rome, with a clean slate, free to pursue against the papacy itself the underground campaign he had pursued against the papists in England, he was by now short of an employer: Walsingham was dead, Elizabeth seems to have turned against him, and Henri IV had not proved to be the hammer of popery he had anticipated. If he had simply grown sick of dissimulation, I should think it would have given him a good deal of gratification to come out with the Fagot story at last. It would have been quite a *coup de théâtre* to have trumpeted the triumphs of Fagot as the faggots were rising on the Campo dei Fiori. Bruno made no such revelation. True, in the Campo itself he was gagged, but he had had the opportunity beforehand to ventilate the wrath he had been bottling up for seven years. He still did not crow about Fagot. Hence I presume that it meant something to him to go into the fire with that secret intact.

I have left to the last one final item in the reckoning between Fagot and the Campo dei Fiori, which it would have been decent not to mention had not Bruno made so much of it himself. He was accused of holding that the only worthwhile moral rule was to do as you would be done by; he probably had said this, but since I do not find it stated in his writings I cannot claim that it is a rule on which he ought to be judged.[8] What he had quite constantly said was that people ought to be done by as they did; and this he believed. The belief accounts for his resistance to justification by faith and his obsession with the transmigration of souls; from the *Candelaio* to the *Cabala*, practically every one of his writings included a lively example or defence of it.[9] He rewrote the Sermon on the Mount to say that if somebody gave you a box on the ear you should give him one back.[10] But he did not believe that the rule ought to apply to himself, or he would not have claimed, to Castelnau of all people, that no one could ever charge him with ingratitude.[11] Since it turned out that it did, there is room for saying, after more sympathetic things, that it served him right.

8 *Documenti*, pp. 60, 107; *Sommario*, no. 198. The nearest thing I have found in Bruno's writings is in the dedication (to Rudolf II) of the *Articuli adversus mathematicos*, 1588 (*OL* i³), p. 4; but this advocates universal philanthropy, which is something else.

9 *Candelaio*, act v; *Sigillus*, pp. 181–2; *Cena*, sonnet p. 5/65; *Causa*, pp. 199–201/37–8; *Spaccio*, pp. 626, 652–3. Cf. above, pp. 149–51.

10 *Cena*, second version, p. 79 n/142: 'Prudenzio... Si quis dederit tibi alapam; tribue illi et alteram.' As Aquilecchia observes, this is a witty conflation of Matthew 5: 40 ('Si quis percusserit te in dexteram maxillam tuam, praebe illi et alteram') with John 19: 3 ('Et dabant ei alapas'), which almost without changing the text makes it say the opposite of what it says: the original is, of course, about turning the other cheek. This is one of Bruno's best jokes, I think, and puts in a nutshell his view that Jesus was a wimp. It is also a fine example of his creative way with quotations, of which there is another at the end of *Texts*, no. 11.

11 *Causa*, p. 177/7 (dedication): 'Io, dunque, qual nessun giamai poté accusar per ingrato . . .'

PART III
Texts and Notes

My object has been, except in the cases of Nos. 1 and 12, to make as scholarly an edition of Bruno's pieces or probable pieces as possible, while providing translations for the less exacting reader. In the pieces by William Herle (Nos. 5–8), where quite the same precision does not seem called for, some inconsistencies will be found in my response to his irritating habit of doubling a high proportion of his consonants.

I have observed these rules:

1.   I have expanded abbreviations, putting additional letters in italics.

2.   I have placed author's alterations (deletions, insertions, etc.) inside square brackets, [ ], adding the appropriate description in italics; likewise [*sic*].

3.   Where something is missing from the Ms., letters, etc., which have been supplied are placed between solidi, /   /, and italicised.

4.   Where, as in Nos. 5–8 and 18 (none of them by Bruno), I have given part of the letter in abstract, the abstracted parts are given between solidi, but not italicised; passages quoted in full inside the abstract are placed between inverted commas.

5.   In Nos. 11 and 11a *only*, where Bruno makes extensive use of solidi, single and double, in his own punctuation, I have followed him.

References accompany the original texts, not the translations, though most reference numbers occur in both.

I

Bruno's Account of his Life in Paris and London,
1581–1586, as given to his Inquisitors in Venice,
20/30 May 1592, translated

Documenti, pp. 84–5.

After [teaching in Toulouse for two and a half years], on account of
the civil wars I left and went to Paris, where I undertook a course of
extraordinary lectures to make myself known and as a trial run; I
gave thirty lectures on the thirty divine attributes, taken from the
First Part of St Thomas [Aquinas' *Summa theologica*].[1] After that,
being invited to give an ordinary course, I declined, because the
public readers in that city are required by statute to go to mass and
other divine services, and I have always avoided this, knowing that I
was excommunicate because I had left my order and abandoned the
habit. True, I had taught a similar ordinary course in Toulouse, but
this was not an obligation of the post, as it would have been in Paris
if I had taken on the ordinary course. While I was giving my
extraordinary lectures, I acquired such a reputation that King Henri
III sent for me one day, and asked me whether the memory which I
possessed and taught was acquired by natural means or by magic. I
gave him satisfaction on this point, and by what I told him and the
proofs I gave him he recognised that it was not done by magic but by
natural knowledge. After this I published a book on memory, called
On the Shadows of Ideas, which I dedicated to his Majesty; and as a
result of this he made me an extraordinary reader, with a salary, and I
continued to read in that city, as I have said, for perhaps five years.[2]

1 Bruno meant Pars Prima, qu. ii-xi, but thirty was his own invention; cf. Yates, *Art of
Memory,* pp. 178 ff, 205 ff.
2 This is misleading, probably on purpose. Assuming, with Yates, *Bruno,* p. 190, that Bruno
arrived in Paris at the end of 1581, he cannot have actually taught there for much more than a
year before he went to England and, if at all, six months after he came back. Spampanato,
Vita di Giordano Bruno, p. 307, must be right in saying that he was trying to play down his
period in England; he also stretched his stay in Toulouse by a year (ibid. p. 303). On *De
umbris idearum,* Yates, *Bruno,* pp. 192–9; *Art of Memory,* pp. 197–227.

Because of the troubles which arose later, I took leave of absence, and with a letter from the king went to England, to stay with his Majesty's ambassador, who was called the Seigneur de Mauvissière, by name Michel de Castelnau; in whose house I had no position, except that I acted as his gentleman. I stayed in England two and a half years, during which time, although mass was said in the house, I did not go to it, nor did I go outside to mass or to sermons, for the reason already stated. When the ambassador returned to the court in France, I accompanied him to Paris, and there I remained another year, staying with those gentlemen whom I knew, but most of the time at my own expense. I left Paris because of the troubles, and went to Germany . . .

2

18/28–19/29 April 1583:
Giordano Bruno to Sir Francis Walsingham,
London, Salisbury Court

BL Cottonian Caligula C vii, f. 214. Calendared in *CSP Scotland 1581–1583*, pp. 431–2.

Copy in a secretary hand, evidently by a clerk in Walsingham's office; there is no sign of the original. A date, '29 April 1583', seems to have been added later.

The first piece of news on the verso, beginning 'Le vᵉ Monsieur du Boys . . .', must have been copied by the clerk from a later piece: the date implies that it was originally on a separate sheet of No. 3, which the clerk mixed up with No. 2.

Advertisements touchinge the Scottish affayres

Le xxiiiiᵉ apvril 1583 contant en la facon de France pour les jours qui se content par le commandement du Pape Jehan Meusnier, post ordinaire du Roy de France est arrive a Londres au logis de Monseigneur l'Ambassadeur lequel a apporte le pacquet du Roy, dont en icelluy pacquet Monseigneur le Duc de Guyse a envoye une lettre a mondict Seigneur l'Ambassadeur se recommandant a luy et luy prie bien fort de mener les affaires de la Royne d'Escosse le plus secretement qu'il pourra en Engleterre et pour ce faire luy a donne ung prevoste qui est en son gouvernement de St. Dizier vallant par chacun an audit Seigneur Ambassadeur la somme de xv cens livres francoises

Votre bon serviteur
Henry Fagot.

Plus ce jourdhuy xxviiiᵉ Apvril 1583 se fait conte de France ung nomme Foulan Escossois lequel hante presque tous les jours au logis de Mondit Seigneur L'Ambassadeur ayant la cognoissance de tous les principaulx ministres Escossois comme je croy et le cognois fort bien qu'il dissimule en en [*sic*] sa Religion ayant ordinairement des nouvelles d'iceux ministres, et est gaige du Roy de France, parquoy Mons*eigneu*r l'Ambassadeur connoist tout ce qui se faict par Escosse.[1]

Votre serviteur
Henry Fagot.

Plus le lendemain il y a ung autre homme nomme Pierres dont je ne scay le surnom d'Icelluy homme fort aage lequel a apporte NB une *lett*re particulierement a mon*dit* Seign*eu*r Cãvillasade [*sic*: l'Ambassadeur] le tout secretement pour envoyer au Roy d'Escosse laquelle faict mention comant il prie bien fort sa Ma*jest*e de prendre encores pacience quelque temps et luy prie ensemble au*dit* Roy de luy envoyer unne couple des bonnes pistolets

Votre bon serviteur,
Henry Fagot.

f.214v/   Le ve Mons*ieu*r du Boys[2] parta de Londres pour s'en retourner en Flandres pour trouver son Altesse Il dict a Mons*eigneu*r l'Ambassadeur dedans la gallerie qu'il ne trouvoit plus d'amitie en la Royne d'Angleterre, et qu'il falloit que Mon*dit* Seign*eu*r l'Ambassadeur creust fermement que son*dit* Altesse esperoit estre espouse a une des filles du Roy d'Espagne et qu'il ne falloit dire mot du tout.

Votre Serviteur,
Henry Fagot

Ce jourdhuy xxix^e Apvril 1583 Mons*ieu*r frocquemorton a disne au logis de mondict Seign*eu*r l'Ambassadeur, lequel a envoye ces jours passez a la Royne d'Escosse xv cens escus sol de quoy Mon*dit* Seign*eu*r l'Ambassadeur est respondant.

Votre Serviteur
Hen: Fagot.

1   William Fowler: ex-minister of the Church of Scotland; had spent some time in France and written against Catholicism; also a minor poet and uncle of William Drummond of Hawthornden (*DNB*). There are numerous reports from him to Walsingham about Castelnau from November 1582 to July 1583 in *CSP Scotland, 1581–1583*, pp. 196–569. Conyers Read (below, p. 197) transcribes the name 'Foulair', which would be the natural thing, but Fagot always uses an *n*.
2   Jean du Bex, the Duke of Anjou's agent in England. He had arrived on 7/17 April: Martin, *Journal of Sir Francis Walsingham*, p. 48.

Plus cedit jour le Millord Henry Catholique Romain et papiste est veu [*sic*] au logis de mond*it seigneu*r l'Ambassadeur justement sur les douze heures lequel a adverty Mons*eigneu*r l'Ambassadeur quil avoit ou [*sic*] dire qu'il tenoit un Escossois pres de luy que l'on menacoit de mettre en prison pour sa Religion et pour avoir este en une maison d'un gentilhomme Irlandois apres que led*it* Irlandois estoit mis en prison.[3]

Vo*tre* Serviteur
H. Fagot.

In translating this and the following piece I have omitted all but the last of Fagot's signatures.

24 April 1583, counting in the French manner according to the new calendar instituted by command of the pope, Jehan Mousnier, the ordinary post for the King of France, arrived in London at the ambassador's house, bringing the king's packet. In the packet the Duke of Guise has sent a letter to the ambassador, commending himself to him and earnestly begging him to manage the affairs of the Queen of Scots in England as secretly as he possibly can. In return he has given him a benefice in his governorship of St Dizier, worth 1500 livres a year.

Today, 28 April 1583, French style, a Scot called Fowler, who haunts the ambassador's house practically every day, [arrived]. I think he knows all the principal ministers of [the Church of] Scotland, and I know very well that he dissimulates in his religion. He has regular news from these ministers, and is also paid by the King of France; whence the ambassador knows everything that goes on in Scotland.[1]

The next day, another man called Pierre whose surname I do not know, a very old man, brought a private letter to the ambassador to be sent secretly to the King of Scots. It says that he [*sic*] earnestly begs his Majesty to be patient a little longer, and also asks the king to send him a good pair of pistols [*possibly*: asks the ambassador to send the king a good pair of pistols].

On 5 [May], M. du Bex[2] left London to return to his Highness [Anjou] in Flanders. He said to the ambassador in the gallery that he found no further amity in the Queen of England; that the

3　I have no idea who this Scot was, and wonder whether he was not Bruno's predecessor as chaplain. The Irish gentleman was perhaps the 'Monsieur Huton' who appears in No. 9, in the Fleet prison and being visited by Bruno.

ambassador should realise that his Highness [now] hoped to marry one of the daughters of the King of Spain; and that this was absolutely confidential.

Today, 29 April 1583, M. Throckmorton dined at the ambassador's house. He has recently sent the Queen of Scots 1500 *écus sol*, which is on the ambassador's account.

This same day Milord Henry [Howard], a Roman Catholic and papist, came to the ambassador's house on the stroke of midnight. He informed the ambassador that he had heard that he kept a Scot in his house who was being threatened with imprisonment for his religion, and for having been discovered in the house of an Irish gentleman after the Irishman had been put in prison.[3]

Your servant,
H. Fagot

22 April/2 May – 25 April/5 May 1583:
Giordano Bruno to Sir Francis Walsingham,
London, Salisbury Court

PRO SP 78/9, ff. 216–17 (no. 96). Well translated in *CSP Foreign 1583*, pp. 291–2.

Holograph hand FA. Written on the back: '[*small*] ♃. Advertis*ements* by Henry/ Fagott./ [*large*]♃ [*and*] 1582'. The second♃ has been written later, and the date I think still later, or at least at another time: it is self-evidently wrong. The symbol ♃ is also to be found on the back of No. 4 (below, p. 197); in both cases it was written in the top left-hand corner of the portion of the back of the letter which served as the front cover when it was folded up. Hence I think that it was not, in either case, part of the endorsement or written by Walsingham's clerk Laurence Thomson, who wrote this one, or by whoever wrote the next one: in neither case is it obviously in the same hand. I think it was in fact, in both cases, the address, and written by Bruno himself; it would therefore be a symbol agreed between himself and Walsingham. The larger version may have been added by Walsingham, either to remind himself that the letter was from Bruno or because the original one was not very visible. The symbol is, I am told, the planetary sign for Jupiter, which may well be relevant to the choosing of it; but I think it was in fairly common use in ciphers and codes, hence we probably ought not to suppose that Bruno wanted to identify himself in that way.

If, as I presume, the fourth item in No. 2 was originally sent with this, this cannot have been sent earlier than 25 April/5 May. It is of course possible that that item was the beginning of a third letter, but if so one would have expected the clerk to have copied the rest of it with No. 2. If a copy of this present letter was made, I have not found it.

Le ii^e may 1583 ung nomme Yerle est venu chez nous lequel a faict report [quil a entendu *deleted*] a monseigneur lambassadeur quil savoit fort bien que lon faisoit des fadesses[1] aux fransoys mais que ceulx qui pense ce [fe *deleted*] faire aus*ditz* francoys sont fort trompez et quil savoit fort bien que le Roy despaigne et celuy de france sont

---

1 *Fadaises*: rubbish, tripe.

pour donner remedde a tout et disoit tout cela en ytallian. [le *deleted*]
Nottez quil est facteur de monseigneur lambassadeur et ne ce fie
gueres en luy.

Votre affexione
Henry Fagot

Cedit jour yl ya lung des gentilhommes de lambassadeur despaigne
flamang[2] lequel a raporte a monseigneur lambassadeur de france quil
connoissoit fort bien que son altesse ne requert aultre chosse que
saprosscher pres le Roy despaigne et [quel *deleted*] quil estoit envoye
de la part [de *deleted*] dudit ambassadeur despaigne pour anoncer
cesdites parolles ce que je luy ay ouy dire a luy mesmes

votre serviteur
henry fagot.

Nottez Ce jourdhuy iiii[e] dudit moys ung nomme foulan escossoys a disne
en la maisson de monditseigneur lambassadeur lequel a [monstre
deleted] aporte deulx [bages *deleted*] bagues dor enchassez dont
je ne connoist les pierres[3] lesquelles sont envoye [z *deleted*] en la
Royne decosse de la part du duc de Lenox dont[4] mondit seigneur
lambassadeur en a la charge de luy les envoyer

Votre serviteur
henry fagot.

f.217v/ Cedit jour monseigneur lambassadeur a receu lettres de madame de
mauvissiere lesquelles font mention coment elle a espoir destre de
retour de bref en ce Royaullme et quelle prie fort que mondit
seigneur lambassadeur soit le plus segret quil pourra en ses affaires et
quelle a ouy dire a Monseigneur de guisse quil a espoir destre en
escosse [le *probably deleted*] plustost que mondit seigneur lambassadeur
ny elle ne pensent mais [ce *inserted*] [pend *deleted*] pendant quil

---

2 I am inclined to identify this man with the Fleming 'qui hantoit fort chez [M.] de
   Mauvissière', and was arrested shortly after Castelnau's departure for carrying letters from
   the Duke of Parma to Catholics in England: Châteauneuf to Villeroy, 3/13-x-1585 (BN ff
   15571, f. 34). He may also, possibly, have been the Antwerper called Alexander described
   in No. 16.
3 Cf. *Causa*, p. 243/77: Bruno on precious stones. He claimed that they were animate and had
   an influence on the soul.
4 This appears to be more or less the word intended, but it is not what is written. The word
   appears to begin with *do*, but I cannot read it.

entretienne la Royne dangleterre le plus amiablement quil pourra et que le Roy decosse est tousiours cathollique en son cuer et que mond*it* seigneur lambassadeur done [bon *deleted*] tousiours bonne consolation en la Royne decosse [Q *deleted*] et quil luy mande ce le plus segrettement quil pourra.

V*ot*re serviteur
henry fagot.

Cedit jour je ouy dire a mons*eigneur* lambassadeur quil craignoit pres que destre en ce Royaulme dautant quil voyoit des chosses qui ce [prep *deleted*] preparent aud*it* Escosse et que lon voyroit chosses mervilleusses avant quil soit gueres dautant quil y a plusieurs seigneurs qui sont en grande [?inimite *deleted*] inimitie et que mondit seigneur le duc de guisse et le duc de Leno ont le mott du guet de tout cela et contoit cela entre luy et ung lord dangleterre dont je ne peu avoir le no*m* dicelluy.

henry fagot

The 2 May 1583 someone called Herle came to our house and told the ambassador that he knew very well that [the English] were trying to make the French believe a lot of rubbish, but they were mistaken in thinking that the French would swallow it. He was sure the Kings of Spain and France would [get together to] put an end to all this nonsense. He said all this in Italian. Note that he is an agent for the ambassador, but does not trust him [*possibly*: but the ambassador does not trust him].

The same day one of the gentlemen of the Spanish ambassador, a Fleming,[2] told the French ambassador that he was well aware that his Highness would be only too pleased to come to an agreement with the King of Spain, and that he had been sent by the Spanish ambassador to say this. I heard him say this himself.

Today, 4 May, a man called Fowler, a Scot, dined at the ambassador's house. He brought two gold rings mounted with stones which I did not recognise;[3] they are being sent to the Queen of Scots from the Duke of Lennox and the ambassador is to convey them to her.

This same day the ambassador had letters from his wife saying that she hopes to be back in England shortly, and begs him to be as secret as he possibly can in his affairs. She says she has been told by M. de Guise that he hopes to be in Scotland sooner than either the ambassador or she expect; that in the meantime he is to entertain the Queen of England as amiably as he can; that the King of Scots is still a Catholic at heart; and that the ambassador should keep the Queen of Scots in good heart, and correspond with her as secretly as he can.

This same day I heard the ambassador say that he was almost afraid to be in England, since he could see what was brewing in Scotland; we should see wonderful things there soon, because there were many lords there at great enmity with each other, and the Dukes of Guise and Lennox have the password to all that. This was said between him and an English lord whose name I could not discover.

Henry Fagot

4

[Between about 20/30 May and about 31 May/10 June 1583]: Giordano Bruno to Sir Francis Walsingham, London, Salisbury Court

PRO SP 53/12, ff. 152–3; there is a copy, by the same hand as that of No. 2, in BL Cottonian Caligula C vii, f. 211. Calendared, not very successfully, in *CSP Scotland 1581–1583*, pp. 430–1; there is a more accurate transcription of part of it in Conyers Read, *Walsingham*, ii, 381 n. 2.

Holograph hand FA. Written on the back: '⧾Aprill 1583 /Fagot/ *in another, but contemporary hand, below* [T *changed to*] Quere'. See above, p. 193, for the symbol.

Date I am sure that the date of the endorsement is wrong. The reason for it may be that Nos. 2–4 came into Walsingham's office together, and that the clerk, lacking a date for this, deduced from the beginning of it that it was the first of the three. I date it after Nos. 2 and 3: 1) because of the experimental form and character of those letters, compared with this one; and 2) because the later items in this letter seem to presuppose items in Nos. 2 and 3. This is particularly so of the reference to Lord Henry Howard, whose name Bruno did not know when he wrote No. 2; it seems the natural reading of the references to Fowler and Mendoza. I date it more exactly by reference to the first sentence, where I take 'longtemps' to mean 'a good while after 25 April/5 May'; and to Bruno's departure for Oxford with Laski and Sidney not later than about 7/17 June. Courcelles began to pass letters to Walsingham somewhere about the beginning of July, NS. I think it is likely to have been written shortly after William Herle's letter to Hatton of 20/30 May (above, pp. 26 f). It is impossible to say whether the 'query', which may conceivably be by Walsingham himself, refers to the date on the endorsement.

The date of this letter is extremely important, because if the endorsement is correct it would be the first of the series as we have it, as the editor of *CSP Scotland* supposed; there would then have been earlier letters which have not survived, and we should have to date the beginning of Fagot's career as a spy a great deal earlier. In that case he could not be Bruno.

Bruno probably got back from Oxford on the 15/25 or 16/26 June, and hence the letter might date from after that. However, 1) one might have thought he would have mentioned being away as an excuse for not writing; 2) this would not leave much time for Walsingham and Courcelles to make their arrangements; 3) Bruno may have stayed longer in Oxford. (Above, p. 24.)

Monseigneur Je este longtemps sans vous escripvre la cause pourquoy estoit que je ne trouvois pas chose qui meritast vous escripvre. mais mon seigneur ayant trouve mintenant chose qui est meritoire je vous le veulx faire entendre Cest quil [h *deleted*] ya deux marchans de livres papistes en la maison de monseigneur lambassadeur dont ung est cuisinier et lautre est son som*m*elier tellement que de deux moys en deulx moys ne faillent a faire chacun leur tour en france pour faire tel traffic tant pour aller revendre des ornemens deglisse quil achettent en ce royaulme que pou*r* raporter livres papistes pour vendre Il y a ung certain conducteur pour iceulx qui est nom*m*e pierres pitou fran[c *changed to*]soys et mesager ordinaire Ung aultre qui ayde a vendre les*d*its livres nom*m*e mestre herson lautre qui decouvre les ornem*e*ns et qui les trouve a achepter qui son no*m* est Jehan Folk dit Renard en fransoys et le portier de notredicte maison qui est [angloys *deleted*] marie en ce royaul*m*e a une angloyse qui est encorres le pire de tous. Monseigneur je vous advise quil sont mintenant en grande peyne et a son guet par quelques rechercheurs qui sont allez en Sodoark [en se *deleted*] ensengne du croysant dont est le lieu ou lesditz livres doibvent decharger[1] mais cenestoit si tost com*m*e il pensoint dont il en sont fort aysent et ont donne grand deniers au maistre dud*it* coissant [*sic*] pour ce taire et le puis bien con*n*oistre pour lavoir [oy *deleted*] ouy dire en notredict somelier qui en est le marchant. les coffres ou sont lesdictz livres ne sont aud*it* logis du [cross *deleted*] croissant et charchent no*m*bre damis pour les faire server segrettement et disent qu'il vouldroint qui leur eust couste cent cinquante livres sterlins et que [les *deleted*] lesditz coffres ou sont leurs livres feussent encores a paris. Ce considerant monseigneur il me semble quil est bon den faire bonne revisitation
f.152v/ dautant que je leur ay ouy dire quil graissent fermement les mains

---

1   John Fisher, Deputy Keeper of Prints and Maps at the Guildhall Library, London, has most obligingly investigated for me the whereabouts of the 'Croissant'. He tells me, on the authority of B. Lillywhite, *London Signs*, 1) that inns with the sign of a Crescent were practically always described as the 'Half Moon'; and 2) that there was, at least as far back as 1648, a Half Moon in Upper Ground, on the south side of the river a little upstream from the present Blackfriars Bridge, and so exactly opposite Buckhurst Stairs and Salisbury Court. I think there is really no doubt that this is our inn, and have (belatedly) altered the text accordingly. The Half Moon will have been situated at the extreme western end of Bankside, near the pleasure garden known as Paris Garden, and just before the beginning of the dog-walkers', anglers' and courting-couples' path known as Narrow Wall which went up by the river with Lambeth Marsh on the inward side. The row of houses which will have included it can be seen on the 'Agas' map in Prockter and Taylor, *A to Z of Elizabethan London*, p. 21; or Fisher, *A Collection of Early Maps of London*, sheet 6. It is just off the bottom of the section of this reproduced in Figure 1, and would have found a place on the Map, Figure 4, if I had known where it was at the time. The reader, if the book is his own, may like to draw it in, facing Buckhurst Stairs. Both Castelnau and Girault are known to have had rendezvous in the area, and no doubt Bruno did as well (William Fleetwood to Sir Thomas Heneage, 12-vi-1578: PRO SP 12/125, nos. 20–4).

aux rechercheurs tant de larye que des autres [h *deleted*] lieux qui
sont de pasage mesmes que je con*n*ois quil ont faict traffic en
ornemans deglise [le *deleted*] de plus de six cens livres sterlins lesquelz
ont fort bien passe en france et sans difficulte nulle et ce vantent que
cest pour autant quil contentent ceulx qui sont les rechercheurs.

Monseigneur je vous advertis aussy que si v*o*tre exelence veult que
je tiens le segraitaire de monseigneur lambassadeur pour tant mon
amy que [l *deleted*] sil est considere de quelque peu de mon*n*oye quil
ne cest faict rien quil ne me le don*n*e a conoistre et que tout ce qui ce
fera touchant la Royne decosse et le segret et lecripture qui ce escript
par l*e*ttre quartalle et fault que sachiez quapres que v*o*tre exelence a
visite auchun pacquet pour adresser vers icelle qui ne laisse a y en
remectre dautre dans le*d*it pacquet et que cela nest [conge *deleted*]
congneu nullement[2] Je le [puis *deleted*] say de par luy.

Le grand facteur de la Royne decosse est le S*ieu*r frocquemorton et
le milord henry hauard et iceulx ne vienent jamais raporter chosse
dicelle que la nuict et monsieur lambassadeur [aut *deleted*] au cas
pareil.

Lambassadeur despaigne a faict son conte en n*o*tre [?maisen *deleted*]
maison que monsieur le duc sen va marier lune des filles du Roy
despaigne.

V*o*tre tres humble et loyal serviteur
Henry fagot.

    donn*e*z vous bien de garde sil vous plaist dung escosoys dont son f.153r/
no*m* est foulain car il est fort traistre Car le segraitaire de mon*d*it
s*eigneur* lambassadeur vous le mande de par moy

Monseigneur,
    I have been a long time without writing to you. The reason was
that I found nothing worth writing; but, Monseigneur, now that I
have found something worthwhile I should like to let you know.

    There are two merchants of popish books in the ambassador's
house, his cook and his butler. Every two months each of them
makes a trip to France to do business, both in selling church
ornaments which they buy in England, and in bringing back popish
books to sell here. They have a carrier who is called Pierre Pithou
and is the ordinary messenger. One who helps to sell the books is
called Master Herson; the other, who digs out the ornaments to buy

---

2 For the translation of this obscure passage, see above, p. 20 and n. 12.

here is called Jehan Folk [?Foxe], Renard in French. He is the porter of our house, and is married here to an Englishwoman; he is the worst of the lot.

Monseigneur, I inform you that they are at the moment very worried and on the alert because of some searchers who have gone to the sign of the Half Moon in Southwark, which is where their books are to be landed;[1] but they have not come as soon as expected, which is a great relief to them. They have given a great deal of money to the landlord of the Half Moon to keep quiet, as I know, because our butler, who is running the traffic, told me so. The chests containing the books are not [yet] at the Half Moon, and they are seeking numerous friends to distribute them secretly. They say they would give £150 sterling for the chests of books to be still in Paris.

Considering this, Monseigneur, it seems to me that it would be a good idea to make a very thorough search for them, as I have heard them say that they liberally grease the palms of the searchers at Rye and other ports. I know that they have sent church ornaments worth more than £600 sterling, which have passed over into France without the least difficulty; they boast that this is because they satisfy the searchers.

Monseigneur, I also advise you that, if your excellency wishes, I have made the ambassador's secretary so much my friend that, if he is given a certain amount of money, he will let me know everything he does, including everything to do with the Queen of Scots and the cipher which is used with her. He tells me that, after your excellency has inspected any packet addressed to her, he can put something else in it without anybody knowing.[2]

The chief agents for the Queen of Scots are M. Throckmorton and Lord Henry Howard. They never come to bring things from her except at night, and the ambassador does the same [when he is sending to her].

The Spanish ambassador came to our house to say that M. the Duke [of Anjou] is going to marry one of the King of Spain's daughters.

Your very humble and loyal servant,
Henry Fagot

Keep a close eye, I beg you, on a Scot called Fowler; he is extremely treacherous. The ambassador's secretary told me to tell you this.

5

15/25 November 1583: William Herle to Lord Burghley, London, The Bull's Head without Temple Bar

BL Lansdowne 39, ff. 190–2.

Holograph   Address but no endorsement.

R*ight* honorable good L*ord*   f. 190r/
/The Earl of Bedford has moved Burghley in a suit in H.'s favour.
Burghley has shown himself favourable, and promised him some
relief for his 'poor estate'. Thanks to his 'dear Patron'. Would have
come to thank him in person, but did not want to take up his time.
Will serve him even with his life: owes all he has to Burghley.

Since his last Burghley will have come to agree with what he
said about Keith, the Swedish ambassador.[1] Douglas and Keith
intriguing together, but Douglas too clever for Keith. Keith 'tempers
to be grateful to the Scottish Queen' and means to visit Scotland on
the way home; but James hates the Swedes./

The sayd Archeballd Duglasse is to be looked unto, for he is a very
practiser: of the Scottish Q*ueen's* faction, and yett insynnuates him f. 190v/
sellf into an oppynion of her Ma*jes*ty's service, being in truth a
countermyner (under colour therof) of all the occasyons and secretes
that he may reche unto, for the advancement of the said Scottish
Q*ueen* his mistresse Tytell, and her pr*es*ent raigne yf it might be. He
hath dellt conninglye with som men of good sorte, to drawe theme
to the Scottishe Q*ueen's* party, and mi selfe have byn offred money

---

1   Herle to Burghley, 27-x/6-xi-1583 (BL Lansdowne 39, ff. 178–80). This reported the
    arrival of some ambassadors from Sweden, one of whom was a Scot called Keith. They had
    come to discuss a marriage to King James. Herle said that Keith was alleged to be a
    supporter of Queen Mary, and that one might take the allegation as proved if he were
    found to be in touch with Archibald Douglas in London. There is no sign of Bruno in this
    or Herle's previous letter (29-ix/9-x-1583: ibid. f. 165).

largely, presumyng belyke that I find neede, and theruppon yf I had tasted ones of that liberality, som matter haply might have byn imparted with me, which otherwise they wolld make me a stranger in. I know som of his instrumentes, and part of his hauntes.

The cheiff marck that is shott att, is her Majesty's person, whom God doth and will preserve, accordying to her confydent trust in him. The duke of Guyse is the director of the actyon, and the Pope is to conferre the kingdom by his gyfte, uppon suche a on as is to mary with the Scottish Queen so as she shall nott be [establisshed *deleted*] estemed Queen by her own right and pretensyons, butt meerly by the Popes collacion, wherby the fere of the yong Scottish k*ing's* religion, is provyded for, and he barred by and mayne.[2] Our practisers wolld be ayded of suche a forein power, as shoold not afterwardes be hable to commande themme hence, yet directed by suche heddes for martiall skill, as shoold supplie in the number of their own, what wanted in strangers, presumyng gretelie of wellthe and multitude, which practises (under pardon of mi zele) will hardly cesse, while the knowen serpent is norisshed in the bosom of our Reallme, having the Arte to enchaunte all her kepers, and brethes nothing elles butt poyson, which abrode butt hissing (her uglynes ones truly sene) wolld torne to her owne ruyne and theires who were most tender of her. The Duke of Guise, yf her platt here (which God confound) were erected, he sholld be in the redy waye to assure him sellf of the crown of Fraunce, the valew and hope of the house of Valoys beyng so nere extinguisshed, and the tytell of the k*ing* of Navarre, beyng so ferefull and dangerous bothe for Rome and Spayne, yf Monsieur[3] or the Frenche k*ing* were outt of the waye. Which in substance is the somm of ther present trecheryes and proiectes to be hatched, butt that God doth miraculously discover and dyvert their malyce, and is the absolute defendor of her Majesty. The rest, and the premisses allso I humblie lay down before your wisdom, and do pray pardon for mi boldness, but with condycyon that my carkasse might serve for a plaster allso for any dedlye sore that might conserve the kyngdom or magistrate, within religion, God and dutye to her Majesty I utter in all humble zele and truth. The Lord Henry Howard is supposed to be a preest, wherof there be mani presumpcyons, and that [further *inserted above*] he is in the secrett register of the popes cardynalls. Ytt is he that advised Symiers to procede by the papistes to establish his master[3] here, and to purge religion by the blood of sondry of our gretest houses in England, and that he should stand stoutly to have the article of fredom for religion graunted, for that her Majestie he

---

2 *By and main*: a term from the card-game Hazard, meaning 'altogether'.
3 The Duke of Anjou, called 'Monsieur' as heir to the French throne.

sayd, was nott resollved of whatt religion yett to be of, A voyce that
savored of his own Blasphemy, and vyle nature.

There is one of his blood,[4] that this sommer hath received letters
and reliques from beyonde the seas, and hath att this present a notable
Jesuite [(among all the Jesuites) *inserted in the margin*] desgised in his
servyce, of whose name and partycularityes besyde, your Lordship
shall with convenyent speede be secretely and faythfullie advertised,   f.191v/
for whye[5] it importes her Majestie to be well informed therof, and
so do I deliver it to your Lordship a grete Councellor, *sub sigillo*
confessionis. [*Marginal note*: I do send on into the country specially
about this.]

Of Fraunces Throckmorton, I advertised Master Secretary this last
sommer, whatt secrete resortes he had to the Frenche ambassador,
whatt long and pryvate conferences, att seasons suspicious, and of
his being att masse there att severall tymes. He is a partye very busy
and an enemye to the present state. His kinseman Sir Nicholas's elldest
son, dyned on Sonday (if I mistake nott the day) with the Frenche
Ambassador, and cam att suche tyme as the Table was sett, beyng
muche made of them and respected, entrying into private conference
with the sayd Ambassador after dyner.[6]

Fraunces Throckmortones brother[7] and on digbye of Lyncollnes
Inn, bothe papists, and noted to carye ill and busy myndes, do intend
to depart the reallme within these 3 dayes as slylye as they may, who
in mi oppynion wolld be observed well att the houre of their
passayge. And thus havyng trobled your Lordship overmuche, I crave
hartly humble pardon for the same, And in case that your Lordship do
finde me fitt to be employed in ani matter, that the tyme or her
Majesties service may [now *inserted above*] require, I will faythfully
discharge whatt your Lordship shall plese to commande me in that
behallf, praying God most hartly upon mi knees to blesse her
Majestie with his grace and long lyfe and your Lordship [with
inserted] hellthe continuallye to preserve her. Mi lodgyng. The 15
of November 1583. The Bullshed without Temple Barre.

> Your Lordship's most Bounden
> W. Herle

---

4 Evidently Philip Howard, Earl of Arundel. Convicted of treason, Howard died in the
   Tower in 1595, and has been canonised.
5 *Forwhy*: 'because'.
6 Arthur Throckmorton, Francis's first cousin: *DNB*, Throckmorton, Sir Nicholas; much of
   Rowse, *Ralegh and the Throckmortons* is based on his recently discovered diary: he later
   became Ralegh's brother-in-law and acquired a copy of Bruno's *De gli eroici furori* (Sturlese,
   Bibliografia, no. 12. 32; Rowse, p. 339). Above, p. 31.
7 I assume that this means Thomas, but see above, p. 102 and n. 10.

Yesterday arrived on Don Gaston de Spinola a Sicylian here out of the *Prince* of Parma's camp who att his departyng was at Ecklow 5 leages beyond Bruges in Flanders. The sayd Gaston departeth from hence into Spayne directly to the *king*.

6

16/26 November 1583: William Herle to Lord Burghley, [London]

BL Lansdowne 39, f. 193.

Holograph Addressed and endorsed. Someone has added, mistakenly: 'The Lord Thomas Howardes supposed book against prophesies'.

Right honorable good Lord, Since the sendyng of mi letter to your Lordship yesterday I wolld butt humblie putt you in remembrance to have the censure of som lerned man, that were asswell quallefied in state causes, as devynity, touching the supposed Lord Henry Howardes booke agaynst prophesyes, for that the sayd booke is conseved by som of good judgement to conteyne sundrie heresies and spyces withall of Treson, though somwhatt closelie caryed as the Author imagynes.

/Hears from Sluys that the Prince of Orange has collected 3000 soldiers in Holland, who have recaptured the Sasse [van Gent], and sundry passages between the land of Waes and the enemy. Parma put out.

Don Gaston come from Parma; going to Spain. A man reputed of action, about 33, one-eyed, resolute. 'His father was a genevoys, his mother a spaniard, and [by *inserted*] his country a Sicylian, which is the worst commixture that ever was.' Keep an eye on him tomorrow, being a solemn day (Accession Day). /

7

[23 November/3 December 1583: William Herle to Lord Burghley, London]

BL Cottonian Caligula C viii, ff. 204–6.

Herle's handwriting. No address or endorsement. There is a sort of signature of two symbols. Somebody, possibly Herle himself, has added a date '23 November 1584' in the margin at the top of the piece, and three other attempts have been made to give a year to it. But from the contents the date is perfectly clear to within a few days, and we may assume that the date given is for some reason simply a year out. Calendared in *CSP Scotland 1584–1585*, p. 426, under 23 November 1584, and there attributed to William Davidson.

The Frenche Ambassador on Thursdaye mornyng, being the 21 of this moneth, had Archeballd Duglasse brought secretely to him by Corselles into his chamber, where after long and ernest consultation had bettwen theme, which cheefly concerned the late letter *received* from the Scotishe Queen, the said Archeballd was secretly dismissed agayn.

They ii[1] do holld for certayn, that *Master Secretary* Walsyngham opened the Scotishe *Queen's* packett, before it cam to the Ambassadors handes, and imparted the secretes therof to the *Queen's Majestie* which makes theme the more respectyve mani wayes, and therfor debated of the maner and matter, how to dele with her *Majestie* touchyng Audyens: desirous by som course of Terrification, to withdrawe her *Majestie* from procedyng to far in examynyng these Actyons, that ar broken furth, and the deciphering of their greater frendes, nott yett discovered. /Archibald Douglas's plots; they are communicated to Guise, and to be executed by Mary and her friends. His connections in Spain and Rome. 'He was ever a countermyner and unfaythfull . . . ever a practiser and irreligious and a reveler in the end of all secretes to serve his own Torne . . .' King

1 Castelnau and Courcelles.

James's arrest of pro-English Scots, and his summons to the Earl of Angus,[2] suggest that he is conniving with his mother. A long string f.204r of complaints against the earl from Duffield, a minister. His slender f.205r answers.

Discovery of Hall the priest; Hall and Somerville.[3] Knows the f.205v feelings of a lot of gentlemen in the country about the queen; hears the sighs of the good, that no difference is made between them and the bad. Compare Pericles, who favoured the *bene merentibus*./

The Scottish faction doth presse on a pace in number and view, and those with theme that desire noveltyes. The on and the other affirming that Cuthbert /*Armorer's* in binding/ late dispatche into Scotland is but intertaynment to occupye a chilld with, and that a hope or glemse of a mariage under this is handled, to drawe the young *king* from his disseygnes and settled frendes, butt that the affinitye [of deleted] with H. is to weke a Calamite to attracte so grett an effect from his own Sphere.[4] In lyke sorte we intertayne the *king* f.206r/ of Spayne is syd and his Ambassador with accomplementes now, to devyde or weken the Tempest prepared and coming.

I am glad to knowe unto mi selfe, in respect of publyck securitye to our gracious soveraigne, that she is furnisshed with matter of her sellf to convynce the Lord Henry Haward criminallye, when she pleseth to extend it. His spirite otherwise is within no compasse of quiett dutye, and his own side saye of that travailling mynde of his, that *aut non capiendus aut non relaxandus*.

I here it agayn confirmed, whatt Tryumphes were made in Spayne, uppon the brute of her Majesties dethe. Spayne, Fraunce, and the Pope, do now labour by all menes (*postposita fide et virtute*) to prevail *per sicarios et proditores*. /Saw Charles Arundell[5] buying gloves and perfumes at a new perfumier's in Abchurch Lane of late; thought he meant to use them to poison the queen, 'she having her sences of smellinge so perfect, and delyted with good savors, butt God will defend her I knowe, for she trustes in him. And to the rest I dare pronounce even from Goddes mouthe that cruelty and trecherie is

2 Alexander Douglas, 8th earl; nephew of James, Earl of Morton, Regent of Scotland 1572–81, and relative of Archibald Douglas. He had organised the overthrow of the Duke of Lennox's regime earlier in the year.

3 John Somerville, a Warwickshire Catholic gentleman of unsound mind who was arrested in October 1583 after having announced his intention of going up to London to assasinate the queen, Hugh Hall, a priest who was allegedly implicated with him, was an expert on gardening who was being employed by Sir Christopher Hatton to establish the garden of his great house at Holdenby in Lincolnshire; he was interrogated in the aftermath of Throckmorton's arrest, 31-xii-1583/10-i-1584: PRO SP 12/164, no. 77. *Leicester's Commonwealth*, p.173 and n., p.219.

4 'H' is Lord Hunsdon, relative and councillor of Elizabeth and governor of Berwick at this time: he had sent Armorer to Scotland to float the idea of a marriage between James and a daughter (or niece) of his (*CSP Scotland 1581-1583*, pp.369, 466, 683; Read, *Walsingham*, ii, 232). *Calamite* is an Italianism - *Calamíta*: 'the adamant or magnet stone' (Florio).

5 Above, pp. 33, 157 n. 55.

highlyest promisse[d] and revenged with breche of faythe, even yn the gretest that ar disposed therunto.'[6] John Gilpin told me over two years ago that when he was sent after Lord Percy in France[7] he met Hall at Rouen with trees and plants, and naughty books concealed in reams of paper. He had a list of people to sell them to. The book contained a slanderous description of practically the entire English nobility, except for the Earl of Sussex.[8]/

Thus I presume to advertys mi knowlege in the premisses to your *Lordship* wherin yf eyther I be to tedyous or bolld, I submytte me sellf humblie to your own censure. Curyous I am nott, butt gelous [for her *deleted*] over her *Majes*ty's securitye and quyetnes which mi lyfe and mi dethe shall ever testefie.

6 This sentence is perhaps not wholly intelligible: my gloss on the second part of it would be 'that one may expect the most brutal and dishonourable kinds of vengence and treachery from great men who think that they have been offended'. I would think Herle means that the assassination of the queen would be a retaliation by members of the Percy and Howard families for the execution for treason in 1572 of Thomas Percy, seventh Earl of Northumberland (brother of the present, eighth, earl), and of Thomas Howard, fourth Duke of Norfolk (brother of Lord Henry Howard, father of the Earl of Arundel, and second cousin of Charles Arundell). Cf. below, Text no. 8: 'those Italyen Erlles', where 'Italian' presumably means 'prone to *vendetta*'.

7 Henry Percy, eldest son of the eighth Earl of Northumberland; he was probably still in France at this time. He succeeded to the title when his father died in the Tower, seemingly by his own hand, in June 1585. He became a notable patron of scientists, and a collector of the works of Bruno: Hilary Gatti, 'Giordano Bruno: the texts in the library of the 9th Earl of Northumberland', *Journal of the Warburg and Courtauld Institutes*, xvli (1983), 63–77. John Gilpin was a servant of the 8th earl, one of the 'greater friends' mentioned above, and p. 32; there is a letter from him to Herle, Rouen, 24–x–1580, describing the doings of English *émigrés* there, in *CSP Domestic: Addenda 1580-1625*, p. 20.

8 The book sounds like the *Treatise of Treasons against Queen Elizabeth,* but this would be the wrong time and place for it: Thomas H. Clancy, *Papist Pamphleteers* (Chicago, 1964), index.

8

22 December 1583/1 January 1584: William Herle to Lord Burghley, London

BL Lansdowne 39, f. 194.

Holograph Addressed and endorsed.

Right honorable Lord,
   I talked yesternight at good leysure with my Lord of Lecester, after I departed from your Lordship of those Italyen Erlles and of other thinges. Which he took in very good parte. I forgatt to aske of your Lordship whether ther had nott byn delyvered to you som whiles since, certayn verses unadvowed, which conserned your sellf, and were in nature of an infamous libell, which yf ani suche thing were, I knowe how to com nere the knowlege of theme, for such verses have byn shewed furth of late, and it may haplye bryng furth these new libelles withall, of whom I hope to have hallf a gesse before it be to morow att night. I wolld have wayted on your Lordship this mornyng to this effect, but that I have taken physick. Ytt may plese you to signefy me your plesure touching the verses before mencyoned, for I depend wholly upon you and have dedicated mi selfe and all mi offices to you, prayeing your Lordship to burne this paper when you have read it.
   /Recommends the Mayor of Dover, who is in juridictional dispute with Dover Castle./

9

Early or mid-January 1584, OS: Giordano Bruno to Sir Francis Walsingham, London, Salisbury Court

PRO SP 12/167, f. 155 (no. 58).

Holograph   hand FA. No address. Endorsed: '1583/ Jan. /secreat Advertisments of Henry Fagot/ Maurice servant to Master Comptroller advertiser to the French Ambassador'.

Dated by the mention of the New Year at the end of the letter, and of the arrival of Girault, which must have been well before 24 January/3 February, when he wrote to his wife in Paris from Salisbury Court (PRO SP 12/168, f. 12 (no. 5)); above, p. 34, n. 33.

The manuscript is damaged on the right-hand side; see preliminary Note to *Texts*.

Monseigneur ceste pre*sen*te servira pour vous advertir en assurance que monsieur le grand contrerolleur[1] tient ung serviteur que ce nomme mons*ieur* morice lequel gouverne mon*sieur* lambassadeur et luy rapporte nouvelles de la court de tout quil peult entendre de son maistre a [qui *deleted*] qu/il *and perhaps something else cut off*/ maict tout son segret et mons*ieur* lambassadeur lu/ *y*/ donne argent pour savoir nouvelles dicelluy [mor/*ice*/ *inserted above*] d /*e*/ tout ceulx quil con*n*oist en la court, dont m/*on*/s*ieur* lambassadeur layme
Nota extresmement et lapel /*le*/ son compaigno*n* et bon amy et Icelluy morice est grand Papiste et amy de mons*ieur* tindalle, et vous promes que sil est faict Inquisition de luy quil dira b/*?ien*/ beaucoup de choses et sur toutes choses donne*z* vous gar /*de*/ dicelluy.

Je vous advertis que vous doniez de garde de Mons*ieur* du Glas car il est pe*n*cionaire pour mons*ieur* lambassadeur.

Henry Fagot

Iil ya ung certain hom*m*e prisonier au Flit lequ/*el*/ [m *deleted*] est grandissime papiste lequel ma dict quil remercioit dieu de ce que

---

1   Sir James Croft. Above, pp. 33, 107.

Mons*ieur* frocquemort/*on*/ naviot pas dict la verite de ce quil saviot et
que si cela fust advenu que tous les papistes es/*toient*/ tous perdus a
jamais le no*m* dicelluy est mo/*nsieur*/ huton gentilhom*me* yrla*n*dois.[2]

Laurens ferno*n* a receu argent de mons*ieur* lambassa/*deur*/
Mons*ieur* lambassadeur faict son conte de aller en esco/*sse*/ mais
don*n*ez vous de garde de cela.

Je vous en garde quelque chosse de segret que Je/*vous*/ diray plus
ce a*m*plement

tout cecy est veritable par ma foy.

In margin

N*ot*re somellier est venu lequel a apporte force livres dont
mons*ieur* papinton[3] en sera le marchant.

Il vous plaisra me don*n*er mes estraines a ce bon an et Je [fer *deleted*]
priray le bon dieu pour v*ot*re exelence.

Ne vous fiez a pitou.

Monseigneur,

This present letter will serve to advise you with certainty that M.
the Grand Controller [of the Queen's Household][1] has a servant
called M. Morris whom the ambassador runs: Morris brings him
news from court about everything he hears from his master, who
entrusts him with all his secrets. The ambassador gives him money
to have intelligence from him and all those he knows at court, for
which the ambassador is exceedingly fond of him and calls him his
companion and good friend. This Morris is a great papist and a
friend of M. Tindalle, and I promise that if he is interrogated he will
tell many things. Watch him very closely.

I advise you to watch M. Douglas, for he has a pension from the
ambassador.

Henry Fagot

There is a man in prison in the Fleet, who is a very great papist,
who told me that he thanked God that M. Throckmorton had
not told the truth of what he knew, and that, if he had done, all
the papists would be in the soup. His name is M. Huton, an Irish
gentleman.[2]

2 Perhaps the man mentioned in No. 2.
3 Anthony Babington, leader of the eponymous plot in favour of Mary in the summer of
   1586, and executed in consequence.

Laurent Feron has received money from the ambassador. The ambassador counts on going to Scotland, but take care that he does not.

I have kept back something secret which I will tell you more of [later].

All this is true, on my faith.

Our butler has arrived, with a lot of books which M. Babington[3] will sell for him.

Please give me my bonus at this New Year, and I shall pray God for your excellency.

Do not trust Pithou.

[Middle to late February 1584, OS]: Notes dictated by William Herle, or more probably copied from his own notes, presumably in the office of Sir Francis Walsingham

PRO SP 12/167, f. 154 (no. 57).

Plain secretary hand. No heading, endorsement or date.

This immediately precedes No. 9 in the PRO volume, but must be later, since Mendoza, who left London about 21/31 January, must still have been in London when No. 9 was written. It must date from some while after Mendoza's departure, and its connection, via Courtois, with No. 11 suggests a date not very long before 16/26 March.

The reference to 'the partie' and 'this partie' is crucial in identifying Fagot/Bruno as the source of much or most of the information in Nos. 5–7, and in establishing the nature of his relation with Herle.

There is one that hanteth the frenshe Ambassador, that lyeth by the Spittel[1] where the Spanishe Ambassador laye, by all circumstances that I can gather it is one Curtois for that the partie taketh him to be a Spaniarde.[2]

There cometh also continually to the Ambassador Scory the Bushop's sonne and hath secreat and longe conference with him and this partye harde him saye that yf his father were deade and his goodes solde he woold not tary.

There is allso one Victor a frenshe monke sarvinge one Noel[3] who

1 St Bartholomew's Hospital.
2 This may possibly have been Zubiaur rather than Courtois, for Zubiaur was certainly 'haunting' Salisbury Court as this time, as is shown by No. 11 and by Scory's confession, 14/24-ii-1585 (PRO SP 12/176, no. 53), and Courtois is not recorded as having done so. However, Bruno is unlikely not to have known Zubiaur's name by now, and Courtois does appear in No. 11 as well.
3 Henry Noel, a prominent courtier and, according to Thomas Fuller, 'one of the greatest gallants of those times': *DNB*, Noel, Sir Andrew. He was also mentioned in Scory's confession as the recipient of a copy of *Leicester's Commonwealth*. The poet Thomas Watson, probably in 1585, dedicated to him a book on the art of memory, saying that it was not worth comparing with those of Bruno and Dickson: Salvestrini, *Bibliografia*, no. 258; Yates, *Art of Memory*, p. 274 and n. 64.

frequenteth muche the Ambassador, by whome he receaveth greatt intelligences from Courte.

Corsailes hanteth secreatly the Courte in the nyght season.

There is a servante of one Semyn [?Hemyn] dwelling in St. Clemence parishe withoute Temple Barre who dooth ordinarely come into the Ambassador and hereth his Masse gyvinge him great intelligences.

[Probably 16/26 March 1584]: Giordano Bruno to Queen Elizabeth, London, Salisbury Court

BL Harleian 1582, ff. 390–1.

Holograph   hand FA. No address, except as in the text, or endorsement.

Date   In the context of an Easter confession and communion, both Zubiaur and Bruno must have been thinking in new style: their date for Easter Sunday was 22 March/1 April. Zubiaur had asked Bruno to hear his confession 'several times'; all or most of these must have been since the beginning of Lent (5/15 February). Bruno sounds as if he had put him off as long as he decently could. The confession was made on a Sunday, and the last Sunday before Easter was 15/25 March, Palm Sunday NS. This is the natural reading of what Bruno says. What makes the date still likelier is that Zubiaur was proposing to make his Easter communion 'next Wednesday'. I think we can take it from No. 11a that he was anxious to keep his feast days as nearly as he could; in that case the Wednesday in question would be either the Wednesday before Easter (18/28 March) or the Wednesday after (25 March/4 April). I have assumed in the text the first of these, though the second would be liturgically more suitable. Which of them we choose does not affect the date of the confession, which will be Palm Sunday in either case; but it does affect the date of Bruno's letter. In the first case Bruno's references to 'ce jour de dimenche dernier' and to 'mercredi prochain' make Monday 16/26 March the only possible date. In the second case the date would be between Thursday 19/29 (I think we can exclude Wednesday) and Saturday 21/31. I plump for the first on the grounds: 1. that '*ce* jour de dimenche dernier' is a form of expression almost or quite impossible to use on the following Thursday, Friday or Saturday, even for Fagot, whose French was actually rather elegant in this letter; and 2. that it would hardly have been in keeping with Bruno's story to leave the letter until four or five days after the confession.

En la serenissime Royne dangleterre france et yrlande salut bonne longue et heureusse vie amen

Madame je veulx fort bien advertir vo*t*re honorable et prudent conseil a qui dieu maintiene bonne perfexion quil cest presente ung quide*m* espaignol nom*m*e Sibiot facteur du sir bernadin de mendosse Jadis enbassadeur pour le Roy despaigne en vo*t*re Royaulme

dangletere lequel cest presente par plusieurs foys vers moy pour
loyr en confession ce que Je lay reffuse jusques a ce jour de dimenche dernier lequel [ma *deleted*] Sibiot ma confesse chosses fort
iniominieusses, et qui me contrangnent de vous dire la pure et vraye
verite dautant que [Je *deleted*] Jaymes votre longue et heureusse vie: et
aussy comme il a tousiours pleu a votre sacre majeste me favorisser
non seullement de bouche mais aussy de coeur et de vos bons moyens
a quoy je veulx tousiours continuer pour [votre *deleted*] la protexion
et saulvegarde de votre exelente Majeste/ Notez cest quil [ma dict quil
?avoyt *and perhaps another word deleted*] ma dict quil a la charge dudit
sieur de mendosse [de vous *deleted*] avec quattre aultres dont je ne say
le nom synon que dung nomme Courtoys de vous faire mourir [par
poisons *added in the margin*] soit par armes, par boucquets, par linge
par senteur par heauf[1] ou par quelque moyen que ce soit, et le tout
avant quil soit peu de tems [en ate *deleted*] et que peult estre il sera la
plus grande berthelemy que onques on a oy parler et quil ny a dieu ny
diable qui lempesche luy ou ses conseillers de ce faire qui est une
chosse fort grandement pitoyable et pour autant Madame que je este
[linstrument pour vous *deleted*] le chercheur de beaucoup de chosses
qui ce sont congneus [veritables *inserted and deleted*] a votre bon
conseil lesquelles ont este trouvez veritables et aussy comme [Jayme
deleted] Jaymes mieulx mourir [au quas *deleted*] au cas que ne vous die
le peure et cincere verite

f. 390v/   Nottez madame que je lay interrogue le plus quil ma este pocibble.
et premierement sur les dix commendemens de la loy laquelle chosse
cest fort bien confesse hors mics sur non occides/ car il a tousiours
ceste volonte vers votre Majeste et luy ay faict les plus belles [Res
deleted] Remonstrances du monde sur cela/ mais il a respondu en
somme que cestoit pour la tranquilite de la [R *changed to*] vraye
Religion catholique [apos *deleted*] apostolique et [*word beginning* Roy
deleted] Romayne et que resolument quil croyoit que son ame yroit
tout droict en paradis quant il nauroit faict aultre chosse que cela: et
semble quil soit enrage en ce confessant comme il grichoit les dentz et
me faisoit peur en le voyant: Notez quil ma promis de me amener les
aultres mais il y en a deux qui vienet en brief despaigne ce quil atent/
quant est dung quidam nomme Courtoys il ne vault pas mieux que
son compaignon et a telle volonte/ il doibvent faire leurs pasques
mercredi prochain et leur reconsillier

Votre humble affexione
Celuy que connoissez

---

1   Fagot may have meant to write *heaux*, but what he actually wrote was *f*. The likeliest thing
is that he remembered that *eau* does not take *s* in the plural, but had a blackout about what
it does take. But he did not normally have difficulty with plurals in *x*.

Written beside signature
Deus adjuvat te et maneat tecum omnibus diebus vite tue Amen

Written below signature
gardez mon segret car Je vous suys fidelle et decouvriray aultres choses
Vide humilitatem meam et laborem meum: [et dimitte omnia *deleted*] f. 391r,
[et cono *deleted*] et cognoce me, quia ego sum pauper sed fidelis[2]   at top/

To the most serene Queen of England, France and Ireland, health, and a good, long and happy life. Amen.

Madame,
I wish to advise your honourable and prudent Council, whom God keep in perfect prosperity, that a Spaniard called Zubiaur has presented himself to me; he is agent for Don Bernardino de Mendoza, formerly ambassador for the King of Spain in your kingdom. He has come to me several times to hear his confession, but I always refused him until this last Sunday. This Zubiaur has confessed to me most ignoble things, which oblige me to tell you the pure and simple truth, because I wish for your long and happy life; and also because it has always pleased your Majesty to favour me not only with your mouth but also with your heart and your resources, in which state I wish always to continue for the protection and safety of your excellent Majesty.

It is to be noted that he told me that he had the charge from M. de Mendoza, with four others whose names I do not know except for one called Courtois, to procure your death very shortly by arms, by poisons, bouquets, underclothes, smell, waters or by any other means; that it will be the greatest St Bartholomew's Day there has ever been; and that neither God nor Devil will stand in the way of their doing it. This is an appalling thing, and in so much, Madame, as I have been the discoverer of many things which have become known to your good Council and found to be true, and would sooner die than tell you anything but the pure and sincere truth:

Note, Madame, that I interrogated him as closely as possible, and

2 Cf. Psalm 24 (Vulgate): 16–18.
   Respice in me, et miserere mei; quia unicus et pauper sum ego.
   Tribulationes cordis mei multiplicatae sunt; de necessitatibus meis erue me.
   Vide humilitatem meam et laborem meum, et dimitte universa delicta mea.
   (Look thou upon me, and have mercy on me; for I am alone and poor.
   The troubles of my heart are multiplied; deliver me from my necessities.
   See my abjection and my labour; and forgive all my sins.)

first on the Ten Commandments of the Law, on all of which he confessed very well, except on *Thou shalt not kill*, for he persists in this intention against your Majesty. I made the finest remonstrances in the world to him about it; but he replied, more or less, that it was for the tranquillity of the true Catholic, apostolic and Roman religion, and that he believed firmly that his soul would go straight to Heaven if he had done nothing else but that; and he seems to have worked himself up into a rage while confessing this, for he was grinding his teeth, and it made me quite frightened to look at him. Note that he has promised to bring me the others, but he is waiting for two of them who are coming from Spain. As for one of them called Courtois, he is no better than his companion, and has the same intention. They are to make their Easter duties next Wednesday, and reconcile themselves.

Your humble affectionate
He whom you know

[*Latin*] May God help you, and remain with you all the days of your life. Amen.

Keep my secret, because I am faithful to you and will discover other things.

[*Latin*] Take account of my humility and my labour, [and forgive all (my sins) (!) *deleted*] and acknowledge me, for I am poor but faithful.[2]

11a

Enclosure in No. 11, presumably meant for
Walsingham only

BL Harleian 1582, f. 269.
Holograph hand FA. No endorsement.
See No. 11.

Ensuit la confession de N.

Et premierement Interrogation a luy faicte combien il y avoit
quil navoit esta [*sic*] confesse/ Responce diceluy quil y avoit cinq
moys et plus. Interrogation sy la confession laquelle il avoit faicte
dernierement par son dernier confesseur avoit este parfaicte et entiere/
Responce que ouy au mieulx quil y estoit pocible/ Interrogation a
Icelluy sur les dix commendemens de notre mere saincte [*sic*] assavoir/
unum crede:[1] que depuis sa derniere confession sil avoit bien faict son
debvoir de aymer dieu et de croyre a ung seul dieu aussy/ *Réponse*/
quil croyoit fort bien a ung seul dieu mais quil ne lavoit pas si bien
ayme ny observay ses saint commandementz comme ung vray fidelle
catholique [debvoit *deleted*] doibt faire/

Interrogation/ *nec jures vana per ipsum*/ Responce quil avoit jure par
plusieurs foys et prins le nom de dieu en vain et de ses sainctz et
sainctes de paradis ausy/ Interrogation savoir: *Sabbata sanctifices*/
Réponse/ quil avoit observe et garde les festes du commendement de
leglise le mieulx quil luy a este pocible mais non pas en telle devotion
comme il debvoit: Interrogation *charos venerare parentes*: *Réponse*/ quil
navoit pas porte honneur ny reverence a ses superieurs comme il
debvoit assavoir comme aux gens deglise et a aultres tant de plus
grande dignite et calite quil nestoit// Interrogation: *Non sis occisor*.
Réponse/ quil navoit tue personne mais que vray est quil en a la

---

1 This and the following Latin phrases attached to the questions are from a Latin doggerel
   intended to remember the Ten Commandments by.

volonte et que sil estoit pocible que dieu luy donnast ceste grace et faveur que ce seroit pour une grandissime ediffication du peuple et que il croyoit fermement quil seroit la cause de la salvation [de *deleted twice*] dames infinies et que iceluy nest pas le seul qui le veult entreprendre mais ausy quil y a quattre autes [*sic*] qui sont ses coadiuteurs/ Interrogation qui cestoit qui vouloit occire/ Réponse/ quil voulloit et avoit intention que ausy tost quil y en auroit troys venus qui sont avec le prince de palme qu'il avoint delibere de tuer la Royne qui est une chose fort pitoyable.

The last paragraph seems to have been added as an afterthought between the above and the signature
Interrogation: *Testis iniquus:*/ quil [na *deleted*] avoit porte fault tesmoignage [alenct *deleted*] alencontre de lung de ses beaux freres[2] pour une chose laquelle estoit de grande importance mais que cestoit pour une paix milleure/

henry fagot

The Confession of N. follows:
Interrogation first made of him: How long since his last confession? *Reply*: Something over five months.

Interrogation: Was his last confession perfect and complete? *Reply*: Yes, to the best of his ability.

Interrogation on the Ten Commandments of Holy Mother [Church] [*sic*]. First commandment: Since his last confession had he done his duty in loving God and believing in one God? *Reply*: He believed firmly in one God, but he had not loved him nor observed his ten commandments as a true faithful Catholic ought to do.

Interrogation: second commandment. *Reply*: He had sworn several times and also taken in vain the name of God and those of his saints.

Interrogation: third commandment. *Reply*: He had kept the feast-days commanded by the Church as well as he could, but not with such devotion as he ought to have done.

Interrogation: fourth commandment. *Reply*: He had not given honour and reverence to his superiors as he ought to have done, that is, to churchmen and to those of higher place and dignity than himself.

Interrogation: fifth commandment. *Reply*: He had not killed any-

---

2   The alternative translation is inspired by an account of the ceremony, similar to that attributed to Zubiaur and his friends, gone through by William Parry in Paris the previous December; here Cardinals Vendôme and Joyeuse are described as Parry's 'beaupères': *Holinshed's Chronicles*, iv, 582.

one, but it was true that he had the will to do so. If it were possible that God should give him this grace and favour it would be greatly to the edification of the people, and he firmly believed that it would be the cause of the salvation of an infinite number of souls. He was not proposing to undertake it on his own but with the assistance of four others.

Interrogation: Whom did he wish to kill? *Reply*: He wished and intended, as soon as three others had come from the Prince of Parma with whom he had determined to kill her, to kill the queen; which is a most appalling thing.

Interrogation: eighth commandment. [*Reply*:] He had borne false witness against one of his brothers-in-law [*possibly*: one of his fellow-conspirators][2] in a matter of great importance, but with the intention of making a better peace between them.

Henry Fagot

12

Two Passages from the Second Dialogue of La cena de le Ceneri, *March–April 1584*, translated

DI, pp. 53–7, 82–4.

i The Trip on the Thames

/Bruno (Nolanus), not having received the expected invitation to lunch on Ash Wednesday, goes off to visit some Italian friends and does not return to Salisbury Court until well after dark. There he finds Florio and Gwynne standing outside the house looking for him. After some discussion he agrees to go with them to supper at Greville's lodgings in Whitehall. /

Teofilo: 'Off we go then,' said the Nolan, 'and let us pray God will be with us this murky evening, on so long a journey and by such dangerous ways.' Although we were on the straight road [to Whitehall], we thought we should do better to take a short cut, and turned down towards the Thames to get a boat that would take us to the palace. We came to the stairs at Buckhurst House and there, shouting and crying 'Oars!' (that is, 'Gondolieri!'), we spent as much time as would have sufficed to get by the road at leisure to our destination and do a small piece of business into the bargain. In the end two boatmen answered from a long way off and, with inordinate slowness, as if they were on their way to be hanged, rowed to the bank; where, after a great deal of questioning and answering about the whence, the whither, the why, the how and the how much, they finally drew the bow of the boat up to the bottom step of the stairs. Then one of the two, who looked like the ancient helmsman of the kingdom of Tartarus [Charon], stretched a hand to the Nolan, and the other, who was I think the son of the first though he was a man of about sixty-five, helped the rest of us on board.

Then you might have said that, though it had taken on board neither Hercules nor Aeneas nor Rodomonte king of Sarza,[1]

> 'gemuit sub pondere cymba
> sutilis, et multam accepit limosa paludem.'
> (The ill-found boat groaned beneath the weight, and
> shipped a great deal of muddy water.)[2]

Hearing this music, the Nolan said: 'Please God this fellow be not Charon; I believe this is the boat called the Emulous of *Lux Perpetua*. It may easily rival in antiquity Noah's Ark and, by my faith, it must surely be one of the relics of the Flood.' The planks of the boat winced whenever you touched them, and at the slightest movement trumpeted all together. 'I think', said the Nolan, 'that it is no fable that the walls of Thebes, as I remember, had voices, and sometimes sang true music.[3] If you do not believe it, listen to the piping of this boat, which sounds like a set of bagpipes with all the drones and shrills the river makes coming in through seams and holes on every side.' We laughed but, God knows, as

> Annibal, quando a l'imperio afflitto
> Vedde farsi fortuna si molesta,
> Rise fra gente lacrimosa e mesta.
> (as Hannibal, when he saw so hard a fate befalling his afflicted
> country, laughed amid the weeping of his companions)[4]

Prudenzio: That is called a Sardonic Laugh.

Teofilo: Inspired by such sweet harmony, as by the pains of love, the times and the seasons, we joined in the consort with song. Master Florio, as one recollecting his loves, sang 'Dove, senza me, dolce mia vita?' (Ah! Where, without me, sweetness of my life, hast thou remained so young, so beautiful?)[5] Then the Nolan chimed in with 'Il Saracin dolente, O femenil ingegno' (The mournful Saracen said: 'Oh, mind of woman, how easily you change!');[6] and so on.

Thus we went forward, little by little as the boat permitted. Time and woodworm had eaten it away till it might have floated like a cork fender; yet it seemed to move, hurrying slowly, as if it was made of lead. The arms of those two ancients were worn out, and

---

1 The Moorish malcontent in Ariosto's *Orlando furioso*; cf. above, pp. 123 f, nn. 56–7.

2 Virgil, *Aeneid*, vi. 413–4: a description of the effect on Charon's boat of taking on board a load of the souls of the dead. The river here is the Styx.

3 Bruno seems to be elaborating the story of Amphion, harpist and founder of Thebes, who built its walls by moving the stones with the power of his music.

4 Petrarch, *Rime*, ccii: the reference is to Hannibal abandoning his Italian campaign and sailing back to Carthage to defend it against Scipio Africanus.

5 Ariosto, *Orlando furioso*, viii, 76; above, p. 122.

6 Ibid. xxvii, 117.

though they limbered up their bodies as if for a powerful stroke, they pulled extremely short with the oars.

Prudenzio: Excellently described: *festina* for the frantic backs of the boatmen; *lente* for the result with the oars. Like feeble workmen of the Garden God [Priapus].

Teofilo: In this manner, as time went on apace and our journey little, we managed something less than a third of the way. At this point, a little upstream from the place called the Temple, our grandfathers[7] instead of getting up speed pointed the boat towards the shore. The Nolan asked us: 'What are these people up to? Maybe they need to get their breath back?' We had to explain to him that, as they said, they were not going any farther, because that was where they lived. Begging and praying did no good, for they were the kind of peasant in whose breast the Cupid of the Unwashed has emptied all his arrows.[8]

Prudenzio: Since the beginning of time, Nature has made every kind of peasant such that he will do nothing for the love of virtue, and next to nothing for fear of punishment.

Frulla: There's another saying about peasants:

> Rogatus tumet,
> Pulsatus rogat,
> Pugnis concisus adorat.
> (Beg him, he preens himself;
> Thump him, he begs;
> Thrash him, he grovels.)[9]

Teofilo: To end: they packed us off; and when we had paid and thanked them (for, in this city, when you get a kick in the teeth from such *canaille*, you have to thank them for it) showed us the best way to get up to the Strand . . .

ii   *The Drinking-Cup (Urcivolo)*

/They sit down at table in Greville's rooms./

Teofilo: Here, by the grace of God, I did not have to witness that ceremony of the drinking–cup or glass which they have a custom of handing round the table: high to low, left to right, or in any old direction, without other order than is indicated by acquaintanceship and highland manners. After the person who starts the game has

---

7   *Patrini*, literally 'godfathers'.
8   'Emptied' is a cautious translation of *spunta*, meaning 'blunts'. On the alternative senses of this, above, p. 123, n. 54.
9   On the history and versions of this rhyme, *DI*, p. 57, n. 1.

taken it from his mouth, leaving a film of grease around it which would do excellently for glue, another drinks and leaves a morsel of bread on it, the next deposits on the rim a small piece of meat from between his teeth, and somebody else sheds into the cup a hair out of his beard; and thus everybody partakes of the drink higgledy-piggledy, and no one is so impolite as not to leave you some generous offering from the remains he displays around his moustache. And if somebody does not feel like drinking, either because he cannot stomach the thought or because he wants to act the great man, it is sufficient if he simply puts the cup to his mouth, leaving you just a suspicion of skin off his lip.

The reason why they do this is that, just as they have all come together to make of themselves one carnivorous wolf by eating the selfsame flesh of a lamb, goat, sheep or Grunnio Corocotta;[10] so, by applying every one his mouth to the one pot, they may succeed in turning themselves into one single blood-sucking leech, in token of one community,[11] one brotherhood, one infection, one heart, one stomach, one gullet and one mouth. And the whole thing has to be done with certain rituals and little performances, so that it is the best comedy in the world to see it, and the most painful and stomach-turning tragedy for a civilised man to find himself in the middle of it, since he will suppose that he is obliged to do as the rest do, on pain to be thought discourteous and ill-bred. For this is the *ne plus ultra* of their civility and courtesy. But since this observance, though still kept up at the vilest tables, is no longer to be found elsewhere except in certain pardonable instances, we shall without more ado leave them to their supper . . .

10 A sucking-pig famous in school text-books since classical times as the author of a comic will. The reference is to the institution of the eucharist at the Last Supper as a *novum testamentum* (Matthew 26: 28; Luke 22: 20; 1 Corinthians 11: 25), which is repeated in the consecration of the chalice at mass. Bruno could conceivably have been referring to Luther's interpretation of *testamentum* as 'will' in the *Babylonian Captivity of the Church (Martin Luther: Selections from his Writings*, ed. J. Dillenberger (Garden City, N.Y., 1961), pp. 272 f); but I doubt if he was familiar with it.

11 *Urbanità.*

13

[Latish February 1585, OS]: Giordano Bruno to Sir Edward Stafford, Paris

BL Cottonian Nero B vi, ff. 315, 320.

Holograph hand FB. Signed with a signature reminiscent of the French royal signature: 'Henry'. The bottom of this has been cut off, presumably when the Cottonian volume was bound up, but I have no doubt that this is the reading. It is obvious from the contents that the writer was the same man as the writer of Nos. 4 and 15. Address, in the same hand: 'Advertissement/ A Monsieur lembassadeur dangleterre'. Endorsement: '8 [M *rubbed away*]arche 1585./ Seacrette advertisementes./△'.

Date Since there is no date on the letter, I imagine that the date of the endorsement is the date of reception in London: i.e. 8/18 March 1585. Hence it would have been written about a fortnight earlier. It must have been written before Thomas Morgan's arrest on 27 February/ 9 March, and I presume that it was sent by Stafford from Paris with his letter to Walsingham of 1/11 March reporting the arrest: above, pp. 55–6. 26 February/ 8 March would be possible, but I can see no reason for the endorsement being in new style. The triangles were meant to draw Walsingham's attention to the passage underlined.

The manuscript is damaged at the edges; see preliminary Note to *Texts*.

Monsieur je vous prie recevoir le presant advertissement, pour tout certain et ne le mespriser, attandu qu'il importe beaulcoup a la conservation de lestat dangleterre, comme lon a coigneu par expeiance [*sic*] par les advertissemens qui vous en ont este cidevant donnez sur le mesme subiect ou lon a descouvert, le malheureux et perfide dessaing des ennemys de lestat, qui ne desirent que la perdition toutalle d'icelluy, et par une guerre civille, revolter et esmouvoir le peuble dangleterre. contre leur princesse, par le moyen des mauvais bruictz: et li [v *corrected to*] bres papalz diffamatoires, et contraires a la religion; qui y sont transportez de france, a la suscitation de ceulx qui sont en fuite dud*it* pays, et de lembassadeur despaigne et aultres leurs adherans, comme des libres a dire Messe, aultres libres diffamatoires composes par les Jesuistes, heures, et aultres libres servans a leur intantion. Lesquelz libres sont transportes de ce pais, au pais dangleterre, par les serviteurs domestiques[1] de Monsieur de Mauvissiere embassadeur pour le roy [en *deleted*] aud*it* pais et dud*it* pais ilz rapportent en france des chappes et ornemens de leglise papalle quilz achaptent depardela a peu de pris pour apres les revendre en ce pa/*is*/ bien cherement et aussi des bas destame,[2] Lesquelz trafficquans se nom/*ment*/ l'un, qui est le principal dud*it* traffic, Gerault de la Cassaigne somellier[1] ordinaire dud*it Sieu*r de Mauvissiere, et laultre Rene Leduc son cuysinier, lesquelz s'en sont enrechis: et senrechissent tous les jours dud*it* commerce /*au*/ detrimant de lestat, duquel ilz desirent la subversion, et mesmes vendent lesdictz livres au logis dud*it Sieu*r embass/*adeur.*/ Ledict delacassaigne someiller,[1] est tous les jours entretenu /*et*/ conseille par ung anglois naturel, qui se tient aupres leglise sainct ylaire dumont, et aussi par ung aultre gentilhomme qu/*on*/ dict estre parent de la Royne,[3] Lesquelz leur donnent mo/*yen*/ de faire tenyr lesdictz livres, et principallement ledict Mo/*rgan*/ lequel faict estat, tous les jours de banquier: pour faire t/*enir*/ [de *deleted*] les deniers quilz voient, estre besoing pour la perfection, de /*leurs*/ monopoles, et se sert led*it* Mourgan: ordinairement pour /*faire*/ tenyr ses le*tt*res, plus seurement d'ung des principaux se/*cretaires*/ de Monsieur de Villeroy, lequel les envoye et enclost da/*ns les*/ pacquetz du Roy qui sont envoyes a son embassadeur a/*udit*/ pais dangleterre, lesquelles le*tt*res led*it* embassadeur, rent /*aux*/ aultres traistres, depardela, affin quelles ne puyssent /*estre*/ descouvertes, Ilz ont promys ausd*its* delacassaigne et l/*educ*/ someiller[1] et cuysinier, que silz peuvent venyr a bout /*de*/ leurs dessaings, ilz les feront grands, et riches a jamais, /*Et*/ detant f.315v/ que led*it*/ de Mauvissiere est prest a sen revenyr /*en*/ france et que en son lieu, le Roy y envoye Monsieur /*de*/ laubespine,[4] dans peu de tempz Ledict delacassaigne /*s'en*/ yra dans quelques jours, pour luy faire apprester /*un*/ logis depardela, aupres de celluy dud*it Sieu*r de Mauviss/*iere*/ du long de ceste riviere: auquel lieu il se faict fort d'en trouver qu'lqu'un [e *deleted*], a louage. et mesmes le pourvoir de serviteurs a sa devotion, tous faictz de sa main, pour tousjours avoir moyen, de continuer leur traffic, et engendrer, de tout leur pouvoir, queque malheur aud*it* pais, estant certain, que tout le mal et trahison qu'on a descouvert, ne procede que d'avoir loge led*it* de Mauvissiere,

---

1 Here Bruno has added two extra loops to the 'm', and may have intended to double it.
2 This might suggest that Bruno had read Girault's letter of 24-i/3-ii-1584 (above, p. 34, n. 33), since that is the only other reference to such a traffic that we have; but it was no doubt common knowledge in the house.
3 From 'conseille' this passage has been underlined, more strongly as far as 'dumont', and a triangle placed against it in the margin. The two men were Thomas Morgan and probably Charles Arundell, who was the queen's cousin.
4 The family name of Châteauneuf.

du long de lad*ite* riviere, auquel lieu ilz font transporter de nuyt.
tant, li [v *changed to*] bres le*ttre*s pacquetz, que aultres choses, enquoy
ilz se peuvent servir, pour la ruyne dud*it* pais, et icelles danrees,
sont secreptement vendues au logis, dud*it* Sie*u*r embassadeur, par
les susd*its* serviteurs domesticques estant besoing pour le bien
du pais, d'empecher quilz ne se logent, en ce quartier, ny aultre
qu'on coignoistra, estre suspect, et ou ilz puyssent continuer leurs
monopoles, ou entreprises meschantes, Ledict delacassaigne n'oze
passer la mer du coste de dieppe, a cause qu'on le coignoist trop bien,
mais sen va a presant, passer du couste de calais, Il seroit besoing
d'advertir, d'un coste et daultre, affin de luy faire faire, tel traicte-
ment qu'il merite, et aussi a son compaignon, et aultres qui sen
vouldront mesler, affin d'empecher la continua*ti*on, de leur meschant
dessaing, qu'est de vous faire tous perdre, Estant aussi besoing
davoir doresnavant le cueur qu'on ne laisse passer de jour, ny
de nuyt, aulcunes pacques, paquetz, coffres, muys, ny tonneaux,
adressans aud*it* Embassadeur, ny aultres de sa maison, et encores
moings a nul des marchans dud*it* pais, allans ny venans, sans estre
vizites, et ce faisant il se descouvrira beaucoup de choses, au profit de
lestat, quest lendroit ou je priere le createur, vous maintenyr

Monsieur en parfaicte sanite longue et heureuse vye.

Vo*tre* seviteur [*sic*] plus affectionne
Henry

/*Je vo*/us suppl*ie* croire le contenu cy dessus /*et ne*/ le negliger ains
leffectuer et vous /*fe*/res ung singulier bien pour le /*re*/pos public de
vo*tre* patrie

Monsieur,

I beg you to receive the present information as quite certain, and
not to despise it, since it matters a great deal to the conservation of
the state of England, as has been found by experience through the
advices which have hitherto been given to you on the same subject;
in these I have revealed the miserable and perfidious design of the
enemies of the state, who desire nothing but its total ruin, and to
raise and stir up the people of England against their princess by a civil
war. This they do by means of evil rumours and defamatory books,
popish and contrary to religion, which are transported into England
from France at the instance of those who are in flight from their
country, and also of the Spanish ambassador and of others who
favour them: such as Mass-books, other [*sic*] defamatory books
written by Jesuits, books of hours and other books serving their

purpose. These books are transported from this country to England by the domestic servants of M. de Mauvissière, ambassador for the king there; they import into France from England vestments and furnishings of the popish Church, which they buy there cheap and sell dear in this country, and also worsted hose.[2]

The principal trafficker is called Girault de la Chassaigne, ordinary butler to M. de Mauvissière, and the other is René Leduc, his cook; they have made and continue to make themselves rich by this trade, to the detriment of the state, the subversion of which they seek: they sell the books at the ambassador's house. De la Chassaigne is continually maintained and advised by a natural Englishman who lives by the church of St Hilaire-du-Mont, and also by another gentleman who is said to be a kinsman of the queen.[3] These give them means to carry the books, and especially Morgan, who acts as a banker for them, giving them the money they need for the execution of their schemes. To pass his letters more securely, Morgan regularly uses one of the principal secretaries of M. de Villeroy, who encloses them in the packets sent by the king to England; the ambassador gives them to the other traitors there, so that they cannot be found out. They have promised De la Chassaigne and Leduc that if their designs are successful they will make them great and rich for ever. Now that M. de Mauvissière is ready to return to France, and the king will shortly send M. de l'Aubépine[4] in his place, De la Chassaigne will leave in a few days to get a house ready for him somewhere near that of M. de Mauvissière, beside the river. He is confident of finding one to let there, and is busy filling it with servants of his own kidney, so as to be able to continue their traffic and do everything in their power to bring some disaster upon the country. It is a fact that all the evil and treason which have been discovered have come from giving M. de Mauvissière a house beside the river, to which they are able to carry by night books, letters, packets and all sorts of other things to serve for the ruin of the country. The goods are secretly sold at the ambassador's house by his aforesaid domestic servants, and it is necessary for the good of the country to prevent them living in that quarter, and in any other regarded as suspect, where they would be able to continue their schemes or wicked enterprises.

De la Chassaigne dare not cross the Channel via Dieppe, because he is too well known [there], but is going off now to cross via Calais. I suggest that you advise people on both sides, so that he can be given the treatment he deserves, and likewise his companion and anyone else who meddles in it, so as to prevent the continuation of their wicked design, which is to ruin you all. You must also take care from now on not to let pass, by day or night, any bales, packets, chests, hogsheads or barrels addressed to the ambassador or to anyone else in his house, still less to or from any merchant in the country, without inspecting them; if you do this you will discover many things for the benefit of the state. At which point I shall pray the Creator to keep you,

Monsieur, in perfect health a long and happy life.

Your most affectionate servant,
Henry

I beg you to believe what is contained above and not to neglect it but to act upon it, and you will do a singular service to the public repose of your country.

14

[Probably Spring 1585]: copy presumably sent to Sir Edward Stafford, Paris

BL Cottonian Nero B vi, ff. 322–4.

Hand FB with some modifications. No address. Endorsed: 'Garnac'.

The placing of this piece in the Cottonian volume would suggest that it was an enclosure in No. 13; but I see no sign that it has been folded, and this and the differences in handwriting imply that it was given to Stafford at another time. As it was perfectly innocuous, there was no reason why Bruno should not have taken it along in person. It seems natural to date it somewhat after No. 13. It may well have nothing to do with Bruno at all; but to my mind the location and handwriting speak fairly strongly in favour.

The spelling 'lh' for 'll', which is a south-western form, makes it certain that the piece came from Bordeaux or thereabouts. The reason I suggest (above, p. 57) that Bruno may have got it from Girault is that Delachassaigne (which was also the name of Michel de Montaigne's wife) is a name common in this region. But Girault's own spelling does not seem to be regional. My former colleague Dr Jonathan Powis, now of Balliol College, Oxford, has been my guide in these regional matters.

Jehanne garnac damoyzelle filhe de dixhuict a vingt ans du pays dangletere Apres la mort de sa merre qui estoict catolique et lavoict instruite en mesme religion continuoit tousiours en icelle et trouvoit tousiours excuze alandroit de Monsur son pere pour naler ouyr le ministre tant elle estoit affectionee en ladite religion catholique et principallement par linstruction dung prestre deguise et dung cathesime [*sic*] que luy avoict donne Et pource quelle voyoit quelle estoit pressee de sondit pere pour aller ouyr le ministre quelle detestoit beaucoup craignant interesser sa consiance print resolution de quiter le pays et sen venir en france a rouan pour estre religieuze au couvant de leur nation qui estren ladite ville de rouan comme elle f.322v/ avoit ouy dire Et de faict ung jour ayant demande conge a sondit pere pour aller voir une siene parante print une garce et luy bailha ung petit paquet quelle avoit faict pour le porter apres elle Et estant en

chemin et non loing du lieu ou elle alloit et cestant retiree ung peu
alesquard ayant prins ledit paquet en print des habilhemans dhomme
et cestant tondue avec des siseaux quelle portoit se couvrit dune
calote et prontemant sen va par ung autre chemin layssant ladite
garsse et sans la voir et sen all [e *changed to*] a tout le jour et le
lendemain tant quelle peust jusques a ce quelle vint en [Islarnde
deleted] Isrlande questoit en caresme prenant et y demeura tout le
caresme alant a lescole du lieu avec les enfans pour aprandre et
noublier ce quelle savoit escrire et lire et apres pasques se mist dans
ung navire en forme de matelot pour sen venir en france pour voir
ses parans comme elle disoit Et quelques jours apres estant arivee
a Bourdeaux sans que jamais son sexe feust descouvert estant sortie
du navire et ayant seu apres estre enquize y avoit deux prebstres
f.323r/ Isrlandois quil beneficies en leglize saint michel et en ayant trouve
ung nomme Messire Adam Hode luy feist almosne et donna moyen
de vivre par lespasse de troys ou quatre jours et apres la mena a
lhospital appelle de saint Jammes quy recoit les pellerins allant a saint
Jaques auquel est surintandant le provincial des Jesuistes pour fere
nourir lesditz pellerins ou elle demeura plus dung mois malade dune
enflure de pied Mais portant ne bougeoit de leglize dudit saint
Jammes a prier Dieu Et apres il advint questant pres que guerie de
ladite enflure elle feust recognue estre une filhe par lhospitaliere dudit
hospital et le dit incontinant audit provincial Dequoy adverty ledit
provincial feist venir ledit hode prebstre pour savoir mieux quelle
estoit et pourquoy avoit deguize son sexe Et ayant [*one word omitted*]
au long et plus que nest dit dessus dou elle estoit et aqui elle
apartenoit et comme elle avoit faict pour estre venue jusques audit
f.323v/ lieu de Bourdeaux et audit hospital et ayant cognu sa pudicite et
chastete entiere et que ny avoit fraude en elle mais seullemant ung
bon zelle de vivre en sa religion et [dentr *deleted*] de se randre
religeuze feust mise au couvant des religieuzes dudit Bourdeaux
apelle de la nun[c *changed to*]tiade par la conduite dudit provincial et
de gens dhonneur qui la feirent recepvoir audit couvant par pitie et
misericorde et le jour de lentree audit couvant Messieurs larchevesque
de Bourdeaux et evesque dacqz et deux honorables damoyzelles la
presenterent comme leur filhe audit couvant en faisant loffice et
sermones acoustumees et en presance de troys ou quatre mille
personnes et par lesditz sieurs et damoyzelles luy feust fourny ce que
luy estoit bezoing pour sadite entree Et ung an et demy apres en
fisrent de mesmes a sa profession ou elle est pour sa vie avec une fort
bonne compagne [*sic*] de religieuzes et fort aymee comme estant fort
honneste vertueuze et devote Laquelle a este visitee par aucungs de sa
nation et par gens dhonneur qui en pouront porter le tesmognage et
savent dou elle est et ont cognu les siens et ont parle aladite filhe

Since this piece was not written by Bruno and may not have been copied or abstracted by him, there is no point in translating it. It recounts the story of a girl of 18 or 20 called Jane 'Garnac', who ran away from home in England in order to avoid going to church and to join an English convent in France. She disguised herself as a boy, went to Ireland, and shipped as a sailor in a boat to Bordeaux. There she spent some time in the hospital of St James, was discovered to be a girl, and was placed by the Jesuit provincial in the convent of the Annonciade with a dowry provided by the local élite and a grand public ceremony.

15

[Beginning of September 1585, OS]: Giordano Bruno to Sir Francis Walsingham, London, Salisbury Court

PRO SP 12/206, ff. 197–8 (no. 80). The letter has been bound in a volume for December 1587.

Holograph hand FA. At the end of first three paragraphs the space left is filled up with a wavy line; after the rest there is a straight line. No address. Endorsed: 'Secreat Advertisements'.

Date I assume that the interview occurred shortly before 6/16 September and that the letter was written immediately afterwards. On that date Florio came to an agreement with Châteauneuf to move out of the house, while remaining his servant: Yates, *Florio*, pp. 65, 67. Florio must have had an interview shortly before this, and presumably Bruno, as a more important member of the household, would have been interviewed earlier. Florio being a Protestant, the discussion about Protestants in the house suggests that the two interviews occurred at much the same time; and Bruno was in jail between say 8/18 and 10/20 September. Above, pp. 58–61, 76–8.

Monseigneur Je vous advertis fort bien que Monsieur de chasteau neuf ma interrogue fort comment lon traictoit les papistes dengleterre et qui sil y avoit point de craincte pour moy par aller par les Rus pour autant que lon connoissoit que je estois [le pr *deleted*] cestuilla qui debvoit estre [?congnue *deleted*] congnu entre tous les autres Je luy ay faict la responce que jamais lon ne ma dict ny faict nul mal pour mon office, en apres il ma demande de ceulx qui frequenteist en la maisson de monseigneur lembassadeur et mesmes de ceulx de qui il se failloit garder craignant quil ne feusses traistres ou bien espions pour [*sic*] le Roy de france Je luy ay respondu sur cela que Je nen savois rien et que Je ne menquestes pas de ceulx la et que je ne ay que faire avec iceulx

davantaige il ma demande si Jen conoisses quelques uns de moy mesmes ou par ouy dire. Je luy ay respondu que non.

Sur cela il ma demande si je connoisses en ma consience monsieur du glas nestre point ung traistre Je luy ay dict que Je nen savois

rien, et m'a demande pourquoy il conferoit tant souvent avec
l'embassadeur   Je luy ay dict que je nen savois rien et me respondit
que Je le savois bien mais que je ne voulles rien dire.

En apres il ma demande de M*aît*re Geffroy le medicin sil nestoit
point un espion et quil avoit ouy dire en france quil ne se falloit fier a
icelluy ny a laure*n*s feron ny a fleuriot et quil estoit pour [cestuilla
deleted] cestuilla ung espion [pour *deleted*] contre le Roy de france et
pour le pape et quil savoit bien quil mordoit des deux costez.

Davantaige [il *deleted*]

Sur ces propos ung certain Itallian nomme brancallion avoisna sur   f. 197v/
cela et dist a mond*it* sieur de casteau neuf quil avoit este a une place[1]
la ou on luy a dict que la Royne dangleterre estoit infiniment marrye
quil failloit que Monseigneur de Mauvissiere sen retournast en france
et quelle vouldroit payer grand nombre dargent et que laustre ne fut
en ce Royaulme et sur cella Monsieur de Casteau neuf luy dist quil ne
dist rien plus.

En apres monseigneur de casteau neuf me demanda com*m*ent je me
gouvernois et que je don*n*asses linstruxion a ses prestres com*m*ent il
falloit quil ce gouvernassent et quil me seroit chosse salutaire et qu'il
avoit amene deux lun pour prescher fust en Itallian ou en fransoys
pour autant quil y a plusieurs Itallians qui[l *deleted*] vienent en la
messe et icelluy prestre est Itallian et mechant lequel ma [de *deleted*]
fort bien dict quil ce fauldroit a composer ung livre de tout ce quil ce
fera en ce Royaulme tant quil [demeura *deleted*] demeurera icy.

Ceans led*it* sieur de chasteau neuf ma jure et promis sa foy que
jamais ne endurera en son logis daultres gens synon que ceulx de sa
religion et quil savoit fort bien que mond*it* Seigneur de Mauvissiere
en avoit en la siene qui le traissoient et que cestoit une grande villenie
et ung grand scecandalle [*sic*] pour luy et quil craignoit que le Roy de
France [len reprent et quil *inserted above*] en estoit fort bien adverti et
mesmes que cella luy est deffendu dud*it* Roy de n'en tenir daultres en
sa maisson que de sa Relligion.

davantaige il m'a demande sil y avoit pas dornemens deglisse a   f. 198r/
vendre en Londres ou aultres places[1] qui feussent a bon marche pour
donner a quelques eglisses en france   Je luy ay dict que jen conoisses
quelques uns et luy ay promis de luy les faire monstrer a lundi
prochain

davantaige il ma dict que Girault somellier qui est pour le pr*es*ent
le sien y a gaigne beaucoup plus il ma dict et interrogue pourquoy
je ne faises coment luy et que je ne faises [?ve *deleted*] venir force
livres comment Girault et sachez quil y en a troys coffres tous plains

---

1 *Place* is an Anglicism. Brancaleone was still serving Châteauneuf, and conveying letters
from English *émigrés*, in 1588 (report of Roger Walton: PRO SP 12/209, no. 57).

dont il y en a ung la ou il y a des livres nouvellement composez contre la Religion dengleterre et faictes estat que Icelluy Girault que cest le plus mechant homme qui soit en la france et le plus grand dissimulateur et que cest une peste en ce royaulme.

Monseigneur je vous supplie de croirre et de faire estat que je vous suys et seray toutte ma vie votre loyal et fidelle serviteur et ay espoir de vous servir en France plus quen engleterre car je seray tous les jours pres de ceulx du conseil et vous supplie au nom de Dieu m'en escripvre ung petit mot comment il fault que je my gouvernes

Dieu saulve la bonne Royne dangleterre avec son bon conseil

Henry Fagot

In margin
Ne me oubliez sil vous plaist.

Monseigneur,

I advise you that M. de Châteauneuf has closely interrogated me how the papists are treated in England, and whether it was not dangerous for me to go about the streets, since it was known that I was the person who ought to be known above all others. I replied that nobody had ever spoken or done any harm to me on account of my office. After that he asked me about those who frequented the ambassador's house and those of whom one ought to be careful on the grounds that they might be traitors or spies for [*sic*: evidently means 'against'] the King of France. I replied that I knew nothing of those matters and did not inquire into such people, and that it was not my business to deal with them. Then he asked whether I knew any of them (to be spies) on my own account or by hearsay. I said no.

Thereupon he asked me whether, on my conscience, I did not know that M. Douglas was a traitor. I said I knew nothing about it. He asked me why he had such frequent conferences with the ambassador. I said I had no idea, and he replied that I certainly did, but did not wish to tell him.

After that he asked me whether Maître Geoffroy the doctor was not a spy: he had been told in France not to trust him, nor Laurent Feron nor Florio. He said that Geoffroy was a spy against the King of France and for the pope, and that he [Châteauneuf] was well aware that he was a double agent.

At this point an Italian called Brancaleone came up and said to M. de Châteauneuf that he had been at a house where someone had told him that the Queen of England was extremely upset that M. de

Mauvissière had to return to France, and that she would have given a great deal of money not to have had [Châteauneuf] come in his place. M. de Châteauneuf told him to say no more.

After this M. de Châteauneuf asked me how I conducted myself [as a priest], and that I should give his own priests instruction on how to behave here; this could do me some good, he said. He had brought two priests, one of them to preach in both Italian and French, since there are numerous Italians who come to mass here. This priest is an Italian and a troublemaker; he said to me that he intended to write a book about everything that happened in England while he was here.

Hereupon M. de Châteauneuf swore to me that he would never tolerate any people in his household except those of his own religion. He said that he knew perfectly well that M. de Mauvissière had some [Protestants] in his house who had been betraying him; there had been great knavery and it was a great scandal for him, and he was afraid the King of France would reprimand him for it. The king knew all about it, and had forbidden him [probably meaning Châteauneuf] to have anybody in his house but Catholics.

He also asked me if there were not church ornaments to be bought cheap in London or elsewhere to give to churches in France. I promised to go and show him them on Monday. He said that Girault the butler, who is now his own butler, had made a lot of money in this business, and asked me why I did not do as Girault did and bring over a lot of books. You must know that there are three chests full of them here, and in one of them there are books recently written against the religion of England; remember that Girault is the most evil man and the greatest dissimulator in France. He is a perfect plague in this realm.

Monseigneur, I beseech you to believe and remember that I am and shall be all my life your loyal and faithful servant. I hope to be able to serve you better in France than I have done in England because I shall be continually close to members of the king's Council. I beg you in God's name write me a line to tell me what to do.

God save the good Queen of England and her good Council.

Henry Fagot

Please do not forget me.

16

[Probably about New Year 1586]: Giordano Bruno to Sir Francis Walsingham, Paris

PRO SP 78/14, no. 90 bis (no folio number, but between ff. 195 and 199). Calendared, with some errors, in *CSP Foreign 1586–1588*, p. 675.

Holograph   hand FA. No address, except as in the text, or endorsement.

Date   This must have been written some while after Bruno's arrival in Paris with Castelnau early in November, NS, 1585, and one might suspect that it was another request for a New Year's bonus (cf. No. 9). But I can see no grounds for dating it at all exactly.

Monseigneur, je vous doibz beaucoup dobligation pour les bene-fices et biens que je receuz journellement de vous et sans lavoir merite mais il vous plaisra monseigneur de croisre a ce coup que vous trouverrez que au besoing qui fidelle serviteur vous sera [*sic*] si dieu me faict la grace de jamais[1] estre en france comme Monseigneur le duc de Montpensier ma retenu pour estre son omosnier pour le suyvre comme chacun sait bien cella qui est au grand regret de monseigneur de mauvissiere mon premier maistre et sachez que nous serons souvent ensemble le plus souvent le grand omosnier de Guisse et moy ensemblement. La ou je vous jures et prometz la foy dhomme de bien que je ne vous feray faulte de vous escripvre tout ce quil ce fera ou en sera faict ou dict car led*it* omosnier est de mon pays et est fort bien mon bon amy et est celuy qui est la cause davoir este que je suys mintenant a mond*it* ?S*eigneu*r duc de Monpensier. [Je v *deleted*] Des nouvelles je vous advise fort bien que je congneu et connoist fort bien pour un espion un petit flemang qui est danvers nomme alexendre dem*eurant* en n*o*tre maison lequel ma dict quil avoit beaucoup de chose a dire au sieur bernardin de mendoce luy estant en

---

1   *Jamais* seems to be an Italianism – 'giamái': 'never or at no time; also ever or at any time' (Florio).

france et que ledit de mendoce luy a promis de luy faire faire [un *deleted*] ung voyage vers le prince de parme qui luy vauldroit beaucoup mais tant y a que led*it* alexendre parle flamang espagnol Itallian almang angloys et fransoys qui est fort rusé et prendray garde sur luy en france car il ne vault rien du tout.[2] Je vous advise fort bien que le somellier de mond*it* seigneur de Mauvissiere a bien faict ses choux gras avec ses livres et cest vanté que[sa *deleted*] la venue de Monsieur de Chasteau neuf luy vault plus de cinq ou six [ses *deleted*] cens escus de proffict.

Je vous advertis quil est facteur pour les papistes dangleterre en france et les soudoye dargent en france car luy il prent de la marchandisse a londres et en baille largent en france   Voilla mintenant sa ruse et ce faict nommer estre le somellier de monseigneur de chasteau neuf prendz garde a luy il y a ung prestre Itallian demeur*ant* au logis de mond*it* chasteau neuf lequel trionfe de prescher et a invente une escripture [qu *deleted*] ainsy quil ma dict quant lo*n* escripvera chose de consequence vers le pape et cro*y* quil est vray ce quil dict dont je vous en feray participant de son chiffre aultre chose ne vous puys que mander sino*n* que je prie dieu

Monseigneur quil maintiene en bonne prosperite longue et heureusse vie en la noble et vertueusse princesse la serenissime Royne dangleterre et a vous et aussy a tout son bon conseil ame*n*

Je vous requers au nom de dieu monseigneur avoir souvenance du pauvre hom*me* qui sera tousiours le vostre et de le considerer sil vous plaist.

Icy est le chiffre [de *deleted*] du p*re*stre Itallian

a e i o u   il fault prendre b pour a /
b f k p x   il fault prendre f pour e / il fault
                      k pour i / p pour o / x pour u.

Dkfx dpknt bpnnf xkf et lpngxf b
Mpnsfkgnfxr
Mpnsfkgnfxr lf sfgrbttbkrf
Pxxbl Skngbng

Monseigneur,
I am greatly obliged to you for the benefits and favours which I have received daily from you without having deserved them, but please believe, Monseigneur, that you will now find, if you need me, what a faithful servant I shall be if God gives me the grace

2 Perhaps the man mentioned in No. 3, n. 1.

to remain in France. The Duke of Montpensier has retained me as his almoner. As everyone knows, this entails accompanying him in his train, which is a matter of great regret to my former master M. de Mauvissière.

You must know that I shall be often in the company of the grand almoner of the Duke of Guise, and I swear to you as a man of honour that I shall not fail to write to you everything that is said and done in that quarter, for the said almoner is from my country, and is a very good friend of mine; it was he who got me my present position with the Duke of Montpensier.

As for news, I advise you that I know and have known for a long time that a little Fleming called Alexander, who lives in our house, is a spy. He has told me that he has given Don Bernardino de Mendoza a great deal of information since Mendoza came to France, and that Mendoza has promised to send him on a trip to the Prince of Parma, which would be worth a lot of money to him. He speaks Flemish, Spanish, Italian, German, English and French, and is extremely cunning; I shall keep an eye on him in France, because he is a dangerous man.[2]

I advise you that M. de Mauvissière's butler has made a fortune with his books; he has been boasting that the arrival of M. de Châteauneuf has been worth five or six hundred *écus* profit to him. He is the agent in France for the English papists, and supplies them with money here by receiving goods for them in London, and paying the money here. This is his system. He has contrived to be appointed butler to M. de Châteauneuf. Keep an eye on him.

There is an Italian priest living in M. de Châteauneuf's house who boasts of his talent as a preacher. He has invented a cipher, so he told me, to write important matters to the pope in. I think this is true, and will tell you what the cipher is. I have nothing else worth saying except to pray God,

　　　Monseigneur, to keep in prosperity, and a long and happy life, the noble and virtuous princess the most serene Queen of England; likewise yourself and all her good Council. Amen.

I beseech you in God's name to remember the poor man who will always be yours, and to please give him something.

Here is the Italian priest's cipher. You put 'b' for 'a', 'f' for 'e', 'k' for 'i', 'p' for 'o', and 'x' for 'u'.

Address/signature in the cipher

17

[Late October or early November 1586, NS: Giordano Bruno to Sir Edward Stafford, Paris]

BL Cottonian Nero B vi, ff. 388–9.

Holograph   hand FC. No address. Endorsed: 'Secrete french advertismentes'.

The date and address are established by No. 18. Above, pp. 65–7. The authorship is discussed on pp. 83–97. I imagine that Stafford sent it to Burghley with No. 18, and Burghley must have passed it on to Walsingham, or it would not be where it is.

The text is made up as follows:

1.   p. 241, l.1 to p. 242, l. 24. Advice in French concerning the Netherlands.
2.   p. 242, ll.25–7. Comment on the above by the writer to Stafford; French.
3.   p. 242, l.28 to p. 243, l.16. Italian translation of (1), slightly abridged, and evidently done on the spot. It is very incorrect; the writer gives the impression of being Spanish.
4.   p. 243, ll.17–end. Passage from the writer to Stafford, including a marginal 'Note'; French.
5.   p. 244, ll.1–7. Extract from an Italian letter written from Lyon to somebody in Flanders, 16/26 April 1586, and presumably intercepted.
6.   p. 244, ll.8–26. Copy of a Latin letter from (I presume) Piero Delbene to the writer, written in Paris about April 1586 and reporting the contents of an Italian letter from Giovanni Cavalcanti in Rome to Jacopo Corbinelli in Paris: see 'A Note on Cavalcanti', no. 2, and above, p. 91.
7.   p. 244, l.27 to p. 245, l.4. Final passage from the writer to Stafford, about Morgan; French.

Les bledz estants prests à couper il faut faire embarquer quatre ou cinq mil hommes en Zelande, et les faire descendre à l'Escluse, et Ostande   Ceux ci commenceront a donner le gast au pais, qu'on appelle [*blank*] qui est depuis ledict Ostande iusques aupres de l'Escaut vers Envers, et brusleront toute la moisson presque meure, et ravageront tout devant que l'ennemi s'y puisse opposer

Il n'y a point de doubte que l'ennemi ayant entendeu cest embarquement et ladicte descente, et le commancement du gast prendra en diligence, ou toute son armée, ou la meilleure partie d'icelle pour aller rencontrer ce camp volant. A lors au mesme instant il faut avoir autre quatre ou cinq mil hommes prests du costé de Berghes, ou aux environs, lesquels tout aussi tost qu'ils auront veu partir lennemi, et marcher au devant des susdicts se ietteront dans la Campigne, et y donneront semblablemant le gast bruslant et ravageant tout.

Lennemi aux nouvelles du gast qui se faict devant et derriere luy, sera contraint d'attaquer le plus proche ennemi, et celuy auquel il pensera faire plus de mal.

Que s'il vient pour attaquer ceux d'Ostande, et s'ils se voyent chargez rien ne les empesche de faire une seure retraicte iusques a leur vaisseaux ayant desia faict le plus grand dommage qu'ils auront peu.

Que si l'ennemi ne les attaque point, ils poursuivront le gast à loisir et se viendront retirer comme dessus.

Si donques l'ennemi tourne visage pour attaquer ceux qui se seront iettez en la Campigne, s'ils ne veulent venir aux mains avec luy, ils ont semblablement le moyen de se retirer, et neantmoins amuzer l'ennemi de ce coste là. Et cependant les autres qui se seront desia retirez a Ostande, et l'Escluse voyant l'ennemi occupé en la Campigne s'en iront faire autant au pais de Tournay, Hainault, l'Isle et Artois, gastant, bruslant, et ravageant tout, et puis s'en revenir à leurs vaisseaux en toute seurté: n'y ayant aucun ennemi en ces quartiers là, qui se puisse opposer a eux, et les engarder de donner le gast par tout.

C'est le seul et unique moyen de reduire l'ennemi à la fain, et le pais a la contraincte de se randre, et de voir bien tost la fin de la guerre.

Italiano.   el medesimo

Gli frumenti essendo venuti à maturita, bisogna imbarquar quatre ove cinque mille huomini in Zelandia, et far descendere al paeze de l'Escluze, et Ostanda. Aquesti comminciarano el guastamento del paeze chiamato [blank] cioe dapo Ostanda appresso lEscaut verso Antuerpia, et abbrugiarano el tritico ia maturo dinanzi que l'inimico puote opponersi.

Non e dubio que linimico avendo inteso aquest[o *altered to*]e imbarquamente, et sapendo que gli Anglesi sono descenduti al paeze de l'Escaut, et que guastano el tritico, [su *deleted*] subito pillara ove tota larmata, ove la meglior parte per opponersi al campo volante. In medesimo tempo bisogna havere quatre ove cinque altri mille huomini apparecchiati de la banda de Berghes, ove intorno, liquali subito que linimico sara partito per opponer si a gli [supr *deleted*] sopraditti, comminciarano medesimamente de guastar el paeze di Campigna, abbrugiando gli frumenti, et altre munitione.

Linimico vedendo el guastamente de drietto, et dinanzi, sara sforsato d'assaltar el piu vicino, et quello que pensara piu facilmente incommodar.

Si vene assaltar aquelli d Ostanda, et vedano non assai, possono con securita retirar si à le nave, avendo ia abbrugiato gli frumenti

Si linimico non hardisce d'assaltar [l'armata Inglesa, *deleted*] loro, possono continuar el guastamente, et retirar si, alle sue nave.

Si linimico ritorna per assaltar quelli que sono in Campigna, possono medesimamente retirarsi, et nondimeno intretenirlo da quella parte. In tanto gli altri que si serano retirati à Ostanda et l'Esclusa, vedendo linimico occupato in la Campigna, farano el medesimo al paeze de Tournay, Hainault, l' Isle, et Artois, guastando, abbrugiando ogni bene, et dapo ritornarsi alle sue nave con securita, nessuno inimico puotendo opponersi.

Pource qu'on tasche de nuire et affoiblir son ennemi en toutes sortes qu'on peut, il y a deux aultres moyens, parlesquel/*s*/ ont [*sic*] le peut beaucoup endommager.

Le premier est de mettre le feu dans lArsenal d'Envers. Ce que promet exequuter un gentilhomme francois de la religion, lequel a fait beaucoup de voyages en ce pais la:

Le second est d'assaillir l'estat d'Italie. Ce qu'est plus facile qu'il ne semble. Premierement pource qu'il est presques tout denué de garnizo/*ns*/ lesquelles ont este employées à lexpedition qu'a faict l'Espagnol tant [*inserted above*] contre Monsieur Drach, que contre les flamants. Le moyen de l'assaillir est aussi facile sans y employer beaucoup d'argant, ni de temps. C'est qu'en un mesme temps qu'on levera une armee en Alemagne pour france il en faudra lever une pour l'Italie, faizant semblant que toute ceste armée doyve fondre sur la france. Car iamais l'Italien ne sen doubtera   Partant sera facile dassaillir ceux qui n'y pensent point, de gaigner ceux qui sont tyrannizez, gehennez et en leur biens, et leur consciences. Il y a aussi un grand seigneur en france qui depuis nagueres a visite tout ce pais la. lequel conduira tout laffaire.

Marginal note to preceding paragraph
No*ta* On scait pour certain que le Roy d'Espagne a contre mandé quinze cents chevauls qu'il [en *deleted*] envoyoit en flandres, et les a rappele [z *added*] depuis Nice pour aller contre monsieur Drach. Ce qui monstre la faute qu'il a de soldat.

La paix aussi qu'a faicte le Duc de Savoye avec ceux de Geneve monstre le mesme

f.389r/   Copie d'une lettre Italiene

doverano costa havere inteso la mala nuova venuta de i danni fatti dal corsaro Inglese nell'isola di san domingo, liquali Dio voglia che restino qui, et che si ci possa provedere presto. Et le provigioni per costa (id est per fiandra) sara facile che si vadino allentando con il piu urgente bisogno che vi sara di far quella impresa, massime temendosi che quest anno non siano per venir le flotte. De Lion le 26 dApvril.

Heri vidi literas Roma allatas in quibus scriptum est, ac diserté, Romanos illos rerum dominos id agitare quomodo et Genevam aggrediantur et Reginam Angliae opprimant. Horum verborum memini. Si tratta per tutte le vie et per ogni modo di percuoter la, et se ne fanno grandi preparamenti, et solo [saspettano *deleted*] saspettano le risolutioni di Spagna, lequali per lo piu sogliono essere molto lunghe: summa literarum huc redit illos ancipiti consilio distineri priúsne Allobrogica*m* illam urbem, an Reginam invadant. Utrum consilium alteri praevortatur usque adhuc in incerto est: sed propediem res palam futura est. Ille idem scribit Germanicum equitatum non fore in Gallia ante Calendas Septembres. Suadet pacem, si saperemus. Nostri foederati satis audacter polliciti sunt Pontifici id se praestaturos nequis haereticus sequenti anno in Gallia hiscere audeat: sed illis nemo credit, ne Romae quidem. Episcopus Placentinus prudens machinator bellorum civilium, Caesare nequicquam, et aliis Germanis repugnantibus, missus est ad aulam Caesaream, qui illic partes Pontificis agat: in illo magnam spem Pontifex habet. Ut Romanensibus artibus evertat consilia Protestantium, et Germaniam conjiciat in teterrimum bellum civile. Haec habui. Tu vale.

Ceste entreprinse contre la Serenissime Royne dAngleterre est confirmée par le dire de Morgan, lequel a affirmé à un honeste homme, qui le visite quelques fois com*m*e malade, qu'il y a une grande coniuration contre sadicte maiesté, delaquelle conspiration il dict que l'Evesque de Glasco est le principal intermetteur, comme estant pensionaire de quatre mil ducats du Roy dEspagne. Qu'est la cause que mons*i*eur de Guize le va voir bien souvent a son logis au college St. Jehan de Latran a Paris.

    Laquelle conspiration on est apres à decouvrir tant par la bouche de Morgan, que par toute autre moyen. Iceluy Morgan promet de reveler plusieurs choses, [pourve *deleted*] s'il plaist à la serenissime
.389v/ Royne [de *deleted*] le delivrer de prison, [et de semployer *deleted*] Il y a apparence qu'il tiendra sa promesse   Premierement pour sa

delivrance Item se voyant neglige de ceux, lesquels l'ont employé en cest affaire, qui ne procurent point sa delivrance. Plus la longue prison a dompté ce zele papistic. Outre plus, Il y a un Conte du pais de Poictou, nomé le Conte de la Magnane, de la religion, en mesme prison, lequel tasche par iournelles admonitions, et exhortations luy deraciner ceste volonté qu'il pourroit avoir contre sa maiesté.

I give abstracts of the advices, and translate Bruno's accompanying remarks.

/Scheme, in French, for defeating the Spaniards in the Netherlands by sending two English armies, one by water from Zealand (i.e., presumably, from Flushing, where Sidney was now governor), the other by land from Bergen-op-Zoom, to lay waste the harvest in Flanders and the Campine of Brabant./

This is the only way to reduce the enemy to starvation, force the country to surrender, and so bring the war to a rapid end.

/Scheme then repeated in Italian./

Since we are seeking to damage and weaken the enemy in every possible way, there are two other means by which we can do them a great deal of harm.

The first is to set fire to the arsenal at Antwerp; a French Protestant gentleman who has travelled a lot in that part of the world says he can carry this out.

The second is to invade Italy, which is easier than you might suppose. Firstly, because the country has been practically denuded of garrisons, which have been used to make up the Spanish forces sent against Drake (in the West Indies) and the Dutch. The way to attack it is simple, and would not take much money, or time. All you have to do is, at the same time as you are raising troops in Germany to fight in France, to raise some more for Italy, while giving out that the entire army is intended for France. The Italians will never suspect anything. So it will be easy to attack people who are not expecting any such thing, and to win over those who live under tyranny, tortured for their property and their consciences. There is also a great lord in France who has recently visited the whole country, and would lead the invasion force.

[*Marginal note*]

Note. It is known for certain that the King of Spain has countermanded (the despatch of) 1500 horse whom he intended to send to Flanders, and called them back from Nice, to be sent against Drake. This shows how short of troops he is. So does the peace which the Duke of Savoy has made with Geneva.

/Italian letter from Lyon reporting the damage done by Drake in the Indies, and the effect this will have in delaying reinforcements to the Netherlands, since troops will have to be despatched to America and the silver fleet may not sail this year.

Delbene's(?) letter about papal enterprises in prospect against Geneva and/or Elizabeth. Not clear which is the priority. Doubts whether the German troops will arrive in France before September. The envoys of the League in Rome say there will be no Protestants in France by next year; nobody believes them. The Bishop of Piacenza (Sega) sent to the imperial court in Prague to stir up a civil war in the Empire./

This enterprise against the most serene Queen of England is confirmed by Thomas Morgan, who has said to an honest man who sometimes visits him (in the Bastille) on account of his sickness, that there is a great conspiracy afoot against her Majesty. The Bishop of Glasgow is the chief organiser of it; he has a pension of 4000 ducats from the King of Spain. This is why the Duke of Guise visits him so often at his lodgings at the college of St-Jean-de-Latran in Paris.

This conspiracy has recently been exposed, both by Morgan and by other means; Morgan promises to reveal many things if the queen is prepared to get him out of prison. I think it is likely that he will keep his promise. First, to get out of the Bastille. Also because he regards himself as having been abandoned by those who employed him in this matter [i.e. the conspiracy: meaning Beaton and Guise] who do nothing to procure his release. Further, long imprisonment has got the better of his popish enthusiasm. Further still, there is a count from Poitou called the Comte de la Magnane, who is a Protestant and in the same prison, who is trying by daily admonitions and exhortations to uproot the evil will he has against her Majesty.

6/16 November 1586: Sir Edward Stafford to Lord Burghley, Paris

PRO SP 78/16, f. 139 (no. 72). Calendared in *CSP Foreign 1586–1588*, p. 125.

Holograph   Words between asterisks in cipher or code.

My very good Lorde, I hope and I dare assure myselfe thatt your Lordships care of thankfulnes and your sonnes to the cardinall shall be dischardged as effectually and secretly accordinge to your Lordship's meninge as kanne anye waye be devysed. /Received new cipher codes, mainly for Catholic *émigrés*./ For my parte my lord I am with your lordship's opinion thatt those bad companions thatt are left on this syde have further fetches in theyr hedds then anye yett be discovered and for my parte I doe whatt I kanne to discover them and have a meanes in hand to see yff by one thatt is greatt with *Morgan* and doeth sometymes hawnte him *in the Bastile* theire is under hope of fayre promyses and hope of libertye (for he is very weary to be wheire he is) anyethinge to be drawen butt *Master Secretary* thatt wille lett nothinge thatt good is to be donne by my meanes, I am afrayed will bothe crosse me in the matter, and alienate the parsons mynde, whome he is acquainted withall, thatt dealeth in ytt. I feare ytt because sutche things have beene donne to me twyse or thryse alredy both with thatt parson that dealeth in this and others that have delt with me in other things, and with thatt disgrace that wheras afore he delt and imployed some heere, when they made ytt knowen unto him thatt they hadd accesse to me and dessired to be delt withal by my meanes, he made ytt by his countenance knowen thatt he lyked ytt nott and wolde never deale with them after . . .

A Note on Castelnau's House

The house was identified by William Boulting, *Giordano Bruno* (London, 1914), p. 89, as in Butcher Row, on the north side of the Strand outside Temple Bar. He has been followed by Gentile, *DI*, p. 17 n. 1, by Yates, *Florio*, p. 61, by Singer, *Giordano Bruno*, and by all writers since. Singer gives, p. 50, an illustration of a pair of modest dwellings bearing fleur-de-lis and other symbols from E. Walford, *London* (1875–80). This cannot be right, as Castelnau's house is described by three separate witnesses as being in Salisbury Court. They are: William Herle, to the Earl of Leicester, 14-viii-1579 (HMC *Bath*, v, 200): coming up from the river, Herle found Castelnau walking under his lodging with a guest; Lord Henry Howard, examination of 11/21-xii-1583 (*CSP Scotland 1581–83*, p. 679); Edward Dodwell, one of the youths taken off Girault's boat at Dover, confession of 15/25-ix-1585 (PRO SP 12/182, no. 18). The house in Butcher Row sounds like the residence of Christophe de Harlay, Comte de Beaumont, ambassador from 1602 to 1605: H.B. Wheatley, *The Story of London* (London, 1904), p. 392.

As for the exact location of the house in Salisbury Court: the map of London by Richard Newcourt and William Faithorne (published in 1658, but drawn rather earlier) is reproduced in *A Collection of Early Maps of London* (Harry Margary, Lympne, Kent/Guildhall Library, London, 1981), sheets 11–18, and discussed in John Fisher's introduction. Figure 9 is an enlargement of part of sheet 13. The correct location is given in John Leake's 'Exact Surveigh' of 1666: ibid. sheet 21, index no. 159 ('Salsbury Court and Dorset House'); Buckhurst House became Dorset House in 1604 when Lord Buckhurst became Earl of Dorset, and the index only refers to buildings, so 'Salsbury Court' must mean the house and not the court itself (Figure 10). No map except Newcourt's gives anything resembling our house on the north side of the court, or any space for it; the Braun-Hogenberg and 'Agas' maps of about 1560 show a tallish house in the right place, abutting on to Buckhurst House in its original castlelike form, and also the garden: ibid. sheets 3 and 6 (Figure 1). On Newcourt's map Dorset House occupies the whole south side of the court, and its garden the whole area between the court and the river. This must be wrong: it looks to me as if, having left no space for Salisbury Court and its garden in the right place, but feeling that it ought to be shown, Newcourt put it in where he had some room, on the north side of the court. My instinct is that he gave a moderately accurate view of the garden front of the house. The reason for thinking that the house may have been extended after 1566 is that the Braun-Hogenberg and 'Agas' maps show it only adjoining its garden at the south-west corner of the house ; but this may be reading too much into these early maps, and seems incompatible with Castelnau's statement about the age of the house (to Walsingham, 10/20-viii-1584; *CSP Foreign 1584–85*, p. 15). His successor, Châteauneuf, said that it was small and smelly (to Walsingham, 18/28-ii-1586: ibid. *1585–86*, pp. 384 f), but he may have had delusions of grandeur.

The history of the property can be put together from *DNB*, Sackville, Sir Richard, and Paulet, William, 1st Marquis of Winchester; from A. Prockter and R. Taylor, *The A to Z of Elizabethan London* (Harry Margary, Lympne, Kent/Guildhall Library, London, 1979), p. 52 (Sackville bought Salisbury House in 1564); and from Castelnau's letters concerning the riot of August 1584 (above, pp. 49–51). These contain a good deal of information about the house and its neighbourhood.

Figure 11 shows the area as it appeared on 2 October 1989. Castelnau's house would have occupied most of the frontage on the south side of what is now Salisbury Square, between the corner of the steps (replacing the original exit to Water Lane) and the corner of Dorset Rise (cut through the site of Dorset House); its garden would have covered most of the space occupied by the present Salisbury House, and some more towards the river. The river bank would have been somewhere to the south of the present Tudor Street. Since the house stood at the top of quite a steep slope, most of which was covered by its garden, it would have had a good view of the river, despite the buildings along the bank. Bruno, in the *Cena* (*DI*, p. 159), speaks of eating grapes from London gardens, so perhaps there was a vine growing up the slope.

Figure 9. Salisbury Court and vicinity, c. 1647. From the map of Richard Newcourt and William Faithorne (enlarged). See above pp. 248–9, for my conjecture that the house shown across the top side of the court is meant to be Castelnau's house, but has been put in the wrong place. The fine building along the bottom side is the new Dorset (ex-Buckhurst) House.

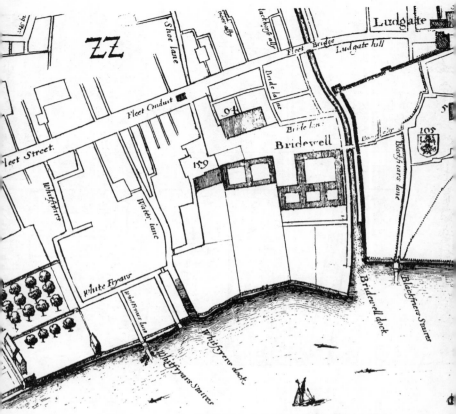

Figure 10.   Salisbury Court and vicinity, 1667. From the 'Exact Surveigh' of John Leake and others, made immediately after the Great Fire (enlarged). The area is in white because all the buildings had been burned down. The map is extremely accurate. No. 159 refers to 'Salsbury Court and Dorset House': the two houses can be clearly distinguished and their relation to each other, to their gardens, and to the court observed.

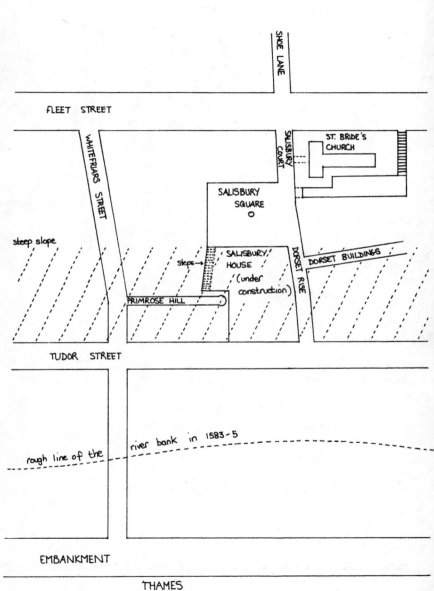

Figure 11. Salisbury Square, 1989.

A Note on Giovanni Cavalcanti and his Roman Newsletters

Giovanni Cavalcanti can be identified as Corbinelli's Roman friend from the originals of the letters used by Calderini De-Marchi, *Corbinelli* (BA T 167 sup, ff. 17, 106, 135, 170 (printed by Calderini De-Marchi, pp. 237 f), 183 f, 189). In the first of these (15-viii-1572) Corbinelli describes him as 'participe e executore di quel poco che m'occorre volere'.

The Cavalcanti were a Florentine family going back to the thirteenth-century poet Guido. Lucrezia's mother was a Gondi and she married, in France, Albizzo Delbene, who died in 1563. She made a great deal of money farming the *gabelle* with the Gondis. She had two surviving sons, Piero (our *abbé*) and Alessandro, who became secretary to Pierre de Gondi, Bishop of Paris (*DBI*, Cavalcanti, Lucrezia). Giovanni Cavalcanti may have been her nephew. In 1583 his father, whose Christian name is not given, was in Paris, apparently working for the nuncio (Corbinelli, in BA T 167 sup, f. 106; Stafford, in *CSP Foreign 1583–84*, no. 311); this would seem a likely trip for Madame Delbene's brother. However, Stafford said that this Cavalcanti was the brother of one Guido Cavalcanti, a fairly well-known servant of both Catherine de Medici and Queen Elizabeth, and Madame Delbene had only one brother (*DBI*).

The sequence of letters, so far as it can be reconstructed from Walsingham's papers, is as follows:-

1. 18/28-ii-1586, Latin abstract, on the same sheet as no. 2a which is inaccurately headed as having been written in October (*CSP Foreign 1586–88*, p. 123; PRO SP 101/72, f. 55 (no. 28)).
2. March or April 1586, Latin abstract made, I presume, by Piero Delbene, with one passage left in Italian (*Texts*, no. 17; BL Cottonian Nero B vi, f. 389); dated by its reference to the departure from Rome of a nuncio who had arrived in Prague by 12/22-iv-1586 (*CSP Foreign 1585–86*, p. 622).

254 *Giordano Bruno and the Embassy Affair*

2a.   Truncated copy of no. 2; see no. 1.

3.   12/22-iv-1586, copy of Italian original (*CSP Foreign 1585–86*, p. 545; PRO SP 101/72, f. 54 (no. 27)). The reference to 'your League', rendered in the Latin abstract no. 2 as 'nostri foederati', makes it clear that the recipient of the originals was in France.

4.   About 25-iv/5-v-1586, copy of Italian original, described as 'de Cavalcanti di Roma', sent with a copy of a letter from Frangipani to Corbinelli of that date (*CSP Foreign 1585–86*, p. 582; PRO SP 85/1, f. 47 (no. 14)). The peculiar shape of the final 'e's, which have a sort of quiff (ƌ), suggests that the copy of the letter and its enclosure was made for Stafford by Delbene himself, of whose writing this is a regular feature. It became common in print, but seems to me unusual in handwriting, except for very formal script in Latin. Comparison with three letters of Delbene (to Lipsius, 3/13-iii-1587; to Walsingham, 6/16-ix-1587; and to Bellièvre, 19/29-ix-1588: Colliard, *Pierre d'Elbène*, facsimile facing p. 336; PRO SP 78/17, f. 260 (no. 118); BN ff 15909, f. 180) shows him using the form fairly often, as in the signature of the second item, or something rather similar. But I cannot testify that the handwriting in general is the same, so I cannot be sure that Delbene wrote this piece himself. I think the external evidence is strong enough to show that it came from him, or from as near to him as makes no difference.

5.   30-iv/10-v-1586, Latin letter from Rome, which sounds like a sequel to the previous one (*CSP Foreign 1585–86*, p. 609; PRO SP 101/95, f. 73 (no. 30)). This was sent via Venice, which the others do not seem to have been, so it may be from a different series.

The substance of the newsletters is very close to what was being passed on to the French court by Cardinal d'Este, the Cardinal Protector of France, at this time: BN ff 16042 (d'Este) and 16045 (Saint-Goard, the ambassador). I see no sign that Cavalcanti was in the cardinal's household, but it sounds as if he had access to it.

The main destination for Cavalcanti's news was the French councillor Bellièvre. The reasons for supposing this are: 1.   that Corbinelli was Bellièvre's client and referred to him in his Paduan correspondence simply as 'the councillor' (Calderini De-Marchi, *Corbinelli*, p. 219 n; Yates, 'New Documents', p. 185, assuming that Bellièvre is the 'consigliere'; BA T 167 sup, f. 146); 2.   That Corbinelli had been passing news from Rome to Bellièvre since at least 1580 (to Bellièvre, 20-x-1580: BN ff 15905, f. 496); and 3. Frangipani's letter to Bellièvre, 23-i/2-ii-1586 (BN ff 15908, f. 93; above, p. 90 and n. 26), saying that they have been communicating through 'Signor Jacomino', who will tell Bellièvre many things not suitable to be put into writing. They seem to me conclusive.

The reader may ask why Bellièvre should have wanted a special source of information from Rome, when most of it seems to have come from Cardinal d'Este, who was writing regularly to the French court in any case. The answer is that d'Este wrote to Villeroy, the secretary of state responsible for Roman affairs, and Bellièvre had different views from Villeroy about the proper relationship between France and Rome: E.H. Dickerman, *Bellièvre and Villeroy* (Providence, RI, 1971), p. 9.

A Note on Fagot's Handwriting, and Bruno's

I have discussed this matter above, pp. 81–83, but the description, though I hope sufficient for the purpose and perhaps as much as the text could bear, may well leave the reader unsatisfied. I therefore add here an analysis of the handwriting of both Fagot and Bruno so far as we have it, with a view both to providing the full description lacking in the text, and to discovering what can be said on pure handwriting grounds about Fagot, Bruno and their relation to one another. I shall be discussing their general style and letter-forms, not being competent to distinguish anything more arcane. The reader may like to look at Plates I–X before starting.

Fagot

The hand which I have described as FA is a French secretary hand.[1] It had a fairly neat version, as in No. 11 (Plate IV), but when used freely was a rough, rapid and untidy effort. It was small and level, but had a tendency to spread, and on two occasions developed into something large and upward-sloping at the ends of Fagot's pieces and in signatures.[2] Its letters were secretary letters (*ℐ* for *e*, *ℭ* for *c*, *ʋ* for *y*, etc.), but it often used italic initial *s*'s (*ʃ*) and *f*'s (*f*), and

---

1 On secretary hand, consult G.E. Dawson and L. Kennedy-Skipton, *Elizabethan Handwriting, 1500–1650* (London, 1968) and A.G. Petti, *English Literary Hands from Chaucer to Dryden* (London, 1977). For the French version of it. A. de Boüard, *Manuel de diplomatique française et pontificale* (Paris, 1929), volume of plates, nos. vi, xiv, xl and xlix. Plate vi (1584) is a good example of a small, non-official French secretary hand, and the nearest thing here to a model for FA. In English sixteenth-century usage the humanistic hand now described as italic was described as Roman, and the distinction between sloping italic and upright roman was not made; I describe the hand in general as italic, and use 'Roman' only where a word for the upright (and printed) version is needed, as in reference to Bruno's hand described below as BB.
2 *Texts*, nos. 11 and 16.

sometimes medial ones; it used r for a final s, and a small capital for initial r and sometimes for others. It resembled the current hand of many Frenchmen who wrote a lot without being professional writers. It was highly cursive and obviously written very quickly.

Fagot's first surviving use of it is No. 3, written towards the end of April (OS) 1583 (Plate I); it had presumably been the hand of No. 2, written a few days earlier, of which we only have a copy. He used the same hand for Nos. 11 and 11a, for Nos. 15 and 16, and indeed for all the pieces which he signed; but in Nos. 4 and 9 he tried variations. In No. 4, written about late May 1583 (Plate II), he attempted a version of the French official hand of which he must now have seen a good deal at Salisbury Court.[3] What he was aiming at was a neat, shapely hand, more italicised than the classic form, which would have had a similarly pleasing effect on the page. For most of the first page of his letter he managed it to some degree; but he could not keep it up, and by the middle of the second side he had fallen back on the scribble of No. 3. We can test him on final s and y. Final s in FA, I have said, is practically always r; there are no exceptions in No. 3, and not many later. In No. 4 Fagot wrote 22 italic final s's to 48 r's, but twenty of these were on the first side, and fourteen in the first ten lines; after this r resumed its sway. The point about y is the direction of the tail: in secretary hand, and in normal FA, it turns to the right and is joined to the next letter; in italic and in improved FA it turns to the left and is separate. In Nos. 3, 11, 11a, 15 and 16 there are very few left-turning y's; in No. 4 there are 13 left-turners to 19 right-turners. Eight of the left-turners occur in the first ten lines of either side 1 or side 2 of the letter, and no right-turners occur before the tenth line of either side. The general appearance of the first side of the letter is not unsuccessful, and could have encouraged Fagot to make further efforts in the genre; but it looks as if he needed more practice, both in the particular hand he was attempting, and in the art of creative penmanship in general.

In No. 9 (January 1584: Plate III) he tried something less ambitious: the hand is a heavy and square version of No. 3, and leans to the right. Except for two *vous*'s, one in the first line, final s is always r, but most of the y's turn left, and some have long straight tails. The effect is extremely ugly. In Nos. 11 and 11a he simply wrote the natural hand more neatly than usual: there are almost no italic final s's

---

3 Examples of this can be seen in de Boüard, *Manuel*, plates xiv, xl and xlix (1566–7); and in BL Harleian 1582, ff. 363, 365, 367 – all I think by Laurent Feron, the embassy clerk, for whom see above, p. 34, n. 33. Italic letter forms were creeping into the French official hand, as in de Boüard's plate xl: f, y and s are the letters affected here, and so they are in our No. 4, hence I imagine that Fagot had some kind of a model for it. But the model was not Feron, since there are no italic forms in his official hand.

or left-turning *y*'s. There are more of both in the Walsingham version (No. 11a) – Walsingham's piece is, oddly, a lot neater than Elizabeth's – but nearly all of them are in the first few lines, or in Latin quotations, and they have no effect on the style.[4]

During the year between No. 11 and No. 13 (March 1584 to February 1585) Fagot must have worked hard at his French calligraphy, or he would not have achieved the brilliant success of the later piece (Plate V).[5] The style is both extremely attractive in itself, finely achieved from start to finish, and totally different from any of his previous efforts that we have. In detail it is not absolutely perfect, though the details do not affect the general appearance, and have to be looked for carefully. Final *s* is italic in the huge majority of cases, and in most of the few where it is not it is in the form ᛒ, which is characteristic of French official hands; this is not really appropriate in what is really an italic hand with French decorations, and gets him into a few difficulties. But there are also three final *ſ*'s (*libres* and *lettres* on side 2, l.14, and *coffres* in line 31: above, p. 228 ll.2 and 16); two single secretary medial *s*'s and one double, and also one secretary double *f*. All of these are on the second side. *y*'s are left-turning and elegantly shaped, with five exceptions: *promys* at the bottom of side 1; *muys* and *ny* (twice) towards the bottom of side 2; and *vye* just before the signature (above, pp. 227, l.25; 228, ll.15, 16 and 21). Most of these errors are connected with other secretary forms: the three *ſ*'s follow secretary *e*'s; two of the *y*'s precede French secretary *s*'s, and one precedes a secretary *e*. Likewise *r*. All *r*'s here are italic (*r*), except for some ᛔ's, which like ᛒ come from French secretary hand; but there are four cases of the small capital from FA. Three are final *r*'s of an *er*, where the *e* is secretary in two cases: one is before the final secretary *es* in *libres*. Finally there is a scattering of secretary *e*'s, as well as those which have been mentioned already: eighteen all told.

Since we can be sure from its contents that Fagot wrote this letter, we can interpret the errors he made in it with some confidence. It is a very well-learned but not quite spontaneous hand, behind which his normal secretary scribble can be seen emerging from time to time, the more as he gets tired. We have here, in short, a residual version of what had happened in his first attempt at elegant writing, No. 4. I think he was probably copying a draft written in FA, which would help to explain his success.[6]

---

4   In No. 11, 4 x *s* to 56 x *ſ* ; 1 x *y*-left to 39 x *y*-right; in No. 11a, 7 to 30; 9 to 23.
5   I should think he had had some tutoring from Feron, whom we can observe in BL Harleian 1582, f. 338 (the first of two ff. so numbered in the volume) polishing up his italic script, e.g. the royal signature 'Henry'.
6   Cf. below, p. 270 (Moscow Ms., f. 5v), for Bruno's rough draft of what will have been an elegant letter to the authorities of Frankfurt.

I ignore No. 14, in which there are no flaws at all; Nos. 15 and 16 are unadulterated FA; with No. 17 (Plate VI) we are back with something of the same order as No. 13.[7] The hand is an almost entirely uncursive sloping italic, diversified by some fairly flowery capitals of a secretary-ish kind. It is attractive, legible, consistent through three languages, and quite different from No. 13. It makes only one mistake in final s, and none in y; indeed it has a new y (y) which is used interchangeably with the usual left-curling one.[8] One has to look very hard for chinks in its armour. Still, there are some to be found. As in No. 13, a few medial or initial secretary s's and f's have slipped into the otherwise infallible sequence of the long italic form. There is a furtive secretary initial f towards the bottom of side 2 (faizant: above, p. 243, l.30). In the Italian translation of the advice about the Netherlands there are two double s's in possono, and a single where he was probably correcting (to be exact, discorrecting) a z (sforsato); there are two more singles in the Latin letter of Delbene. In the Italian translation he had to correct a q and a p which he had written with straight tails instead of tails curling to the right like all the others (above, pp. 243, ll.4, 9, 11, 12; 244, l.14 (summa), l.21 (Episcopus)). At this point in the composition, where he was translating off the cuff into Hispano-Italian, we may well suppose that he had other things on his mind. But the strongest signs that the hand is not spontaneous do not appear here: there are two of them.

The marginal 'Note' at the bottom of side 2 (above, p. 243, ll.36–42: Plate VI) has been one of our indications of Fagot's authorship, and the handwriting rather confirms this. It was perhaps written more quickly than the main text, either after the adjacent passage or after he had finished the whole piece. In the (original) fourth line, where he was conveying the news that Philip II was withdrawing some cavalry he had intended for Flanders, the en at the beginning of envoyoit (in /les/ chevauls qu'il envoyoit) came out in secretary hand and had to be crossed out. The nine original lines of the 'Note' also contain a secretary n, of which there is a corrected example elsewhere;[9] a secretary x (x not x), of which there is another in the last line but one; and two secretary c's (c) to join three in the Italian translation, papistic just before the end and a couple of others. They contain a joined ct in faicte which is mistaken in itself and probably secretary in inspiration.[10] The last mistake is in the

7   For No. 17 see above, pp. 65–7.
8   Used by Feron in his 'Henry' (above, n. 5).
9   These are: (final) y, in On, in the Note; and (medial) u, corrected to $\bar{u}$, in allentando, above, p. 244, l.5. The capital n of Nota is odd ($\mathcal{N}$); perhaps a J of Je was originally intended.
10 Above, p. 243, l.40. The joined ct in faicte has a resemblance to the italic form used in Bruno's Helmstedt letter (below, p. 269), but I think it is actually a secretary form. Cf. faict in the adjacent text (p. 243, l.25), where the c is secretary, but does not join the t.

copy of the Delbene letter, where Fagot wrote a *partes* (above, p. 244, l.24) of which the *r* and the *es* are in rough secretary hand. What had happened, just as in *libres* in No. 13, was that the *r* had slipped into the capitalised form, and the later letters had followed. He probably did not notice what he had done; if he did, he probably thought it better to leave the word as it was than to make a rather obvious correction, as he had done in the 'Note'. We emerge from our investigation of No. 17 with a collection of errors which is modest but distinctive, like a set of footprints.

This is as careful a description I can make of the handwriting of Fagot's pieces. The conclusions I draw from it are of two sorts; one of them is very agreeable to the argument of this book, the other is more of a problem. The first sort are conclusions about Fagot, of which there are three.

1.   Fagot wrote Nos. 3, 11, 11a, 15 and 16 in his original hand, more or less unchanged except that in No. 11 and particularly in No. 11a he made an effort to tidy it up. He also wrote the latter part of No. 4 in it and, we may presume, the whole of No. 2. This is properly what I have called FA, of which therefore examples occur between April 1583 and January or February 1586.

2.   In Nos. 4 and 9 he attempted to write in different styles. In No. 9 he set his sights fairly low, and achieved what he wanted, though the result is only a stiff version of normal FA. In No. 4 he had been a good deal more ambitious: he had tried a version of classic French secretary hand. He could not manage it, and gave up halfway through the letter.

3.   In Nos. 13 and 17, the two pieces written to Stafford in France, he succeeded rather brilliantly in doing what he had failed to do in No. 4. Considering the difficulty I have had in establishing that he actually wrote No. 17, this assertion needs to be defended, and I defend it as follows.

Nos. 13 and 17 are in different hands: the handwriting evidence is therefore at first sight in favour of their having been written by different people. However, carefully inspected, they reveal a corpus of errors or singularities in the handwriting which are similar in type and substance. This resemblance constitutes a case for their not having been written by different people. I recommend a comparison of the errant *partes* in No. 17 with *libres* and *coffres* in No. 13 (above, p. 258); of the deleted *en* in No. 17 with the two cases of *lieu* in No. 13 where the *e* is in secretary hand (above, pp. 227, l.32; 228, l.1); and of the two *possono*'s in No. 17 with *passer* in No. 13 (above, p. 259; pp. 243, ll.9 and 11; 228, l.8). In most of these instances the incorrect usages are close to other examples where the word has been written correctly: hence they would appear to be genuine mistakes. I do not argue that these resemblances suffice to establish that Nos. 13 and 17 were written by the same hand. I think that they are of sufficient negative force to neutralise the assumption that the two pieces were written by different people, and to leave the field open for arguments in favour of positive identification.

The handwriting evidence itself indicates one of these, which is founded on the character of No. 4. Here Fagot attempted to write an official French secretary hand, and did not succeed. So we know that he was prepared or anxious, for whatever reason, to attempt other hands than the spontaneous one. We have to suppose that during a period of nearly two years he put in enough practice to ensure that Nos. 13 and 17 were a success, where No. 4 had been a failure. This is a credible story. It is supported by the facts that the hand of the errors in Nos. 13 and 17, which looks like the same hand, also looks like the spontaneous hand into which No. 4 subsided, i.e., normal FA; and that the proportion of errors was similar. I take the example of double s.

In normal FA, this can be either secretary ($\mathcal{ff}$) or italic ($\mathcal{ff}$ or $\mathcal{ff}$), but the secretary form is the usual one. In No. 3 all double s's are secretary; in Nos. 11a and 15, all except one; Nos. 11 and 16 are divided, with a majority of italic forms – twelve to six or seven in No. 11; five to four in No. 16. In all cases where elegance is attempted, the case is different. In No. 4 all double s's except one are italic; so they are in No. 13; in No. 17 all except two. I conclude that for Fagot italic double s was a criterion of an elegant letter. In the three attempts it was achieved fairly consistently; a small number of errors was made on each occasion, in the same form and also in the same kind of word.[11]

Does this point convert my credible story into a true one, and positively oblige us to agree that Fagot wrote No. 17? Obviously not. It makes the story more plausible, indeed pretty probable; but it does not make it true. It hardens up the case for the two pieces not having been written by different people, but does not positively establish that they were written by the same person. Nothing of a handwriting kind could establish this except the certainty that the hand of the errors in the two pieces was the same hand. Presumably some quantity of errors, if they continued to be in the same style, might provide that certainty; I do not think the available number is enough. All I can claim, I think, is that the authors of both No. 13 and No. 17 were people who wrote naturally in French secretary

---

11   In No. 4, 15 italic and 2 secretary; in No. 13, 28 and 1; in No. 17, 20 and 2. All the errors were in verbs: *feussent* in No. 4, *passer* in No. 13, *possono* (twice) in No. 17. Compare Bruno's usage, below, p. 265.

hands which had a number of similarities and which they were both trying not to write in. I do claim this.

The positive evidence which would identify the author of No. 17 as Fagot will have to be sought elsewhere than in the handwriting. It has been set out in the text,[12] but there is a good reason for setting it out again. Much of what I have said about the authorship of No. 17 depends on the previous identification of Fagot as Bruno: I think we should ignore that here. We can also ignore the similarity in the contents of the two letters, in so far as they are both about Thomas Morgan, and probably both connected with his imprisonment: any English spy working in Paris would be looking for news about Morgan. We are left with two arguments: the argument from Stafford's description of the author of No. 17 as a man who had already worked for both Walsingham and himself and had passed from one to the other; and the linguistic argument from the similar flaws in the authors' French, and from the presence in No. 17 of Fagottesque singularities like *icelluy* and the penchant for 'Notes'.

I did not think that by themselves these two arguments were sufficient for a positive identification of the author of No. 17 as Fagot: hence it seemed more promising in the text to proceed by seeking to identify the author directly as Bruno. Now that we have a handwriting analysis to go on, we can approach the matter from Fagot's end again. We have three new considerations.

1.   The handwriting evidence reduces the presumption in favour of different authorship for Nos. 13 and 17 arising from the difference of hands, to a degree where it is no longer the formidable obstacle it seemed to be; it lowers the threshold of proof required on the other side. It may perhaps lower it to the point where the two arguments already given become sufficient.

2.   The handwriting evidence strengthens the second argument, especially in regard to the Note. A Note is a Fagot-like characteristic in itself; a Note which shows a strong tendency to slip into secretary hand is a very Fagot-like characteristic.

3.   A new argument is added, the handwriting argument itself: the argument from the similarity of the errors and corrections, and from Fagot's earlier effort (No. 4) to write another hand of the same general – that is, calligraphic – type.

The author of No. 17 is then to be described as a man who had previously worked for Walsingham and had transferred his services to Stafford; who was probably Italian; who wrote French like Fagot and showed a penchant for Notes; and who in addition had a spontaneous French secretary hand which, like Fagot in No. 4 and

12   Above, pp. 83–97.

No. 13, he was trying not to write in. I think the argument against identifying the author of No. 17 as Fagot has now shrunk to vanishing point, and that we can affirm more positively than before that Fagot wrote it. That is my first conclusion.

Bruno

The second conclusion is a negative one, and concerns Bruno in his own person. In so far as I have established that Bruno and Fagot were the same person, I now have another, and clinching, argument for holding that Bruno wrote No. 17. But the argument from handwriting pursued above does not directly help to establish this; on the contrary, it turns out to be an argument against it. The argument has been that Fagot, and therefore Bruno, had a 'natural' or spontaneous French secretary hand which he was likely to fall back on when attempting to write in other styles. The implication is that the pull of normal FA was very strong. This amounts to saying that FA was Bruno's natural hand, or one of his natural hands, or his natural hand between 1583 and 1586. He cannot therefore have invented it or even, as I have said in the text, 'adopted' it at the time he adopted the alias Fagot. He must have arrived in England with a good deal of experience in using it. Since it is a French hand, and since everything we know him to have written in it was written in French, we can probably conclude that he had picked it up in France and had used it there for writing French. We must also conclude that he continued to use it in England for writing other things than Fagot's letters, for it had not become rusty between 1583 and 1586.

There are three difficulties about this.

1.   Bruno had, as we know, a 'natural' or spontaneous hand which was quite different.

2.   The one piece of his handwriting we possess from before his arrival in England, and the one surviving sentence written in his own person during his stay there, imply that this was his original hand and the hand he used in England and France.

3.   There is no sign in what we possess written in it of any tendency to drift into FA. Nor is there any real sign of a tendency for FA to drift into it. If Bruno wrote both what we have in his own handwriting, and also what we have in Fagot's, he must have had two spontaneous hands, and composed two corpuses of handwriting, which were quite different. Simply on handwriting grounds this is not, as a modern reader may suppose, impossible for a sixteenth-century writer; but we shall need to make a powerful case to show it.

I have described Bruno's known handwriting above (pp. 81–3).[13] Further examination has added little to what I say there, except to persuade me that there is a stronger family resemblance between the various examples than I had felt at first sight. Thus the first version of the album verses (Wittenberg, September 1587), where Bruno seemed to be trying a new hand, includes one case of an odd form of *es* joining an italic *e* to a secretary *s* to produce ⲥ/ʄ, ⲯ/ʄ for *est, esse*, etc. This is the constant usage of the Moscow manuscript, and one must therefore take it as what Bruno normally wrote. The Geneva signature, though very different from the Helmstedt one, is virtually reproduced (apart from its use of the name 'Philippus' instead of 'Jordanus') in the two versions of the album verses, the dedications and the text of the Helmstedt letter. We can redistribute the variations as follows.

1.   The underlying hand is the cursive Italian italic of the Moscow Ms., ff. 1–5 (*De vinculo spiritus*, draft: Plate IX) and 162–8 (*Medicina lulliana*: Plate X). The Helmstedt letter (Plate VIII) can be taken as an elegant version of this which excludes, except occasionally, the secretary forms of *s* and *f* which are usual in the rapid version. I shall now call this BA.

2.   Otherwise, when wanting to write something more impressive (Geneva signature, dedications, second version of the verses, most headings in *Medicina lulliana*) he resorted to a Roman or upright italic hand which, except in the Geneva signature, is printed, not cursive (Plates VIIa, VIIb and X). I shall call this BB.

3.   The only piece which seems to fall rather outside this pattern is the first version of the verses (Plate VIIc), though it has, as I have said, other Brunonian characteristics. We have no reason to call it anything.

These variations are considerable, and I think it is proper for me to describe them as different hands; but none of them gets us anywhere at all near Fagot, in either his rapid or his elegant efforts. There is, for example, no case in Fagot of anything like the *est* or *esse* just described, nor of the *a* from mediaeval court hand (ⲁ), a feature of BB which also seems eccentric. The forms which Fagot slips into by mistake are from Fagot's secretary hand, FA, not from Bruno's italic BA.

It is true that there is a qualification to be made: some of the secretary forms which Fagot falls into when he is trying to write something else are also secretary features of Bruno's own hands. This is the case with two of the criteria I have used for catching Fagot

---

13   I subjoin a list of the sources for Bruno's handwriting, with references, at the end of this Note.

in error: secretary double s (ff) and small capital r. Both of these are to be found in some quantity in the Moscow Ms. and elsewhere in Bruno's authentic handwriting.

Secretary double s, as I have explained, is Fagot's normal usage except where he is trying something special. It is also Bruno's normal form: it appears in the Geneva signature, in one of the dedications, and fifty-four times in the Moscow Ms. against ten for the italic form. As in Fagot, the italic predominates where some elegance is attempted. In the diagram on f. 6 of the Moscow Ms. the italic form is used (twice) on the diagram itself, the secretary form (three times) in he marginal notes to it. In the Helmstedt letter, a venture into elegance of a kind not unlike Fagot's Nos. 13 and 17, s and double s are in general carefully italic, but despite its smooth appearance the letter was actually written rather rapidly, and two secretary ss's (out of five), as well as two secretary st's (out of twelve) slipped out by mistake. R is a different case, in that Bruno normally wrote it in the cursive italic form ($\mathcal{R}$), or as $\mathcal{T}$ or $\mathcal{r}$. However, the small capital appears quite often in the Moscow Ms.: twenty-nine times in *De vinculo spiritus*, five times (I think) in *Medicina lulliana*, and once in the diagram, f. 6. There is one case in the Helmstedt letter. In Bruno it is not so well developed or so angular as in Fagot, and ranges from a full $\mathcal{R}$ to a skeletal $\mathcal{K}$; but in the middle of a cursive italic hand this may not mean much.

So far we might argue that what Fagot was failing to conceal in Nos. 13 and 17 was not FA but Bruno's rough hand, BA. This is not a line which is doomed from the start: FA and BA have a fair number of common letter-forms, particularly among consonants, and these can sometimes bring them very close to each other: compare *dissimulatione* in *De vinculo spiritus*, f. 3r, l.34, with *dissimulateur* in No. 15, p. 3, l.17 (above, p. 236, l.4). But it will not really do. In BA double s and small capital r are members of an isolated group of non-italic forms, which includes single s, single and double f, x and mediaeval a; for two of the principal forms I have cited in this argument, secretary e and secretary final s, there are no cases whatever in Bruno's hand as we have it. It was not the odd secretary letter, but a whole secretary hand that Fagot was falling back on.

This is perfectly obvious in No. 4, and obvious enough in No. 13, with its scatter of secretary e's and final s's to add to the rest. It is not obvious in No. 17, but does emerge from close examination. We can argue that the underlying hand is FA, but not that it is BA. In the description I have given above of No. 17, I count twelve different kinds of error, corrected or uncorrected. Six of these (p, q, small capital r, medial s, double s and x) could equally well have come from FA or BA; two (secretary c, secretary f) could have come from either, but probably came from FA; but four (secretary *e*, *n*, final *s* and *ct*) could have come from FA but not from BA. We can see the difference if we compare No. 17 with Bruno's Helmstedt letter (Plates VI and VIII). Here the errors are in *ss*, *st* and small capital *r*, and there is a form of *ct* which, unlike the mistake in No. 17, is italic and derived from BA, or vice versa. The underlying hand is certainly BA. Our failure to find in No. 17 any *letter*-forms indisputably from BA is perhaps the more interesting in that there is a *spelling*-form in No. 17 which seems striking enough to remark on and is repeated elsewhere in Bruno: *exequuter* in the French of No. 17, *exequutorem* and *exequutionem* in the Latin of the Helmstedt letter, *esequtione* in the Italian of the *Cena de le Ceneri*.[14] We must conclude by returning to our previous judgment. What Fagot was falling back on in Nos. 13 and 17 was a systematic secretary hand. But Bruno did not, so far as we know otherwise than from Fagot, have a systematic secretary hand. We have not made much impression on this problem.

It seems to me that this is something we are going to have to live with. The likeliest avenue towards solving it would be the proposal that Bruno wrote a secretary hand when he was writing currently in French, and that he had developed and practised this between his stay in Geneva and his arrival in England. Since, as Fagot, he was posing as a Frenchman, the hand was the natural one for him to write in. Writing the language more or less phonetically he would, for example, be less likely to slip from his secretary *est* into the bastard *est* which he generally wrote in Latin. This is an attractive idea, and if we are already persuaded that Bruno and Fagot were the same person I think it is what we shall have to assume. But until somebody discovers something (else) written by Bruno in French, which turns out to have been written in FA or something like it, it cannot be more than a speculation.

There is another difficulty about it. I have taken it for granted that Bruno wrote his intelligence letters in FA, as he signed himself 'Fagot', in order to disguise his authorship. But if FA was his normal hand when writing in French, and if, as my previous argument leads us to believe, he continued to write in it after he had come to Salisbury Court, the disguise would have been extremely thin. Supposing that he had papers written in FA in his room, the not

14 Above, p. 243, l. 21; Helmstedt letter, ll. 3 and 7; *Cena* (Aquilecchia), p. 62, l. 8. Since this spelling equates *qu* with hard *c*, it was presumably a gallicism. *Qu* is similarly used in the 'Italian' translation in No. 17, in *imbarquar*, *imbarquamente* and *que* (above, p. 242, ll. 29, 33, 36, etc.); I have argued that here it was an (intentional) Hispanicism. Fagot had occasional difficulty with *qu* = *k*, as in No. 11 (above, p. 216, l. 22) and 11a (p. 219, l. 21); but he had domesticated it most effectively, to the extent that he was inclined to over- rather than to under-use it.

unlikely conjunction of a leak at court and a curious servant or visitor at the embassy might easily have dished him. He probably did not have much occasion to write in French while he was in London, but the argument requires that he had or made sufficient occasion to keep the hand in working order throughout the time he was there. It is walking a tightrope to claim that he wrote enough in it to keep it up, but not enough for Castelnau, if one of the Fagot pieces got out, to have recognised it as his.

I really have no answer to this, except that something like it must have happened. There is in favour of it the evidence that he did not think that FA was altogether secure. Hence his efforts, as early as No. 4, to try a different hand, continued more successfully in Nos. 13 and 17. There is the difficulty that he must surely have had some help (I have assumed from Feron) in learning the elegant style achieved in No. 13, whence it would have been known in Salisbury Court that he was practising French calligraphy; but after No. 4 he did not try anything like this when writing as Fagot in London. Perhaps we can also infer insecurity about FA from the fact that copies of his early communications were made in Walsingham's office, and the original of the first of them apparently destroyed. Indeed the only cases where further concealment of the hand was not attempted are Nos. 11-11a, 15 and 16. By the time he wrote No. 15 he was about to leave England, and may have thought that extra precautions were unnecessary (but he was planning to continue his career in France); No. 16 was written from France, and not signed. When he wrote No. 11, much the most likely of his London communications to have been leaked, he was perhaps too euphoric to bother: the authorship of the piece would have been instantly obvious to almost anyone who could read it, and Walsingham did well to keep it in a drawer.

I come at length to my handwriting story. It is that Bruno arrived at Salisbury Court with fluency in a French secretary hand which he did not generally use; that he used it from time to time while he was there, on what occasions I do not know; that he adopted it for his communications with Walsingham because these were written in French and because it was the opposite of his usual hand or hands; that despite his justified faith in the security of Walsingham's arrangements he was nervous that the hand might be brought home to him, and therefore thought he had better try something different; and that his experiments in trying something different led him to take a course in French and italic calligraphy. This he exploited in his communications to Stafford, who had a reputation for lack of security, written in Paris and including No. 17. I add that Bruno's experiments in calligraphy, so far as we know them – an italicised

French official hand, a cursive Gallo-Roman, and an uncursive italic – may seem to be carefully avoiding the two elegant hands he used in his own person: the cursive italic of the Helmstedt letter and the uncursive Roman of the dedications.

This is not a simple story, though possibly the more lifelike for that. It would, if true, accord with the knowledge that many of the writers of Shakespeare's age, English writers at least, wrote spontaneously in a variety of hands: we have come across the point, quite near home, in the tale of Francis Throckmorton and his conspiratorial papers. Bruno would be an appropriate addition to the company of those who illustrated the 'poetycall fiction of Bryareus the Gyant', who had a hundred hands.[15] That is as may be, but it is nothing like the powerful case we have been looking for. I cannot claim that my handwriting story is sufficiently persuasive in itself to confound a moderately determined sceptic, and shall have to concede that the more thorough handwriting analysis here attempted, while it confirms the argument of the book from one point of view, distinctly muddles it from another. It is just as well that my claim that Fagot and Bruno were the same person has not depended on their handwriting.

Not to end in a minor key, I insert here a piece of knowledge which emerged in the course of this investigation but has nothing to do with handwriting. In three pages of *Medicina lulliana* (ff. 162v–163v) Bruno makes use four times of a locution which will remind us of Fagot: 'Ulterius est notandum quod . . .'; 'Et notandum. . .'; 'Est tum notandum quod . . .'; 'Et nota . . .'. This will take us back to the margins and text of Nos. 2, 3, 9, 11 and 17, and particularly to No. 11, the confession letter to Elizabeth. 'Notez cest quil . . .' is visibly an effort to translate 'Est notandum quod . . .' (Plates IV and X)[16] It would be extremely silly of me to take this as a special usage of Bruno's; but as a special usage of Fagot's which is also a usage of Bruno's it is worth its 'note'.

15 Petti, *English Literary Hands*, pp. 19–20; Dawson and Kennedy-Skipton, *Elizabethan Handwriting*, p. 9 and plate 16, are, properly I suspect, rather more cautious. Petti's remarks are exploited for absurd purposes ('a revolution of the signifier') in Jonathan Goldberg, *Writing Matter* (Stanford, Cal., 1990), pp. 239 ff, cf. pp. 53 f, 234, 273; but the book contains much useful information, including (p. 129) the quotation from Thomas Fuller, borrowed here, about the writing-master John Davies of Hereford. On Francis Throckmorton, above, p. 83.

16 Above, p. 216, l. 9.

Sources for Bruno's Handwriting

The surviving corpus of Bruno's handwriting known at present is as follows; details of secondary works will be found above, p. 81, n. 5 and in *Sources and Literature*, below.

GENEVA SIGNATURE

Livre du Recteur of the Academy of Geneva, 20-v-1579.
Bibliothèque publique et universitaire de la Ville de Genève, Ms. fr. 151, under date.
Documenti, p. 36.
Plate VIIa.

DEDICATIONS

i.   Of *De umbris idearum* to Alexander Dickson, probably late 1583.
University College Library, London: Ogden A 50.
Sturlese, 'Un nuovo autografo del Bruno' (facsimile at p. 390).
Plate VIIb.
ii. Three others, to *a*. Jacob Cuno, *b*. Tycho Brahe, and *c*. Caspar Kegler, 1587–8.
From Gotha, Prague and University College, London.
Sturlese, *Bibliografia*, nos. 17.8, 20.45 and 20.25; Salvestrini, *Bibliografia*, nos. 225 and 226 bis (facsimiles of *a*. and *c*.); Sturlese, 'Su Bruno e Tycho Brahe'; Aquilecchia, 'Un autografo sconosciuto' (facsimile of *c*.). I have not seen a copy of *b*.

VERSES

Two examples of a version of Ecclesiastes 1: 9–10 ('Quid est quod est? . . . Nihil sub sole novum'), entitled *Salomon et Pythagoras*, written for friends in Wittenberg, 18/28–ix–1587 and 8/18–iii–1588. From Stuttgart and Florence.
Salvestrini, *Bibliografia*, nos. 224 and 226, with facsimiles.
Plate VIIc is a copy of the first, from Württembergische Landesbibliothek, Stuttgart, Cod. hist. 8° 10, f. 117r.

HELMSTEDT LETTER

Bruno to the Pro-rector of the University of Helmstedt, 6/16-x-1589. Holograph. The only legitimate surviving letter of Bruno apart from the draft in the Moscow manuscript (below).

Herzog-August-Bibliothek, Wolfenbüttel: Cod. Guelf. 360 Novorum 2°, f. 49.
Above, p. 82, n. 6; text in *Documenti*, p. 52. There is no published facsimile that
I know of.
Plate VIII.

MOSCOW MANUSCRIPT

A notebook containing a variety of original manuscripts written between 1589 and
1591, in Helmstedt, Frankfurt and Padua, by Bruno himself, his amanuensis Jerome
Besler and one other hand; put together at some later date.
Lenin State Library of the USSR, Moscow: Ms. Φ 201, no. 36. Often known as
the 'Noroff Ms.' from A.S. Norov, the nineteenth-century collector who acquired
it. Printed in *OL* iii.

Bruno's own contributions are:

> ff. 1r-5r Draft of *De vinculo spiritus* (*OL* iii, pp. 637–52)
> f. 5v Draft of a letter to the Senate of Frankfurt, just before 2/12-vii-1590
> f. 6r Sketch diagram of influences on the human body
> ff. 162r-168r First part of *Medicina lulliana*

Possibly also:

> f. 161 ??Diagram for a box-cipher (above, p. 83, n. 7). A version is printed in
> *OL* iii, p. xx; I have not seen the original.
> f. 180 Described as missing in *OL* iii, p. xvii. A Latin prescription or recipe,
> interesting because written in a hand with secretary characteristics, but unlikely to
> have been written by Bruno.

Discussed in *OL* iii, pp. xvii-xxix; facsimile of ff. 167v–168r after p. 706.
I have used a set of photographs of those parts of the manuscript written by Bruno
most generously provided by the Lenin State Library.
Plates IX (f. 2v) and X (f. 163r). Transcriptions in *OL* iii, pp. 642–44 and x–xi.

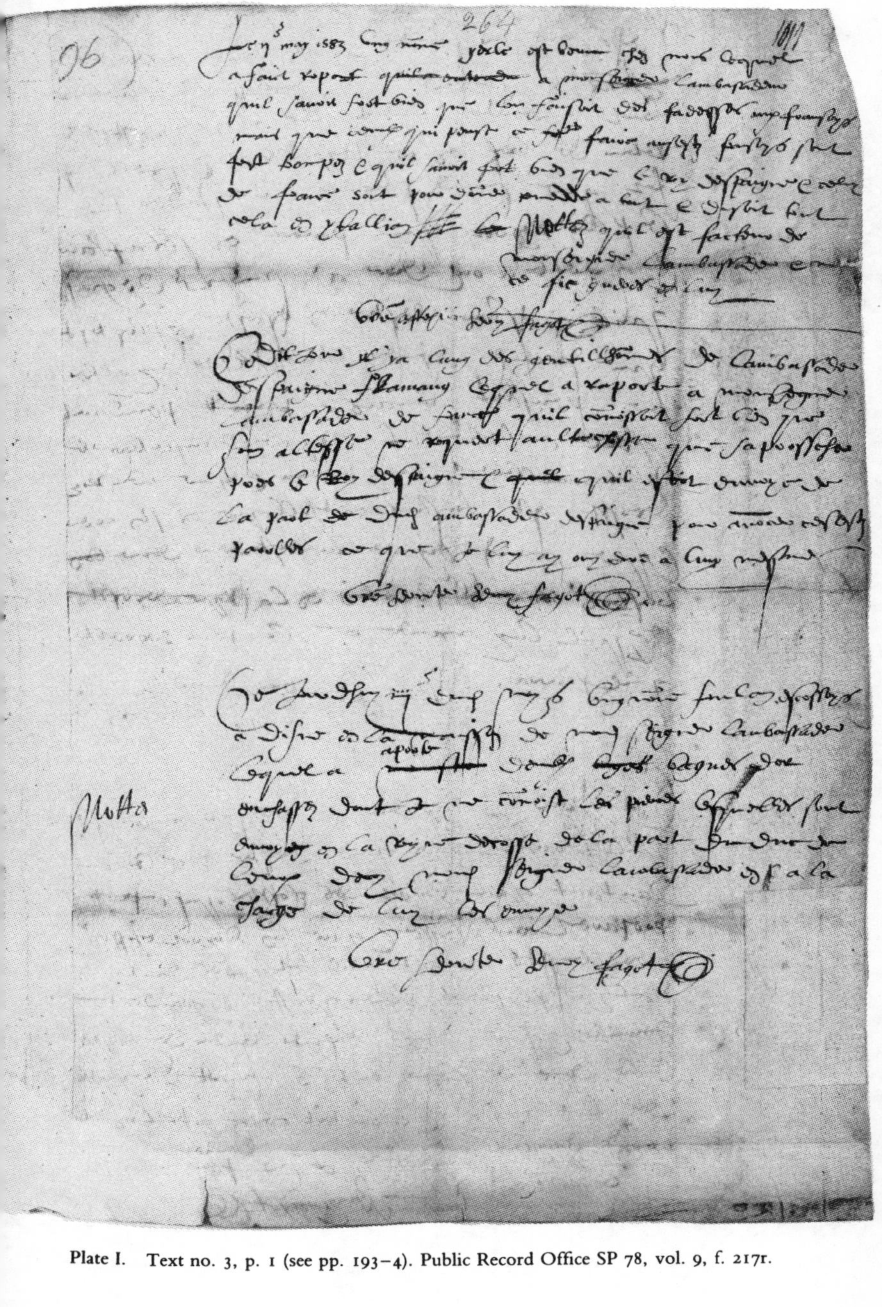

Plate I. Text no. 3, p. 1 (see pp. 193–4). Public Record Office SP 78, vol. 9, f. 217r.

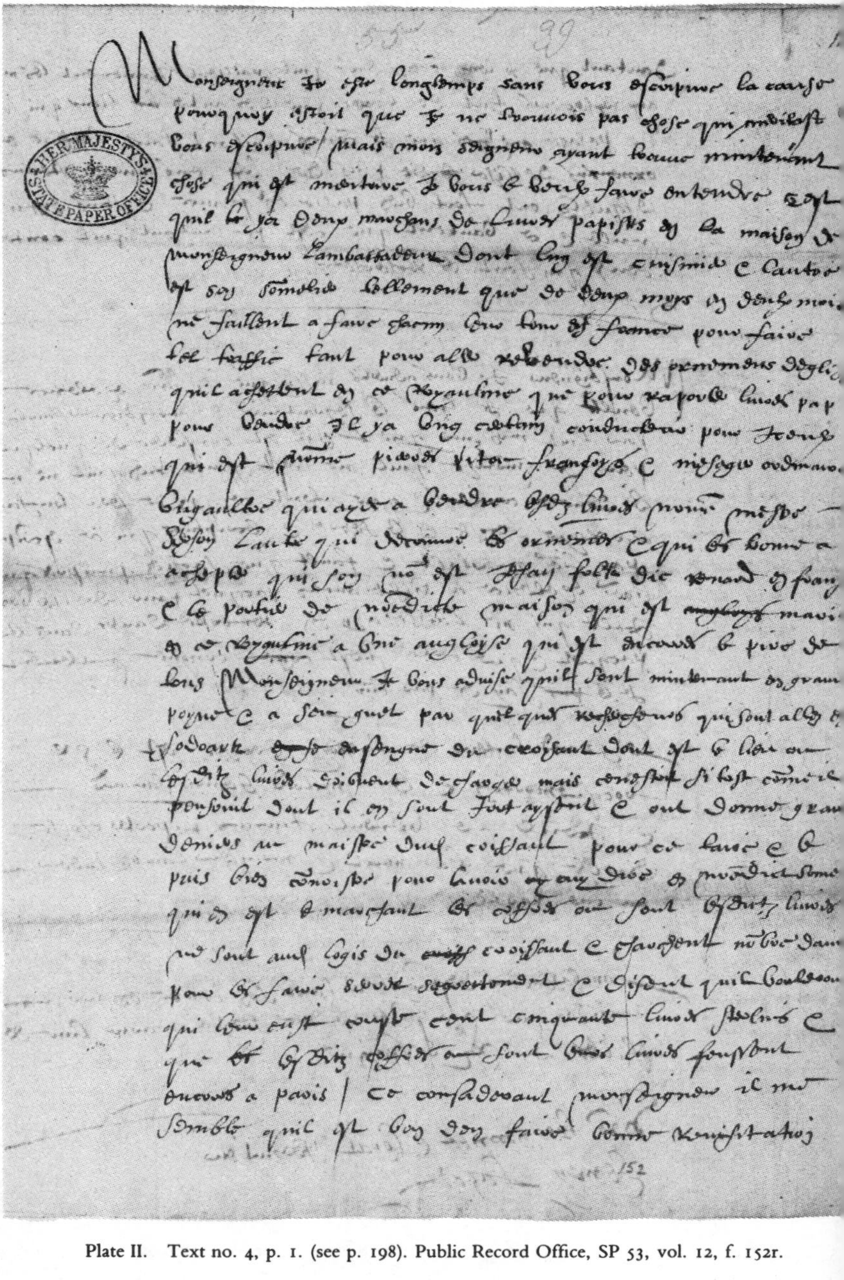

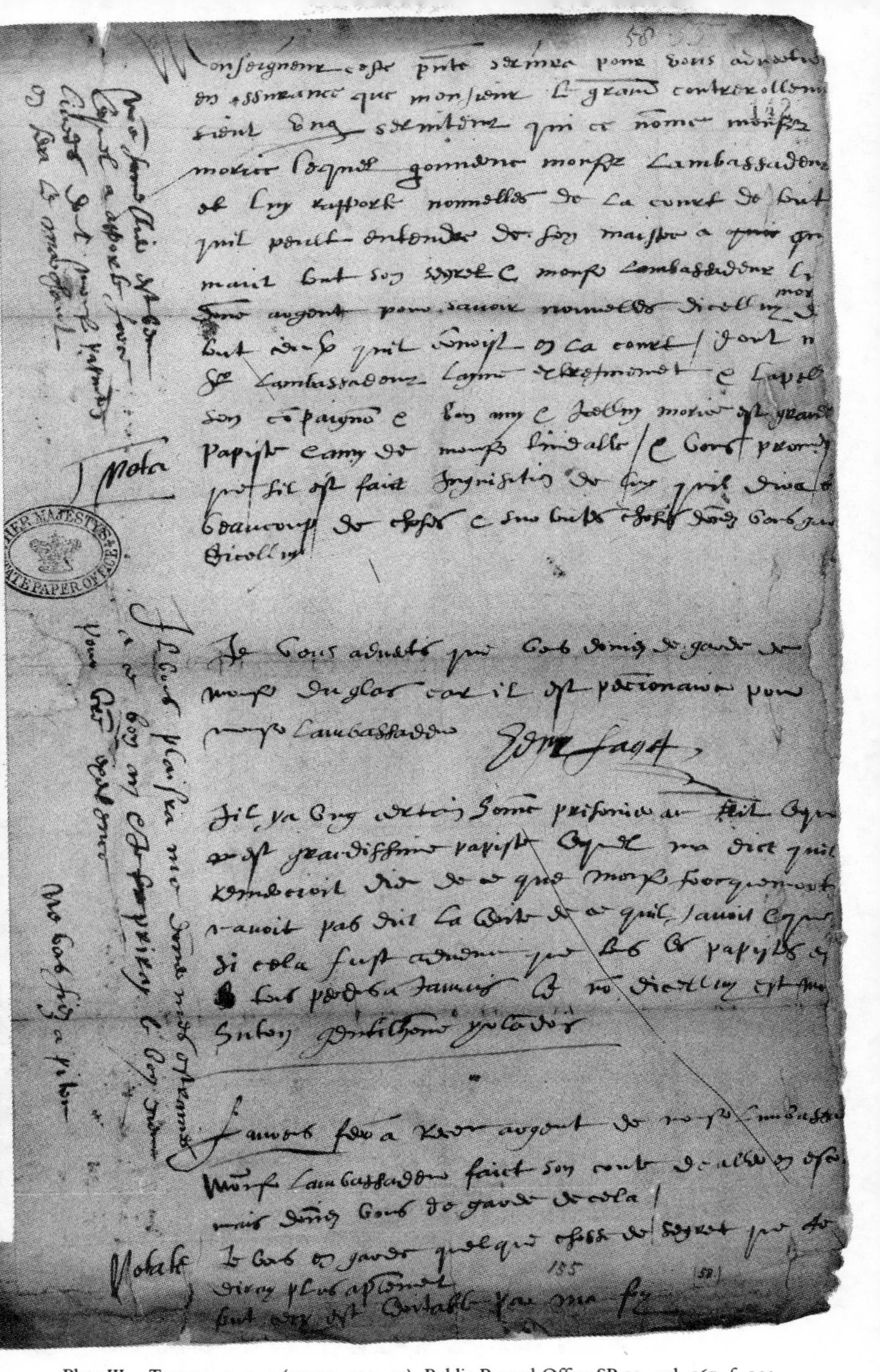
Monseigneur ceste presente servira pour vous advertir
de assurance que monsieur le grand controlleur
tient ung serviteur qui se nome monsr
Molier lequel gouverne monsr lambassadeur
et luy rapporte nouvelles de la court de tout
quil peult entendre de son maistre a quoi [illegible]
mais tout son secret et monsr lambassadeur luy
donne argent pour savoir nouvelles diceluy [illegible]
tout ce quil [illegible] en la court / dont [illegible]
[illegible] lambassadeur [illegible] et [illegible]
son compaigne et bon amy et [illegible] Molier est grand
papiste amy de monsr [illegible] / et [illegible]
[illegible] fait [illegible]
beaucoup de chose et [illegible]
diceluy

Je vous advertis que [illegible] de garde de
monsr Duglas car il est pensionaire pour
monsr lambassadeur
Henry Fagot

Il y a ung [illegible] prisonnier [illegible]
qui est grandissime papiste [illegible] ma dict quil
[illegible] de ce que monsr [illegible]
navoit pas dict la verite de ce quil savoit [illegible]
[illegible]
[illegible]
[illegible]

Jaurois [illegible] argent de monsr lambassadeur
monsr lambassadeur faict son conte [illegible]
mais donnez vous de garde de cela /
[illegible] quelque chose de secret [illegible]
[illegible] plus a plein
[illegible]

Nota

Notable

Plate III. Text no. 9, p. 1 (see pp. 210–11). Public Record Office SP 12, vol. 167, f. 155.

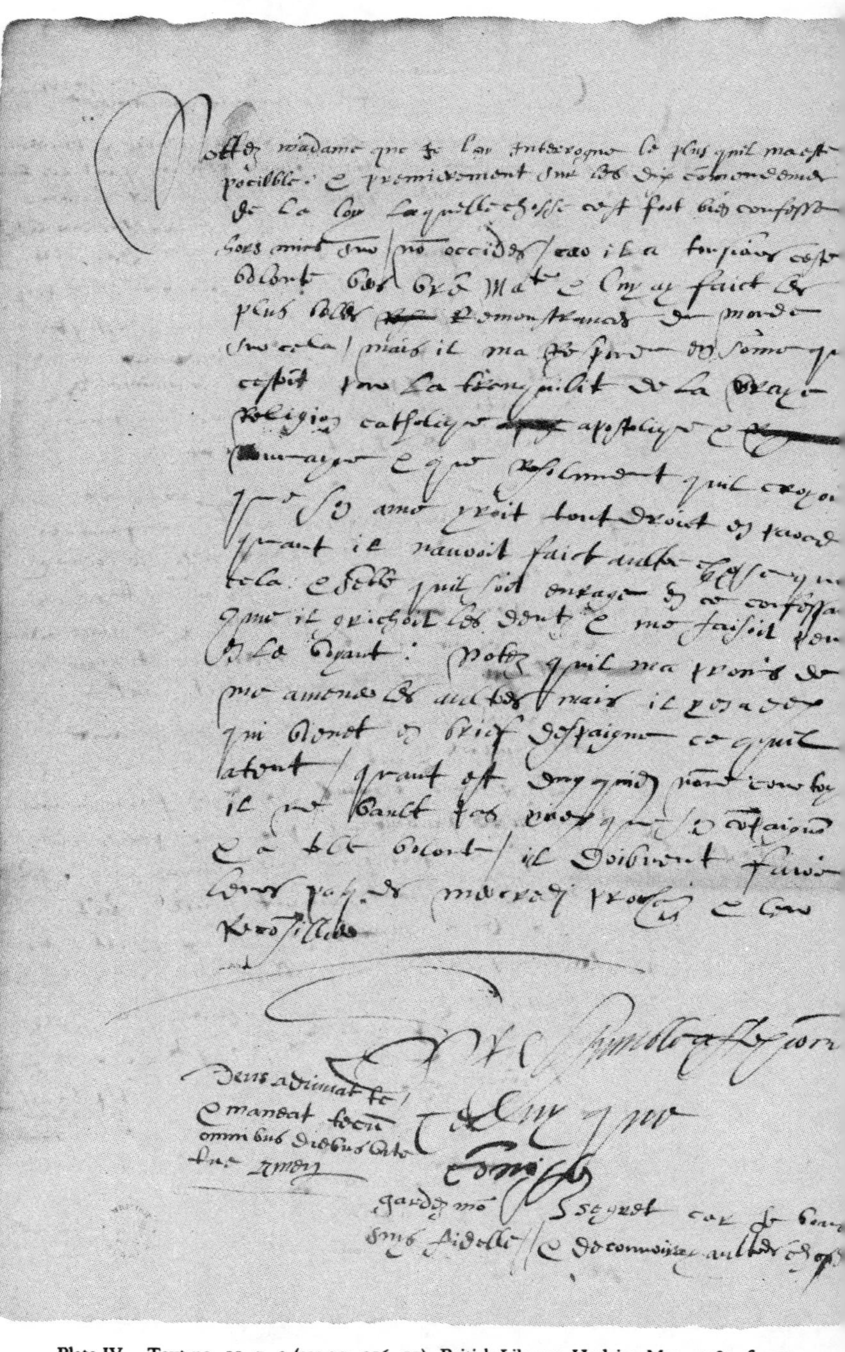

Monsieur Ie vous prie Recevoir le presant advertissement, pour tout
certain, et ne le mesprisen, Attandu quil Importe beaucoup a la
conservation de lestat daugleterre, comme Ion a coigneu par l'experien
par les advertissemens q[ui] vous y ont este cidevant donnez, sur le
mesme subiect on l'a descouvert, le malheureux & perfide dessaing
des ennemys de cestat, qui ne desirent que la perdition tout[e] e—
d'Icelluy, et par vne guerre Civille, &molter et esmouvoir le peuble
daugleterre, contre leur princesse, par le moyen les mauvais bruict[z]
& libres papal[z] diffamatoires, et contraires a la religion;
qui y sont transportez de france, a la suscitaon[s] de ceulx qui
sont en fuite dud[it] pais, et de lembassadeur despaigne et
aultres leurs adgerans, comme des libres a dire messe, aultres
libres diffamatoires composés par les Jesuistes, heures, et
aultres libres servans a leur Intantion, lesquelz libres
sont transportes de ce pais, au pais daugleterre, par les serviteu[rs]
domestiques de monsieur de maunissiere embassadeur pour
leroy oud[it] pais & dud[it] pais & rapportent en france
des eschappes & ornemens de leglise papalle qu'ilz aceptent
depardela a peu de pris pour apres les revendre en ce pa[is]
bien cherement & aussi les bas destame, lesquel[z] Ie croi[s]
l'un qui est le principal dud[it] traffic, s'enault de la
Campaigne sommellier ordinaire dud[it] s[eigneu]r de maunissiere,
l'aultre Rene ledut son cuysinier, lesquel[z] s'en son[t]
enrechis: et s'enrechissent tous les Iours dud[it] commerce
detriment de lestat, duquel Ilz desirent la subvers[ion]
et mesmes vendent lesd[ict] Livres au logis dud[it] s[eigneu]r embass[adeur]
Ledict delacampagne sommellier, est tous les Iours entreten[u]
Conseille par vng Anglois natureL, qui se tient aupres de leglis[e]
sainct ylaire dumont, et aussi par vng aultre gentilhomm[e] qui
dit estre parent de la Rogue, lesquelz luy donnent moy[en]
le faire tenyr lesd[ict] Livres, et principallement ledict mon[sieur]
Lequel faid estat, tous les Iours de banquier: pour faire te[nyr]
les demers qu'ilz doivent estre besoing pour la perfection de
monopoles, & se sert les morgan: ordinairement pour
tenyr ses tres, plus souvent dung des principaux se[rviteurs]
de monsieur de villeroy, lequel les envoye & encloist dan[s]
parquetz du Rey qui sont envoyes Ason embassadeur a[u]
pais daugleterre, lesquelles tres les embassadeur, renf[erment]
aultres traistres, depardela, affin qu'elles ne puissen[t]
Segommertes, Ilz ont promis & aussi delacampaigne & c[uisinier]
sommeller et cuysinier, que librement benyr A bou[t]

58

Plate VIIa. Signature in the *Livre du Recteur* of the Academy of Geneva, 20 May 1579. Bibliothèque publique et universitaire de la ville de Genève, Ms. fr. 151, under date.

Plate VIIb. Dedication of *De umbris idearum* to Alexander Dickson, probably late 1583. University college London Library, Ogden A 50.

Salomon. et Pythag[oras]

Quid est q[uo]d est? Ipsum q[uo]d fuit

Quid est q[uo]d fuit? Ipsum q[uo]d est.

Nihil sub sole novum

SALVS.

†

Jordanus Brunus
Nolanus Witeb[ergae]
18 7bris

Plate VIIc.   Verses written in the Album of Hans von Warnsdorf, Wittenberg, 18/28 September 1587. Württembergische Landesbiblothek, Stuttgart, Cod. hist. 8° 10, f. 117r.

Amplissime et R[everendissi]me D[omi]ne Prorector

Jordanus Brunus Nolanus, per Helmstadensis eccl[esi]ae primarium pastorem, et superintendentem, in propria actione et inaudita causa factum iudicem, et exequutorem in publicis concionibus excommunicatus. tenore praesentium a' Magnificentiae R[everendissi]mae vestrae claritate, et ab universis Amplissimi senatus dig[nita]te in publico consistorio humiliter adversus iniquissimae et privatae illius sententiae publicam exequutionem, expostulans audiri petit. ut si quid iure g[ene]ra ipsius gradum et dignam existimationem academiae saltem iuste accidisse cognoscat. quamvis iux[ta] Senecae S.

Qui statuit aliquid parte inaudita altera,
Aequum licet statuerit, haud aequus fuit.

Quamobrem et ipsum R[everendum] Pastorem Excell[entissi]ma amplit[udini]s v[estrae] authoritate citandum rogat: ut et illud (si deo placuerit) constare possit, non ex privata vindictae libidine sed ex boni pastoris [e]t muneris pro ovium suarum salute profectam fulmen illud esse. Datum Helmstadij sexta Octobris 1589

Jordanus Brunus Nri sup[...]

Plate VIII. Bruno's Helmstedt Letter. Bruno to the Prorector of the University of Helmstedt, 6/16 October 1589. Herzog-August Bibliothek, Wolfenbüttel, Cod. Guelf. 360 Novorum 2°, f. 49.

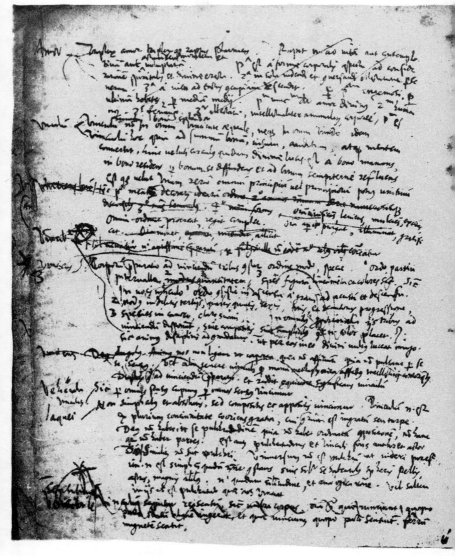

Plate IX. Moscow Manuscript, A Rough Draft. *De vinculo spiritus*, probably Frankfurt, 1590. Lenin State Library of the USSR, Moscow, Ms Φ 201, no. 36, f. 2v.

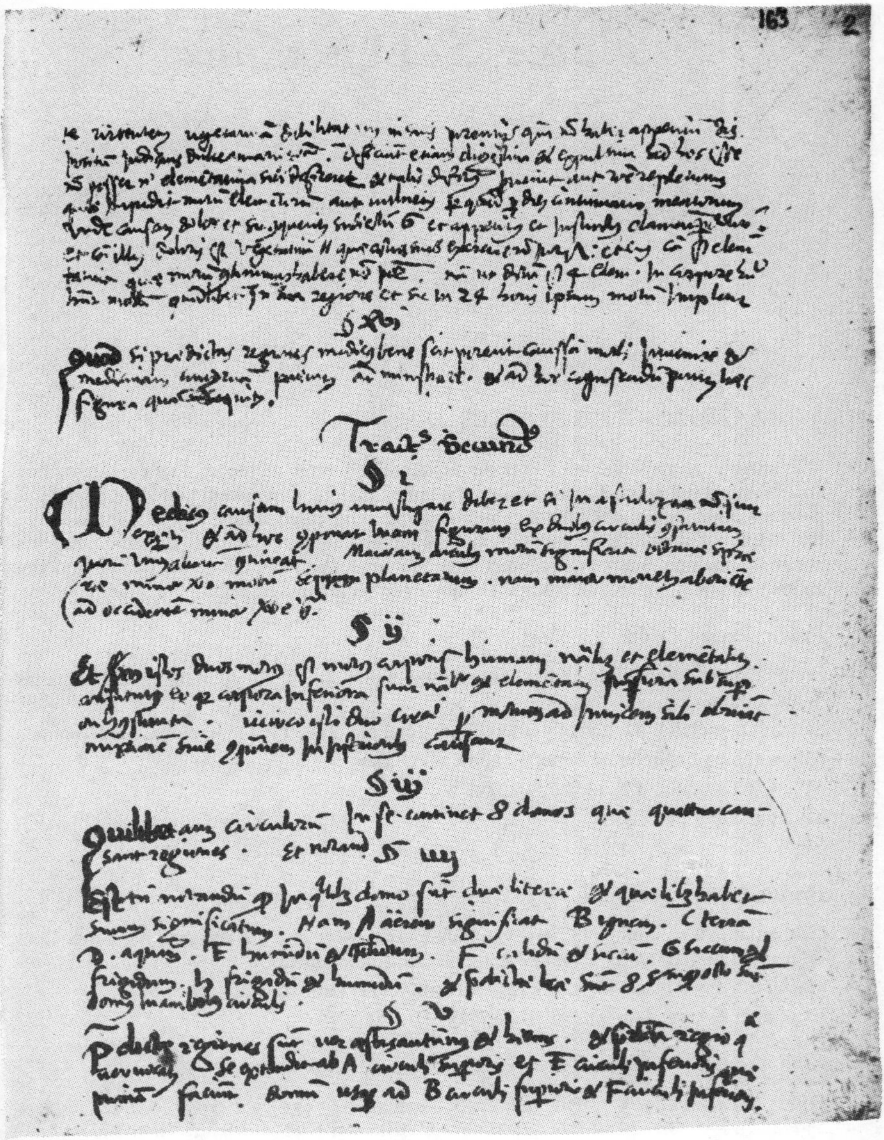

Plate X.   Moscow Manuscript, A Fair Copy. *Medicina lulliana*, probably Padua, 1591. Lenin State Library of the USSR, Moscow, Ms Φ 201, no. 36, f. 163r.

Sources and Literature

1. MANUSCRIPT SOURCES

It is simple, if artificial, to list these separately: I refer at the end of each series or collection to the related calendar or other publication, which will be found in section 2 unless otherwise stated. All Arabic numerals refer to volumes; where known I give the origin of the volume or collection. I have italicised volumes in which Fagot's communications, scattered far and wide through the Public Record Office and the British Library, are to be found. I omit a few eccentric items.

Public Record Office, London

State Papers, Elizabeth. All these volumes are from the papers of Sir Francis Walsingham.

SP 12 (Domestic): 92, 147, 151, 155, 163, 164, *167*, 168, 176, 182, *206*. *CSP Domestic.*

SP 53 (Mary, Queen of Scots): *12*, *13*. *CSP Scotland.*

SP 78 (France): *9*, 13, *14*, 16, 17, 19, 20.

SP 85 (Italian States): 1.

SP 101 (Newsletters): 72, 95. *CSP Foreign* for all three.

British Library, Department of Manuscripts

Cottonian Mss.: *Caligula C vii*, *Caligula C viii*, *Nero B vi* (Walsingham); Titus C vi (Henry Howard). *CSP Scotland* for the Caligula volumes.

Harleian Mss.: *1582* (Walsingham, probably via Thomas Phellippes).

Lansdowne Mss.: 29, 31, *39* (Burghley).

Bibliothèque Nationale, Paris, Département des Manuscrits

Fonds français: 3305, 4736, 15973 (Castelnau); 15571 (Villeroy); 15892, 15905, 15908, 15909 (Bellièvre); 16042, 16045 (Cardinal d'Este and Saint-Goard).

Cinq Cents de Colbert: 337, 472, 473 (Castelnau).

Biblioteca Ambrosiana, Milan

Manuscripts: T 167 sup (Corbinelli). Consulted in a microfilm kindly made available by the Institute of Mediaeval Studies, University of Notre Dame, Indiana. Calderini De-Marchi; Yates 'New Documents', section 4.

2. PUBLISHED COLLECTIONS OF DOCUMENTS

Blet, P. (ed.), *Girolamo Ragazzoni, évêque de Bergame, nonce en France . . . 1583–1586* (Acta nuntiaturae gallicae, ii; Rome/Paris, 1962).

Calendar of State Papers, Domestic, 1581–1590, ed. R. Lemon (London, 1865).

Calendar of State Papers, Domestic: Addenda, 1580–1625, ed. M.A.E. Green (London, 1872).

Calendar of State Papers, Foreign: 1581–1582, ed. A.J. Butler (London, 1907); *1583–1584; 1584–1585; 1585–1586; 1586–1588*, ed. S.C. Lomas (London, 1914, 1916, 1921, 1927); *1586–1587 (Holland and Flanders)*, ed. S.C. Lomas and A.B. Hinds (London, 1927); *January–July 1589*, ed. R.B. Wernham (London, 1950).

Calendar of State Papers, Scotland and Mary, Queen of Scots: 1581–1583; 1584–1585; 1585–1586, ed. W.K. Boyd (Edinburgh, 1910, 1913, 1914).

Calendar of State Papers, Spanish, Elizabeth: 1580–1586, ed. M.A.S. Hume (London, 1896).

Chéruel, A., *Marie Stuart et Catherine de Médicis* (Paris, 1858): correspondence of Castelnau, 1582–4, pp. 226–355. Printed from a Ms. in the archives of the D'Esneval family, now in the possession of the De Broglie family at the Château of Pavilly, Normandy. By the kindness of the owners and of M. François Burckard, *conservateur-en-chef* of the *Archives départementales* of the Seine-Maritime at Rouen, I have been able to check Chéruel's work against a microfilm of the original, and found it immaculate.

Dasent, J.R. (ed.), *Acts of the Privy Council: new series*, xii (London, 1896).

Historical Manuscripts Commission, *Calendar of the Manuscripts of the Marquis of Salisbury at Hatfield House*, ii–iii (London, 1888–9), for the years 1572–89.

Historical Manuscripts Commission, *Calendar of the Manuscripts of the Marquess of Bath*, v (London, 1980).

Hughes, P.L. and Larkin, J.F. (ed.), *Tudor Royal Proclamations* (3 vols; New Haven/London, 1964–9).

Labanoff, A. (ed.), *Lettres, instructions et mémoires de Marie Stuart, reine d'Écosse* (7 vols; London, 1844).

Le Laboureur, J. (ed.), *Mémoires de Michel de Castelnau*, 3 edn by J. Godefroy (3 vols; Brussels, 1731).

Murdin, W. (ed.), *A Collection of State Papers relating to the Affairs of Queen Elizabeth/from the papers of/William Cecill Lord Burghley* (1571–96) (London, 1759).

Ogle, A. (ed.), *A Copy-book of Sir Amyas Paulet's Letters* (?London, 1866).

Pollen, J.H. and MacMahon, W. (ed.), *The Venerable Philip Howard, Earl of Arundel* (Catholic Record Society, xxi, 1919).

Pollen, J.H. (ed.), *Mary Queen of Scots and the Babington Plot* (Scottish History Society³, iii; Edinburgh, 1922).

Teulet, A. (ed.), *Relations politiques de la France et de l'Espagne avec l'Écosse au XVIe siècle* (5 vols; Paris, 1862).

3. SOURCES FOR BRUNO

LIFE

The non-literary sources for Bruno's life, as then known, were collected by Vittore Spampanato and published in his *Vita di Giordano Bruno* (Messina, 1921), pp. 599–

786, and reprinted by Giovanni Gentile in *Documenti della vita di Giordano Bruno* (Florence, 1933), which I use; the most important of them was the text of the Venetian *processo* (to 1592), which occupies pp. 59–136 of this volume. Since then the chief additions have been the abstract of the whole of Bruno's inquisitorial process up to the end of 1597, published by Angelo Mercati, *Il sommario del processo di Giordano Bruno* (Studi e Testi, ci; Vatican City, 1942); and the letters of Corbinelli used by Yates, above section 1.

WORKS

Latin writings

Jordani Bruni Nolani opera latine conscripta, ed. F. Fiorentino and others (3 vols in 8 parts; Naples and Florence, 1879–91). I have used:

i, part 1, ed. F. Fiorentino: *Oratio valedictoria*; *Oratio consolatoria*; *Camoeracensis acrotismus*; *De immenso et innumerabilibus*, book 1.

i, part 3, ed. F. Tocco and H. Vitelli: *Articuli adversus mathematicos*, dedication to Rudolf II.

i, part 4, ed. F. Tocco and H. Vitelli: *Figuratio aristotelici physici auditus*, dedication to Piero Delbene.

ii, part 1, ed. V. Imbriani and C.M. Tallarigo: *De umbris idearum*.

ii, part 2, ed. F. Tocco and H. Vitelli: *Ars reminiscendi*, *Triginta sigilli et triginta sigillorum explicatio*, *Sigillus sigillorum*; *De lampade combinatoria lulliana*, preface; *Animadversiones circa Lampadem lullianam*.

ii, part 3, ed. F. Tocco and H. Vitelli: *De comparatione imaginum*.

iii, ed. F. Tocco and H. Vitelli: editors' introduction on Bruno's manuscripts and handwriting, and facsimiles. *De vinculo spiritus*; *De vinculis in genere*.

Due dialoghi sconosciuti e due dialoghi noti, ed. G. Aquilecchia (Rome, 1957), prints the dialogues about Fabrizio Mordente published in Paris in 1586.

Italian dialogues

Dialoghi italiani, 3 edn by Giovanni Aquilecchia (2 vols continuously paginated; Florence, 1958) of the first two volumes of the *Opere italiane*, ed. Giovanni Gentile (Bari, 1907–8). Essential.

Scritti scelti di Giordano Bruno e di Tommaso Campanella, ed. Luigi Firpo (2 edn; Turin, 1968) contains the *Cena*, part of the *Eroici furori*, Bruno's 'Autobiography' (i.e. *Documenti*, pp. 76–87), and a chronology of Bruno's life.

SINGLE EDITIONS

La cena de le Ceneri, ed. Giovanni Aquilecchia (Turin, 1955).

English trans. by A. Gosselin and L.S. Lerner, *The Ash Wednesday Supper* (Hamden, Conn., 1977).

De la causa, principio e uno, ed. Giovanni Aquilecchia (Turin, 1973).

French trans. by Émile Namer, *Cause, principe et unité* (Paris, 1930).

English trans. by Sidney Greenberg, in *The Infinite in Giordano Bruno* (New York, 1950), pp. 76–173.

De l'infinito universo e mondi: English trans. by D.W. Singer, in *Giordano Bruno: his Life and Thought* (New York, 1950), pp. 225–378.

Spaccio della bestia trionfante, ed. Michele Ciliberto (Milan, 1985), for its polemical introduction.

English trans. by Arthur D. Imerti, *The Expulsion of the Triumphant Beast* (New Brunswick, N.J., 1964).

De gli eroici furori: English trans. by P.E. Memmo, *The Heroic Frenzies* (Chapel Hill, N.C., 1964).

Il Candelaio: I have used the handy edition by I. Guerrini Angrisani (Milan, 1976).

4. OTHER WORKS: OTHER CONTEMPORARY OR LITERARY TEXTS; SECONDARY WRITINGS; WORKS OF REFERENCE

Anon., *A Discovery of the Treasons practised and attempted . . . by Francis Throckmorton* (1584), in *Harleian Miscellany* (10 vols; London, 1808–13), iii, 190–200.

Anon., possibly Arundell, Charles, Parsons, Robert and others, *Leicester's Commonwealth: The Copy of a Letter Written by a Master of Art of Cambridge* (1584), ed. D.C. Peck (Athens, Ohio, 1985).

Aquilecchia, Giovanni, 'La lezione definitiva della "Cena de le Ceneri" di Giordano Bruno', *Atti dell'Accademia nazionale dei Lincei: Memorie, Classe di scienze morali, etc.*[8], iii, no. 4 (1950), 209–43.

——————, 'Un autografo sconosciuto di Giordano Bruno', *Giornale storico della letteratura italiana*, cxxxiv (1957), 333–8; also ibid. cxl (1963), 148–51.

——————, Lo stampatore londinese di Giordano Bruno', *Studi di filologia italiana*, xviii (1960), 102–28.

Ariosto, Ludovico, *Orlando furioso*, ed. L. Caretti (Milan/Naples, 1954).

Aston, Margaret, *England's Iconoclasts, i: Laws against Images* (Oxford, 1988).

Aubrey, John, *Brief Lives*, ed. R. Barber (Woodbridge, Suffolk, 1982).

Bacon, Francis, *Essays*, ed. M.J. Hawkins (London/Melbourne, 1972).

Baguenault de Puchesse, G., *Jean de Morvillier* (Paris, 1870).

Barbera, M.L., 'La Brunomania', *Giornale critico della filosofia italiana*, lix (1980), 103–40.

Barnavi, Élie, *Le Parti de Dieu: étude sociale et politique des chefs de la Ligue parisienne, 1585–1594* (Brussels/Louvain, ?1980).

Battaglia, S., Barberi Squarotti, G. and others, *Grande dizionario della lingua italiana* (14 vols to date; Turin, 1961–).

Battista, C., and Alessio, G., *Dizionario etimologico italiano* (5 vols; Florence, 1950–7).

Bodin, Jean, *Six livres de la République* (1583); abridged trans. by M.J. Tooley, *Six Books of the Commonwealth* (Oxford, n.d.).

Bossy, John, 'English Catholics and the French Marriage, 1577–1581', *Recusant History*, v (1959), 2–16.

——————, 'The Character of Elizabethan Catholicism', in T. Aston (ed.), *Crisis in Europe, 1550–1660* (London, 1965), pp. 223–46.

Boüard, A. de, *Manuel de diplomatique française et pontificale* (Album of Plates: Paris, 1929). I have not seen the text.

Boucher, Jacqueline, *La Cour de Henri III* (n.p., 1986).

Butler, E.C., and Pollen, J.H., 'Dr. William Gifford in 1586', *The Month*, ciii (1904), 243–58, 348–66.

Buxton, John, *Sir Philip Sidney and the English Renaissance* (London, 1954).

Calderini De-Marchi, Rita, *Jacopo Corbinelli et les érudits français* (Milan, 1914).

Cappelli, A,, *Cronologia, cronografia e calendario perpetuo* (5 edn; Milan, 1983).

Champion, Pierre, *Charles IX: la France et le contrôle de l'Espagne* (2 vols; Paris, 1939).

Cheney, C.R., *Handbook of Dates for Students of English History* (London, 1945).

Chéruel, A. See section 2.

Ciliberto, Michele, *Lessico di Giordano Bruno* (2 vols continuously paginated; Rome, 1979).

————, 'Asini e pedanti', *Rinascimento*², xxiv (1984), 81–121.

————, *La ruota del tempo: interpretazione di Giordano Bruno* (Rome, 1986).

————, *Giordano Bruno* (Rome/Bari, 1990).

Clancy, Thomas H., *Papist Pamphleteers* (Chicago, 1964).

Cloulas, Ivan, 'Les Rapports de Jérôme Ragazzoni . . . avec les ecclésiastiques . . . (1583–1586)', *Mélanges . . . /de l'École française de Rome*, lxxii (1960), 509–50.

Cobbett, William (ed.), *State Trials* (2 vols; London, 1809).

Colliard, Lauro A., *Un dottore dell'Ateneo patavino alla Corte di Francia: Pierre d'Elbène (1550–1590)* (Verona, 1972).

Corsano, Antonio, *Il pensiero di Giordano Bruno nel suo svolgimento storico* (Florence, 1940).

Cross, F.L., and Livingstone, E.A., *Oxford Dictionary of the Christian Church* (2 edn; London, 1974).

Daniel, Samuel, *The Complete Works in Verse and Prose*, ed. A.B. Grosart (5 vols; 1896, repr. New York, 1963).

Dawson, Giles E., and Kennedy-Skipton, L., *Elizabethan Handwriting, 1500–1650* (London, 1968).

Devlin, Christopher, *Robert Southwell* (London, 1956).

Devoto, G., and Oli, G.C., *Dizionario della lingua italiana* (Florence, 1971).

Dickerman, E.H., *Bellièvre and Villeroy* (Providence, R.I., 1971).

Dio Chrysostom, ed. and trans. J.W. Cohoon (5 vols; London, 1932–51, repr. 1961–4).

Ditchfield, Simon, 'Brunomania in Italy, 1886–1890' (unpublished essay, Warburg Institute, London, 1986).

Durkan, John, 'Alexander Dickson and S.T.C. 6823', *The Bibliotheck* (Glasgow), iii (1962), 183–90.

Evans, R.J.W., *Rudolf II and his World* (Oxford, 1973).

Firpo, Luigi, 'Il processo di Giordano Bruno', *Rivista storica italiana*, lx (1948), 542–597; lxi (1949), 1–59; reprinted as *Quaderni della Rivista storica italiana*, i (Naples, 1949).

Fisher, John, intro., *A Collection of Early Maps of London, 1553–1667* (Lympne Castle, Kent/London, 1981).

Florio, John, trans., *The Essays of Michel de Montaigne* (1603), ed. L.C. Harmer (3 vols; London, 1965 edn.).

Florio, John, *Queen Anna's New World of Words, or Dictionarie of the Italian and English Tongues* (1611; repr. Menston, Yorks., 1968).

French, Peter J., *John Dee: the World of an Elizabethan Magus* (London, 1972).

Gatti, Hilary, 'Giordano Bruno: the Texts in the Library of the 9th Earl of Northumberland', *Journal of the Warburg and Courtauld Institutes*, xlvi (1983), 63–77.

Gentile, Marino, 'Rileggendo il Bruno', *Humanitas* (Brescia), iii (1948), 1154–64. (I have not yet succeeded in seeing a copy of this piece, for which see above, *Epilogue*.)

Ghisalberti, A.M. and others (ed.), *Dizionario biografico degli italiani* (36 vols to date; Rome, 1960–).

Godefroy, F., *Dictionnaire de l'ancienne langue française* (10 vols; Paris, 1880–1902; repr. 1969).

Goldberg, Jonathan, *Writing Matter* (Stanford, Cal., 1990).

Greengrass, Mark, 'Mary, Dowager Queen of France', *The Innes Review*, xxxviii (1987), 171–88.

Halliwell, J.O. (ed.), *The Private Diary of John Dee* (Camden Society, xix, 1842).

Hamilton, A.C., *Sir Philip Sidney: a Study of his Life and Works* (Cambridge, 1977).

Hicks, Leo, 'An Elizabethan Propagandist: the Career of Solomon Aldred', *The Month*, clxxxi (1945), 181–90.

——————, 'The Strange Case of Dr. William Parry', *Studies* (Dublin), xxxvii (1948), 343–62.

——————, *An Elizabethan Problem: Some Aspects of the Careers of two Exile-Adventurers* (London, 1964).

Hofmeister, P., 'Die Strafen für den Apostata a Religione', *Studia Gratiana*, viii (1962), 423–46.

Holinshed, Ralph, *Chronicles of England, Scotland and Ireland* (6 vols; London, 1807–8 edn).

Hollar, Wenceslaus, *A Long View of London from Bankside, 1647* (London Topographical Society, publication no. 112; London, 1970).

Holt, Mack P., 'The Household of François, Duke of Anjou', *French Historical Studies*, xiii (1984), 305–22.

Howard, Henry, *A defensative against the Poyson of supposed Prophecies* (London: John Charlewood, 1583).

Hubault, G., *Michel de Castelnau, ambassadeur en Angleterre, 1575–1585* (Paris, 1856; repr. Geneva, 1970).

Hughes, Philip, *The Reformation in England*, iii (London, 1954).

Imbs, P., *Trésor de la langue française*, xii (1986), for *Patrie*.

Ingegno, Alfonso, *La sommersa nave della religione: studi sulla polemica anticristiana di Giordano Bruno* (Naples, 1984).

Jensen, De Lamar, *Diplomacy and Dogmatism: Bernardino de Mendoza and the French Catholic League* (Cambridge, Mass., 1964).

Jones, C.P., *The Roman World of Dio Chrysostom* (Cambridge, Mass./London, 1978).

Kerman, Joseph, *The Masses and Motets of William Byrd* (London, 1981).

Luther, Martin, 'The Babylonian Captivity of the Church', English trans. In John Dillenberger (ed.), *Martin Luther: Selections from his Writings* (Garden City, N.Y., 1961), pp. 249–359.

Martin, A. Lynn, *Henri III and the Jesuit Politicians* (Geneva, 1973).

Martin, C.T. (ed.), *Journal of Sir Francis Walsingham from December 1570 to April 1583* (Camden Society, civ part 3, 1871; repr. New York/London, 1968).

Nicolas, Sir Harris, *Memoirs of the Life and Times of Sir Christopher Hatton* (London, 1847).

Ordine, Nuccio, *La cabala dell'Asino: asinità e coscienza in Giordano Bruno* (Naples, 1987).

Pastor, Ludwig von, *The History of the Popes from the Close of the Middle Ages*, English ed. and trans. by F.I. Antrobus and others (40 vols; London/St Louis, Mo., 1928–41; repr. 1938–61). Vols xix–xxii (1930–3; repr. 1952) cover the years 1572–90.

Peck, D.C. *See* Anon.

Peck, Linda Levy, *Northampton: Patronage and Policy at the Court of James I* (London, 1982).

Petrarca, Francesco, *Rime, Trionfi e Poesie latine*, ed. F. Neri and others (Milan/Naples, 1951).

Petti, Anthony G., *English Literary Hands from Chaucer to Dryden* (London, 1977).

Pollard, A.W., and Redgrave, G.R., *A Short-Title Catalogue of Books Printed in England . . . 1475–1640*, 2 edn by W.A. Jackson, F.S. Ferguson and K.F. Pantzer (2 vols; London, 1986).

Pollen, J.H. *See* Butler, E.C.

Prockter, A., and Taylor, R., *The A to Z of Elizabethan London* (Lympne Castle, Kent/London, 1979).

Read, Conyers, *Mr. Secretary Walsingham and the Policy of Queen Elizabeth* (3 vols; Oxford, 1925–7; repr. 1967).

——————, *Lord Burghley and Queen Elizabeth* (London, 1960).

——————, 'The Fame of Sir Edward Safford', *American Historical Review*, xx (1915), 292–313.

Rees, Joan, *Samuel Daniel* (Liverpool, 1964).

Rowse, A.L., *Ralegh and the Throckmortons* (London, 1962).

Salvestrini, Virgilio, *Bibliografia di Giordano Bruno, 1582–1950*, 2 edn by Luigi Firpo (Florence, 1958).

Sidney, Sir Philip, *The Countess of Pembroke's Arcadia*, ed. M. Evans (London, 1977).

Singer, D.W., *Giordano Bruno: his Life and Thought* (New York, 1950).

Spampanato, Vincenzo, *Vita di Giordano Bruno* (Messina, 1921).

Stephen, Leslie, and Lee, Sidney (ed.), *Dictionary of National Biography* (1885–1901; repr., 22 vols; London, 1949–50).

Stone, Lawrence, *An Elizabethan: Sir Horatio Palavicino* (Oxford, 1956).

Strong, Roy, *The English Icon: Elizabethan and Jacobean Portraiture* (London/New York, 1969).

Strunk, Oliver, *Readings in Music History: ii, The Renaissance* (London/Boston, 1981 edn).

Sturlese, [M.] Rita [Pagnoni], 'Su Bruno e Tycho Brahe', *Rinascimento*[2], xxv (1985), 309–33.

——————, *Bibliografia, censimento e storia delle antiche stampe di Giordano Bruno* (Florence, 1987).

——————, 'Un nuovo autografo del Bruno', *Rinascimento*[2], xxvii (1987), 387–91.

Tilley, M.P., *A Dictionary of the Proverbs in England in the 16th and 17th Centuries* (Ann Arbor, Mich., 1950).

Wernham, R.B., *Before the Armada: the Growth of English Foreign Policy, 1485–1588* (London, 1966).

Williams, Neville, *Thomas Howard Fourth Duke of Norfolk* (London, 1964).

Wilson, Charles, *Queen Elizabeth and the Revolt of the Netherlands* (London, 1970).

Wilson, F.P., *Oxford Dictionary of English Proverbs* (3 edn; Oxford, 1970).

Wind, Edgar, *Pagan Mysteries in the Renaissance* (London, 1958).

Yates, Frances, *John Florio: the Life of an Italian in Shakespeare's England* (Cambridge, 1934).

—————, 'The Religious Policy of Giordano Bruno', *Journal of the Warburg and Courtauld Institutes*, iii (1939–1940), 181–207; repr. in *Collected Essays* (below), i, 151–79.

—————, *The French Academies of the Sixteenth Century* (London, 1947; repr. with introduction by J.B. Trapp, London, 1988).

—————, 'Giordano Bruno: Some New Documents', *Revue internationale de philosophie*, xvi (1951), 174–99; repr. in *Collected Essays*, ii, 111–30.

—————, *Giordano Bruno and the Hermetic Tradition* (London, 1964).

—————, *The Art of Memory* (1966; London, 1969 edn used).

—————, *Collected Essays*: i, *Lull and Bruno*; ii, *Renaissance and Reform: The Italian Contribution* (London, 1982, 1983).

Index

Since ample reference to them is given in Parts I and II, I have not made reference to the *Texts* here, except where they, or their introductions and notes, contain matter that does not appear in the body of the book. Names of modern scholars are italicised.